THE
PRESIDENCY
IN A SEPARATED SYSTEM

THE
PRESIDENCY
IN A SEPARATED SYSTEM

SECOND EDITION

CHARLES O. JONES

BROOKINGS INSTITUTION PRESS
Washington, D.C.

Copyright © 2005
THE BROOKINGS INSTITUTION
1775 Massachusetts Avenue, N.W., Washington, D.C. 20036
www.brookings.edu

Library of Congress Cataloging-in-Publication data
Jones, Charles O.
    The presidency in a separated system / Charles O. Jones.—2nd ed.
      p.   cm.
    Summary: "Examines the organizational, political, and procedural challenges faced by postwar U.S. presidents, from Truman through George W. Bush, working in a separated system of government"—Provided by publisher.
    Includes bibliographical references and index.
    ISBN-13: 978-0-8157-4717-8 (isbn-13, paper : alk. paper)
    ISBN-10: 0-8157-4717-9 (isbn-10, paper : alk. paper)
    1. Presidents—United States—History.   2. Separation of powers—United States.   3. United States—Politics and government.   I. Title.
JK516.J66 2005
352.23'0973—dc22   2005009334

9 8 7 6 5 4 3 2 1
The paper used in this publication meets minimum requirements of the American National Standard for Information Sciences—Permanence of Paper for Printed Library Materials: ANSI Z39.48-1992.

Typeset in Times

Composition by R. Lynn Rivenbark
Macon, Georgia

Printed by R. R. Donnelley
Harrisonburg, Virginia

To

SAMUEL C. PATTERSON

and the memory of

RICHARD E. NEUSTADT

Contents

Tables

Figures

Preface to the Second Edition

I was reluctant to prepare a second edition of this book. I find it painful enough to revisit what I have written, continually questioning how I might better have expressed an idea or reported findings. And yet the Clinton and Bush 43 presidencies offered enticing cases for the arguments made in the first edition. The Clinton years provided three instances of a Democratic president and Republican Congress, the first such party split since 1946 and the only straight run of three such splits since the founding of the modern two-party system. The Bush 43 presidency may set many records before its completion, but the role of the U.S. Supreme Court in the 2000 election, a tie in the Senate (then the switch to Democratic control), net increases for congressional Republicans in the midterm and presidential elections, and the advancement of narrow-margin politics are in themselves sufficient to merit an examination of Bush's presidency in the separated system.

I have sought to achieve two major purposes in this revision. First, I refine the concepts, having thought and written more about separationism in the decade after the publication of the first edition. Notably, I incorporate points made in my presidential address to the American Political Science Association in 1994 and in my inaugural lecture as the John M. Olin Visiting Professor of American Government at the University of Oxford, 1998–99. Additionally, I have published two books of relevance to separated system politics: *Passages to the Presidency: From Campaigning to Governing* (Brookings, 1998) and *Clinton and Congress, 1993–1996: Risk, Restoration, and Reelection* (University of Oklahoma Press, 1999).

Second, I integrate Clinton and Bush 43 into the comparative analysis of postwar presidencies. These cases provide still more variations in split-party government and, as well, illustrate emerging narrow-margin politics and permanent campaigning. I add six cases of lawmaking that contribute refinements to my earlier treatment of partisan strategies and offer more evidence of system production under variable institutional, political, and policy conditions.

I acknowledge the help and support of several persons. My colleagues and friends in the Department of Political Science, University of Wisconsin-Madison and the Brookings Institution provided the backing that scholars may merit but often don't receive. Byron E. Shafer, then Mellon Professor of American Government at Oxford, invited me to Nuffield College for an ideal postretirement year as Olin Professor. As so many American scholars know, Nuffield nourishes the mind, body, and, if reachable, the soul. Karen M. Hult, Virginia Polytechnic Institute and State University, and Matthew W. Dickinson, Middlebury College, read the revision and provided very helpful comments and suggestions. I took their good advice in every instance, as would any presidential scholar from talented reviewers.

Brookings Institution staff provided their usual excellent assistance in moving this project along. First to be mentioned is Nancy D. Davidson, now retired, who urged me for years to prepare a revision. Chris Kelaher and Mary Kwak shepherded the manuscript through the several stages required to get it in print. Tanjam Jacobson provided a thorough editing of my prose. Carlotta Ribar proofread the pages, Julia Petrakis prepared the index, and Beth Schlenoff designed the cover.

The first edition was dedicated to my dear friend of over fifty years, Samuel C. Patterson. That mark of loyalty is not diminished by adding a tribute to Richard E. Neustadt. I came to know Dick well during the writing of the first edition, for which he sent several pages of comments to make me look better in print. We corresponded frequently after that, exchanging manuscripts and comments on presidential doings. I always got the better of the deal. In 2002 I had the intellectually exciting opportunity of writing about his career. My preparations included two interviews, one in London, the other in our home in Cross Plains, Wisconsin. I was ecstatic when his reaction to the article was, "You got it right." Like so many others, I miss him greatly. Never having had the opportunity of studying with him, I am nevertheless his devoted student. I trust that learning is evident in these pages.

Preface to the First Edition

In mid-July 1985 I was working at the Gerald R. Ford Library in Ann Arbor, Michigan, sorting through documents related to the major reorganization of federal energy agencies before and after the oil embargo by the Organization of Petroleum Exporting Countries. In April 1973 the Nixon administration had proposed the creation of a Federal Energy Administration, an Energy Research and Development Administration (ERDA), and a Department of Energy and Natural Resources. As I tracked the White House memos relating to ERDA that had been written in the summer and fall of 1974, two observations occurred to me: the work on ERDA took place during an institutional crisis of historic proportions, and virtually no trace of this unprecedented crisis appeared in the communications I was reviewing. The creation of ERDA was progressing at a level substantially below that of presidential goings and comings. The relevant participants in the complex energy policy network were hard at work building support for the proposal. The paperwork involved surfaced only occasionally in the Oval Office, as evidenced by presidential initials. While news stories were being written about the virtual collapse of the government, ERDA was approved by Congress and signed into law by President Gerald Ford on October 11, 1974. The presidency, it seems, is not the government.

I vowed at that time to correct what I perceived to be a common misunderstanding about the role of the president in the policy process. I began that endeavor by writing a paper exploring the role of presidents in agenda setting, seeking to identify how presidents varied in their capacities to manage the continuing agenda and to supervise policy alternatives. At a conference

xiii

at Brown University, the paper played to mixed reviews; in truth, the reactions were more negative than positive and more resistant to an altered interpretation than I had anticipated. For me, however, it was an initial effort in exploring the significant differences among presidents' personal, political, institutional, and policy strengths for governing.

In 1987 I proposed to Paul E. Peterson, then director of the Governmental Studies program at Brookings, that I write a book for Brookings on the role of the president in the policy process. Brookings accepted my proposal. I wrote to Peterson, "I want to understand much better than I do what it is that the White House contributes to policy development and approval. And I want to specify some of the more important conditions associated with what I assume to be variable policy functions and performance." Still motivated by my observations while working with the Ford White House files, I initially planned to study how weak or weakened presidents perform in office. Thus my focus at first was on so-called lame duck presidents and those, like Ford, who had very limited resources. At this early stage, the study was called "Governing When It's Over." Ultimately I found that it was necessary to compare all presidents in the post–World War II period. It was difficult to define weakness apart from strength. Further, it was apparent that every president faced the problem of "governing when it's over," of seeking a place in the permanent government. This understanding essentially brought me back to where I had started: the continuity of governing in a separated system and the variable role of the president.

I do not presume in this book to treat all dimensions of presidential power. I concentrate on those features I know best. In policy terms, that means focusing more on domestic than on foreign policy. I expect that a portrayal of post–World War II presidents based primarily on foreign policy would vary somewhat from that produced here (though that portrayal would have to reflect the greater role played by the contemporary Congress in foreign and national security issues). In institutional terms, I focus primarily on presidential-congressional relations. Obviously the president's interactions with the bureaucracy and the courts are of equal interest in a fuller understanding of the role of the president in governing. I would welcome a study of how postwar presidents have oriented themselves to the bureaucracy. If anything, the separateness of the presidential and executive branches is more obscure and misunderstood than that of the president and Congress.

In this book I often challenge the interpretations of analysts who rely on the criteria of a presidency-centered, responsible-party perspective in evaluating the national political system. For the most part, these are persons judged to be substantially more influential than political scientists: journalists, bureau chiefs, editors, political activists and reformers, Washington insiders, even presidents and their staffs. It is not clear why they cling to this perspective in light of the historical fact and daily reminders of separationism as the central feature of our government. I muse about that curiosity in chapter 8. It suffices here to speculate that people commonly reach for simple explanations in the face of complex phenomena. Because the American way of governing is the most intricate ever devised, a perspective that promises code-like explanations is attractive. When political scientists or historians advise that the complex cannot be made simple by proclamation, a common response is that the system should be reformed to make it more "responsible." However, a separated system is a bulwark against major change, as the history of reform efforts demonstrates. Political and institutional reformers are therefore typically frustrated even when they manage to enact change, mostly because their failure to comprehend fully the nature of the system leaves them at a strategic disadvantage in designing and implementing effective reform. Meanwhile, along the way there is adaptation as the separated system surveys and acts on social and political developments. Exactly how that adaptation takes place is worth studying, since it would reveal the workings of the American style and form of governing.

I wish to acknowledge my substantial debts in the preparation of this book. They are identified here in no order of importance as all were vital to the design and execution of the research. Several graduate students provided essential research tasks, most notably Katie Dunn Tenpas and John B. Bader. Few scholars have been better served. I am very grateful for their efforts as well as the good humor with which they carried out any number of tedious tasks. Others who assisted at different stages were Joanne Dunkelman and Rickey Vallier.

In the development of the project itself, I conducted a number of conversations and interviews with presidential and congressional scholars, journalists, politicians and former public officials, and various "think tankers" who have had experience in government. These exchanges were of inestimable value in providing context and conceptual direction. Included among the scholars were Bruce Buchanan, Colin Campbell, Louis Fisher, Erwin C. Hargrove Jr., Anthony King, Paul C. Light, Michael J. Malbin, Richard E. Neustadt, Roger G. Noll, Mark A. Peterson, James P. Pfiffner, Bert A. Rockman, and Stephen G. Wayne. As with all my research efforts, I consulted frequently with my friend of forty-five years, Samuel C. Patterson, to whom the book is dedicated. The journalists included Dom Bonafede, Richard Cohen, Janet Hook, Albert Hunt, Dick Kirschten, Neil MacNeil, Cokie Roberts, Steven Roberts, Gerald Seib, and Juan Williams.

The Brookings Institution more than met my need to talk with scholars with experience in government. I had extensive, recorded conversations with Warren I. Cikins, Stephen Hess, Sidney L. Jones, Lawrence J. Korb, Bradley A. Patterson, Joseph A. Pechman, A. James Reichley, Robert D. Reischauer, Charles L. Schultze, James L. Sundquist, and Joshua M. Wiener. I profited as well from less formal, but frequent, discussions with Robert A. Katzmann, Thomas E. Mann, Pietro S. Nivola, and R. Kent Weaver. Other recorded interviews were held with Robert E. Hunter, Suzanne R. Garment, Norman J. Ornstein, and Isabel V. Sawhill.

Conversations and formal interviews were also conducted with several former and present public officials. The purpose was to explore the variable role of the president in the national policy system with persons known to be reflective on such issues. Included were Charles Brain, Lawrence Eagleburger, Stuart Eizenstat, Bill Frenzel, Steven Hofman, Michael Jackson, Nicholas A. Masters, Philip Odeen, Harold Seidman, Charles Whalen, and Donald Wolfensberger. Some of these talks were tape recorded, and Vera M. Jones transcribed most of the taped interviews. I also had the privilege of attending the seminars for new members of the 101st, 102nd, and 103rd Congresses in Williamsburg, Virginia, where many of the issues treated in this book were discussed.

Some years ago, Stephen Hess conducted several interviews with public officials on subjects of relevance to this study. He graciously allowed me to listen to these tape-recorded sessions. Mark Rozell also permitted me to read interviews he conducted with officials of the Ford White House. The oral history interviews at the Lyndon Baines Johnson Presidential Library were an immensely useful source for background material on many post–World War II presidencies, and I am grateful for the cooperation of the library staff in making the relevant interviews available for my use.

A number of persons who know a great deal about the subject of this book kindly read and evaluated the manuscript. An initial set of readers included Richard F. Fenno Jr., Anthony King, and Bert A. Rockman. Their comments were invaluable in the first round of revisions. The second set of readers included Paul C. Light, Richard E. Neustadt, and Nelson W. Polsby. Thomas E. Mann, director of the Governmental Studies program, provided comments along the way and then offered an overview of the critiques as well as suggestions from his own reading of the manuscript. Leon D. Epstein read the manuscript in its final form. I wish to express my appreciation for the efforts of these scholars and friends. Their careful reading resulted in needed improvements in what is written here and how it is presented.

THE
PRESIDENCY
IN A SEPARATED SYSTEM

CHAPTER 1

Perspectives on the Presidency

The president is not the presidency. The presidency is not the government. Ours is not a presidential system.

I begin with these starkly negative themes as partial correctives to the more popular interpretations of the U.S. government as presidency-centered. Presidents learn these refrains on the job, if they do not know them before taking office. Consider what President George W. Bush knew of executive power prior to his taking the oath of office on January 20, 2001. He witnessed firsthand his father's problems in governing with a Democratic Congress, 1989–93, culminating in his father's defeat in 1992. He observed the struggles of President Bill Clinton throughout his eight years in the White House, battles that intensified with Republican majorities in Congress, 1995–2001. He learned about the limitations of executive power on the job as governor of Texas. And his own election was a bitterly fought contest that extended beyond election day. One of the closest races in history was finally ended on December 12, 2000, when the U.S. Supreme Court effectively stopped the recount in Florida, thus giving the state's electoral votes to Bush by fewer than 600 popular votes. A deeply disappointed Al Gore conceded the following day. Gore actually won the popular vote and lost the Electoral College by just four votes.

Joining Bush in Washington was a Republican House of Representatives, by the narrow margin of 221 to 212 (with two independents), and a Senate that was a dead-even split. The Democrats failed to win majorities in either chamber but had net gains in both.

George W. Bush proceeded to form his presidency with the least political standing of any president in the post–World War II era and with relatively weak legislative standing as well (see table 2-3 on page 52). The popular vote was a 50.3–49.7 percent split of the two-party vote in favor of Gore; the Electoral College vote, 50.4–49.6 percent in favor of Bush; the House of Representatives, 50.8 percent Republican to 49.2 percent Democrat and other; and the Senate, fifty Republicans (plus one vice president) to fifty Democrats. It was "the perfect tie," as one book had it.[1] But Bush won the tie and therefore had the responsibility of governing. Lacking political stature, he capitalized on *position,* the status of being president.

In 1992, President-elect Bill Clinton's circumstances contrasted sharply with those of Bush in 2000. He won handily in the Electoral College but received just 43 percent of the popular vote in a three-way race. Democrats maintained majorities in both houses of the 103rd Congress but had net losses of seats in each. As the leader of the first one-party government in twelve years, Clinton was under pressure to produce. Yet exercising influence required adjusting to its limitations. At a news conference shortly after his election, the president-elect acknowledged the challenge of converting campaign promises into legislative accomplishments.

> It's all very well to say you want an investment tax credit, and quite another thing to make the 15 decisions that have to be made to shape the exact bill you want.
>   It's all very well to say . . . that the working poor in this country . . . should be lifted out of poverty by increasing the refundable income tax credit for the working poor, and another thing to answer the five or six questions that define how you get that done.[2]

These lessons are not exclusive to presidents who enter office with constrained political standing. President Lyndon B. Johnson during the early years of his administration had the most impressive political advantages of any chief executive in the post–World War II era. An outpouring of grief for John F. Kennedy, an anxiety on Capitol Hill to enact legislation as a legacy for the young, assassinated president, a landslide win for Johnson in 1964, and two-thirds majorities for Democrats in both the House and the Senate, combined to provide huge benefits. However, President Johnson, too, understood that the president is not the presidency and the presidency is not the government. In his "perspectives on the presidency," Johnson reflected later on what is required to realize the potentialities of the office.

> Every President has to establish with the various sectors of the country what I call "the right to govern." Just being elected to the office does not guaran-

tee him that right. Every President has to inspire the confidence of the people. Every President has to become a leader, and to be a leader he must attract people who are willing to follow him. Every President has to develop a moral underpinning to his power, or he soon discovers that he has no power at all.[3]

For presidents, new or experienced, to recognize the limitations of office is commendable. Convincing others to do so is a challenge. The names of presidents become convenient labels for marking historical time: the Johnson years, the Nixon years, the Reagan years. Media coverage naturally focuses more on the president: there is just one at a time, executive organization is oriented in pyramidal fashion toward the Oval Office, Congress is too diffuse an institution to report on as such, and the Supreme Court leads primarily by indirection. Public interest, too, is directed toward the White House as a symbol of the government. As a result, expectations of a president often far exceed the individual's personal, political, institutional, or constitutional capacities. Performance seldom matches promise. Presidents who understand how it all works resist the inflated image of power born of high-stakes elections or short-term policy successes and seek to lower expectations. Politically savvy presidents know instinctively that it is precisely at the moment of great achievement that they must prepare themselves for the setback that will surely follow.

Focusing too much on the presidency can lead to a seriously distorted picture of how the national government does its work, the identification of weaknesses that are not there, and hence the proposal of inapropriate reforms. The plain fact is that the United States does not have a presidential system. It has a separated system. It is odd that it is so commonly thought of as otherwise, since schoolchildren learn about the separation of powers and checks and balances. As the author of *Federalist* 51 wrote, "Ambition must be made to counteract ambition." No one, least of all presidents, the Founders reasoned, can be entrusted with excessive authority. Human nature, being what it is, requires "auxiliary precautions" in the form of competing institutions, their legitimacy grounded in differing forms of public support and representational behavior.

The acceptance that the United States has a separated, not a presidential, system prepares one to appraise how politics works, rather than being simply reproachful and reformist. Thus, for example, for one political party to win the White House, while the other wins majority control of Congress (referred to here as split-party government) would be acknowledged as a potential or even likely outcome in a separated system, its legitimacy rooted in the separation of elections. Failure in recent decades to admit the authenticity of the split-party condition has fostered criticism and reform, often to the exclusion of analyzing what actually gets done. The post–World War II record shows that bills are passed and signed into law, executive orders issued, revenues collected, standards promulgated, military actions taken, under both one- and split-party arrangements. And so-called gridlock has occurred either way.

Simply put, the role of the president in this separated system of governing varies substantially, depending on his resources, advantages, and strategic position. My strong interest is in how presidents place themselves in an ongoing government and are accommodated by other participants, notably those on Capitol Hill. The central purpose of this book is to explore these adaptations. In pursuing this interest, I have found little value in the presidency-centered, party government perspective, as I will explain below. As a substitute, I propose a separationist, diffused-responsibility perspective that I find more suited to the constitutional, institutional, personal, political, and policy conditions associated with the American system of governing. First, however, I offer dramatic cases of how a president's role can change during his term in office, stories of the highs and lows of serving in the White House.

Landslides, No Slides, and Presidential Power

Surely if any president is to command the government, it will be one who wins so overwhelmingly that no one in Washington can deny his legitimacy for setting and moving the agenda. Two postwar presidents illustrate that a big win is no protection against changing conditions. Lyndon B. Johnson in 1964 and Richard M. Nixon in 1972 triumphed at the polls. Both then suffered dramatic losses in their capacity to lead. Johnson decided not to seek reelection in 1968; Nixon resigned in disgrace in 1974.

Election does not guarantee power in the American political system. Rather it legitimizes the effort of a president to lead, "to establish . . . the right to govern," in President Johnson's words. Leadership itself depends on opportunity, capability, and resources. By intent, the U.S. government performs within a set of limits designed to prevent it from working efficiently. There is substantial evidence that Americans continue to support the principles of mixed representation, separation of institutions, and distribution of powers, with all the checks and balances associated with those structural features.

Johnson won by a landslide in 1964. His opponent, Senator Barry M. Goldwater (R-Ariz.), won the electoral votes of just five Deep South states (those won by Dixiecrat candidate Strom Thurmond of South Carolina in 1948) plus a narrow win in his home state. On the day following Johnson's triumph, a *New York Times* editorial expressed the prevailing optimism. The predominant interpretation was that voters had expressed trust in Johnson, disaster had been averted with the defeat of Goldwater, and a mandate had been sanctioned. It was a "good election" by the criteria of the model of party government preferred by many analysts.

> The American people have given emphatic notice that they want to move forward constructively along the road of international understanding and domestic progress. . . .
>
> Rejected is the thesis that the challenges of an era of dynamic, relentless change in domestic and foreign affairs can be met by dismantling the Federal Government or by shaking a nuclear fist at the rest of the world. No more decisive rebuke could have been administered to the right-wing extremists whose command of the Republican national machinery plunged that great party into its destructive course. . . .
>
> The strong mandate for flexibility of approach now given to the man in the White House offers some hope, in contrast to the despair that would have been engendered throughout the world—especially among America's allies—by a Goldwater victory.[4]

Johnson's victory was amplified by the gains of congressional Democrats. Their already impressive margins in each house increased, producing better than two-to-one Democratic majorities. It was a victory akin to those of the Franklin D. Roosevelt era. No one doubted that President Johnson had the right and the responsibility to govern. Yet upon leaving office he pondered that such an election guaranteed only the responsibility; the right had to be established, then continually nurtured. In fact, Richard E. Neustadt recalls that Johnson himself was aware that he had two years of grace. Summarizing a meeting in December 1964, he wrote that Johnson understood the nature of his win, that it was "a sharp defeat for screwballism and an endorsement of sanity, but by no means an overwhelming mandate for a Hundred Days, à la 1933."[5] At the same time, Johnson predicted that there would be pressure for a bold agenda, with the columnists "watching, counting days, and keeping score."

Conditions changed substantially as a result of the midterm elections of 1966. Republicans realized a net gain of forty-seven House seats (their greatest gain since 1946) and four Senate seats. They also won back several state houses. This significant Republican showing brought rather different editorial comment in the *New York Times*: "There is a widespread dissatisfaction and uneasiness about the course and the prospects of the Vietnam War. . . . As a result of Tuesday's victories, the Republican Presidential nomination in 1968 now seems very much worth having and the number of potential claimants was increased."[6]

By the final year of the Johnson administration, the commentary could be described as "doleful." David S. Broder of the *Washington Post*, in discussing the 1968 State of the Union message, compared the mood of 1964 with that of 1968: "Above all, the optimistic 'can-do' President of 1964 had been transformed into a sober, slow-talking man who puzzled aloud about the 'restlessness' and 'questioning' in the land."[7] The message from a spent president emphasized crime control legislation.

Johnson himself clearly felt every bit of the burden detected by Broder and others. Here is how he described that last year in his memoirs:

> As I look back over the crowded diaries listing the telephone calls and meetings of 1968, as I reread the daily headlines that jumped so steadily and forebodingly from one trouble spot to another, as I review the memos and the intelligence reports, I recall vividly the frustration and genuine anguish I experienced so often during the final year of my administration. I sometimes felt that I was living in a continuous nightmare.[8]

There are few better illustrations of how changes in the political and policy configurations influence the confidence, capacity, dedication, and fever for governing. But there are other interesting cases.

Richard M. Nixon was reelected in 1972 by stunning popular and Electoral College margins. His percentage of the popular vote was nearly as great as Johnson's in 1964; his Electoral College count was greater (520 compared to 486). His opponent, George McGovern, won the electoral votes of Massachusetts and the District of Columbia. Editorial comment, however, deemed this a less significant result than for Johnson in 1964. Why? Primarily because congressional Republicans did not do as well as had congressional Democrats in 1964. In 1972, the Republicans realized a net gain of twelve House seats and a net loss of two Senate seats, failing to produce majorities in either chamber. Some called it the "empty landslide." "What the election appears to say through Congress is: All right, four more years—but only with the continued safeguard of checks and balances in liberal doses."[9] Arthur Krock of the *New York Times* concluded that "in the wide meaning of the term, he [Nixon] has no mandate at all."[10] Imagine, a forty-nine-state win and "no mandate at all."

Less than nineteen months after his second inaugural, President Nixon resigned as a consequence of the Watergate scandal. The reactions were a mixture of pity and relief.

> The resignation of Richard M. Nixon . . . comes as a tragic climax to the sordid history of misuse of the Presidential office that has been unfolding before the eyes of a shocked American public for the last two years. . . . What is important is that here was a man who failed his public trust. Never before in American history has there been such a failure at so high a level. This is the sorrow and the tragedy.[11]

The disgraced president returned to California, where he suffered an attack of phlebitis. He had an operation and was in serious condition.

> I was a physical wreck; I was emotionally drained; I was mentally burned out. This time, as compared with the other crises I had endured, I could see no reason to live, no cause to fight for. Unless a person has a reason to live for other than himself, he will die—first mentally, then emotionally, then physically.[12]

The Johnson and Nixon cases are particularly dramatic examples of how political, personal, and policy conditions can change during a presidency. But all presidents face ups and downs in their status and influence. There are no exceptions. More recently, George H. W. Bush had record job performance ratings at the height of the Gulf War, only to see these numbers plummet with the downturn in the economy. Bill Clinton's election in 1992 was greeted with enthusiasm after twelve years of Republican control of the White House. As one analyst put it, "the stars are really aligned right for the next four years."[13] Yet in 1994 the Democrats lost their House and Senate majorities. And subsequently Clinton himself, reelected in 1996 by a comfortable margin, became the first elected president to be impeached. George W. Bush lacked a popular majority and faced serious doubts about his abilities to lead and to govern, especially in regard to foreign and national security issues. The terrorists' attacks on September 11, 2001, dramatically changed his status and his presidency: his approval ratings soared to record highs. Later, however, they declined dramatically with the prolonged insurrection in Iraq. In 2004 he narrowly won reelection.

Nowhere in the Constitution is there a guarantee that election by a wide margin ensures a president advantages through a term in office, nor that a president who barely ekes out a win can never gain an edge in the governing process. The election is but one in a series of events that variably affect presidential power. Likewise, high public approval ratings at one point are no guarantee either of political success at that time or of subsequent high ratings. Breathtaking shifts can and do occur. Presidents must be ever attentive to the inconstant nature of their strategic position. Most presidents in the postwar period have hardly needed this advice. Truman, Eisenhower, Nixon, Ford, Reagan, Bush 41, Clinton, and Bush 43 served with split-party control between the White House and Congress (one house or both); Truman, Kennedy, Nixon in 1968, Carter, Clinton, and Bush 43 won by narrow margins or less than 50 percent of the popular vote. That leaves just Lyndon Johnson. And he learned that political support can deteriorate: "A President must always reckon that his mandate will prove short-lived. . . . For me, as for most active Presidents, popularity proved elusive."[14]

Pictures in Our Heads

If the presidency is to be a major source for understanding American politics, then it is convenient to have a set of expectations by which to test performance. Richard Rose points out that several "portraits" have been used in recent years—some more idealistic, some more iconoclastic. "The overall effect is confusion rather than understanding; balanced portraits are relatively rare."[15]

Two types of expectations are frequently relied on by analysts, particularly those in the media, who necessarily produce short-term commentary and evaluations. Presidents are tested first by the broader criteria associated with judgments about the role of the presidency in the political system. The specifics may vary from one president to the next, but, in Walter Lippmann's marvelous phrase, we carry "pictures in our heads" that serve as cues for evaluating behavior: "what each man does is based not on direct and certain knowledge, but on pictures made by himself or given to him."[16] Often reactions based on these images are not fully or systematically articulated as models of behavior. Rather, they are formed by judgments made along the way. Sometimes these are traceable to positive evaluations of one president: Franklin D. Roosevelt is a frequent model, and surprisingly, given how he was judged at the time, so is his successor, Harry S Truman. Or judgments can be traced to comparisons with a predecessor of the same political party: Dwight Eisenhower for Richard Nixon, Lyndon Johnson for Jimmy Carter, Ronald Reagan for George H. W. Bush, or George Bush the father for George Bush the son.

The second type of evaluation measures a president against himself. This test is based on who the president is (or who the evaluator judges him to be), what his record has been to that point, and what he has said in gaining office. Mark J. Rozell spotted this form of assessment in his study of President Carter's press relations.[17] Journalists' conceptions of how Jimmy Carter ought to perform as president were based on what they thought they knew about him; in a sense, they were testing him by their understanding of his own performance criteria.

If integrated, these two sources provide the basis for a balanced judgment about presidential performance. Often, however, the two are drawn on separately and may conflict. For example, it might be argued that President Carter should compromise in order to get legislation enacted because that is what a president should do as political leader in a separated system; yet a compromising Jimmy Carter is out of character and thus he loses credibility. President Ford should restore the leadership of the White House; yet a vetoing Gerald Ford is out of character with his image of establishing harmony. Each President Bush (father and son) should offer an extensive legislative program; yet activism is out of character with the men and their limited or nonexistent mandates.

There also are contrary expectations associated with split-party government. Hopes are expressed for reduced partisanship even as conditions usually promote partisanship, such as when one party controls the White House and the other, Congress. Here, for example, is editorial analysis following the 1946 elections in which the Republicans recaptured both houses of Congress for the first time since 1930:

> The greatest danger is that a purely partisan approach to the 1948 Presidential campaign, now hardly a year and a half off, will stultify the work of this Congress. The hope must be that the President and the majority and minority leaders will realize that a narrow partisanship will hurt, not help, them in 1948.[18]

As it happened, of course, the 80th Congress was intensely partisan. President Truman used that fact in the 1948 campaign. He won a surprising victory, the Democrats recaptured control of Congress, and the *New York Times* then expressed "gratification . . . in the emergence of a unified National Government."[19] Ignored was the fact that the 80th Congress had enacted ten pieces of major legislation, including the Marshall Plan and the Taft-Hartley Act.[20]

Likewise, when the Democrats won so overwhelmingly in 1974, increasing their margins substantially in both houses, President Ford was advised "to temper partisanship in favor of collaboration with the opposition party." "A similar spirit of constructive collaboration" was expected from the Democrats.[21] In effect, it was recommended that separated system politics be dismissed in favor of the politics of harmony as the preferred picture in our heads.

These various impressions or expectations are not models in the scientific sense. But they do serve a similar function by creating standards for testing presidential performance. Even when presidents exceed the expectations, there often is a return to the home base of prior judgments. In some cases, as with Carter, those evaluations may result in less credit than is actually due; in other cases, as with Reagan, they may result in more. That is, Carter's and Clinton's penchant for hyperbole led to tests that were unrealistic; Reagan's tendency to support the inevitable earned him praise for a positive record with Congress that was in fact quite limited beyond his first year in office.

Behavior or performance that exceeds expectations is treated as just that—exceptional. Thus it is difficult to get an adjusted reading. The case of George W. Bush is pertinent. While Bush has been frequently judged not to be legitimate as president (for failing to win the popular vote in 2000 and the controversy over the Florida recount) or competent (for questions about his experience and intelligence), evidence to the contrary, such as strong public support or able decisions, was treated as transitory and unusual. As subsequent challenges arose, expectations reverted to the lesser view of Bush's status and ability. Ironically, the rather consistent low expectations lowered the bar for him in making the next decision. The notion that a presidency is the composite of accommodations to changing people, politics, and policy issues is, perhaps, too demanding and best left more to historians than contemporary analysts or critics. It was decades before a more positive score was computed for Truman.

The Dominant Perspective:
Unitarianism and Party Government

The pictures in our heads are impressions, not well-thought-out theories of governance. The images set forth above, however, are consistent with a dominant and well-developed perspective that has been highly influential in evaluations of the American political system. I refer to it as "unitarianism" and it varies in important ways from "separationism," which I discuss below. The unitarian perspective supports party government, typically led by a strong and aggressive president. Its advocates prefer a system in which political parties are stronger and more integrated than they normally can be in a system of separated elections. Accountability and responsibility are the primary objectives. Accordingly, split-party outcomes are anathema because both parties win and are then encouraged to share credit and avoid blame. This lack of clear and direct accountability is viewed as a deficiency that naturally fosters a reformist mood among party government advocates. James L. Sundquist refers to it as "the constitutional dilemma."[22] Roadblocks built into the system often prevent ideological policy positions, conservative or liberal, from being enacted into law:

> A president is expected to lead the Congress, but its two houses are independent institutions and, most of the time of late, one or both are controlled by his political opposition. And when a president fails as leader—whether because the Congress chooses not to follow or because of the many possible forms of personal inadequacy—the system has no safeguard.[23]

Sundquist quotes Douglas Dillon, secretary of the Treasury in the Kennedy administration and cochair of the Committee on the Constitutional System (a group dedicated to reforming the Constitution), in identifying the insufficiencies of the U.S. system:

> Our governmental problems do not lie with the quality or character of our elected representatives. Rather they lie with a system which promotes divisiveness and makes it difficult, if not impossible, to develop truly national policies. . . . No one can place the blame. The President blames the Congress, the Congress blames the President, and the public remains confused and disgusted with government in Washington.[24]

The unitarian or party government perspective is best summarized in the recommendations made in 1950 by the Committee on Political Parties of the American Political Science Association.

> The party system that is needed must be democratic, responsible and effective. . . .
> An effective party system requires, first, that the parties are able to bring forth programs to which they commit themselves and, second, that the parties possess sufficient internal cohesion to carry out these programs. . . .
> The fundamental requirement of such accountability is a two-party system in which the opposition party acts as the critic of the party in power, developing, defining, and presenting the policy alternatives which are necessary for a true choice in reaching public decisions.[25]

Note the language: party in power, opposition party, policy alternatives for choice, accountability, internal cohesion, programs to which parties commit themselves. As a whole, it forms a test that a separated system is frequently bound to fail.

Oddly, the report did not envisage strong presidential leadership for the party. Rather, the emphasis was on creating a powerful party council with whom the presidential candidate and the president would be expected to cooperate.[26] This council would play a major role in determining the party platform and in interpreting the platform as applying to current problems. The ultimate goal was to create party structures that would overcome the divisions inherent in a separated system. Put otherwise, an effort was made to make party an independent rather than dependent variable.

I know of very few contemporary advocates of the two-party responsibility model. But I know many analysts who rely on its criteria when judging the political system, for example, in interpreting elections and evaluating presidents once in office. By the standards of unitarianism, the good campaign and the good election have the following characteristics:

—Publicly visible issues that are debated by the candidates during the campaign.

—Clear differences between the candidates on the issues, preferably deriving from a party ideology as expressed in the platform.

—A substantial victory for the winning candidate, thus demonstrating public support for one set of issue positions.

—A net increase in congressional seats and state houses, indicating a win for the party (not just the president) and its positions.

—A greater than expected win for the victorious party, preferably at both ends of Pennsylvania Avenue.

—A postelection declaration of unity from the congressional leaders of the president's party.

A good president, from this perspective, is one who makes government work, one who has a program and uses his resources to get it enacted. A good president is an activist: he sets the agenda, is attentive to the progress being made, and willingly accepts responsibility for what happens. He can behave in this way because he has demonstrable and dependable support within his party. There is unity and therefore the likelihood of accountability—the very essence of unitarianism.

It is not in the least surprising that the real outcomes of separated elections frustrate those who prefer responsible party government. Ordinarily these demanding tests will be met only by coincidence. Even an election that gives the same party control of the White House and both houses of Congress in no way guarantees a unified or responsible party outcome. And even if a president and his congressional party leaders appear to agree on policy priorities, the situation may change dramatically following midterm elections, which do not involve the president. Robert A. Dahl and Charles E. Lindblom described the effects of the constitutional electoral provisions this way:

> The strategic consequence of this arrangement, as the Constitutional Convention evidently intended, has been that *no unified, cohesive, acknowledged, and legitimate representative-leaders of the "national majority"* exist in the United States. Often the President claims to represent one national majority, and Congress (or a majority of both houses) another. The convention did its work so well that even when a Congressional majority is nominally of the same party as the President, ordinarily they do not speak with the same voice.[27]

Understandably, advocates of party government are led to propose constitutional reform. Coincidence is not a reliable basis for ensuring their preferred outcome. Still, recent developments on Capitol Hill may be encouraging. Party unity has strengthened, especially with the Republicans' success in the South and their majority status in the House of Representatives from 1995, after forty years in the minority.[28] President George W. Bush even found it advantageous to have the disciplined House Republicans act first on his proposals, as pressure on the Senate. As it happened, however, narrow margins there enabled the Senate Democrats to obstruct passage in many instances. In this case the president working with a strengthened party organization on Capitol Hill brought limited results— and, oddly, frequent media and Democratic criticism of House Republican leaders for failing to be more accommodating to the Democrats.

There is no standard formula under present constitutional arrangements for governing from the White House. Presidents identify their strengths and evaluate their weaknesses in negotiating with Congress or otherwise attempting to lead. They seldom have the advantages desired by advocates of party government, though party strength in Congresses waxes and wanes. Even in those cases where appearances would suggest "responsible party" leadership (for example, in 1932, 1936, and 1964), it is by no means certain either that the appearances are the reality or that the advantages can be long sustained. The tests of performance should account for the variations in party splits and in the political and policy advantages available to the president and Congress.

Variations in Party Splits

Split-party control between the White House and Congress has been characteristic of national politics since the founding of the present two-party system and has been featured a majority of the time in the post–World War II period. It is, of course, a wholly constitutional result in a system of separated elections for three elected institutions (president, House of Representatives, and Senate). With the establishment of a well-fixed two-party system, there are eight potential combinations of governance: two with one party in command of the three institutions and six split-party arrangements. The voters have frequently exercised their option of producing split-party government. All six split-party combinations have been experienced since 1856. Table 1-1 lists the cases, the first of which was in 1858. Although split-party results were frequent in the nineteenth century, they tended to arise from midterm elections. That is, a president would first be elected with a Congress under the control of his party, which would then lose one or both houses at the midterm. In only three cases (Hayes, 1876; Garfield, 1880; and Cleveland, 1884) did a president begin his administration under split-party conditions, and in each instance the president's party only failed to achieve a majority in one house. These three instances did occur in sequence, however, producing the longest period of split-party government in history—fourteen years (see table 1-2). It was also rare in the nineteenth century for the president's party to be in the minority in both houses. The two cases (Hayes, 1878; Cleveland, 1894) occurred as a result of midterm elections (table 1-1).

There are but three instances of split-party control in the early twentieth century: Taft, 1910; Wilson, 1918; and Hoover, 1930. Only under Wilson did the president's party lose its majority in both houses. These three instances of midterm losses presaged substantial defeats for the president's party in the subsequent presidential election. Perhaps the contemporary presidency-centered, party government perspective derives from analysis of this period, particularly given the expansionist outlooks of Woodrow Wilson and Franklin D. Roosevelt (the quintessential strong president, by which others are typically measured). It may also be that analysis of this period encourages the view of divided or split-party government as a corruption—a condition associated with the failure of party and policy leadership by presidents and therefore to be prevented.

In the period from 1946 to 2004 there has been split-party government a majority of the time. In contrast to earlier eras, in this third period presidents have often entered office when their party was unable to command majorities in Congress: Eisenhower in his second term, Nixon and Reagan in both terms, Bush 41 in his single term, and Clinton in his second term. In 2000, Bush 43 had a Republican majority in the House, a tie in the Senate. During

Table 1-1. *Split-Party Control between the White House and Congress, 1858–2002*

President and year	Type of split control		Election establishing split control	
	Both houses of opposite party	One house of opposite party	Presidential	Midterm
Buchanan (D) 1858		House		x
Grant (R) 1874		House		x
Hayes (R) 1876		House	x	
Hayes (R) 1878	x			x
Garfield (R) 1880		Senate[a]	x	
Arthur (R) 1882		House		x
Cleveland (D) 1884		Senate	x	
Cleveland (D) 1886		Senate		x
Harrison (R) 1890		House		x
Cleveland (D) 1894	x			x
Taft (R) 1910		House		x
Wilson (D) 1918	x			x
Hoover (R) 1930		House[b]		x
Truman (D) 1946	x			x
Eisenhower (R) 1954	x			x
Eisenhower (R) 1956	x		x	
Eisenhower (R) 1958	x			x
Nixon (R) 1968	x		x	
Nixon (R) 1970	x			x
Nixon (R) 1972	x		x	
Ford (R) 1974	x			x
Reagan (R) 1980		House	x	
Reagan (R) 1982		House		x
Reagan (R) 1984		House	x	
Reagan (R) 1986	x			x
Bush 41 (R) 1988	x		x	
Bush 41 (R) 1990	x			x
Clinton (D) 1994	x			x
Clinton (D) 1996	x		x	
Clinton (D) 1998	x			x
Bush 43 (R) 2000[c]		Senate	x	

Source: Calculated from data in Harold W. Stanley and Richard G. Niemi, *Vital Statistics on American Politics*, 3rd ed. (Washington: CQ Press, 1992), table 3–17; and various Internet sources for later presidencies.

a. The situation following the 1880 elections was extraordinary. The Senate was split evenly: thirty-seven Democrats, thirty-seven Republicans, two independents. After much maneuvering and two Republican resignations, the Democrats appointed the officers and the Republicans organized the committees.

b. The Republicans, in fact, won a majority of House seats (218-216), but by the time the Congress first met, a sufficient number had died to permit the Democrats to organize the House.

c. The Senate was split evenly. Vice President Cheney broke the tie to allow Republicans to organize. Five months later, a Republican senator switched to Independent, voting with the Democrats to organize.

Table 1-2. *Split-Party Control between the President and Congress,*
by Historical Period, 1856–2006

| Period | Number of splits | | Total years | | Consecutive years |
	Both houses of opposite party	One house of opposite party	Number	Percent	
1856–1900 (44 years)	2	8	20	45	14 (1874–88)
1900–1946 (46 years)	1	2	6	13	0[a]
1946–2006 (60 years)	14	4	36	60	12 (1980–92)[b]
1856–2006 (150 years)	17	14	62	41	. . .

Source: Calculated from data in table 1-1.
a. There were three Congresses with split control (1911–13, 1919–21, and 1931–33), but no two were consecutive.
b. There were two other lengthy periods of split control: 1954–60 and 1968–76.

the postwar era, Republican presidents had seventeen opportunities to capture full control of the government; they did so three times (in 1952, 2002,
and 2004). The longest sequence of split-party government in this period—
twelve years—does not quite match the fourteen-year spell in the nineteenth
century, but in combination with the eight-year span during the Nixon and
Ford presidencies, it represents an extraordinarily high percentage for a
twenty-four-year period (83 percent).

In summary, it is apparent that split-party control can hardly be labeled
an aberration, at least as measured by frequency of occurrence. It has been
the result in two out of five elections since 1856 (see table 1-2). The period
that appears to serve for many analysts as a model for testing effective government (1900–46) had the fewest years of split control. Divided government occurred 54 percent of the time in the other two eras combined.

Also noteworthy are the differences between the first and third periods.
Instead of serving as a corrective check at the midterm, as was so frequently
the case in the nineteenth century, split-party government has been legit-
imized from the start of a presidency in the contemporary period. There
must be a point at which an event that is repeated frequently is misdiag-
nosed as exceptional or even as a corruption. In the third period voters have
had seven opportunities (1948, 1956, 1972, 1976, 1984, 1992, and 2002) to
make adjustments from an incumbent split-party government to a single-
party government. They did so four times, once providing congressional
majorities to an incumbent Democratic president (Truman, 1948), once

switching the Senate from the opposition to the president's party (Bush, 2002), and twice giving an incumbent Democratic Congress its own president (Carter, 1976; Clinton, 1992). Interestingly, in each of these cases the president himself emerged from a narrow election win with, at best, an ambiguous charge. In 1980, the voters chose to go in the opposite direction—from an incumbent single-party government (that of the Carter presidency) to a split-party government (a Democratic House and Republican Senate for Reagan). The 2000 election was a special case in which the Republicans barely won the White House, kept their majority in the House, and had a tie in the Senate that was lost a few months later.

Variations in Presidential Advantages

The variation in political status and strategic positioning does not end with having identified presidents with single-party or split-party governments. Presidents in each situation differ substantially in the advantages they have beyond those associated with their party's being in the majority in the House and the Senate. These advantages may derive from the election itself and how it is interpreted, the actual number of House and Senate seats held by the president's party, public and media support (typically measured by job approval ratings), midterm results, and the nature of the issues. Thus, for example, there is a substantial difference between Jimmy Carter's single-party government in 1977 and that of Lyndon Johnson in 1965; and equally, between Richard Nixon's split-party government in 1969, that of Ronald Reagan in 1981, and that of Bill Clinton after the 1994 midterm election.

These advantages and their effects will be identified in subsequent chapters. Suffice it for now to state that sometimes when the president has few resources, the Congress has many (or members are led to believe so). The Republicans in the 80th (1947–49) and 104th (1995–97) Congresses, for example, believed that they were on their way to single-party government in the subsequent presidential election and acted aggressively in pursuing that goal, unsuccessfully in both cases. Similarly, congressional Democrats in the post-Watergate era (1975–77) acted confidently on policy issues and carried this behavior over into the Carter presidency, often challenging a president of their own party. The variations foster distinctions among governments: those that are *presidential* because of extraordinary White House advantages and the wit to use them; those that are *congressional* because of weakness in the White House and strong leadership capabilities on Capitol

Hill; and those that are *balanced,* with advantages more or less evenly distributed at both ends of Pennsylvania Avenue.

Taken together, party splits and different institutional advantages prepare the analyst for the varied circumstances under which presidents seek to govern. Political parties simply lack the structural status to override these distinctions, to compensate for the limitations experienced by elected officials within the executive and the legislature. Nor should one expect political parties in a separated system to exercise power they do not or cannot possess.

The variations in conditions for governing are clearly consistent with a separation of powers anchored by distinct elections. The independent sources of power for each institution often lead to different interpretations of the agenda and what is required to cope with the problems it lists. As noted above, occasionally one or the other institution is dominant. More typically, however, the White House and Congress must "act in tandem," as Mark A. Peterson correctly asserts. He views the two as a partnership and conjures up the image of a tandem bicycle. "On matters of domestic policy, the president may sit at the 'front' of the process, providing direction by influencing the policy agenda . . . but the choice of direction lacks significance without a synchronized response from the 'rear'."[29] This metaphor is appropriate enough under some conditions, but the variations noted above suggest that the president will not be riding up front at all times or on all issues. They also suggest that before tandem-ness there may be competition for who rides up front and, more than likely, for how credits are shared for a race well run.

It is difficult to maintain a distinction between partisan and institutional differences when seeking to understand how the government works. Is it a case of a Republican president versus a Democratic Congress? Or is it simply the president versus the Congress? The puzzlement is a consequence of the constitutional and political structure itself. Not all dilemmas were resolved in Philadelphia; in fact, several were generated there. To take the case of split-party government, the president obviously cannot appeal solely to his political party under most circumstances (sustaining a veto is an exception). Meanwhile, the majority party in Congress may well appeal to institutional identification in seeking support from members of the president's party. I can promise no more than attentiveness throughout this book to the distinction between conflict that is more strictly partisan and that which is more strictly institutional.

What can be said about responsibility for policy and governing within this system? At least two interpretations are evident: that responsibility is either assignable or not, and correspondingly that it is focused or diffused. Neither interpretation presumes an empirically demonstrable responsibility, as would suit the criteria set forth by party government advocates. The first simply proposes that under certain conditions (typically single-party government) analysts will be inclined to assign responsibility to the president's party when it has majorities on Capitol Hill. And the second proposes that under other conditions (typically split-party government) analysts will find it difficult to assign responsibility, though they will often, nonetheless, hold the president accountable for whatever happens "on his watch." The consequence is more focused with the first, diffused with the second.

I make no judgment at this point about a preferred interpretation. The immediate purpose is to encourage the reader to accept both assignable and nonassignable responsibility as legitimate interpretations associated with electoral outcomes and institutional shares of powers. Acknowledging the legitimacy of both types is particularly important for the postwar period, since the preferred outcome of the party responsibility advocates—single-party control and superior White House advantages—is an uncommon occurrence. Analysts limited to presidencies under those conditions have an *N* of 1 to work with in the postwar period—the presidency of Lyndon Johnson, and then for just two years, 1965–67. Remaining to be explained are the fifty-eight years of that period when, by a wholly constitutional process, voters produced split-party government or single-party government with ambiguous electoral messages.

The intention then is to establish a framework that permits analysis of relative presidential and congressional political, institutional, and policy advantages, reserving judgments about the workability of the system for the time being. The party responsibility model provides little or no aid either for describing a significant portion of the politics since 1946 or for predicting policy developments in the period. An alternative perspective is needed: one more suited to the political, institutional, and policy conditions of the time.

An Alternative Perspective: Separationism and a Government of Parties

An alternative perspective for understanding American national politics is bound to be unsatisfactory to party responsibility advocates. By the rendition promoted here, with separationism, responsibility is individualized, not collectivized. Accordingly, it is diffused, not focused. Representation is not pure and unidirectional; it is mixed, diluted, and multidirectional. Further, the tracking of policy from inception to implementation discourages the most devoted advocate of responsibility theories. This alternative perspective accepts the rationale and reality of separate institutions competing for shares of powers. It does not pursue means for overcoming these features. Party government is not considered likely; rather a *government of parties* is presumed commonly to exist. By this perspective, there is no overarching political party apparatus, nor can an effective one be fashioned by reforms. Multiple party units operate throughout the elected national government—in the House of Representatives, the Senate, the White House, the national party headquarters. Accordingly, a president finds that he must negotiate with leaders of his own party, as well as those from the other party.

Separationism advances a government of parties, which, in turn, tends to diffuse responsibility. The presidency and Congress and multiple party units and leaders share credit when things go well and make it difficult to pinpoint who was wrong when things go badly. For the mature government (one that has achieved substantial involvement in social and economic life), much of the agenda is self-generating, that is, it results from programs already on the books. Thus the desire to propose new programs is often frustrated by demands to sustain or expand existing programs, since resources are often limited because of growth in entitlements and defense. Much of the modern agenda then tends to be reformist in nature, altering what exists more than enacting what is new.

Additionally there is the matter of who should be held accountable for what and when. This is not a novel issue by any means. It is a part of the common rhetoric of split-party government. Are the Democrats responsible for how Medicare has worked because it was a part of Lyndon Johnson's Great Society? Or are the Republicans responsible because their presidents accepted, administered, and revised the program? Is President Carter responsible for creating a Department of Energy or President Reagan responsible for failing to abolish it, or both? At what point should a new president be held accountable for the decline of the economy when the downturn started in the previous administration? The partisan rhetoric on deficits continues to blame the Democrats for supporting spending programs and the Republicans for cutting taxes. It is noteworthy that this level of debate fails to treat more fundamental issues, such as the constitutional roadblocks to defining or assigning responsibility. In preventing the tyranny of the majority, the Founders also made it difficult to specify accountability.

It is understandable that critics will conclude that the American political system lacks responsibility in the classic sense. Yet this view is typically based on a collective notion of responsibility, as identified with parliamentary systems. A separated system will fail this test for structural reasons. Having a president, representatives, and senators elected separately and for terms of different lengths tends to individualize responsibility. A composite or collective party accounting may be possible by examining the individual records and behaviors of those seeking reelection. But it takes a shrewd and calculating voter to stitch together an accounting of party performance through sequences of presidential and congressional elections.[30]

Here are the reasons why. Presidents are electorally accountable after a first four-year term, if they choose to run again. The Twenty-Second Amendment precludes an electoral accounting after the second term except by assignment to the successor candidate of his party, for example, Bush 41 for Reagan or Gore for Clinton. Elected representatives are accountable every second year, and all along the way, according to David R. Mayhew in *Congress: The Electoral Connection*.[31] Collective accountability for the party's record in the House is at least potentially possible because all districts have elections. In practice, however, members seeking reelection are normally held responsible for their record and behavior during the two-year span, not for the record of their party. No such potential exists for senators, given the constitutional provision that one-third of the body is up for reelection every two years. This feature complicates accountability in other ways too. With two senators and three elections in a six-year period, every state will have one of those biennial elections without a senatorial contest. Additionally, the classes of senators up for reelection vary substantially in two respects: regional representation and population. For example, the class standing in 2000 was weighted heavily toward the Northeast, representing states with about 70 percent of the national population; the Midwest and South dominated the 2002 class, representing states with just half of the population; and the 2004 class had more regional balance, again representing about 70 percent.[32]

Diffusion of responsibility, then, is not only a likely result of a separated system but may also be a fair outcome. Accordingly, one has to doubt how reasonable it is to hold one institution or one political party accountable for a program that has grown incrementally through decades of varying single-

and split-party control and through disparate sequences of elections. Reforming a government program is bound to be an occasion for holding one or the other of the branches or parties accountable for wrongs being righted. If, however, politics allows crossing the partisan threshold so that both parties are on the same side, as may be possible in split-party government, then agreements may be reached that will avoid blame and permit credit taking and, potentially, significant policy change. This is not to say that both sides agree from the start about what to do. Rather it is to suggest that diffusion of responsibility may permit policy change that would have been much less likely if one party had to absorb all of the criticism for past performance or blame should the reforms fail when implemented. The forging of a major welfare reform package between President Clinton and congressional Republicans in 1996 is but one notable example (see chapter 7).

Institutional and partisan competition is an expected outcome of the constitutional arrangements that facilitate mixed representation and variable electoral horizons. For forty years (1954–94), this competition was reinforced by Republicans frequently winning the White House, Democrats comfortably maintaining majority status in the House of Representatives, and, in the 1980s, both parties hotly contending for majority status in the Senate. Bargains struck under these conditions may have the effect of perpetuating split control by denying opposition candidates the issues upon which to campaign and the means for defining accountability. To take an example from the 104th Congress: If a President Clinton reaches agreement with congressional Republicans on welfare or immigration reform, as he did, then split-party government may be perceived as working. Why not, then, return the Democrat to the White House and the Republicans to Congress? That was the outcome in 1996.

The participants in this system of mixed representation and diffused responsibility naturally accommodate their political surroundings. A government of parties is a working system, after all. Gridlock is possible, but it is by no means inevitable. Competition can facilitate resolution of issues if the participants are motivated to enact laws. It is useful to be reminded that the Founders were seeking to create a government. In *Federalist* 47, Madison cited a provision of New Hampshire's constitution that exquisitely reveals the governing purposes of separationism: "The legislative, executive, and judicial powers ought to be kept as separate from, and independent of, each other *as the nature of a free government will admit; or as is consistent with that chain of connection that binds the whole fabric of the constitution in one indissoluble bond of unity and amity.*"[33] Seemingly, the

Founders were sensitive to the possibility that separate institutions competing for and sharing powers could produce a stalemate.

Much of the above suggests that the political and policy strategies of presidents in their dealings with Congress will depend on their advantages at the time. One cannot employ a constant model of the activist president leading a party government. More often than not, presidents participate in a government of parties—one defined more by the principle of separation than by unity. Conditions may encourage the president to work at the margins of presidential-congressional interaction (for example, where he judges that he has an advantage, as with foreign and national security issues). He may allow members of Congress to take policy initiatives, hanging back to see how the issue develops. He may certify an issue as important, propose a program to satisfy certain group demands, but fail to expend the political capital necessary to get the program enacted. Or he may seek to escape the trying politics of split control and issue executive orders when feasible. My point is that having been relieved of testing the system for party responsibility, one can proceed to analyze how presidents perform under variable political and policy conditions.

In reprise, separationism was designed as a means of governing, one that promotes competition, multiple legitimacies, mixed representation, and institutional sharing of powers. In stark contrast to the preferences of the unitarian, for the separatist the good election is one that preserves the incentive to share powers and to compete in the lawmaking process. Party landslides are worrisome, leading as they do to declarations of mandates and unwarranted interpretations of advantages in the competition for powers. The period following World War II has been a separationist era that has both encouraged reform and frustrated its realization.

The Neustadt Formulation

In 1960 a book on the presidency was published that was destined to become one of the most influential works on a political institution. Richard E. Neustadt worked as a "political-level bureaucrat" in the Truman White House and was headed for a career in government and politics. But when the Republicans took charge of Washington in 1952, Neustadt left to begin professional life in academia. He found scholarly work on the presidency "to be very remote from what I had experienced." And so he set about writing *Presidential Power: The Politics of Leadership* "to fill the gap between the academic literature . . . and my experience."[34]

The separation of powers, or as Neustadt interpreted it "separated institutions *sharing* powers," is bedrock to how the presidency is analyzed. Presidents seek influence in a government that mostly cannot be led by commandments. Presidential power, then, is the power to persuade and to bargain. Optimally, the president makes an effort to convince other power holders that what he wants is what they should want, as suited to their authority in the separated system. Sources of persuasion include the president's "vantage points in government, together with his reputation in the Washington community and his prestige outside."[35] It follows that these sources must be nurtured, protected, and, when possible, enhanced.

I have proposed modifications to Neustadt's interpretation of the separation of powers and to "vantage points" as a source of power, alterations that in conversations and correspondence he agreed were consistent with his formulation. The first modification simply adds competition to the dynamics of the separated system: separated institutions sharing and competing for powers. That competition both complicates and helps to define the tasks of presidents exercising personal influence. The second modification enlarges Neustadt's first and basic source of power, the vantage points in government, by adding the qualities or status of being president. The vantage points are more objective; the qualities more subjective but very real. I apply the label "position" to this combination of advantages. As noted below, I have found the concept of position to be particularly useful in analyzing the presidency of Bush 43, both in his first year, when he had few other advantages, and later, when the war in Iraq came to threaten his status as a leader.[36]

Also basic to the Neustadt formulation is a distinction between *power* and *powers*. Power is personal influence, that is, what a president can do to get his way within a separated system populated by others equally anxious to exercise their own influence. Powers are those designations of authority to the president by the Constitution, Congress, or custom. Having powers is no guarantee of the effective wielding of personal influence. For that, a president depends on the sources noted above (vantage points, professional reputation, and public prestige) and his leadership skills in applying them.

Neustadt's formulation was an effort to comprehend the nexus of the personal and the institutional, of what is transitory with what is constant. In personal correspondence, he explained it this way: "My fundamental question remains the same throughout, namely how best to think about the possible effects of one's own choices on one's own prospects for personal influence within the institutional setting of a given office. . . . This amounts to seeking the essence of thinking politically, an endless search since this is so much an instinctive, intuitive process."

By this view, effective presidents continuously calculate the implications of their choices for their personal influence in making subsequent choices. They should think prospectively as they make their own history. And they also learn from their history: "The history you know, the experience you've had are critical. How useful it is if you've had it and how difficult it is to apply if it isn't your history."[37]

Neustadt's formulation has been enormously helpful in my thinking about the presidency in a separated system. We both begin with the reality of separationism. He focuses almost exclusively on the president and his exercise of power; I am more broadly attentive to relations with Congress. He is ever sensitive to the constraints on presidential power coming from Capitol Hill; I describe the sources of these constraints. I widen the lens and he narrows the focus within that broader field, mindful of motion threatening the president's personal influence.[38]

The Politics of Partisan Variations

A main contention so far is that constitutional arrangements for elections and the distribution of powers challenge presidents in their quest to serve effectively. Several combinations of party control of the elected branches of government are possible, thus adding the separation of politics to the separation of powers. Equally, these arrangements invite several patterns of partisan interaction and policy participation between the White House and Congress, as well as between the two houses of Congress and within committees. In fact, one-party government with powerful presidential advantages is an uncommon outcome in the post–World War II period. Therefore, one should not expect to witness straight, or noncompetitive, partisanship—winning with votes from only the president's party—very often. Exercising power as personal influence demands reaching across the aisles as well as down Pennsylvania Avenue.

An alternative perspective to that of party government, as offered above, should encourage a search for other partisan patterns and the conditions shaping those patterns. This approach may even permit a better understanding of institutional reform by identifying the circumstances under which changes can be effective, given the patterns of partisan interaction that obtain.

I have identified five patterns that will be explored further in the chapters devoted to presidential-congressional interaction on legislation: noncompetitive partisanship, competitive partisanship, competitive bipartisanship, bipartisanship, and cross-partisanship.[39] These categories identify the nature of the coalition building that takes place, directing attention to who participates in the lawmaking process, how they do so, and at what point. Most patterns can occur under either split- or single-party government. And there may be differences between how the president interacts with the House and the Senate. As will become evident, the patterns may vary within an administration—either during a particular period or in regard to specific bills. Much depends on the strategic situation: who initiates the legislation, the nature of the support, and what additional support is required.

Noncompetitive Partisanship

In this pattern, bargaining and coalition building occur primarily within the president's party, which has majorities in both houses of Congress. It is the pattern that best suits the conditions of the party government model. Responsibility is presumably focused within the dominant party. The purest example in the postwar period occurred during the first two years of the Johnson administration (1965–67). With two-thirds majorities for the Democrats in the House and Senate, the president had only to satisfy his own party in building majority support for his program. A significant number of major laws were enacted. No one doubted who was responsible.

A most interesting case of partisanship under split-party government developed in the final eighteen months of the Bush 41 administration (1991–93). Oddly, the partisanship was associated with the weakness of both the Republican president and the Democratic Congress. Both lost a basis for bargaining and compromise because their advantages were seriously reduced: public confidence in the president declined dramatically following the Persian Gulf War; Congress experienced a number of humiliating scandals. The stalemate that many predict for split-party government under any circumstances was characteristic of the 102nd Congress. In this case, the leaders of both parties viewed their opponents as vulnerable. Thus deadlock was associated not with strength, but rather weakness. Not surprisingly, little was accomplished.

The Clinton and Bush 43 presidencies also displayed cases of straight, noncompetitive, partisanship (see chapter 7). These instances were very different from those of the Johnson presidency, however. The party margins were narrow but unity was sufficient to win the day. Especially notable was the passage of President Clinton's 1993 economic package by the narrowest possible margins in each house, with no Republicans voting in favor in either chamber. The House Republicans during the first term of the Bush 43 presidency also showed extraordinary party discipline to suit the president's strategy of putting pressure on the Senate, a strategy that had mixed success.

Competitive Partisanship

This pattern is associated with split-party control and is, therefore, commonly featured in the postwar period. Until 1994, the split typically was between a Republican president and a Democratic Congress (there was just one case of the opposite arrangement, 1947–49). In 1994, the Republicans won majority status in the House of Representatives for the first time in forty years and also won the Senate; for the next six years President Clinton faced a Republican Congress. There was an important difference between the two partisan splits. Under the Republican presidents, Congressional Democrats frequently had sizable margins; Congressional Republicans had very narrow margins in the Clinton years.

Under certain conditions, competitive partisanship may characterize single-party government. The Bush 43 presidency is a case in point. With the Senate split 50-50 in 2001, Republicans were able to organize only with the vote of the vice president. Even so, the parties worked under a historic agreement that gave the Democrats special status as a minority. And after Senator James Jeffords (Vermont) switched from Republican to Independent, the Democrats were able to organize the Senate. In 2002, Republicans had a net gain of Senate seats sufficient for a narrow majority (51 to 48, with one Independent). Given the small margins in both houses, it took very few defections for the Republicans to lose a vote. Accordingly, competitive partisanship characterized most major issues on the agenda of the 107th Congress (2003–05).

Competitive partisanship is typified by the parallel development of proposals at each end of Pennsylvania Avenue or by the two parties in each house of Congress. Often these proposals represent different approaches to the problem, with participants in both institutions having sufficient support and expertise to be credibly involved. The increase in analytical capability on Capitol Hill in recent decades has allowed the majority parties in the

House and the Senate to be more active players in all phases of the policy process, thus enhancing their competitive edge.

Bargaining and coalition building can and do occur in competitive partisanship. At some point, the two forces typically try to reach an agreement. Why not simply capitalize on the failure of the other side to compromise? Because both sides identify possible political gains in reaching an agreement, or losses due to stalemate. Acknowledging that the problem requires attention, the participants determine that they can claim credit for success while avoiding blame for failure (past, present, or future). The latter point requires more elaboration. The agenda of a government with mature programs often is dominated by reform proposals or adjunct proposals (that is, those extending particular benefits). As noted earlier, it is difficult to enact reform without partisan recrimination. If, however, the two parties, each in control of an institution, can reach agreement, they can neutralize the issue for subsequent electoral campaigns yet preserve their right to formulate an initial proposal that reflects partisan concerns and group pressures. Competitive partisanship may be expected to work best when there is acknowledged strength in both the White House and Congress, thus creating the bargaining condition. There is less basis for this pattern if one or the other is dominant or if both are weak (as in the Bush 41 case cited above).

Competitive Bipartisanship

Recent developments in narrow-margin politics suggest a variation of competitive partisanship. The classic case is the education legislation in the 106th Congress (2001–03). George W. Bush made education reform a priority issue in the 2000 campaign. Bush invited Senator Edward M. Kennedy (D-Mass.) and Representative George Miller (D-Calif.) to work with the White House in designing legislation for this traditionally Democratic Party issue. The effort was bipartisan in that key representatives of both parties were actively involved during the early stages of crafting a bill. However, Republicans and Democrats had real differences that needed to be reconciled, making the process competitive.

The principal difference between partisan and bipartisan competition is in the stage at which it occurs. In partisan competition, each party develops its own proposal, fights for that plan, and remains sensitive to a point at which compromise is possible. If a bargain can be struck, then a coalition is formed to pass the legislation; if not, stalemate may be the result, especially given that filibusters are frequently threatened in a Senate with narrow margins. In bipartisan competition, the contenders compete throughout in fashioning legislation that can be enacted with a cross-partisan coalition. Stalemate may also occur if the bipartisan working group fails to shape a broadly acceptable bill. In the case of education reform in 2001, a bill eventually passed with 89 percent support in the House and 92 percent support in the Senate (see chapter 7). Several of the bills relating to national security following 9/11 also evidenced competitive bipartisanship; others, straight bipartisan cooperation.

Bipartisanship

There is a tendency to associate bipartisanship with foreign policy and national security issues. The most frequently cited era of bipartisanship—that following the end of World War II—was characterized by certain congressional leaders, most notably Senator Arthur Vandenberg (R-Mich.), accepting the president's leadership and convincing other Republicans to do the same. As used here, bipartisanship refers to the active and cooperative involvement of Republicans and Democrats in several phases of the lawmaking process, from problem definition through program approval. Representatives from both parties work to formulate proposals, fashion compromises, reach agreements, and enact laws. Public interest typically overcomes competitive spirit.

Bipartisanship may occur between the president and Congress or within Congress. The first type is likely to be facilitated when the president and congressional leaders from both parties agree on the need for policy action and cooperate in producing legislation (the Marshall Plan is an example). In the second type, congressional leaders may work together, then convince the president to join them (as on some environmental issues and Social Security reform), or the issue may be substantially congressional in scope, not requiring presidential involvement (for example, budget reform). There may also be cases in which congressional bipartisanship is used as a strategy to counter the president (as with the passage of the War Powers Resolution during the Nixon administration, or resistance to the cuts in water control projects recommended by President Carter in the first year of his presidency). Such cases illustrate institutional conflict—between the legislative and executive branches—over partisan disagreements.

Finally, it is worth noting what bipartisanship is *not*, at least as used here. It is not simply cosponsorship of a bill by a few members from each party or one or more members from one party working with the other party; such activity is classified here as cross-partisanship. Often the term "bipartisanship" will be used strategically to enhance the success of legislation, in the belief that it has a cachet among the public and the media.

Cross-Partisanship

In cross-partisanship an important segment of one party works with or can be counted on for support by the other party. Typically the initiative comes from one party, which then seeks to gain enough support from the other to form a winning coalition. Often it is the president who needs votes from the other party. The "conservative coalition" of Southern Democrats and Republicans illustrates that a cross-party coalition can develop at certain times on some issues. This alliance frequently voted together against legislation, but in 1981 it combined to produce important budget and tax laws. Republican gains in the South have eroded its base as a working coalition.

Cross-partisanship differs from competitive partisanship and bipartisanship in important ways. As noted above, the coalition often forms to stop action, not to initiate it. If there is a proposal, however, it typically comes from the president, who then tries to gain support from a sufficiently large segment of the other party to win. Often he knows in advance whom he can count on. Compromises may have to be accepted, but the process is different from competitive partisanship, where independent proposals are developed along the way, or bipartisanship, where both parties cooperate from the start (often through their leaders).

Two forms of cross-partisanship are pursued in lawmaking. The first, discussed above, arises from knowing in advance where support from the other party is likely. Examples would be the availability of southern Democrats to Republican presidents on certain economic and social issues, and that of northeastern Republicans to Democratic presidents on environmental and social issues (and a larger segment on trade). The process can sometimes look very much like bipartisanship, in that the supportive members of the other party may well be active in the early stages of lawmaking. The difference is in the scope of support.

The second type of cross-partisanship emerges from the playing out of competitive partisanship. As agreements are reached through the lawmaking process, leaders learn who on the other side is willing to support a final bill. Thus it is that competitive partisanship results in a cross-partisan coalition sufficient to pass legislation. As strategies, the two patterns may be interactive. What begins as one may develop into the other as agreements are either forged or fall apart.

Summary

It is apparent from this brief review that lawmaking in the separated system depends on the political conditions of the time. As I show in chapter 2, the political and legislative standing of presidents varies substantially, as do the issues faced by each. These variables have an effect on presidential power and, in turn, on which partisan strategies work best, or work at all.

Change within Presidencies

Research on the presidency is often criticized for being insufficiently comparative, too often focusing on one president and offering limited capacity for generalizion. That criticism itself is revealing of a common practice in the study of American national politics, dividing political and policy time by presidential administrations. Yet people, politics, and issues change during a president's tenure. For example, the Eisenhower years were considered to be relatively calm, yet the last two years looked very different from the first two. Only three members of Eisenhower's original cabinet remained (and Secretary of State John Foster Dulles died early in 1959). The Democrats had nearly two-thirds majorities in both houses of Congress in 1959; the Republicans had slim majorities in both during Eisenhower's first Congress. The federal budget actually decreased during Eisenhower's first two budget years (1954, 1955), but then increased by a third in his last budget year (1961). The unemployment rate went from 2.9 percent in 1953 to 6.8 percent in 1958.

These changes pale in comparison with what happened under subsequent presidents. There were thirty-one changes in cabinet secretarial positions during the Nixon-Ford presidencies, whereas Eisenhower had ten changes during his eight years. And, of course, Nixon himself was gone, as was his original vice president, Spiro T. Agnew. Lyndon Johnson's Gallup poll rating went from 80 percent approval in January 1964 to 35 percent approval in August 1968. The Democrats' two-thirds majority in the House shrank to 57 percent, allowing the reemergence of the conservative coalition between Republicans and southern Democrats. George H. W. Bush achieved record public approval in 1991, only to see it soon dissipate. His effectiveness in the Persian Gulf War was quickly forgotten during the economic recession that persisted through the summer of 1992. And Bill Clinton began with Democratic majorities in both houses of Congress in 1993, but lost those majorities for good in 1994. In 1998, he was impeached in the

House of Representatives, although he survived his subsequent trial in the Senate.

Tracking these changes and their implications for presidential power is not a simple task. And it will not be accomplished here to full satisfaction, to be sure. But this study emphasizes the importance of accounting for change in any effort to locate a president politically, understand how much help he can count on, and estimate what problems he is trying to solve.

There are other, more conceptual reasons for emphasizing change within as well as between presidencies. Developments that carry through from one to another can be explored, and the contribution or function of any one presidency is set in the context of the broader national policy process. Thus, for example, analysis of developments in health care costs as a policy problem may elaborate or modify the notion that the president sets the agenda for Congress. It may show where the president fits within a larger agenda-setting process that precedes and succeeds his service. Finally, attention to changes within a president's term in office increases the number of presidencies to study. There have been eleven post–World War II presidents at this writing but, as will be discussed later, these eleven have had many more presidencies, as measured by their changes in status.

What Is to Follow

This book emphasizes the strategic positions of presidents and how they change. I will rely on the alternative "diffused responsibility" perspective, ever searching for how this nation is governed under the strikingly diverse constitutional arrangements of single- and split-party control. I am interested in the coping and the recouping, the initial efforts to organize and the subsequent adaptations as presidents explore what works best for them, and the variations in the president's role in lawmaking.

There are several expectations stemming from the alternative perspective that help shape the organization of the book from this point forward. Of central interest are those having to do with presidents themselves, White House and cabinet organization, public support, the nature of the agenda, lawmaking, and reform. In a separated system of diffused responsibility, these are the expectations:

—Presidents will enter the White House with variable personal, political, and policy advantages or resources. Presidents are not equally good at comprehending their advantages or identifying how these advantages may work best to influence the rest of the government.

—White House and cabinet organization will be quite personal in nature, reflecting the president's assessment of strengths and weaknesses, the challenges the president faces in fitting into the ongoing government, and the political and policy changes that occur during the term of office. There is no formula for organizing the presidency, though certain models can be identified.

—Public support will be an elusive variable in analyzing presidential power. At the very least, its importance for any one president must be considered alongside other advantages. "Going public" does not necessarily carry a special bonus, though presidents with limited advantages otherwise may be forced to rely on this tactic.

—The agenda will be continuous, with many issues deriving from existing programs. The president surely plays an important role in certifying issues and setting priorities, but Congress and the bureaucracy will also be natural participants. At the very least, therefore, the president will be required to persuade other policy actors that his choices are the right ones. They will do the same with him.

—Lawmaking will vary substantially in terms of initiative, sequence, partisan and institutional interaction, and productivity. The challenge is to comprehend the variable role of the president in a government that is designed for both continuity and change.

—Reform will be an especially intricate undertaking since, by constitutional design, the governmental structure is antithetical to efficient goal achievement. Yet many, if not most, reforms seek to achieve efficiency within the basic separated structure. There are not many reforms designed to facilitate the more effective working of split-party government.

I have chosen to organize this book by the set of topics identified in these expectations: who presidents are and how they differ (chapter 2); organization of the White House and the cabinet, and how both change during a president's time in office (chapter 3); how public support varies and what it means (chapter 4); the continuing agenda and how presidents manage it (chapter 5); how lawmaking works, where the president fits, and how it varies by issue (chapters 6 and 7); and reform in a separated system of diffused responsibility (chapter 8). I will make comparisons among the postwar presidents, constantly endeavoring to identify the variations in governing that this country has experienced. The chapters on lawmaking focus on specific pieces of legislation. I have, however, selected major bills from each administration and also show how patterns of presidential-congressional interaction vary within one administration.

My main mission is to provide a means for understanding how a separated system of government works under the varying circumstances allowable by the Constitution and a two-party structure. I focus on presidents, but my purpose is broader, as I attempt to place them in the continuing process of governing. I am not by nature a reformer. I am, however, eager to see the national government work effectively under all of the conditions sanctioned by the Constitution. Therefore one underlying purpose of this book is to promote a perspective that will encourage analysts to appreciate the unique nature of the American system and to think creatively about how to make it work better.

CHAPTER 2

Presidents and the Presidency

Presidents are the leaders authorized to move into the White House. The presidency is the institution of executive powers. As Edward S. Corwin has written, "What the presidency is at any particular moment depends in important measure on who is President. . . . Yet the accumulated tradition of the office is also of vast importance."[1] The way presidents fit into the presidency and affect it is by no means uniform, but their performance may be judged by criteria based on conceptions of what is presidential. These conceptions, in turn, are rooted in the accumulated tradition of the office. There is, after all, a presidency beyond a president. As Ronald Reagan explained: "Some people become President. I've never thought of it that way. I think the Presidency is an institution over which you have temporary custody and it has to be treated that way. . . . I don't think the Presidency belongs to the individual."[2]

This chapter will explore the different circumstances under which the eleven post–World War II presidents—Truman through George W. Bush— assumed the office. I want to make this simple but immensely important point: presidents are not created equal, politically or otherwise. Some are well prepared, others are not; some have several advantages, others have few; some seek the office, others have it thrust upon them. In most cases, however, expectations of their performance are uniform: analysts rely on a generalized conception of the institution in testing each holder of the office. They seldom make an effort to identify how well prepared the person is to fit into the institution. Many studies of executive leadership focus on the presidency, not on the presidents serving variably as leaders. Even those that treat individual presidents often have as their purpose generalizations about the larger institution, thus reinforcing the tendency to evaluate each performance by an equivalent standard.[3] As it happens, that standard draws from an institution in the making, one to which each president contributes.

The eagerness to rate presidents, so common in biographies and in efforts to evaluate them comparatively through time, reflects this tendency to derive expectations from a concept of the office itself rather than from the personal, political, and policy conditions associated with a president's service. Historian Thomas A. Bailey put it this way: "Judging Presidents is not like judging those who play duplicate bridge; no two incumbents were ever dealt the same hand." For Bailey, "presidential polls are something of a parlor game, and as such should not be taken too seriously."[4] President John F. Kennedy was more blunt: "How the hell can you tell? Only the President himself can know what his real pressures and his real alternatives are. If you don't know that, how can you judge performance?"[5]

One truly noble effort to compare presidents by a set of qualities judged to be related to leadership and job performance is that of Fred I. Greenstein. He evaluates "modern" presidents from Franklin D. Roosevelt to Bill Clinton. These men are tested on their proficiency as a public communicator, organizational capacity, political skill, vision of public policy, cognitive style, and, the most intriguing attribute, emotional intelligence. No president receives an A on all of these qualities. Rather, Greenstein presents a mixed report, a tally of strengths and weaknesses that aid in explaining "the highly personalized nature of the modern American presidency."[6]

The major purpose, then, of the present chapter is to propose what one might realistically expect of the eleven presidents who served between 1945 and 2005. My interest, first, is in the accommodation that is likely to occur between the president and the presidency at the start of his term. Later chapters will examine the extent to which the president influences the presidency, as well as the accumulated experience of exercising power in the same position over time. Of related interest are the changes that occur over the course of a president's term. The president's view of the job may well change during his time of service. Likewise, those with whom a president must deal normally benefit from learning how that president views his responsibilities and responds to change.

How They Came to Be There

There are eighteen cases of taking the oath of office among the eleven presidents of the postwar period. They can be classified into five categories.

Elected presidents: Presidents who were nominated and elected for a first term. There are seven cases: Dwight D. Eisenhower, 1952; John F. Kennedy, 1960; Richard M. Nixon, 1968; Jimmy Carter, 1976; Ronald Reagan, 1980; Bill Clinton, 1992; and George W. Bush, 2000.

Reelected presidents: Presidents who were renominated and reelected. There are five cases: Eisenhower, 1956; Nixon, 1972; Reagan, 1984; Clinton, 1996, and George W. Bush, 2004.

Nonelected presidents: Vice presidents who took over due to the death or resignation of a president. There are three cases: Harry S Truman, 1945; Lyndon B. Johnson, 1963; and Gerald R. Ford, 1974.

Elected vice presidents: Vice presidents who were nominated and elected after serving out the term of their predecessor as a nonelected president. There are two cases: Truman, 1948, and Johnson, 1964.

Elected heir apparent: A vice president who was nominated and elected after serving with his predecessor. There is one case: George H. W. Bush, 1988.

This listing itself evokes assorted expectations of presidential orientations to the job. The first two categories—elected and reelected presidents—isolate those who win the office by virtue of their successful initiatives through a two-stage process of nomination and election. The pledges made along the way are shaped by personal commitments, associations, and the campaign experience. There are differences between running initially (more creative) and seeking reelection (more protective). The next three categories—nonelected presidents, elected vice presidents, and elected heir apparent—differ substantially from the first two. These are people who either did not try to reach the White House on their own or had earlier tried and failed. They are truly presidents of circumstance. First, note how many of them there are: six of the eighteen cases in this period. Second, it is vital to appreciate the strikingly different conditions in which they assumed the office, different from those of the first two categories and different from each other.

Elected Presidents

Elected presidents endure two related campaigns: one within the party for the nomination, the other to win the office itself. There are important

Table 2-1. *Nomination Experience of Postwar Presidents*

President	Run before?	Nomination contested?	Primaries Held	Primaries Entered	Primaries Won	Convention contested?
Elected						
Eisenhower (1952)	No	Yes	13	5	4	Yes
Kennedy (1960)	No	Yes	16	7	7	Yes
Nixon (1968)	Yes	Yes	15	6	6	Yes
Carter (1976)	No	Yes	27	26	17	Token
Reagan (1980)	Yes	Yes	35	33	29	No
Clinton (1992)	No	Yes	41	37	32	Token
Bush 43 (2000)	No	Yes	43	43	36	No
Reelected						
Eisenhower (1956)	n.a.	No	19	14	14	No
Nixon (1972)	n.a.	Minor	20	16	16	No
Reagan (1984)	n.a.	No	...	...	...	No
Clinton (1996)	n.a.	No	...	...	...	No
Bush 43 (2004)	n.a.	No	...	...	...	No
Elected vice presidents						
Truman (1948)	No	No	14	7	7	Yes[a]
Johnson (1964)	Yes	Minor	16	2	2[b]	No
Elected heir apparent						
Bush 41 (1988)	Yes	Yes	38	38	37	No

Sources: *Congressional Quarterly's Guide to U.S. Elections* (Washington: CQ Press, 1975), pts. 1, 2; *Congressional Quarterly's Guide to 1976 Elections* (Washington: Congressional Quarterly, 1977), pp. 5–30; and *Congressional Quarterly Weekly Report,* various issues (1980, 1984, 1988, 1992).

n.a. Not applicable.

a. Many southern Democrats walked out of the convention and formed the Dixiecrat Party.

b. Johnson was a write-in candidate in several primaries.

differences in the nominating experiences of elected and other presidents (see table 2-1). The most impressive difference came with the increase in the number of presidential primaries following the divisive 1968 Democratic convention. Eisenhower, Kennedy, and Nixon ran in less than half of the few primaries held before 1972. Each established front-runner status in these contests, buttressing their efforts inside the party to win the nomination. Eisenhower and Kennedy had to display outside support so as to convince party officials of their credibility as candidates, because both had to run against insider candidates for the nomination (the former against Senator Robert A. Taft, the latter against Senator Lyndon B. Johnson). Nixon was the consummate insider and probably could have been nominated without entering any primaries. It had come to be expected, however, that presidential candidates would participate in the primaries, so Nixon ran and won in six states.

The other interesting characteristic of the three nominating contests held before 1972 is that closure was not achieved in the preconvention period. Since the primaries were not the only means for garnering delegate votes, it was possible for candidates to remain in the race without engaging other candidates, running alongside the favorite and probable nominee. With the expansion in the number of primaries, however, challengers could be defeated outright and left with no other, less engaging and confrontational means for winning delegate support. Eisenhower was strongly challenged by Taft at the convention in 1952. In fact, he did not receive a majority of the delegates on the first ballot (shifts in delegate votes then provided the margin). Kennedy and Nixon both received just over 50 percent of the delegate support on the first ballot.

A result of nonengagement and failure to achieve closure before the convention was that the candidate faced a competing organization within the party. To unite the party for the fall campaign it was necessary to bargain. Rather than being distributed over thirty-five or more primary elections spread geographically and over time, the contest for the nomination was focused on a meeting at which the two or more candidate organizations interacted on policy, political, and personnel issues. Negotiations on the platform, the national party structure, selection of the vice president, and future presidential appointments provided experience for executive leadership, not unlike that required in the White House for negotiating with Congress.

Essentially the system in place since 1972 requires the presidential candidate, once in office, to compensate for not having had to negotiate with governmental (mostly congressional) leaders in the course of winning the nomination. For example, in 1980 Reagan conducted what I have termed a "trifocal campaign"—one designed to look forward from the preconvention campaign to the convention and on to the general election.[7] His party-oriented campaign showed that a high degree of party unity can be achieved under the new, plebiscitary system. George H. W. Bush emulated this approach in 1988 but with less success, due in part to his identity with the moderate wing of the party. His son, George W. Bush, achieved a high degree of party unity in 2000, as he was able to satisfy the more conservative groups to a greater extent than his father had done.

The Democrats have faced a very different problem since 1972. The special interests identified with the party often appear reluctant to cooperate with the prospective presidential candidate. Either the challenging candidates are unwilling to withdraw on schedule—as with Edward Kennedy in 1980, Gary Hart in 1984, Jesse Jackson in 1984 and 1988, and Jerry Brown in 1992—or groups demand that their interests be represented in the plat-form or elsewhere, regardless of the consequences for the fall campaign. Further, one of the two successful Democratic candidates in this set, Jimmy Carter, was not predisposed to conduct a party-oriented campaign. He sought from the start to separate himself from the traditional party organi-zation, including that in Congress.[8]

In 1992, Bill Clinton, too, faced challenges from groups within the Democratic party, but he was more inclined than Carter to work with and through the party apparatus. Like Carter, he selected a well-respected sen-ator as a running mate, but he was in a stronger position than previous can-didates (Carter in 1980, Mondale in 1984, and Dukakis in 1988) to take charge of the Democratic convention, and he did so. Meanwhile, congres-sional Democrats were in a substantially weaker political position than in 1976, primarily because of a series of scandals. Thus they were not a pres-ence at the 1992 convention and were more likely than in recent years to mesh their reelection campaigns with the Clinton campaign.

The pattern is less clear in the general election campaign for elected presidents than in their nominating experiences (see table 2-2). I will dis-cuss them in three groups: Eisenhower and Reagan; Kennedy and Carter; and Nixon, Clinton, and George W. Bush. The first pair could legitimately claim convincing victories; in fact, their wins even encouraged talk of party realignment. Eisenhower won handily, and beyond that, his party won majorities in both houses of Congress, making this the first fully Republi-can government since 1929. What was lacking for the declaration of a man-date was a clearly defined program, apart from Eisenhower's promise to "go to Korea" and end the conflict there.

Reagan's victory was more impressive than Eisenhower's for three rea-sons. First, he defeated an incumbent Democratic president, the first time that had happened in the twentieth century. He won less of the popular vote than Eisenhower, but there was a third candidate, John Anderson. Reagan's percentage share of the two-party vote was almost exactly the same as Eisenhower's. Second, the increase of thirty-three House seats for the Re-publicans was their greatest in a presidential election year since 1920, though still insufficient for the party to attain majority status. In the Senate, the Republicans gained twelve additional seats, a stunning result that gave them majority control of that body. Third, Reagan set forth a clear set of policy priorities during the campaign. No one doubted he would try to enact his proposals into law. The 1980 presidential election was among the most policy oriented in recent history.

Table 2-2. *General Election Experience of Postwar Presidents*

President	Presidential vote (percent)			Congressional seats by president's party		
	Popular	Two-party	Electoral	House	Senate	Control?
Elected						
Eisenhower (1952)	55	55	83	Gain	Gain	Yes
Kennedy (1960)	50	50	56	Loss	Loss	Yes
Nixon (1968)	43	50	56	Gain	Gain	No
Carter[a] (1976)	50	51	55	Gain	No change	Yes
Reagan[a] (1980)	51	55	91	Gain	Gain	Split[b]
Clinton[a] (1992)	43	53	69	Loss	No change	Yes
Bush 43 (2000)	50	50	50	Loss	Loss	Yes
Reelected						
Eisenhower (1956)	57	58	86	Loss	No change	No
Nixon (1972)	61	62	97	Gain	Loss	No
Reagan (1984)	59	59	98	Gain	Loss	Split
Clinton (1996)	50	55	70	Gain	Loss	No
Bush 43 (2004)	51	51	53	Gain	Gain	Yes
Elected vice presidents						
Truman (1948)	50	53	57	Gain	Gain	Yes
Johnson (1964)	61	61	90	Gain	Gain	Yes
Elected heir apparent						
Bush 41 (1988)	53	53	79	Loss	No change	No

Sources: Calculated from data in Harold W. Stanley and Richard G. Niemi, *Vital Statistics on American Politics*, 3rd ed. (Washington: CQ Press, 1992), tables 3-14; 3-17; and *Congressional Quarterly Weekly Report*, various issues.
a. Defeated an incumbent president.
b. The House remained under Democratic control; the Senate shifted to Republican control.

The Kennedy and Carter elections were alike in many respects. Both presidents won by narrow margins—among the closest in history—in the popular as well as the Electoral College votes. The sources of their victories were similar: the Northeast, the South, and a few industrial Midwest states. Further, neither could rightfully claim coattails. Though retaining majorities, House and Senate Democrats had net losses in 1960 and experienced virtually no change in 1976. Both Kennedy and Carter ran behind the overwhelming majority of the victorious congressional Democrats. It was therefore obvious from the start that they would have to work for the support of Congress in spite of the large Democratic majorities.

Those remaining have the fewest common features. Nixon won narrowly in 1968. He won 43 percent of the popular vote in a three-candidate race (a disaffected Democrat, George Wallace, formed a third party, garnering 14 percent of the popular vote and 46 electoral votes). After that election, the Republicans successfully sought to attract the Wallace voters, resulting in a winning coalition in presidential elections until 1992, interrupted only by Carter's narrow victory in 1976. In 1992 Clinton also won 43 percent of the popular vote in a three-candidate race. The third candidate, Ross Perot, captured 19 percent of the popular vote and no electoral college votes. Like Nixon with the Wallace voters, Clinton's aim in 1994 and 1996 was to attract Perot supporters. The most notable difference between these two presidents is that Nixon was the first president in the history of the modern two-party system to enter his first term with the opposition party in control of both houses of Congress. Clinton was more fortunate in 1992: the Democrats won majorities in both houses, though by lesser margins, due to Republican gains.

The election of George W. Bush in 2000 was a happening unto itself. The contest was not resolved on election day; indeed, neither candidate knew whether he would become the president until the U.S. Supreme Court halted the Florida recount on December 12. Bush won a bare majority in the Electoral College and less than 50 percent of the popular vote; he had the least political standing of any entering president in the postwar period (see table 2-3, page 52). Bush did enjoy one advantage over Nixon, however: a Republican majority in the House and a tie in the Senate. Yet Democrats had net gains in both bodies in 2000, thus reducing the positive effect of Republican control.

Two tests can be used to summarize the comparison of the seven elected presidents: Did the election provide the president with special advantages upon entering the White House? Did the congressional elections complement any advantage gained from the president's election? Only Eisenhower and Reagan, two Republicans, had both types of advantages (and only Reagan was prepared to use them in the early months of his presidency). The other five won narrowly and had to establish their credibility with Congress. For them, being inaugurated was but the start of a process of authenticating their right to lead.

Reelected Presidents

Five postwar presidents have been elected to a second term in office. Four—Eisenhower, Nixon, Reagan, and Bush 43—were Republicans, and the renominations and reelections of the first three had many features in common (see tables 2-1 and 2-2). Not unexpectedly, given the relative success of their first terms, the nomination in each case was essentially a coronation. With virtually no opposition (Nixon experienced minor opposition from the right in 1972), they were free to enter many primaries, thus using the preconvention period to promote their reelection campaign. The conventions were rousing kickoffs for their general election campaigns. Meanwhile, the Democrats experienced growing frustration, due to internal disputes that spilled over into the general election campaigns. In 1972 and 1984, for example, the Democratic candidates were unable to concentrate on their Republican opponent because of problems with their vice presidential choices. George McGovern's first choice in 1972, Senator Thomas Eagleton (D-Mo.), was dropped when it was discovered that he had undergone electric shock therapy. And in 1984 Walter Mondale found that his running mate, Representative Geraldine Ferraro (D-N.Y.), had to respond repeatedly to assertions about her husband's financial dealings. The media attention seriously detracted from Mondale's campaign during the crucial first weeks after the convention.

The fourth Republican renomination and reelection, that of George W. Bush, was of a different order. He was unopposed for the nomination, but the Democrats put up an active contest that concentrated on the president's failings in directing an unpopular war and a recovering economy. Senator John F. Kerry (D-Mass.) won early victories in the primaries and started a long, vigorous, and well-financed campaign. During the summer of 2004, the Democratic nominee was frequently ahead in the polls. Although Bush's renomination in the latest-ever-scheduled national convention was a coronation like that of other reelected Republican presidents, few, if any, delegates expected an easy win in the general election.

The only Democrat to be reelected in the postwar era was Bill Clinton, in 1996. His renomination was uncontested, but his first term might well have invited a challenger had there been one with sufficient national standing. Clinton's national health care plan went down to defeat in 1994. And in the midterm elections in that year, Democrats lost their majorities in both the House and Senate, along with many key state houses. The 104th Congress (1995–96) displayed intense, competitive partisanship, culminating in the partial shutdown of the government in fall 1995, because Clinton and the Republicans could not reach an agreement on the budget. However, a turnaround was achieved in 1996. Major legislation was enacted and both Clinton and the Republican Congress were returned.[9]

The general election results in four cases (Eisenhower, Nixon, Reagan, and Clinton) constituted approval of the whole government. The three Republican presidents were overwhelmingly reelected, the campaign issues were primarily those of continuity and reaffirmation, and there was little or no change in Congress, with Democratic majorities returning but for the Senate in 1984. So, too, did the 1996 election validate the existing government. Clinton was handily reelected, as were Republican majorities in Congress. Clinton's win, however, did not match the landslide victories of the three Republicans. In fact, with Perot again on the ballot, Clinton joined Woodrow Wilson as the only presidents in the twentieth century to fail twice to gain a majority of the popular vote.

Like his 2000 election, Bush 43's reelection requires special attention. It certainly did not fit the pattern of being an "approval" election. A wartime president, Bush received 51 percent of the popular vote and 53 percent of the electoral vote. His aides pointed out that he received more popular votes than any candidate in history. But second place in those sweepstakes went to his opponent. No reelected president since Woodrow Wilson in 1916 had received such low percentages of the popular and electoral counts as shares of the two-party vote (in 1996 Clinton had two opponents, Dole and Perot, and received 55 percent of the two-party popular vote and 70 percent of the electoral vote). On the other hand, Republicans had historic gains in the House and Senate in 2004, an outcome that had eluded the other four reelected presidents in the postwar era.

The first four reelected presidents in the postwar period faced a quandary. Their service was impressively endorsed by voters. Yet voters also seemingly endorsed the records of Congresses controlled by the other party (except for the Senate in 1984). Because presidents are term limited, it is highly probable that their status in Washington will erode during their second terms. Therefore they are as challenged as newly elected presidents to develop and nurture their strategic position in working with congresses of the other party. The record shows, too, that opposite party congressional majorities were very active in the final years of these presidencies, clearly anticipating possible presidential victories for the out party with the certain exit of the incumbent. In three of the four cases, the out party did then win, the election of George H. W. Bush being the lone exception (and what an exception, the first vice president to win from that position since Martin Van Buren in 1836).

It remains to be seen at this writing how George W. Bush's second term will develop. It is exceptional. While he lacks the impressive wins of the others, Bush 43 is the only one of the five to have his party in the majority in both houses of Congress. At his first press conference after his reelection, he announced an ambitious domestic agenda, citing the "political capital" that he intended to spend in support of his proposals. Additionally, the war on terrorism continued to be a priority for the president and Congress, ensuring an active second term.

Vice Presidents as Presidents

The three most relevant considerations for comparing the three vice presidents as president are the circumstances under which they assumed the office, the timing of their assumption of office in the presidential term, and the nature of the agenda. Truman and Johnson took over upon the death of the incumbent. How each incumbent died is relevant for the strategic position of the successor. Roosevelt died of natural causes after having served three full terms as president. He was credited for enacting a domestic New Deal and directing the nation's war effort, 1941–45. The nation mourned his death, but the shock itself carried only a limited and short-term advantage for Truman. Rather, Truman was compared unfavorably with the man many consider to be the greatest president of the modern era.

The timing of Roosevelt's death left Truman with nearly a full term— from April 12, 1945, to January 20, 1949. There was no provision for a vice president under these circumstances (the Twenty-Fifth Amendment was ratified in 1967). All attention focused on Harry Truman, and the reviews typically were not flattering. He then had to face a midterm election in 1946 as the leader of a party and a nation that had not selected him for that purpose. The results were devastating to the Democrats. House Republicans had a net gain of fifty-six seats and Senate Republicans a net gain of thirteen seats, giving them control of both chambers for the first time since 1929.

Truman did, however, have a ready-made agenda when he took office. The war was winding down, and with its end came a predictable, if not readily resolvable, set of issues. Truman had to make a number of important decisions, most notably the dropping of atomic bombs on Hiroshima and Nagasaki. Essentially, though, he was expected to carry on in the shadow of his predecessor, yet he was measured by Roosevelt's example. "His Work Must Go On" was the caption of one cartoonist's dedication to Roosevelt.[10] Because Truman was not well known, his accession to the White House sent analysts scurrying for reassurance, as an editorial in the *New York Times* suggested.

> In one of the great moments of American history there steps into the office of the Presidency of the United States, and into a position of world-wide influence and authority such as no other living American has ever held, a man who is less well known to the people of this country than many other public figures and almost totally unknown abroad. This man is a farmer's son from

the Missouri Valley, a veteran of the last war, a self-styled "practical politi-cian," a two-term member of the Senate, a compromise candidate for the comparatively obscure office from which fate, with dramatic suddenness, has now catapulted him to power.[11]

Truman himself expressed it this way to some reporters: "Boys, if you ever pray, pray for me now. I don't know whether you fellows ever had a load of hay fall on you, but when they told me yesterday what had happened, I felt like the moon, the stars, and all the planets had fallen on me."[12]

For Lyndon B. Johnson, the situation was quite different. John F. Kennedy was assassinated in the prime of his life. He had served less than three years and was therefore denied the chance to make his full mark on American politics; indeed, his record of success on Capitol Hill was not particularly impressive. He had prepared an extensive legislative program, however, and it was therefore left to Johnson, the master legislative leader, to guide that program through Congress. That was the expectation and Johnson's natural inclination, as a former leader of the Senate who also had past service in the House.

Johnson did not have to cope with a midterm election. He was free to prepare for the 1964 presidential election by seeking to move as much leg-islation as possible in the time he had available. He was uniquely equipped to do just that. Most analyses were optimistic about Johnson's capability for serving out the term of the slain young president:

> To these tasks Lyndon Johnson brings experience and qualities of character that should stand him in good stead. He is thoroughly at home in the Con-gress, which must now share with him the responsibility of steadying the country through the crisis which confronts it. He is well known in all parts of the country, but no one can really know his qualities as leader until he has had a chance to demonstrate them in an assignment more difficult than any other on earth. He is a man of moderate views, with a talent for bringing concord out of disagreement.[13]

This was considerably more hopeful than popular opinion on Truman. It was this type of support, along with the public desire to honor President Kennedy, that contributed to Johnson's outstanding legislative record in 1964, and subsequently to his landslide election to a full term.

The third vice president as president entered office with the least advan-tages of the three, perhaps of any vice president in history. Gerald Ford had not been elected to the position of vice president; he had been nominated under the provisions of the Twenty-Fifth Amendment after the elected vice president, Spiro T. Agnew, resigned in disgrace. He was confirmed as vice president by the House (387-35) and the Senate (92-3) and took the oath of office on December 6, 1973. When Ford assumed the presidency on August 9, 1974, following Nixon's resignation, his predecessor's program was stalled because of the Watergate crisis. Nixon had had a relatively successful first term, particularly in foreign policy. On the domestic front, his landslide victory in 1972 had encouraged a somewhat more audacious approach, particularly in attempting to curb government growth. Ford, like Johnson, was judged to have the qualities to work with Congress and break the stalemate: "Mr. Ford brings to the White House the tremendous advantage of being able to talk constructively with people who had lost all faith in the previous administration and had broken off relations with it."[14]

Thus Ford had the advantages of a stalled but full agenda, his own experience on Capitol Hill as a leader in the House, and the hopes of those who found him a welcome successor to Richard Nixon. But the Nixon legacy also included Nixon himself possibly having to stand as defendant in a criminal trial. Whatever the burdens of the Roosevelt legacy for Truman or the Kennedy legacy for Johnson, they paled in comparison to what Nixon left for Ford. A full pardon for Nixon was Ford's solution, and it cost him the few short-run advantages that he had. One editorial placed his action within the context of the Watergate conspiracy:

> This newest use of the powers of the presidency to curtail inquiry and to relieve Mr. Nixon of responsibility for this action will strike you as nothing less than a continuation of a cover-up. We do not believe Mr. Ford intended his action to have that as its primary purpose. But that will be its primary effect.[15]

The timing of the resignation, followed by the pardon, could not have been worse for President Ford. Like Truman, Ford had to face a midterm election. Unlike Truman, who had more than eighteen months before the election, Ford had less than three months. Even had he not pardoned Nixon, Ford would have faced the likelihood of standard midterm losses, possibly amplified by a stagnant economy and the first opportunity for the public to express itself on Nixon and Watergate. As it was, the House Republicans suffered a net loss of forty-three seats, and Senate Republicans a net loss of three seats. The House Democrats had a two-thirds majority in the new Congress.

These cases of vice presidents serving as presidents require special attention throughout this book. However well they understand the purpose of having a vice president, few analysts truly consider the likelihood of one serving as president. It therefore will not do to lump them into the other categories. Voters do not elect them as presidents; they did not even elect Ford as vice president. No one of these three could conceivably have won nomination as president at the time they became vice president. Of the three, only Johnson tried, and he lost badly to a junior senator from Massachusetts. Their advantages and disadvantages can be traced to the man they succeeded. To create their own presidency they had to work through and around the direct legacy of their predecessors, including the development and nurturing of power as personal influence, suited to Richard E. Neustadt's formulation (as described in chapter 1). Two of the three vice presidents as presidents were successful in winning on their own and thus had the opportunity to reduce the effect of the past and create their own White Houses. The third, Gerald Ford, came astonishingly close to winning. Had he done so, he would have faced a much greater challenge than Truman or Johnson in authenticating his leadership, since the Democrats were returned with substantial majorities in both houses of Congress in 1976 (67 percent in the House, 61 percent in the Senate).

Elected Vice Presidents

The nomination and general election politics of the 1948 and 1964 campaigns were dramatically different. Presumably, as the argument has gone here, these differences presaged contrasting presidencies. Harry S Truman had to battle all the way. Many Democrats opposed his nomination, but none of them could mount a sufficiently strong challenge. And the opposition took the form more of backroom maneuvering than opposition in the primaries (Truman won the few that he entered). The 1948 convention offered early signals as to what would happen later within the Democratic Party. Some southern Democrats walked out as a result of losing the platform battle on civil rights, leading eventually to the Dixiecrat candidacy of J. Strom Thurmond of South Carolina (one of two third-party candidates in the postwar period to win electoral votes).

The results of the 1948 general election were among the most bizarre in history. Congressional Democrats recaptured control of both houses of Congress (see table 2-2). Their net increase of seventy-five seats in the House ranked among the largest shifts in the twentieth century. And yet it was hard for Truman to take much credit, since his margin was among the smallest ever. The fact that he won at all was his primary advantage. He entered office hoping to translate his surprise win into substantive gains in public policy, perhaps by somehow establishing a linkage between the presidential and congressional outcomes. In his memoirs he points out: "My long campaign against the Eightieth Congress had convinced the voters that a turnover was necessary, and I was given an overwhelmingly Democratic Congress to replace the one which had blocked the administration's domestic progress for two years."[16] Unfortunately, the task of establishing his leadership of Congress was complicated by the fact that he had lost four Deep South states to Thurmond. These four states had 8 of the 57 Democrats in the Senate and 30 of the 263 Democrats in the House. The South would not be his friend on many crucial issues in the 81st and 82nd Congresses; many southern Democrats voted with Republicans to form a conservative coalition.

In sharp contrast, Lyndon B. Johnson swept into office in 1964. In other ways, he, too, was the issue. But the conditions were overwhelmingly positive. Because he had no opposition, Johnson could ignore the primaries, and did so. The convention was, as for a president seeking reelection, a coronation. The Republicans accommodated Johnson further by nominating Barry Goldwater, who was to the right of center in his own party and therefore could not expect full support even within that minority. Thus, again as in the case of a reelected president, the results represented an endorsement of Johnson's style in modifying, expanding, and enacting the Kennedy program. To punctuate this endorsement, voters provided a net increase of thirty-eight House Democrats and two Senate Democrats, bringing the totals in both houses above the two-thirds mark.

President Johnson had extraordinary advantages because of his own election and the results in Congress. His victory and that of Reagan in 1980 came closer to meeting the conditions of the party responsibility model than any other postwar election. Yet Johnson did not always heed Neustadt's warning to think prospectively about the effects of his decisions on his power, especially in regard to the Vietnam War. Consequently his personal influence declined dramatically, as he acknowledged later. President Truman's immediate advantages were less directly translatable into power as personal influence. Yet in time historians came to treat him more positively than they did Johnson.

Elected Heir Apparent

It is said that a category with an N of 1 is not worth discussing. In this case, I beg to disagree. The election of George H. W. Bush in 1988 could be included in the category of elected presidents, but I believe it deserves separate status. Part of the justification is simply the importance of highlighting the special problems for an heir apparent, or sitting vice president, in establishing his leadership of the government. Additionally, it is worth pointing out that three other heirs apparent—Richard Nixon in 1960, Hubert Humphrey in 1968, and Al Gore in 2000—came close to winning the White House.[17] Each would have faced problems similar to those encountered by Bush in following an administration with which they were identified. Nixon and Gore would have likely had to work with an opposition-party Congress, Humphrey would have had a Democratic Congress, but one with many critics of the Vietnam war.

The campaign for the nomination in 1988 was a rather short-lived contest. Super Tuesday, the day on which several southern primaries are held, clinched the nomination for Bush. The general election had few major issues. Bush won handily, and there was virtually no change in the number of seats held by either party in Congress. The results look very much like those of the reelected presidents (see table 2-2). In fact, one might make the case that the voters had approved the return of the same government, with Bush serving as the representative of a president (Reagan) who could not serve a third term. So conceived, the Bush administration could be expected to encounter the same problems of generating enthusiasm and policy proposals that had been characteristic of the relatively sluggish second Reagan term.

Bush was not being reelected, however. He was taking over as a first-term president with the intention of running for a second term. His election did not test well by the two criteria suggested earlier for Eisenhower and Reagan. Given the lack of issues during the campaign, it was difficult to interpret Bush's substantial victory in policy terms. And there was virtually no connection between his victory and congressional results. Thus the heir apparent faced the predicament of separating his presidency from that of his popular predecessor and producing an advantage for influencing Congress that was not available to him as a result of the election. Meeting these challenges was not trouble free. Fashioning his own administration ran the risk of alienating the many Reagan loyalists among Republicans on Capitol Hill, as well as those in the Reagan White House and cabinet who hoped to be included in a Bush administration. The Bush experience is instructive for future heirs apparent because its problems are generic to the system.[18]

Different Challenges

This review of how presidents come to serve in the White House identifies abundant variation in the extent to which the means and nature of succession authenticate the exercise of power. The most striking differences are, of course, between being elected to office and assuming the office upon the death or resignation of the incumbent. Establishing one's independent right to govern as a takeover president is a challenge of a high order.

The optimal conditions for creating presidential advantages once in office include a contested nomination that is satisfactorily resolved, a landslide victory for the presidential ticket, and substantial gains for the president's party in Congress that can be reasonably associated with the presidential campaign. As shown, very few of the postwar elections meet these conditions, reinforcing a point to be reiterated throughout this book: there is nothing automatic about the conferring of power as personal influence on presidents in a separated system. Eisenhower (1952), Johnson (1964), and Reagan (1980) clearly had the most advantages. Truman (1948), Kennedy (1960), Nixon (1968), Carter (1976), Bush 41 (1988), Clinton (1992), and Bush 43 (2000) had many fewer advantages. Eisenhower (1956), Nixon (1972), Reagan (1984), and Clinton (1996) had to seek advantages in elections that reaffirmed split-party government. Bush 43 (2004) had a Republican Congress but not the landslide wins of other reelected presidents. I turn next to a comparative analysis of the political and legislative standing of postwar presidents.

Standing on Entering Office

A president's standing at his inauguration varies, depending on his election results, how his party fared in Congress, and early assessments of his ability to do the job. Most presidents are accorded a so-called honeymoon that is sustained by hopes for change and the freshness of a new start. But the glow of the inaugural period cannot alter or long hide the political facts of who won and how.

Table 2-3 presents scores for the political and legislative standings of postwar presidents at the time of their inauguration. The presidents are ranked in each of the categories—political standing, legislative standing, and combined power score. The scoring relies on standard indicators. Political standing incorporates the president's percentage of popular vote, percentage of Electoral College vote, and initial job approval ratings. Legislative standing is based on the percentage of the president's party in the House and Senate, and a five-point bonus is added for majority status.[19] The scores within each category are added, then combined for a composite power score, with which it is possible to rank the presidents.

Johnson in 1964 is in a class by himself, the outlier among postwar presidents, scoring well above the others. A common case with Republican

Table 2-3. Political and Legislative Standing of Postwar Presidents

President	President's political standing[a]					Party's legislative standing[b]						Combined score	
	Popular vote (%)	Electoral vote (%)	Job approval (%)	Total	Rank	House (%)	Bonus	Senate (%)	Bonus	Total	Rank	Total	Rank
Eisenhower (1952)	55	83	78	216	4	51	5	50	5	111	6	327	2
Eisenhower (1956)	57	86	76	219	2	46		49		95	10	314	5
Kennedy (1960)	50	56	77	183	8	60	5	65	5	135	3	318	4
Johnson (1964)	61	90	71	222	1	68	5	68	5	146	1	368	1
Nixon (1968)	43	56	59	158	12	44		43		87	12	245	14
Nixon (1972)	61	97	51	209	5	44		42		86	13	295	9
Carter (1976)	50	55	66	171	10	67	5	61	5	138	2	309	6
Reagan (1980)	51	91	57	199	6	44		53	5	102	8	301	7
Reagan (1984)	59	98	62	219	2	42		53	5	100	9	319	3
Bush 41 (1988)	53	79	57	189	7	40		45		85	14	274	11
Clinton (1992)	43	69	58	170	11	59	5	57	5	126	4	296	8
Clinton (1996)	50	70	62	182	9	48		45		93	11	275	10
Bush 43 (2000)	50	50	57	157	13	51	5	50	3	109	7	266	13
Bush 43 (2004)	51	53	51	155	14	53	5	55	5	118	5	273	12

Sources: Compiled from data in Michael Nelson, ed., *Guide to the Presidency*, 2nd ed. (Washington: CQ Press, 1996); and various Internet sources for later presidencies.
a. Popular vote is the two-party popular vote. Job approval is upon entering office.
b. Percentage of seats held by president's party. Bonus is added for majority status (three points only awarded for the Senate in 2000 because of a tie).

presidents was for the person to win big and his party to do less well in Congress. Eisenhower and Reagan in their elections and reelections scored well personally; their parties did moderately well in Congress but were far from achieving commanding positions. Nixon improved his political standing substantially upon being reelected, but in Congress his party did not. And George H. W. Bush won convincingly, but congressional Republicans had a net loss of two seats in the House and no gains in the Senate.

Three Democratic presidents—Kennedy, Carter, and Clinton—fit a pattern for their first (for Kennedy and Carter, only) terms: relatively weak personal political status and more robust legislative standing, due to substantial leftover majorities for their party in Congress. In each of these cases the Democrats had a net loss of seats in Congress (very slight for Carter) but had had net gains and comfortable margins in the previous midterm elections (1958, 1974, and 1990, respectively). Clinton improved his political standing in the second term, but by then his legislative standing had deteriorated due to the Democrats' loss of their majorities in the House and the Senate in 1994. The fourth postwar Democratic president, Harry Truman, is a special case. He had low political standing in 1948 by the measures relied on here, but he was not expected to win at all. Nearly as surprising was the recapture of the House and Senate by Democrats, which enhanced Truman's legislative standing from the previous Congress.

George W. Bush is the most unusual case to be considered. Bush ranks dead last in political standing for both election and reelection. In 2000, he had a narrow loss in the popular vote, a narrow win in the electoral vote, and a modest job approval score. He improved marginally upon his popular and electoral vote percentages in 2004, but his job approval at inauguration was less even than in 2000. His first-term legislative standing was better than most other postwar Republican presidents (only Eisenhower ranked higher). Republicans had net losses of seats in both chambers in 2000 but retained their majority in the House and tied with Democrats in the Senate. Net gains were then realized in 2002 and 2004. Still, Bush's first term composite score placed him just ahead of Nixon's first term, and there was no improvement at the start of his second term.

Presidents' political and legislative standing help them define the challenges for developing and implementing lawmaking strategies in the separated system. It is especially interesting to note how few of the postwar presidents had sufficiently high standing to employ noncompetitive partisan strategies. Most were limited to competitive and cross-partisan strategies. Only Johnson in the first two years of his elected term had the commanding status in prestige, reputation, and position to exercise the full potential of presidential power as explicated by Neustadt.

Of the others, Democrats Truman, Kennedy, Carter, and Clinton (in his first term) might well have pursued a more noncompetitive partisan strategy had their party been more unified or Congress more cooperative. The Democrats had an average membership of 62 percent in the House and 60 percent in the Senate as these presidents entered office. However, Truman and Kennedy had to cope with the conservative coalition of southern Democrats and Republicans on several issues. Carter had problems of his own making, given that he often distanced himself from congressional Democrats. And Clinton in 1993 had to manage in a new era of Senate obstructionism, wherein it became necessary to have the support of sixty loyalists for a partisan strategy to be effective (an exception was the 1993 reconciliation package; see chapter 7).

Noncompetitive partisanship was not an option for Eisenhower, Nixon, and Reagan in either of their terms, nor for the two Bushes and Clinton in his second term. The mean standing of their party in the House for these entering presidents was 46 percent, and in the Senate, 48 percent. Only Eisenhower (1953–55) and George W. Bush for five months in 2001 had both House and Senate majorities upon entering the White House (Bush in the Senate by the tie-breaking vote of the vice president). Bush also had Republican majorities in the House and the Senate at the start of his second term. All the rest faced split-party control. On most major issues, it was essential to work with some Democrats in order to achieve a measure of success.

Who They Are

I turn next to the personal characteristics of presidents. James David Barber's analysis of presidential character explores the personal background, political experience, and intellectual development of presidents.[20] He uses his findings to predict performance in the White House. Such an inventive scheme goes far beyond what will be attempted here. My purpose is to offer a brief biographical sketch that places each president in his time and to pose possible effects that his life experiences might have on the perspective he brings to the job. A president's experiences and perspectives aid in judging the extent to which he is able to realize the potential of the politics that brought him to office. A final exercise below proposes governing incentives associated with a president's time, assets, and liabilities.

The postwar presidents can be classified into four groups in terms of the eras of their birth and maturity. Truman and Eisenhower were between centuries; they are of the World War I generation. The period of Truman's childhood was a difficult one, with many labor disputes and economic woes. His first vote for president was in 1908, in a contest between William Howard Taft and William Jennings Bryan. The period of Eisenhower's childhood also spanned some of the financial troubles of the early part of the century, the rise of the Progressive Party as a force, and the resulting split in the Republican Party. His first vote was cast in the three-way race of 1912 between President Taft, former president Theodore Roosevelt, and Woodrow Wilson.

The second group includes Johnson, Nixon, Ford, and Reagan. In their early years they witnessed World War I, the relative calm that followed in the 1920s, and the drama of the stock market crash in 1929. They are of the Depression generation. Johnson and Reagan cast their first votes for president in 1932, both for Roosevelt; Nixon and Ford first voted for president in 1936.

The third group includes Kennedy, Carter, and Bush 41, the World War II generation. Though Kennedy's death has fixed his youthful image in time, had he lived he would at this writing be the oldest of these three presidents. His first vote was in the 1940 election, when he supported Roosevelt, who had appointed his father ambassador to Great Britain. Carter and Bush first voted in the 1948 election between President Truman and Thomas E. Dewey.

The fourth group includes Bill Clinton and George W. Bush, the first presidents of the post–World War II, baby boom, generation. The time span from the birth of Truman to that of Bush 43 is sixty-two years, to that of Clinton, sixty-four years. Chester Arthur was president when Truman was born, and Truman was president when Bush and Clinton were born. Truman was growing into manhood at the time of the Spanish-American War. Later he served in World War I. Clinton and Bush were maturing at the time of the Cuban missile crisis and the escalation of U.S. involvement in the Vietnam War. Clinton avoided the draft; Bush served in the Texas Air National Guard. Clinton's first vote was in 1968, in one of the most troubling and divisive elections ever for the Democratic Party; Bush's first vote was in 1964, an election in which Johnson led the Democrats to a triumphal victory.

Most postwar presidents had very modest backgrounds. An elitist theory of political recruitment and advancement does not fare well with this group. Only Kennedy and the two Bushes were among the well born. The other eight (including the unelected Ford) had humble beginnings. Their schooling varies somewhat, ranging from high school only (Truman) to law degrees (Nixon, Ford, and Clinton) and an MBA (George W. Bush). Nixon attended Whittier College and Duke University Law School. Ford was the only president in this group to attend a large public university—the University of Michigan (and then received his law degree from Yale). Eisenhower and Carter went to military academies (army and navy, respectively). Kennedy, Bush 41, Clinton, and Bush 43 went to prestigious private institutions (Harvard, Yale, Georgetown, and Yale respectively). Clinton also attended Oxford University as a Rhodes scholar, and then Yale Law School. George W. Bush received his MBA degree from Harvard Business School. Johnson and Reagan attended small colleges that lacked prestige even within their respective states.

Presidents have varied substantially in regard to the ages when they first sought elective office and when they entered the White House (see figure 2-1). The age of their first elective political experience ranges from twenty-eight for Johnson to sixty-two for Eisenhower. Johnson was the youngest (twenty-nine) to win an elective office, Clinton was the youngest (fifty-four) to exit the White House (not counting Kennedy), and Reagan was by far the oldest (seventy-eight) to leave. There is also wide variation in the years of experience (not all of it political) between the first election and entering the White House. For Eisenhower, that figure is zero (although, of course, he had decades of military experience); for Johnson it is twenty-seven. The vice presidents who took over (Truman, Johnson, and Ford) had an average of twenty-five years between their first elective office and becoming president. Another two vice presidents who won on their own—Nixon and George H. W. Bush—had nearly the same number of years of experience upon entering the White House (23.5). The rest of the group—Kennedy, Carter, Reagan, Clinton, and George W. Bush— averaged 12.8 years. Bush 43 is second only to Eisenhower for having the least time between first elective office and the presidency.

The limited subnational elective political experience of recent presidents is also shown in figure 2-1. Only one of the eleven presidents started at the local level (Truman was the equivalent of a county executive). Carter started as a state senator and then became governor; Reagan started as a governor; Clinton was first state attorney general and then governor; and George W. Bush started as governor. Eisenhower started right at the top. The other five first got into elective office by running for Congress—the House of Repre-

Figure 2-1. *Age and Political Experience of Postwar Presidents*

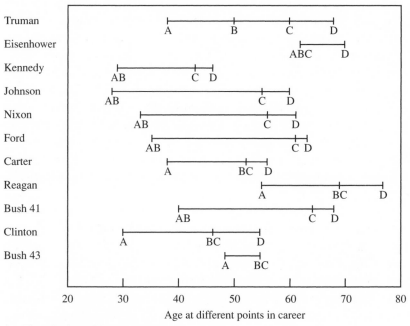

A = First elective poitical experience.
B = First national elective political experience.
C = Enters White House.
D = Exits White House.

Sources: Calculated from data in William A. DeGregorio, *The Complete Book of U.S. Presidents,* 2nd ed. (New York: Dembner Books, 1989); and various contemporary accounts.

sentatives in every case (George H. W. Bush first tried the Senate but was defeated and then was elected to the House).

Such limited state and local experience contrasts starkly with that of the eight other presidents in the twentieth century. All but Herbert Hoover had some elective experience below the national level. Five of the eight were governors, another was a lieutenant governor, four served in the state legislature, and four had local government experience, although not always in an elective position. Conversely, only two had congressional experience (McKinley in the House, Harding in the Senate). No doubt the differences between the two periods represent judgments by politicians as to what represents potentially valuable experience for winning the presidential nomination and the election.

But it may also reflect changes in the agenda, at what level of government that agenda is being treated, and what best prepares someone to manage it. Changes in the political parties and their role in the nominating process also play a part. It would have been difficult in the early years of the twentieth century to win the nomination from outside a political party. Subsequently the outside route to the nomination has been tried by dozens of potential candidates, many of whom have never been elected to any office.

The eleven postwar presidents' experience with legislatures (including that gained as a governor or vice president) ranges from zero (Eisenhower) to almost thirty years (Johnson). If one removes the three vice presidents who served as president (Truman, Johnson, and Ford), the average legislative service drops dramatically—those three had nearly as much total experience (more than sixty-four years) as the other eight (seventy-four years). Two other vice presidents, Nixon and George H. W. Bush, had brief experiences on the Hill (six and four years, respectively), and it is not absolutely certain that either could have succeeded without having served first as vice president; indeed, Nixon lost on his first try, even with that advantage, and George H. W. Bush tried and failed to get the Republican nomination in 1980.

That leaves Kennedy as the president with the most congressional experience among those who successfully sought the presidency and the only postwar president to be elected while serving in Congress. Finally, four of the five most recent presidents at this writing—Carter, Reagan, Clinton, and George W. Bush—gained most of their pre–White House experience as governors, working with state legislatures. This record shows clearly that presidents are not typically elected from Congress. In fact, only two sitting senators (Harding and Kennedy) and one sitting representative (Garfield) have been elected president.[21] Most postwar presidents have had to learn on the job in dealing with Congress.

Progressive ambition—that is, taking advantage of a series of opportunities that lead from one office to the next, higher office—is a very small factor in presidential accession.[22] Only four postwar presidents started at the state level (Carter as state senator and governor, Clinton as attorney general and governor, Reagan and George W. Bush as governors) and they did not then work their way toward Congress. Excluding Eisenhower, all the others served in Congress but, again, Truman, Johnson, and Ford were chosen as vice presidents, not a job one necessarily seeks out of ambition (though some do). Nixon, too, was selected as vice president, although he might have run for president on his own had he stayed in the Senate. Perhaps Kennedy and George H. W. Bush best fit the theory of progressive ambition. Although he did not serve in the state legislature, Kennedy climbed the ladder nationally from House to Senate to White House. And Bush sought to move from the House to the Senate, but was defeated in 1970; he then tried for the presidential nomination in 1980 and lost to Ronald Reagan. But one pure case and one near case do not a theory prove. More persuasive is the view that there is no predictable track to the White House. As shown, presidents enter the White House with strikingly varied political experiences and at different points in their political lives. The challenge is in attempting to understand how these various routes help to explain what happens when presidents assume office.

These eleven presidents also differ in terms of their experience within their respective political parties. There are some interesting pairings. Truman and Kennedy were in Congress but did not rise to party leadership positions. Truman had, however, served earlier as a party leader at the county level. Eisenhower obviously had no direct experience with his party. Indeed, he had not declared his party preference before running for president. Some of those wishing to replace Truman as the Democratic nominee in 1948 suggested Eisenhower (and, in fact, he received a few thousand votes in Democratic presidential primaries in that year). Johnson and Ford had lengthy experience as party leaders on Capitol Hill. Neither held state or local party positions, however, nor did they ever work directly for the national party organization.

The other six presidents—Nixon, Carter, Reagan, George H. W. Bush, Clinton, and George W. Bush—had the most diverse party experiences. Nixon and Reagan probably raised more money for the Republican Party than any other leaders in the history of American elections to that time. Both willingly participated in thousands of party and candidate dinners and other organizational events before becoming president. The senior Bush's association with the party is somewhat different but no less impressive. He is the only postwar president to have served as a county chairman (Truman served for only part of a county). He also participated in an endless stream of party activities as vice president, and he was the chairman of the Republican National Committee during the difficult Watergate months.

Carter's experience looks good on paper—almost as good as that of the other three just discussed. However, he worked alongside or even against the party as much as for it. He wanted to make changes, and it is doubtful that his service as governor encouraged Georgia Democrats to view him as their leader. In 1978 he chaired the midterm campaign committee for the Democratic National Committee. The post was mostly honorary, yet afforded him the chance to travel and make contacts that proved useful to him later, in his presidential bid. Clinton was active in the Democratic Leadership Council, serving as chairman for one year. And George W. Bush worked in his father's campaign in 1988 and served as a catalyst for the growing strength of the Texas Republican Party during his years as governor.

Once in office, presidents' relationships with their political parties differed markedly. Eisenhower, the president with no party experience, relied on Nixon. Truman worked well at the local level: this may even have won him the election in 1948. Kennedy was on a mission to heal party divisions when he was assassinated. Johnson and Ford were primarily legislative leaders serving in the White House, both well connected to their parties in Congress. Carter never blended well with the party apparatus and paid dearly for this tense relationship. Reagan worked well with the party apparatus at all levels: he was arguably the most effective party leader of the postwar presidents. George H. W. Bush was the only one of the presidents to serve as chairman of his party's national committee. Yet he was never fully accepted by the more conservative wing of the Republican party, a fact that plagued him throughout his presidency and in his campaign for reelection. As presidents, Clinton and George W. Bush showed themselves to be effective fundraisers. The mystery case is Nixon. As president he appeared to insulate himself from the party, essentially going into business for himself in the 1972 presidential campaign. He, too, paid dearly in the end, when party leaders in Congress and elsewhere failed to come to his aid in the Watergate scandal.

Governing Incentives

To say that presidents differ personally and in how they enter the White House borders on being trite. To say that these differences are often ignored in the expectations of their performance in office restores interest, however. As a final exercise in this chapter, I catalog the special advantages and weaknesses of the postwar presidents upon entering office and speculate about governing incentives logically associated with each set. I then note mitigating personal factors that either facilitated or altered the realization of achievements related to these incentives.

This exercise bears a resemblance to a broader and more deeply historical treatment by Stephen Skowronek. Neither of us was aware of the work of the other, but our interests converged, if not our subjects. Skowronek's analysis stretches from early in the nineteenth century to late in the twentieth. My attention is directed to the post–World War II era. He insists, as do I, that attention be paid to the conditions under which presidents enter office and the constraints with which they must cope while there. His question is: "How do presidents go about the task of fashioning their place in history, and how amenable are these places to being fashioned according to presidential design?"[23]

For Skowronek, the presidency is order shattering, affirming, and creating through successive presidents. Legacies are altered, used to new purpose, and passed along to the next seeker of a place in history. Skowronek identifies four recurrent "structures of presidential authority": reconstruction, disjunction, articulation, and preemption. Above all, these constructs encourage scholarly attention to when and how presidents settle into the job. His cut of history is very much greater than mine, and therefore he offers intriguing comparisons across time. His emphasis on legacies is also stronger. I pay greater heed to political capital and personal qualities. Yet, as noted above, our results are complementary.

Table 2-4 illustrates my attempt to specify a set of governing incentives. It includes the eighteen times the eleven postwar presidents entered office. The characteristics are drawn from this chapter's review of how presidents came to be in the White House and their personal and political backgrounds. I then deduced governing incentives for each president as reasonably following from the balance of advantages and disadvantages. This exercise produced five incentives:

Assertive: With strongly positive advantages upon entering office, the president has incentives to be aggressive in promoting policy proposals from the start (three cases: Johnson, 1963 and 1964; Reagan, 1980).

Compensatory: With significant disadvantages, and particularly lacking an electoral edge, the president leans toward devising supplementary means for authenticating his leadership (eight cases: Truman, 1948; Kennedy, 1960; Nixon, 1968; Carter, 1976; Clinton, 1992 and 1996; George W. Bush, 2000 and 2004).

Custodial: In assuming the office of a strong predecessor, the president takes custody of an existing agenda (one case: Truman, 1945).

Guardian: Typically associated with reelections; the strongest advantage, a landslide election, is not bolstered by congressional majorities. The president uses his electoral reaffirmation to protect or guard what has been done (four cases: Eisenhower, 1956; Nixon, 1972; Reagan, 1984; George H. W. Bush, 1988).[24]

Table 2-4. *Advantages, Weaknesses, and Incentives of Postwar Presidents*

President	Advantages	Weaknesses	Deduced incentive
Elected			
Eisenhower (1952)	Election by wide margin Congressional majorities Contrast[a]	Lack of Washington experience	Restorative
Kennedy (1960)	Congressional majorities New generation/contrast[a]	Election by narrow margin No connection[b]	Compensatory
Nixon (1968)	Experience Contrast[a]	Election by narrow margin No congressional majority	Compensatory
Carter (1976)	Congressional majorities Contrast[a]	Election by narrow margin No connection[b] Lack of Washington experience	Compensatory
Reagan (1980)	Election by wide margin Senate majority Connection[b] Contrast[a]	Lack of Washington experience No House majority	Assertive
Clinton (1992)	New generation/contrast[a] Congressional majorities	Election by narrow margin Limited connection[b] Lack of Washington experience	Compensatory
Bush 43 (2000)	Available talent Organization Congressional majorities	Disputed election Limited Washington experience	Compensatory
Reelected			
Eisenhower (1956)	Election by wide margin Experience	No congressional majority Runout[c]	Guardian
Nixon (1972)	Election by wide margin Experience	No congressional majority	Guardian
Reagan (1984)	Election by wide margin Experience Senate majority	No House majority Runout[c]	Guardian
Clinton (1996)	Electoral College margin Agenda	No congressional majority	Compensatory to assertive
Bush (2004)	Improved vote totals Congressional majorities	Narrow margins War in Iraq	Compensatory
Nonelected			
Truman (1945)	Congressional majorities Congressional experience	Contrast[a] Preparation	Custodial
Johnson (1963)	Congressional majorities Congressional experience Assassination	None	Assertive
Ford (1974)	Contrast[a] Congressional experience	No congressional majority Appointed Watergate legacy	Restorative

(continued)

Table 2-4. *Advantages, Weaknesses, and Incentives of Postwar Presidents (Continued)*

President	Advantages	Weaknesses	Deduced incentive
Elected vice presidents			
Truman (1948)	Congressional majorities	No connection[b] Party division	Compensatory
Johnson (1964)	Election by wide margin Congressional majorities Connection[b]	None	Assertive
Heir apparent			
Bush (1988)	Experience	No congressional majority Runout[c]	Guardian

a. A favorable or unfavorable comparison with the previous administration.
b. Whether the president's win was perceived as related to his party's wins in Congress.
c. The depletion of the agenda, typically associated with reelection.

Restorative: Due to the stark and positive contrast with his predecessor, the new president has incentives to restore the status of the office (two cases: Eisenhower, 1952; Ford, 1974).

How do these governing incentives compare with the partisan strategies identified in chapter 1? They relate to the conditions that a president faces when entering office. The partisan splits and arrangements are included among those conditions, as are personal, electoral, and other factors, such as succession and the legacy of the previous administration. But the partisan patterns refer generally to how the political parties interact in law making and related processes (for example, appointments), often associated with the extent and nature of competition or cooperation.

Are the governing incentives predictive of the early behavior of the postwar administrations? For the most part the answer is yes. But there are exceptions, seemingly because the president and his team decide to ignore the balance of advantages or to believe in a singular interpretation of their mission. The principal exceptions are Truman (1948), Nixon (1972), Carter (1976), and Clinton (1992). Some analysts might also include Bush 43 (2000 and 2004). Perhaps buoyed by his surprise win and large congressional majorities, Truman's incentive was more assertive than compensatory. Carter also could claim a surprise win, but in capturing the nomination rather than in winning the general election (which he came close to losing). Possibly more important in explaining his greater assertiveness was the fact that he was the first president to be elected in the aftermath of Watergate. He believed that he was entrusted by the people to "do the right thing" once in the White House.

Nixon, too, was more assertive than conditions appeared to warrant. Although he won an overwhelming victory in 1972, its size could reasonably be attributed to the weakness of his opponent and a Democratic Party still fractionated following the 1968 convention. In any event, Nixon failed to bring Republican congressional majorities to Washington. In his own mind, Nixon had scores to settle, and a guardianship strategy was not his preference.

The case of Clinton in 1992 was complicated by Democrats' enthusiasm on having regained the White House and Congress after twelve years. Whereas on paper a 43 percent win for the president and a net loss of Democratic seats in Congress might have suggested the need for a compensatory approach, the pressures to act were substantial, and Clinton was an activist by personality. Against this background he launched an ambitious agenda, including a national health care plan that was unlikely to be passed in Congress.[25]

Some have criticized George W. Bush for being more assertive in his initial months in office than conditions allowed. In contrast with Clinton and his health care plan, however, Bush succeeded in getting sufficient cross-partisan support to enact his priority tax cut in these early months. Still, it is inarguable that Bush sought to capitalize on position (see chapter 1) as an aggressive compensatory incentive, and that this approach alienated many Democrats on Capitol Hill. Upon reelection in 2004, Bush announced an ambitious agenda and claimed the political capital to back it up. Whereas a compensatory strategy might be inferred from a narrow win and small congressional margins, clearly the president intended to be more assertive than political conditions appeared to warrant.

At the very least, these incentives alert one to alternative criteria for evaluating performance. If it is correct that presidents enter office with assorted advantages, then it is reasonable to account for the extent to which they match or exceed the performance plausibly associated with one set over another. That evaluation modifies substantially one that is drawn from an idealized concept of the president as presidency, one that judges each occupant by a standard of assertiveness in leading a party government. The alternative tests ask: What can a president reasonably be expected to accomplish? Does he meet those expectations? These tests are not as benign as one might think. Meeting limited expectations may not be at all what is judged to be necessary for the good of the country, either by analysts or by the public. Therefore, one conclusion may well be that a president operating as expected under severe constraints simply cannot do the job. If he is reelected, however, there should be more concern about the viability of the election system than about the performance of the president in question. Reelection under such circumstances might suggest that the voters were not given a choice, that they were uninformed about the president's capacity to lead, or that they simply preferred a president who was respectful and mindful of the limits on presidential power.

CHAPTER 3

Organizing to Govern
in the Separated System

The separated system of diffused responsibility, mixed representation, and competing legitimacies presents special problems for presidents. They are typically held accountable for many policies and most events, none of which they fully control. Unlike most prime ministers, presidents cannot depend on being well acquainted and connected with others in elected and decisionmaking positions. Neither can they presume upon a standard formula for sharing powers with these others, because none exists. Further, bureaucrats, legislators, and interest group representatives tend to accommodate to changes at the top by developing continuities below. The triangles of power may not be as cozy as in the past, but the connections among the permanent actors are still a formidable challenge to an incoming president, who is expected to take charge of the government. The test can be especially demanding for vice presidents taking over and for elected presidents who have not previously been part of the national government.

Clearly, then, presidents must become larger than themselves to fulfill their responsibilities and meet performance expectations. Organization is one means through which they can accomplish these goals. They have a measure of discretion in making appointments and in structuring access to the Oval Office and decisionmaking in the Executive Office. This organization will depend to a considerable extent on the personal, experiential, and political advantages of each president. It is the person as president who must come to life organizationally. If that process is unnatural and forced, it will not work well for achieving the goals of leadership. Of course, the circumstances will vary. Some presidents, like Roosevelt, Eisenhower, and

Reagan, have had the advantages of a fresh start, experience in leading complex organizations, and strong electoral endorsement. Others, like takeover presidents Truman, Johnson, and Ford, had to manage initially within a structure designed to make someone else appear larger than life.

This chapter focuses attention on the variations in organizational challenges and experiences of eleven post–World War II presidents—Harry S Truman to George W. Bush—to determine how presidents take charge and the circumstances in which they do so. I concentrate primarily on the White House staff and cabinet secretaries as representative of two crucial sets of appointments, with the understanding that these appointments represent a small portion of a president's executive staffing apparatus and that this entire workforce is crucial to effective presidential leadership.[1] The White House staff enlarges the person as president to include a group of close advisers and spokespersons. The cabinet secretaries extend the president's reach into the permanent bureaucracy. These more public appointments often come to characterize a presidency.

Most of the government is already organized and in place when presidents take office. Departments and agencies are at work; a huge proportion of government employees stay at their desks. An immediate task facing the president and his associates is to connect with the permanent government as a prerequisite to establishing a degree of influence or control. Bureaucrats are accustomed to this exercise, and indeed, for the most part, they comply with it. But the president's success in establishing connections to "his" government requires more than moving into the Oval Office and making the necessary appointments. Validating the leadership of the White House and encouraging compliance by the bureaucracy and Congress are not one-time activities. Presidents must shape and reshape their means of governing through a temporary and ever-changing organizational design.

The famed Committee on Administrative Management (the Brownlow committee) rightly concluded in 1937: "The President needs help."[2] Bradley H. Patterson Jr., who served on the White House staff for three presidents, concludes that the president needs help more than ever because he "acts in a gigantic theater-in-the-round," with greater demands for coordination among more people and fewer boundaries between issues.[3] Presidents have gotten more assistance, to be sure. But Peri E. Arnold observes: "The plain fact is that no modern president has fully managed the executive branch." He warns that efforts to increase managerial capacities result in a "trap" by "offering increased capacity and influence to presidents but creating even greater expectations about presidential performance." Arnold believes that "the president is not so much a manager of administration; he is a tactician using it."[4]

How the president selects and organizes the White House and the cabinet and puts them to work typically depends on his analysis of goals, personal resources, and needs. After all, it is his White House, if only his government on consignment. The staff represents his effort to find a place within a larger structure that was there when he arrived and will be there after he leaves, albeit influenced in the interim by his presence. In a sense, this staffing process grafts a head onto an existing body. No one can imagine that to be a simple exercise. It starts very personally, when the president shapes an organization to suit his manner and method of decisionmaking. It then may be adapted to what the president and his staff find is necessary to get the government to work as they want it to.[5]

It is surely true that presidents seek to organize the White House to serve them and that those appointed intend to achieve that goal if at all possible. But there is an institutional imperative as well, relating to the growth of government and the emergence of a substantial administrative apparatus attached to the presidency. Upon entering office, presidents can and do cut back staff or conceal staff growth, often to fulfill a campaign promise and compare themselves favorably with their predecessor. These reductions are typically more symbolic than real, however, because of "the recurrent streams of action-forcing questions flowing necessarily to presidents themselves, through regularized procedures."[6] Demands will be made, and the pressure to meet them is substantial. The presidency is increasingly institutionalized, thus placing greater distance between the personal White House staff and the governing departments and agencies, as Paul C. Light has shown empirically in his analysis of "layering" in the modern bureaucracy.[7] As a consequence of the growth and development of the Executive Office of the President during the postwar period, presidents have found they must manage a nearby government surrounding the White House itself. That management task naturally falls to the White House staff and other presidential appointees.

The Presidential Branch

The White House staff includes those close aides whose work is oriented to the president's political, policy, social, and constitutional responsibilities (as well as those of the president's spouse). The Executive Office staff includes people in units, like the Office of Management and Budget, the

National Security Council staff, and the Council of Economic Advisers, that have been created to provide professional advice to the president as well as direction to and coordination of the bureaucracy. Together these staffs constitute the presidential branch—a term attributed to Nelson W. Polsby. During the Nixon presidency, which is generally credited with originating contemporary White House staff operations, the White House staff grew to well over 500 and there were significant problems of coordination. Subsequent presidents have sought to work with a somewhat leaner staff, seemingly acknowledging that an outer limit had been reached during the disgraced Nixon White House.[8]

The Executive Office of the President is a minigovernment of approximately 1,700 professionals who act as the president's contacts with the bureaucracy, Congress, other governments, the public, the party, and the press. This minigovernment is located in the White House itself, in the ornate Old Executive Office Building next door, and in the New Executive Office Building one block away. Polsby describes how it came about:

> Perhaps the most interesting development of the fifty-year period is the emergence of a presidential branch of government separate and apart from the executive branch. It is the presidential branch that sits across the table from the executive branch at budgetary hearings, and that imperfectly attempts to coordinate both the executive and legislative branches in its own behalf.[9]

The emergence of a presidential branch was bound to threaten the regular departments and agencies, not to mention politicize what was originally meant to be neutral and professional in-house advice from the Executive Office of the President. The president is encouraged, if not fully prepared, to go into policy business on his own, without having to depend heavily on advice from cabinet secretaries and other presidential appointees. Thus the status of cabinet secretaries has declined, while that of the president's assistants has increased. These developments have suited those presidents suspicious of the bureaucracy, as most are. Republican presidents (six of the eleven in the postwar era) particularly welcomed an independent source of policy and political advice, since they doubted that certain of their proposals were welcome within many departments and agencies.

The White House staff sits atop this branch and is responsible for its management. One may rightly question whether the whole apparatus has resulted in a net gain of influence for the president. Significant numbers of politically ambitious professional people, many with strong policy commitments, spur in-house competition for the president's time. Independent, self-organizing policy entrepreneurs were not exactly what Louis Brownlow had in mind when he concluded that the president needed help. As John Hart describes it:

> Nowadays, senior White House staffers regularly do what Brownlow said they should not do. They quickly become prominent figures in every administration. They do make decisions, issue instructions, and emit public statements. They do interpose themselves between the president and the heads of departments. They do exercise power on their own account, and, on occasions, certain members of the White House staff have not discharged their functions with restraint. In recent years some have clearly lacked the high competence Brownlow thought essential, and few have displayed much passion for anonymity.[10]

Hedrick Smith contends that "presidents developed their own bureaucracy."[11] But the White House staff is not a standard bureaucracy—far from it. Like aggressive staff personnel on Capitol Hill, many are men and women anxious for credentials that will permit them to move elsewhere. They can enhance their résumés substantially with White House experience, especially if it includes successful encounters with the bureaucracy.

The advent of a presidential branch and an aggressive White House staff is not a cost-free benefit for the president. I have noted the trap that Arnold speaks of: more staff and higher expectations of achieving the unachievable. Adding staff to solve the president's traditional problem of managing and directing the bureaucracy for his own policy purposes can, itself, become a management problem. A former White House staff person who served Eisenhower and Nixon offered a particularly vivid analysis of the consequences of an elaborated staff, as well as how presidents have sought to escape the trap. I quote it at some length because it so well illustrates both the need for and the costs of such staff.

> The president who understands staff work knows that any staff tries to ensnare its victim. Its victim is its leader. . . . The president moves into the White House . . . and they come trotting into the place with a staff around them that helped them with the election. That staff feels as if the president is a personal possession. . . . And they put this into a hermetically-sealed box and try to keep everyone else away from it.
>
> And so you have the first part of the presidency, the inner circle. . . . Then you have middle season when they have to enlarge it slightly and breach that with a crack or two because they become overworked. And they realize in growing desperation they can't handle all the work and so, most grudgingly, they will bring in a newcomer to enlarge their group.
>
> During this season the president gets claustrophobia. He realizes that he's being spoon-fed by just this small clique of people, and he wants to break out; he wants to look out the window and see who's out there.

So he uses devices. President Eisenhower used those famous stag dinners . . . to get around his staff. He would call in people from all across the country . . . and he would sit down to have a very enjoyable dinner and post-dinner conversation. "What's going on in America, boys; tell me what's going on out there?" And they would end up in long discussions and even arguments over the course of America and what's troubling educators, what's troubling businessmen, what's troubling labor. Very valuable to President Eisenhower because he had been on military staffs for many years. He knew precisely what a staff would do to a leader. So he deliberately did that to franchise himself from his own staff.[12]

One need not accept George E. Reedy's admittedly exaggerated image of White House "inner life" as "essentially the life of the barnyard, as set forth so graphically in the study of the pecking order among chickens" to take interest in how the White House is organized and whether it works well in serving the president. Reedy's experience in the Johnson White House led him to believe that "below the president is a mass of intrigue, posturing, strutting, cringing, and pious 'commitment' to irrelevant wind-baggery." He attributed this tendency to the cloak of power associated with the presidency that invited "intrigue, pomposity, and ambition."[13] In over-stating his case, Reedy draws attention to the potential for an unelected staff to act in the name of the president, and therefore to the need for the president and his trusted advisers to exercise control and management. This view is consistent with Richard E. Neustadt's claim that "the institutions that surround the President are, in their way, the usurpers [of presidential power] and enemies. It doesn't matter whether it's the cabinet or the staff. These people have separate agendas because of separate institutions sharing and competing for powers and they're not immune from that."[14]

Simply put, the president faces a dilemma. Government has continued to grow and politics has been separated by frequent split-party arrangements in which the president's party is in the minority on Capitol Hill. If anything, presidents need even more help now than when the Brownlow committee made its recommendations. As Matthew J. Dickinson points out, however, staffing should be based on "the context in which the president operates."[15] He argues that attention should be paid to the president's goals, audience, and preferred bargaining resources. In other words, the operating principle should be his needs as defined by him, not those of a political bureaucracy institutionalized as the presidential branch.

Dickinson recommends "competitive adhocracy" similar to that employed by Franklin D. Roosevelt. With this approach, staffing is, among other things, nonhierarchical, flexible, less articulated, overlapping in functions, much less institutionalized, and kept small.[16] But suggestions for dismantling or dramatically reforming the presidential branch will inevitably be resisted. Specializations develop for a purpose, dependencies are created throughout the government, buildings are erected and space allocated, and expectations are formed around how it was done yesterday.

Organizational Models

What are the options for organizing the White House staff? In 1976, President-elect Jimmy Carter asked Stephen Hess, a senior fellow at the Brookings Institution and a former White House staff person, for memorandums on organizing the presidency. In the first edition of his book *Organizing the Presidency*, which had come to Carter's attention, Hess sensibly emphasized the importance of fitting the organization of the White House to the person who is president. Thus in advising Carter, Hess worked with what he knew about the new president: Carter's stated organizational preferences (for example, that there should be no chief of staff) and his desire to avoid the problems of previous presidents. Hess concluded that "a president need not have a chief of staff—he can divide the duties—but he should not be his own chief of staff. Otherwise he will find that he is spending considerable time on servicing his staff, rather than the other way around."[17]

Hess reviewed two dominant models of organization and proposed a variation that was attentive to preferences that Carter had already expressed. According to Hess, the previous models were the circle and the pyramid. The circle was

> used by FDR and JFK. The president [is] at the hub with staff impinging on him from all points along the circumference. The model can work well in running small enterprises (such as the White House during the early New Deal), but tends to create undue chaos and confusion in the modern presidency, especially over time as new people are added to the staff who lack established working relationships with each other and the president.

The circle is often referred to as the "spokes of the wheel" type of organization, with the Oval Office as the hub.

The pyramid was "used by Eisenhower and Nixon. The president [is] at the apex. Extremely orderly; but may tend to screen out creativity and can lead to excessive secrecy. Only advisable for presidents who have long experience with this model (as did Ike in the military)."[18] The pyramid normally requires a chief of staff, who acts as the checkpoint for what passes through to the Oval Office. Appointing some form of a chief of staff with variable access to the president is generally accepted as the way to organize in the contemporary period. The person in this position is under tremendous pressure and must have the full confidence of the president. He or she may not be able to withstand this pressure for very long. In fact, in fulfilling the function of protecting the president, such a person may have to resign in the event of a breakdown or scandal, for failure to do so implicates the president. The rewards for service as chief of staff are not always obvious. Dick Cheney, who served as President Ford's chief of staff, observed: "If there's a dirty deed to be done, it's the chief of staff who's got to do it. The president gets credit for what works, and you get the blame for what doesn't work. That's the nature of the beast."[19] James A. Baker III, Reagan's first chief of staff, has written that "it is easy to understand why some people also characterize [the position] not just as the second-toughest job in Washington but as the *worst* job in Washington."[20]

Instead of either the circle or the pyramid model, Hess offered a variation for the Carter White House that he viewed as providing "open efficiency" or "orderly access." Resembling an isosceles trapezoid (a pyramid with its top sawed off), it "allows wide access to the president in a structured setting. This assumes that you [Carter] are a highly methodical person who will be ultimately dissatisfied with incomplete staff work or tangled lines of communications, while, at the same time, will wish not to be overly dependent on a small number of aides and as open as possible in your conduct of the presidency."[21]

Others, too, have classified presidential staff management forms as a collegial system or "adhocracy" in place of the circle, and a formalistic or centralized management system in place of the pyramid. The competitive adhocracy approach of Franklin D. Roosevelt is often added to these core types.[22] But as the discussion below of individual presidents will show, these ideal types do not sufficiently account for the variations found in actual practice, as related to differences in personal and institutional demands on the president. The spokes are not always the same length, and therefore produce anything but a circle; pyramids are never that pointed; the trapezoid has not been tried; and multiple advocacy is less a management style than a process of uncovering various policy options.

Cabinet Secretaries: Reaching Within

The terms *government* or *administration* are frequently used to designate the prominent persons who make up the group of presidential appointees.[23]

The first—government—is particularly susceptible to misunderstanding outside the United States, since it is commonly used in parliamentary systems to refer to the prime minister and his or her cabinet. In the parliamentary context it conveys the idea of unity as well as a process within the majority party or coalition for developing that unity. The second—administration—is somewhat less easily misunderstood but it, too, tends to convey more of a collective sense of purpose within the permanent and temporary executive than is constitutionally or politically warranted by the American system.

This strength of unity in other systems presumably derives from processes of integration among those who make up the government and also between these people and the bureaucracy or the legislature. In many parliamentary systems a measure of integration is achieved at the start through a recruiting process that builds on common experiences, typically drawing cabinet ministers from parliament. The potential for unity of purpose in this system is highly accommodating to the demands of party government. It facilitates accountability by encouraging policy and administrative integration; indeed, the government may well be judged on that basis.

In the United States, the top appointees who are considered the "government" or the "administration" are typically not well integrated through prior policy or political experience. In many instances cabinet secretaries and White House staff have had little or no previous association with one another, through either work or politics. The mix of career ambitions represented by presidential appointees may well bring the outside world to Washington, but there is no guarantee that these officials will cohere into a working government. In fact, there is a high probability that they will not. Thus the president is somewhat in the position of the Olympic basketball coach. He may well have talented players but lack a team.[24]

Proper Tests of Presidencies

If a presidency is tested by the criteria of a "government," it will almost always be found wanting. But what is the point in applying those tests? However imperfect by the standards of responsible party government, the separated system persists in the United States. Thus other measures of presidential strength or weakness are needed. The tests of presidential effectiveness—if not exactly strength or weakness—may be the extent to which communication is established between the White House and the departments and agencies, the clarity of the policy messages communicated, and the degree of mutual support that results when the messages are clear. The mixed experience and background of those brought in to manage the permanent government pose a significant communications challenge for the White House. Diversity, however admirable on other grounds, may interfere with building unity of purpose—especially so if appointees act more as group representatives than as team players. In criticizing the American system, analysts often fail to appreciate what it takes to integrate that which has been so carefully separated.

If a presidency is judged as a communications network, a good cabinet is one in which each appointee is sufficiently oriented to the White House and informed of its goals to accomplish policy, administrative, and legislative tasks with clarity and confidence. A president's grade is based on how many officials meet this one-on-one test of contact and communication—president ↔ cabinet official—regarding issues of the moment, not on tests derived from communal or party government decisionmaking.

Viewing the presidency as a set of orientations of cabinet appointees toward the Oval Office (not necessarily toward one another) encourages an analysis of the process by which this happens (or fails to occur), as well as how it may change. It also invites consideration of whether a president is successful in orienting cabinet secretaries to his purposes, and whether the secretaries then represent that orientation in the many individual contacts that they have with other decisionmakers. Dean Rusk, secretary of state for Presidents Kennedy and Johnson, illustrated both points in discussing the demands on cabinet secretaries. "President Johnson was always considerate of his Cabinet officers. I think he felt that they were the ones who shared with him the public responsibility and the constitutional and statutory responsibility of office." This was a successful orientation. "It was the Cabinet officers who had to appear most often before the Congress to defend a program. It was the Cabinet officers who met the press and helped to carry the public explanation of policy, and who had to share the ultimate responsibility."[25]

Cabinet secretaries are, of course, responsible for administering their departments and representing departmental interests within the wider policy process. But, as Rusk states, they are also spokespersons for the administration within their policy areas. Their public responsibility is typically issue specific. A cabinet secretary speaks for a presidency regarding the policies proposed and implemented by his or her department. These policies may be cross-cutting, to be sure, but not even a cabinet secretary who is a close friend of the president is likely either to expound or be listened to on issues outside his or her departmental jurisdiction. Below the level of the president, more general cross-cutting discussion or exposition is likely to come from White House staff, possibly the chief of staff or the director of the Office of Management and Budget.

Variations in Appointments

The variable characteristics of presidents are revealed in the appointments they make, even today, when there is pressure to be more diverse than in the past. Polsby illustrates this point:

> When a new president picks his cabinet, he gives observers the first set of solid clues about the kind of president he intends to be. . . . President Eisenhower's appointment of "nine millionaires and a plumber" gave quite a good forecast of the sort of presidency General Eisenhower wanted to have. When John Kennedy became president he struck a dominant theme of self-consciously moving beyond his own range of personal acquaintance to form a governing coalition. Likewise, his appointment of his brother as attorney general telegraphed a strong desire to keep close control of the civil rights issue.
>
> It is possible to see in Richard Nixon's cabinet appointments a mirror of his emerging view of the role of the president vis-à-vis the rest of the government.[26]

These observations are also applicable to more recent presidencies. Clinton's proclaimed emphasis on diversity, a cabinet like America, clearly reflected his governing principle, as did the executive and business orientation of George W. Bush's appointments.

Implicit in Polsby's comments is the lack of institutionalization of the cabinet. Jeffrey E. Cohen concludes that each president fashions a role for those who serve in the cabinet, that some of these individuals come to have considerable power, and that there may be institutional development within a presidency but not between presidencies. There is little carryover from one president to the next.[27]

It is apparent, then, that cabinets are interesting primarily because they reflect the president's effort to govern within the separated system. When cabinet secretaries are successful, they may expect to share their success with the president, and when there is failure, they may expect to be held accountable, perhaps even to resign or be fired.

These characteristics do not make the position very attractive. In fact, they help to explain the relatively high turnover among cabinet officials. It is not that one cannot profit from the experience (and there always appear to be takers), but only certain people can make the position work for them politically. Getting the proper fit between a department's interest and that of the cabinet secretary may only be a happenstance, particularly when there are pressures to represent different groups in the most publicly exposed positions of a presidency. Unconventional demands, the unstructured nature of the job, and the need to satisfy interests not associated with performance in office may contribute to the familiar pattern of appointees getting in, gaining whatever experience and prestige are allowed, and getting out. The surprise is when turnover is low, as under Clinton and George W. Bush in his first term (see table 3-1 below). Other features of cabinet life include the following:

—A tendency to identify with the interests and clientele of the department the longer one stays ("going native").

—Variable access to the White House, depending on the agenda, personal chemistry between the secretary and the president (or top aides), and presidential policy interests.

—Greater centralization of decisionmaking in the White House or the presidential branch to compensate for the lack of unity or community among the cabinet (amplified even more if a cabinet secretary goes native).

—Pressure to balance presidential policy positions against congressional support for existing programs (particularly characteristic of split-party government between a Republican president and a Democratic Congress).

At the very least, these features prepare one for the variation in the turnover of cabinet secretaries. Table 3-1 ranks presidencies in the twentieth century by the mean and median number of months of service, as well as the number serving throughout a presidency. For purposes of this table, elected and takeover presidents are taken together—for example, Kennedy and Johnson—because a high proportion of cabinet secretaries remain in place for the takeover president. Three categories of presidencies are presented: the three-term presidency of Roosevelt, two-term presidencies (with the combinations noted above), and one-term presidencies.

The number of cabinet-level departments increased from nine at the start of the twentieth century to fourteen at the end (and subsequently to fifteen with the addition of the Department of Homeland Security in 2002). Just one was dropped, the Post Office in 1970, though Navy and War were combined to form the Department of Defense in 1947. Note the substantial differences in both the mean and the median tenures. Among two-term presidencies ranked by mean, there is a difference of twenty months between the top and bottom (Wilson and Roosevelt/Truman); ranked by median, there is nearly thirty months' difference (Clinton and Roosevelt/Truman). Differences are

Table 3-1. *Tenure and Rank of Cabinet Secretaries, 1901–2001*

President	Mean tenure		Median tenure		Serving throughout administration	
	Months	Rank	Months	Rank	Number	Rank
Three terms						
Roosevelt	59.2	1	52.5	1	2	1
Two terms						
Wilson	47.8	1	44.5	3	3	2
Eisenhower	47.3	2	40.5	5	2	5
Clinton	46.1	3	48.0	1	4	1
Roosevelt[a]	44.7	4	43.0	4	3	2
Harding/Coolidge	43.5	5	46.0	2	2	5
Reagan	37.5	6	35.0	6	1	7
Kennedy/Johnson	36.5	7	25.0	7	3	2
McKinley/Roosevelt	29.2	8	24.0	8	1	7
Nixon/Ford	27.1	9	24.0	8	0	9
Roosevelt/Truman	25.4	10	19.0	10	0	9
One term						
Taft	39.0	1	48.0	1	7	1
Hoover	32.0	2	40.0	2	5	3
Bush 41	30.8	3	30.0	3	7	1
Carter	27.5	4	25.0	4	4	4

Sources: Compiled from data on cabinet listings in Michael Nelson, ed., *Guide to the Presidency,* 2nd ed. (Washington: CQ Press, 1996), pp. 1689–97; and various Internet sources for later presidencies.
   a. 1933–41.

equally stark among one-term presidencies, with Taft ranked first and Carter ranked last by both mean and median.

Concentrating on the postwar presidencies, the lowest mean and median number of months of service were under Nixon/Ford (for two-term presidencies) and Carter (for one term); Eisenhower had the highest mean in the postwar period. Those findings fit the general knowledge about those presidencies (see discussion below). The surprise comes with Clinton, who has the third highest mean among all presidencies in the twentieth century, second among postwar presidencies; and the highest median among all two-term presidencies in the twentieth century. Note also that the Clinton presidency featured the highest number of cabinet secretaries serving through the two terms (the proportion was smaller than in some others, however, due to the increase in the number of cabinet secretaries).

Table 3-1 portrays impressive disparities in the makeup and stability of twentieth century presidencies, viewed as collections of top-level appointees. During the Nixon/Ford presidency, a total of forty-three people served as cabinet secretaries (an average of nearly four per department). For Eisenhower, that number was just twenty, or only two per department. Those totals provide important clues about the continuity and stability of these presidencies and the organizational capacity of the presidents themselves.

That the Clinton presidency should rank at the top in cabinet stability by these measures surely requires comment. Disorder was evident on many fronts, including among cabinet secretaries: an impeachment and trial of the president, the president held in contempt of court, and independent counsels appointed to investigate five cabinet secretaries. Nevertheless, it was apparent that several appointees really liked their jobs—a tribute to the president for identifying a good fit. Four—Janet Reno (Justice), Donna Shalala (Health and Human Services), Bruce Babbitt (Interior), and Richard Riley (Education)—stayed for eight years. In addition, the White House staff became preoccupied with damage control in regard to scandals, thus leaving the cabinet secretaries to manage their work more independently. Finally, the president was a policy "wonk," receptive to new ideas. Thus there were rewards for service as a cabinet secretary, notably, access to the Oval Office and the satisfaction of securing the president's attention to a department or agency agenda.

George W. Bush had at least two advantages in creating his cabinet. As the son of a former president, he could rely on several persons with experience in his father's presidency. A partial list includes Vice President Dick Cheney (former White House chief of staff and secretary of defense); Secretary of State Colin Powell (former national security adviser and chairman of the Joint Chiefs of Staff); Secretary of Defense Donald Rumsfeld (former White House chief of staff, secretary of defense, and NATO ambassador); White House chief of staff Andrew Card (former secretary of transportation); Secretary of Transportation Norman Mineta (former secretary of commerce); Secretary of Veterans Affairs Anthony Principe (former deputy secretary and secretary of veterans affairs).

Bush's second advantage was the result of his own previous experience as a governor. He appointed three former governors and four other state and local executives to cabinet positions. These appointments produced a cabinet with impressive executive experience. Stability was a hallmark during the first term, with just two changes each among cabinet secretaries and core White House staff.

Perhaps most striking to foreign observers accustomed to parliamentary systems is the extent to which cabinet secretaries, who represent the president's reach into the permanent government, are drawn from private life or state and local government. Of the postwar elected presidents, only George H. W. Bush appointed to his cabinet a sizable proportion of persons with federal executive experience at the time of appointment. Bush was close to being a takeover president, however, and therefore he reappointed several sitting cabinet secretaries. As noted above, Bush's son appointed a number with previous federal executive experience. Nixon, Reagan, and Clinton initially appointed no one with federal executive experience immediately before their cabinet service, although several of their appointees had previously served as federal-level executives. The other elected presidents did little better. Kennedy, Nixon, and George W. Bush appointed a number of governors; Clinton's cabinet secretaries included several with previous state executive experience, as did those of George W. Bush.

Of course, as presidencies mature, they naturally develop more federal executive experience, and presidents, once in office, tend to make new appointments from the executive branch rather than from the private sphere. Thus, for example, when Nixon made wholesale changes in 1972 and 1973, he drew much more heavily from those with experience in the federal government. And George W. Bush appointed a number of his top White House aides to cabinet posts (including attorney general and secretary of state) in the transition to his second term.

Organizational Experience of Postwar Presidencies

However useful as general descriptions of or prescriptions for the relationships between a leader and staff, common geometric configurations like the circle or pyramid fail to portray how postwar presidents do their work. Moreover, such models imply static conditions when continual adaptations are probable. I identify four organizational patterns associated with the presidents and their terms in office:

—Stable: Periods of substantial continuity in organizational structure and personnel.

—Adjusted: Ordinary organizational adaptation to change.

—Renewed: Major organizational restructuring, with many new appointments.

—Transitional: A transition from an organization in place to one suited to a new president (associated with takeovers).

As shown in figure 3-1, patterns shift during a presidency, typically as a result of experience in office and new priorities. Accepting that a presidential branch has evolved, White House staff organization differs among presidents to exactly the degree one might expect, given its dependency on the president: who he is, how he got there, how he views the job, and what are his organizational preferences. Differences show up on a number of dimensions, not just the degree and trail of access to the Oval Office. In addition, the cabinet secretaries that each president appoints reveal the changing nature of his presidency. It is fair to say that each president has more than one presidency. This change has implications for the president's strategic position and functioning in the separated system; it affects public standing, influence in agenda setting, and status in the lawmaking process. These points are illustrated in a review of the postwar presidents.

Roosevelt to Truman

When Franklin D. Roosevelt died on April 12, 1945, his successor, Harry S Truman, had served as vice president for just eighty-two days. Truman's assumption of the top job was the earliest in a term since Andrew Johnson succeeded Lincoln in 1865. Like Johnson, Truman served nearly a full term as president (April 12, 1945, to January 20, 1949).

WHITE HOUSE STAFF. Truman had virtually no executive experience and little time as vice president to observe how his predecessor managed. Time alone would not have been sufficient, however, either to discern or to emulate Roosevelt's organizational and management style. His techniques were subtle, complex, and suited to his distinctive personality. Neustadt explains:

> In a White House on Roosevelt's pattern, senior aides were called upon to do two things at once: to help their President put his concerns in personal perspective and to help him keep his work informed by other perspectives also. These two are somewhat contradictory; to manage both a man needs empathy and loyalty and self-discipline, all three. For these qualities in combination, Roosevelt looked to old associates from politics and government. . . . Truman followed suit as best he could. Lacking at the start enough reliable associates, he picked most of his best aides young and grew them on the job. . . . In time, this method worked quite well outside the national security sphere.[28]

Initially Truman had the advantage of two exceedingly shrewd Roosevelt advisers, Harry Hopkins and Sam Rosenman. However, Hopkins died in January 1946, and Rosenman returned to New York City early in that same year. Clark Clifford replaced Rosenman as Truman's special counsel. Truman's biographer Robert J. Donovan describes the personal, if

Figure 3-1. *Postwar Presidents, by Organizational Pattern, 1945–2005*

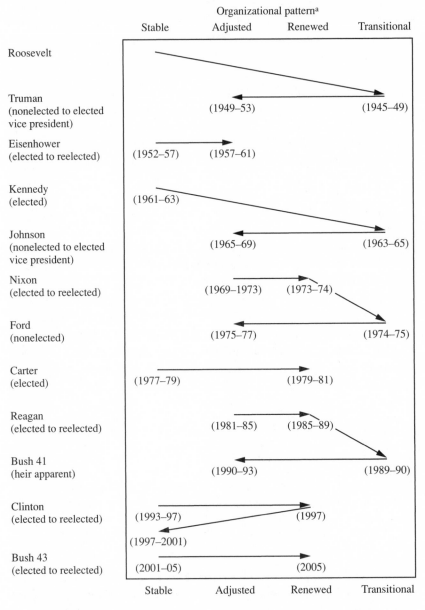

a. See text for explanation of patterns.

sometimes awkward and unformed, manner in which the president related to his staff:

> Truman was his own chief of staff. He chaired the morning staff meeting in his office, parceled out assignments, gave directions, discussed the concerns of the different members, and watched the White House budget. . . .
>
> He was slow to develop the knack of using a staff well. [John] Snyder . . . said afterward that, especially in the hectic early months, Truman drew upon the rudimentary principles of administration he had learned at reserve army summer camps in the twenties and thirties.[29]

In his memoirs, Clark Clifford stresses Truman's preference for equal access among staff aides, a pattern often favored by members of Congress who become president because it is how they had operated on Capitol Hill.

> The manner in which President Truman ran the White House evolved as time went on, but at all times it reflected his informality, his accessibility and openness, and his preference for rapid, intuitive decision making over careful, analytical staff work. His White House could best be visualized as a wheel with spokes: each spoke was one of his key aides, with different (but sometimes overlapping) areas of responsibility. Harry Truman would never have felt comfortable if access to him was controlled by a single person. No organization chart of the Truman White House ever existed.[30]

However equal the access, the infighting between Clifford and Assistant to the President John R. Steelman was well known. Clifford cast the running dispute as that of "liberal versus conservative," explaining, "My other adversary on policy was a member of the White House staff, John Steelman. As time went on, our relationship became increasingly confrontational. To a certain extent, the Presidential staff divided into factions grouped around the two of us."[31] When Clifford left in 1950, he was replaced by Charles Murphy. Well versed in Capitol Hill politics, Murphy became Truman's chief political operative. As Clifford notes, however, "Charlie was comfortable only in the domestic field. . . . Thus for the first time, a clear division between those working on domestic and national security affairs began to emerge in the White House."[32]

The Truman White House staff had a personal, even intimate, quality. It remained relatively inconspicuous to the public. Neither the president nor cabinet officials viewed staff as a barrier to the Oval Office. Indeed, one former aide explained to Stephen J. Wayne that "if any cabinet member had called up and asked for a meeting with the president and been turned off by a staff member, by God that staff member would have been fired within 24 hours by Harry Truman."[33]

CABINET SECRETARIES. The more public extension of the White House during the Truman years was the cabinet. There were three Truman cabinets, as measured by the amount of turnover. The first was that in place at the time of Roosevelt's death. As G. Calvin Mackenzie put it: "Most Presidents, upon coming to the White House, have to form a government. Harry Truman inherited one."[34] Having served for a long time, several cabinet members resigned soon after Truman took over. Of those who did not, Secretary of the Interior Harold Ickes resigned with Truman's blessing and Secretary of Commerce Henry A. Wallace was fired.

Following this inherited cabinet, there were two waves of Truman appointees. For the first wave Truman could draw on a sizable pool of subcabinet and ambassadorial talent from the three-term Roosevelt presidency. Thus, "with little need to 'capture' the government or to redirect it significantly, Truman was able to make a large percentage of his executive nominations from his own circle of acquaintances and from among individuals whose actions and reputations he had been able to observe at close range."[35] The third and last Truman cabinet was the most stable. After Interior Secretary Julius Krug resigned in 1949, there were but three other changes: two in Defense, one in Justice.

In summary, organization during the Truman years was transitional, then adjustable (see figure 3-1). There were many changes in personnel, with among the greatest number serving and highest turnover in the twentieth century (see table 3-1). There was, however, no one point of renewal, of creating a Truman presidency after the initial resignations of Roosevelt appointees. The transition itself was relatively swift, due to the age, perhaps the weariness, of the Roosevelt government. The comparison with the Johnson and Ford presidencies is striking in this regard. There was a substantial foreign and domestic policy legacy. The new president could pick and choose among experienced people in coping with this large agenda. The organization that resulted has been described by Stephen Hess as "a blending of stunningly capable patricians, unimaginative professionals, and incompetent cronies."[36] Fortunately for the country, Truman often chose the best people for the biggest jobs. Unfortunately for his presidency, his poor choices and inelegant style detracted from his contributions, substantially delaying the credit due him for certain courageous decisions.

Eisenhower

As shown in figure 3-1, the eight-year Eisenhower administration moved from a stable organization to one that experienced regular adjustments. In sharp contrast to the Truman years, turnover in the Eisenhower cabinet was among the lowest of any presidency in the twentieth century (see table 3-1).

WHITE HOUSE STAFF. No postwar president entered the White House with as much organizational experience as Dwight D. Eisenhower. Nor have other presidents written so clearly and so directly on the subject. Andrew Goodpaster, staff secretary to Eisenhower, explained: "We had a president who was, if I may say so, the most skillful man when it came to organizing, to performing functions well, with the deepest understanding of the role of organization, of how to use staff, of subordination and decentralization . . . of anyone I've ever known or known of."[37]

Eisenhower's own discussion of the topic reveals more than his preferences; it offers evidence of a well-developed conceptual approach:

> For years I had been in frequent contact with the Executive Office of the White House and I had certain ideas about the system, or lack of system, under which it operated. With my training in problems involving organization it was inconceivable to me that the work of the White House could not be better systemized than had been the case during the years I observed it.[38]

Eisenhower outlined the major functions of a White House staff, stressing the need for coordination, which led him to justify appointing a "responsible head." He "sought a competent administrator and a good friend" for this post, but judged that "it would create in many quarters a suspicion of excessive military influence" to select one of his military friends. After considering former senator Henry Cabot Lodge (R-Mass.) and Sherman Adams, former Republican governor of New Hampshire, Eisenhower selected the latter.

Eisenhower had no intention of serving as his own chief of staff. He fully understood the role to be played by such a person: a chief of staff worked for the president, not the other way around. Eisenhower also had a clear conception of how the operating staff (which he thought should be called the "president's staff," to avoid confusion with the Executive Office of the President) should be organized and work. According to Fred I. Greenstein, Eisenhower used Adams as a top assistant for coordination and communication but also as a deputy. "In this status, an aide was supposed to be fully aware of his superior's policies or be able immediately to get clarification and further instructions." The chief of staff as deputy was a conception developed by Eisenhower as military commander and was designed "to extend [the] superior's impact, making decisions of his own."[39]

The president's concept of and reliance on a chief of staff as deputy was the subject of strong criticism. Beyond the charges that Adams acted arrogantly was Louis Koenig's conclusion that "Adams suffered from, and eventually succumbed to, the hazards of unreviewed judgment."[40] Eisenhower depended too heavily on Adams, thus failing to provide sufficient check on his chief of staff's exercise of power and creating a system that depended too heavily on one person.[41] Adams was forced to resign when it appeared that he had intervened with regulatory commissions for a friend, Bernard Goldfine. The much less aggressive General Wilton Persons took over, denying Eisenhower strong administrative direction during the last two years of his second term.

The presidential branch was first institutionalized during the Eisenhower years. Several innovations in staff organization contributed to that development. Among the positions created and subsequently retained were a special assistant for national security affairs, a congressional relations office, staff secretaries to coordinate the paperwork coming into the White House (with a special secretary for the cabinet), and several special assistants, which served as a way of bringing in prominent outsiders. During Eisenhower's presidency there was substantial continuity in the White House staff (as with the cabinet), and little or no change in his preference for relying heavily on his staff.

CABINET SECRETARIES. Possibly because he was new to the politics of governing, President Eisenhower liked the idea of a cabinet as a functioning body. He found it useful as an orienting instrument. "I not only found a spirit of teamwork and friendship in the Cabinet, but I also found its deliberations and debates enlightening as I faced important decisions." He established a cabinet secretariat to "work up agendas for the discussions and see that all my decisions respecting them were properly reported and communicated to interested parties."[42] A former Eisenhower aide who helped develop the secretariat explained that it "acted as a radar set, constantly scanning what was going on among its staff colleagues, at the departments, in the press, the Congress, the states."[43] Clearly the president believed that if it were organized properly, the cabinet could perform advisory and coordinating functions.

Eisenhower identified the important orienting function straightforwardly at the first cabinet meeting: "I wanted this fine group of men who had signaled their willingness to serve their country, and to help me, *to understand the job as I saw it.*" He expected this fine group of men to contribute to a presidency that he well understood to be his. To this end, he anticipated that they would express themselves on issues beyond those of their immediate cabinet responsibility. "No one was relieved of his responsibility or the opportunity to think broadly and to make suggestions."[44]

Continuity of personnel was a highly desirable feature of a cabinet used in this way. The Eisenhower cabinet was impressive in this regard (see table 3-1). By definition, frequent turnover would adversely affect both the president's confidence in the cabinet and also how others viewed the administration. Unity and clarity of purpose are important features of a military organization. Eisenhower meant to achieve both in his presidency.

There were but three changes in the cabinet during the first term in office, only one in the first two years. Two cabinet secretaries, Ezra Taft Benson in Agriculture and Arthur Summerfield as postmaster general, served the full eight years. Three others—Sinclair Weeks in Commerce, James Mitchell in Labor, and John Foster Dulles in State—served for six years. Of the ten changes among cabinet secretaries, seven occurred in the second term.

Perhaps the most striking feature of the Eisenhower cabinet was the similarity among the secretaries. Compared with more contemporary cabinets, the all-male appointees were virtually interchangeable (a woman, Oveta Culp Hobby, was appointed when the new Department of Health, Education, and Welfare was created). Eight of the original ten were within ten years of Eisenhower's age, six within four years. The secretaries tended to be Protestants and from business, banking, and law. With the exception of Martin Durkin, the secretary of labor who left first and quickly, it was very much a "gray suit" set of government officials.

In one sense the Eisenhower cabinet was like that of the other presidents of this era: it was selected and it functioned to serve the president's orientation to governing. It would be inconceivable in the twenty-first century, however, that a president's orientation would lead him to appoint such a homogeneous cabinet. The contemporary appointment of cabinet secretaries must and will meet a test of representational diversity. That standard of diversity, in turn, modifies the extent to which the president is free to determine how the group will contribute to governing. Cabinet secretaries are presumably at least partially responsive to the clienteles they represent, and a more diverse set of clienteles have access to the halls of power.

Kennedy to Johnson

The shocking assassination of John F. Kennedy created the second postwar transitional presidency (see figure 3-1). Circumstances were very different from those characterizing the transition from Roosevelt to Truman.

Those in the Kennedy presidency were young, not old; vigorous, not weary; anxious to keep going, not retire. The organizational consequences were therefore very different.

WHITE HOUSE STAFF. In organizing the White House, President Kennedy "purposively reverted to the Roosevelt model, but with modifications."[45] As a Kennedy aide explained to Stephen Hess: the president "did not put people in a competition with each other. He was not manipulative in a personal, psychological sense."[46] The highly structured, hierarchical Eisenhower staff was scrapped in favor of a much less structured "buddy" system. Kennedy asked Neustadt and former White House special counsel Clark Clifford for independent memos on the transition, with recommendations for organizing the new White House. Neustadt cautioned against blind acceptance of the Roosevelt model but proposed committing to "the *spirit* of his presidential operation." Clifford favored "a lean and fast-moving White House," concluding that "a vigorous President in the Democratic tradition of the Presidency will probably find it best to act as his own chief of staff, and to have no highly visible majordomo standing between him and his staff (and, incidentally, between him and the public)."[47] Theodore Sorensen, who served as Kennedy's Clark Clifford, approved of this arrangement in reflections many years later: "We had a modified system under which one person on policy and program, one person on national security operations, one person on press, and one person on congressional relations each had equal access to the president. We kept in touch with each other, and I think it worked reasonably well without a chief of staff."[48]

As did Roosevelt, Kennedy worked one on one with staff aides. Many of his closest aides had served with Kennedy in the Senate and through the presidential campaign. Like their president they were young, quick, aggressive, and ambitious. Therefore, "he was infinitely accessible to the Special Assistants," who were his friends, virtually his clones.

> He liked to regard his staff as generalists rather than specialists and had a distressing tendency to take up whatever happened to be on his desk and hand it to whoever happened to be in the room. But a measure of specialization was inevitable, and the staff on the whole contrived its own clandestine structure, taking care to pass on a presidential directive to the person in whose area it lay.[49]

As Sorensen describes it, Kennedy wished to use his staff as an extension of himself, "one that represented *his* personal ways, means and purposes."[50] If the staff were truly socialized to his interests and needs, then he could multiply many times his own capacity to hear, read, and understand what was going on in government.

This approach to organizing the White House was as suited to Kennedy's experience and personal preferences as the more structured version was to Eisenhower's. Kennedy had not previously managed a large organization: the 1960 presidential campaign was really his first such experience. He had been a legislator and was just the second sitting senator ever to be elected president (Warren G. Harding in 1920 was the other). This lack of executive training contributed to a system that was ad hoc and eclectic in its staffing and its style of service. The president preferred that the staff be small, fluid, and organizationally flat, as was suited to service in the Senate.

The untimely death of President Kennedy made it impossible to evaluate the effectiveness of his White House staff operation or to know how stable it may have been over an extended period. Perhaps to an even greater extent than in the case of Truman's takeover in 1945, Vice President Lyndon B. Johnson had to demonstrate continuity. Johnson inherited a substantial agenda and a staff anxious to complete the legacy of the dead president. The new president himself explained in his memoirs that he considered himself "the caretaker of both his [Kennedy's] people and his policies."[51]

Although Johnson shared many of Kennedy's unmet goals, his style was very different. He faced all the problems normally attendant to taking over, yet had the challenge of adapting himself to the Kennedy staff in symbolic recognition of the legacy. All of Kennedy's principal staff aides stayed on for an interim period. Meanwhile Johnson appointed other aides who were given "ad hoc assignments conditioned largely by the immediate needs of the president."[52] In a sense, then, to a greater extent than was the case under Truman, there was a dual staff operation: the Kennedy holdovers and the Johnson ad hoc appointments.

Harry McPherson, special counsel to Johnson, notes that "the potential for savage internecine warfare was very high."[53] And inevitably Johnson worried about the loyalty of the Kennedy staff. Although, as Doris Kearns Goodwin points out, there was a mutuality of need—Johnson profited from their talent and they ensured that there would be a "martyr's cause."—it was hard to sustain the dual arrangement.[54] Among other developments, Johnson himself became suspicious, perhaps even a bit paranoid, about the Kennedys and their loyalists.

Those favoring geometric images (triangles, circles, trapezoids) to understand organizational relationships are bound to be frustrated by the

Johnson White House. In the initial phase one must picture two circles or wheels, with a set of connectors. Johnson's overwhelming victory in 1964 permitted him to become more of his own president, though he was not moved (nor was it politically wise) to define his presidency by making a clean break from the Kennedy legacy. Those Kennedy staff who stayed on melded into one circle of advisers: the classic spokes-of-the-wheel organization, with one important modification. Perhaps more than for other presidents who employed this structure, not all of the spokes on Johnson's wheel were the same length. Further, an individual's spoke could be lengthened quickly, should the president become displeased.

Given what is known about the different leadership styles of Kennedy and Johnson, there was remarkably little reforming of White House operations following the assassination. Even accounting for Johnson's determination to be the "executor of [Kennedy's] will," this continuity was extraordinary.[55] Any changes had to, and did, occur within a context of a reassuring continuity. That this was accomplished encourages an analysis of qualities not typically attributed to Johnson, such as sensitivity, patience, and commitment. Unfortunately for his own legacy, Johnson was unable to succeed in foreign policy as he had in the domestic sphere. By 1968 his handling of the Vietnam War had virtually made him a prisoner in the White House. "In the end, Lyndon Johnson had turned the presidency into a bunker. Then he handed it over to Richard Nixon."[56]

CABINET SECRETARIES. Though well connected to governing elites through political service and family ties, Kennedy was reportedly awed by the task of creating a presidency. The Democrats had been out of the White House for eight years. Therefore the pool of available talent with subcabinet experience was limited. Neustadt recalls the president exclaiming after the election: "People, people, people! I don't know any people. I only know voters. How am I going to fill these 1200 jobs?"[57]

However many close friends one has, they become few when one is faced with the challenge of taking charge of the executive branch. Further, friendships may make a limited contribution to meeting this challenge. The quest is for a workable presidency, as defined by the president and as directed by an organization orienting itself to his style and policy goals. Therefore it is more important in making appointments to determine how this or that person will serve those ends than it is to ensure companionship.

Kennedy achieved impressive continuity among his cabinet secretaries during his short time in office. The initial group was carefully selected, and a number of major appointments were given to persons with whom the president was not well acquainted. The big three—State, Defense, and Treasury—were filled with surprising choices. Dean Rusk (State) had experience in foreign affairs but was unknown to Kennedy. Robert McNamara (Defense) had been recommended by Robert Lovett, Truman's secretary of defense, for either Treasury or Defense. He, too, was unknown to the president. The president did know Douglas Dillon (Treasury), but his executive service had been in the Eisenhower administration, as undersecretary of state for economic affairs. Seemingly, each of these appointments was special and unexpected enough to indicate these men's genuine interest in serving. And by the Polsby test, the cabinet secretaries came to reflect the president's interests and style.

The pattern among cabinet secretaries for the full eight years of the Kennedy-Johnson period is very different from that of the Roosevelt-Truman experience. The longevity within certain departments is impressive. Three secretaries—Orville Freeman, Agriculture; Stewart Udall, Interior; and Rusk, State—served the full eight years, the most for any of the five elected/takeover presidencies. The average length of service in State, Defense, and Treasury was greater even than during the Eisenhower administration. Of the thirteen changes during the eight years of the Kennedy-Johnson presidencies, nine occurred within three departments: three each in Commerce; Health, Education, and Welfare; and the Post Office. Thus remarkable stability was achieved during a period of substantial upheaval (the assassination, conflict over civil rights, and the Vietnam War) and change (the enactment of the Great Society).

It is fair to state that Johnson never did exercise the option of putting a strong stamp of his own on the presidency that he inherited through cabinet secretarial appointments. This was in part due to Johnson's vision of fulfilling the Kennedy legacy. But it was also due to his belief that many in the cabinet were good at their jobs. Eric F. Goldman explains that Johnson made a distinction in judging the cabinet: "There were the JFK men, whom he considered for the most part able, dedicated to public service and quite capable of serving another President loyally. Then there were the RFK men; whether able or not, they were 'sonsofbitches, plotting inside my own house.'" Rusk, McNamara, Udall, Freeman, and Willard Wirtz (Labor) were among the JFK men; the others Johnson proceeded to replace "at a leisurely pace and in ways that expressed his debts, needs and enthusiasms."[58]

Did Lyndon Johnson have a concept of the cabinet as a working unit within his presidency? Doris Kearns Goodwin quotes the president as saying that he expected loyalty but worried that "all too often they [department heads] responded to their constituencies instead of mine." Johnson explained that he "was determined to turn those lordly men into good soldiers." Kearns Goodwin viewed this statement as a familiar Johnson formula for the exercise of power: a "one-sided dependence."[59] Had he originally been elected in his own right, Johnson might have had the opportunity to create this dependence. As it was, however, he was put in charge of another president's White House.

Thus, although it is possible to identify two cabinets for these eight years—the initial Kennedy group adjusted to the eventual Johnson group—the most outstanding characteristic of the period is stability (see figure 3-1). As in the Eisenhower years, initial appointments from the outside were followed by the elevation of several subcabinet personnel to cabinet secretarial status.

Nixon to Ford

The third transitional two-term presidency in the postwar period is the least conventional in history (see figure 3-1). Never before had a president resigned, nor a vice president taken over who was not a part of the elected ticket. The organizational patterns were unusual, to say the least.

WHITE HOUSE STAFF. Stephen Hess describes Richard Nixon as a "management-conscious president" who was constantly tinkering with White House organization.[60] His interest in management was seemingly driven by a concern for order and control, as well as the usual desire to create a structure that would sustain him and his presidency. The president lacked the experience of directing large organizations and thus was never certain what would work best, or indeed whether organization and management could serve the purposes he had in mind.

Nixon, like Eisenhower, expected a lot from formal organization. Organizational charts were back after an eight-year absence. But Nixon also liked "an adversarial proceeding within the staff," according to his chief of staff, H. R. Haldeman.[61] So although he structured his staff like Eisenhower's, from the start Nixon wished to use it in ways that were not necessarily facilitated by a hierarchy. He said he wanted a "dispersal of power" and "multiple advocacy" of policy positions.[62] Yet, in contrast to Roosevelt, he was anxious not to have conflicts in these positions left unresolved on his doorstep. As Haldeman explained:

Nixon wanted these officials to submit their problems in writing or to deal with someone on the staff better able to handle their concerns than the President before they were granted precious Presidential time. And this infuriated them, because the man who said "no" to them was a staffer, me. . . . They vented their fury on me, but every White House insider knew that I was doing this at the President's direct order. And so did most of the outsiders.[63]

An aide who served both Eisenhower and Nixon explained that the Nixon administration became "oddly, far more structured" than the Eisenhower administration.

It was not that way in the beginning. It evolved into a very tight control and it got tighter . . . as time went on. Ordinarily White House staffs start out very tight, very closed in, with a small band of people around the president allowing very few others into that inner circle. As the time moves they find out they can't handle all that business themselves, and the president has claustrophobia, so the band starts to expand and ordinarily by his third year or fourth year, the presidency has been opened up. But in the Nixon instance it went the other way.[64]

The organization of the Nixon White House was every bit as complex as the person it served. For other presidents, staff operations were an extension of their own strengths and weaknesses. Under Nixon it seemed that the structure was a blend of what he truly wanted and what he thought he should have, based on an unarticulated concept of what was right for the "good" president. While this blend reflected his complex personality, it made it difficult to predict the president's intentions, thus greatly complicating understanding on the part of the staff.

Haldeman was clearly in charge as chief of staff, and that was what Nixon wanted. As Haldeman explained: "Instead of having to figure out who to contact on each particular item, he could simply call me in and cover everything on his mind, leaving it to me to follow up with the appropriate people."[65] John Ehrlichman wrote: "The two became complementary, and by 1968 it was hard to tell where Richard Nixon left off and H. R. Haldeman began."[66]

Nixon's other principal close advisers were John Ehrlichman and Henry Kissinger. Both had sources of strength independent of Haldeman that ensured their direct contact with the president. Ehrlichman began as White House counsel and then took over responsibility for domestic policy. He was very close to Haldeman (they had known each other in college and worked for Nixon in the 1960 campaign) and would occasionally fill in as head of the staff on the rare occasions when Haldeman was on vacation. As national security adviser, Kissinger had direct access to the president, though Haldeman typically sat in when foreign policy issues were presented (offering political, not substantive, comments).

Ehrlichman once observed that it took six years for Nixon to settle on how he wanted to organize his government.[67] Most presidents make organizational and staff changes during the course of a presidency. Ordinarily these adjustments are refinements. In the case of Nixon, however, the process appeared to be continual experimentation to have organization work for him, not necessarily with him.

One other more or less independent operation developed in the Nixon White House. Charles Colson was formally responsible for public liaison but acted as a sort of wild card. The open-ended nature of his assignment, along with his access to Nixon, meant that he often operated in other people's substantive areas (usually at the president's behest). Haldeman believed that

> Colson encouraged the dark impulses in Nixon's mind. . . . By 1971 Nixon was using three subordinates—Haldeman, Ehrlichman, and Colson—for three different approaches to some projects. I was the man for the straight, hit-them-over-the-head strategy. Ehrlichman, who loved intrigue, was given the more devious approach. And Colson was assigned the real underground routes.[68]

Following the 1972 election, two developments led to a substantially restructured White House (the renewable pattern, as shown in figure 3-1). First was the perpetual search for the organization best suited to the president's preferences. The reelected president announced wholesale resignations and reassignments of both staff and cabinet members before his second inauguration. Second was the Watergate incident, which led to the resignations of Haldeman, Ehrlichman, and Colson, all three of whom later served prison terms. The new group of staff aides was not close to Nixon, nor did he want them to become so. In any event, they had barely gotten accustomed to their jobs when the president resigned.

Nixon's legacy for Gerald R. Ford was very different from either that of Roosevelt for Truman or Kennedy for Johnson. Truman and Johnson were expected to fulfill the goals of their predecessors; Ford was expected to restore honor to the White House. Ford was under substantial pressure to get rid of Nixon's staff, including strong advice from his longtime aide, Robert Hartmann. He resisted a "Stalin-like purge," feeling that "there were people on the White House staff who had nothing to do with Watergate. For me to have fired them all would have tarred them with the Nixon brush. . . . I made the decision to proceed gradually."[69]

Ford paid a price for this decision. "The press demanded a wholesale cleansing of the White House of all Nixon 'holdovers' and criticized Ford for failing resolutely to take such action."[70] Ford's first press secretary, Jerald R. terHorst, doubted that the president could escape criticism; there had to be some continuity and it would be difficult to find a totally "clean" team. Unbeknownst to Ford, a group headed by Philip Buchen, a long-time friend from Michigan, had begun to meet in anticipation of Nixon's resignation, so as to be able to provide the new president with advice.[71] Among their recommendations was not to have a chief of staff during the early months. This was judged to be a solution to the "Haldeman problem." But they believed that it was important to have a manager or coordinator of the new staff, a person who would not be interested in serving as a chief of staff. Ford selected Donald Rumsfeld, then serving as ambassador to NATO, for this job.

Upon taking over, Ford's White House staff operation borrowed from his congressional experience of managing a relatively small office in which staff aides all typically have access to the boss. He endorsed the spokes-of-the-wheel concept with himself as the hub, serving as his own chief of staff. Rumsfeld and others argued for a more hierarchical structure, "but the president had to go through his period where he got that out of his system."[72]

The initial period of Ford's presidency featured a great deal of staff infighting, due in large measure to conflicts between those who were already close to Ford and those who had served Nixon. Particularly bitter was the running dispute between Robert Hartmann and Haldeman's immediate replacement, General Alexander Haig (who stayed on in the Ford White House as staff coordinator). Ford's eventual solution was to give Haig another assignment and convince Rumsfeld to take Haig's post. In his meeting with the president, Rumsfeld apparently explained the drawbacks of the spokes-of-the-wheel organization, clearly communicating that he would not take Haig's job unless it were more of a chief of staff position. Ford agreed that the system was not working well and made Rumsfeld the chief of staff.

The confusion and uncertainty that characterized staff operations on the domestic side were not repeated on foreign and defense matters, though there were problems. Henry Kissinger carried over into the Ford presidency, initially simultaneously holding the key posts of secretary of state and national security adviser. He himself conceded the awkwardness of this arrangement. He was both in charge of the Department of State and in a position to coordinate that department's recommendations with those from other departments, notably Defense.[73] In the fall 1975, Ford appointed General Brent Scowcroft as national security adviser, a decision that did not sit well with Kissinger, who was reluctant to cede power.

The circumstances of Ford's accession to the White House seemingly offered significant advantages over those of Truman and Johnson in organizational and staff matters. After all, he was not charged with being the executor of the Nixon will—quite the opposite. Yet he was not able to realize the full benefits of the expectations of change because of his own lack of executive experience, the lack of available talent, the need for some continuity, and, perhaps most important, his decision shortly after taking office to pardon Nixon. As a result these factors and his weak political position, the Ford White House was never in a position to gain the offensive in governing.

CABINET SECRETARIES.   In his candid account of life in the Nixon administration, Ehrlichman reflected on the difficulties between the White House and the cabinet:

> What went wrong with the Nixon Cabinet? Surely something did. Most of the Cabinet members were discontented most of the time, and many of them failed to manage their departments well. . . . The President, from 1970 on, spent a significant percentage of time worrying about the Cabinet and tinkering with it. And so did some of us on his staff.
>
> At root were the President's own shifting and variable concepts of the Cabinet—of what it should be and do—and what the President expected from it.[74]

In his memoirs, Nixon explained that he "had strong opinions . . . about the way a President should work," developed during his time as vice president. Eisenhower's staff "had too often cluttered his schedule with unimportant events and bothered him with minor problems." Nixon believed that he could accomplish far more by reading memos than by meeting with cabinet secretaries.[75]

In relating to the department heads, Nixon seemed at times almost suspended between his own strong convictions regarding loyalty and his sensitivity to how his presidency would be viewed by others. Nixon wanted "good managers" who would serve on the "team." "I had . . . seen the hazards of appointing Cabinet members who were too strong-willed to act as part of a team. I wanted people who would fight to the finish in private for what they thought was right but would support my decision once it was made."[76] The private battle had to take place on paper, however, since Nixon did not like face-to-face meetings, surely an odd method of proceeding for a "team." It was little wonder that the cabinet secretaries became confused as to what signals were being sent by the coach to the team. With characteristic candor, Ehrlichman reported:

> The Cabinet men undoubtedly began their jobs with the euphoric and erroneous idea that Nixon reposed great, almost unbounded confidence in each of them. At the time Nixon probably *believed* that he did, but essentially he didn't. He wanted to be reelected and he wanted a place in history as a great President. Because he wanted these things he couldn't possibly give the Cabinet free rein.[77]

Thus it did not take long for dissension to arise between the White House and the cabinet departments. Nixon's failure to make clear his expectations at the start was compounded by his indirectness in conveying how these privately held expectations were modified along the way. Consequently cabinet secretaries often had to guess how their actions might be interpreted within the White House, and several were not very good at doing so.

This same pattern of undelivered yet strong opinions about cabinet members; avoidance of face-to-face meetings; and searches for a publicly acceptable rationale to make changes was to be repeated several times. The first of five waves of changes came in 1970. The next round was breathtaking in scope. It started in late 1971, when Earl Butz replaced Clifford Hardin as secretary of agriculture, and was followed by three other changes in 1972. To that point the changes had been rational, ordinary adjustments, not very different in purpose from those of other administrations. Following his landslide reelection in 1972, however, the president was determined to clean house, to deal more directly and confidently with those "crybabies" in the cabinet, as Nixon was wont to refer to them.[78]

> He got started the day after the election. At 11 a.m. he met with the White House staff. . . . To his National Security Adviser, Henry Kissinger, he appeared withdrawn, "grim and remote." Kissinger sensed his mood accurately: "It was as if victory was not an occasion for reconciliation but an opportunity to settle the scores of a lifetime." Nixon gave perfunctory thanks to the staff, before announcing that the first order of business was to reorganize. "There are no sacred cows," he declared, then changed the metaphor: "We will tear up the pea patch."[79]

Nixon soon left the meeting. Haldeman then asked everyone to submit a resignation immediately and fill out a form declaring the documents in their possession. According to Kissinger, "The audience was stunned. It was the morning after a triumph and they were being, in effect, fired." One hour later the same "wounding and humiliating" procedure was repeated before the cabinet. "It made removal from office appear to be not the result of Presidential reflection about the future but a grudge from the past."[80]

Only three cabinet secretaries remained—Treasury, Interior, and Agriculture. Six resignations were immediately accepted; two others followed some months later. There were ten total changes within the year. The Watergate scandal, which occurred during this period, does not account for all of them—in fact, it really accounts only for the resignations of Richard Kleindienst and Elliot Richardson as attorneys general. More important was Nixon's own intention upon reelection to renew his presidency and to project what he judged to be strong leadership.

Gerald R. Ford was sworn in as the thirty-eighth president on August 9, 1974, just minutes after President Nixon resigned. The new president well understood his precarious political situation: "Most Vice Presidents who become President have buried their predecessors and then gone on to reassure the people by wrapping themselves in the mantle of the men they followed. . . . At the time of his departure, Nixon had no mantle left." Ford also perceived correctly that reporters "harbored a natural skepticism about my talents and skills," and that he "had no mandate from the people, and the Congress understood that."[81] On the other hand, Ford had one substantial advantage: he was not Richard Nixon. That fact helped establish his legitimacy with the American people, and it was also important in restoring the credibility of the executive branch.

Ford's assumption of the White House did represent a stylistic sea change. And the circumstances of the takeover invited greater reflection than usual on White House management of the executive and of congressional relations. Organization may not be the key variable to governing if the president has the advantages of a large electoral victory. But President Ford and his associates had to judge how best to reconnect the White House to a government that had learned to operate in its absence. However, Ford was not the best person to figure this all out. As his close friend and counsel, Philip Buchen, explained, "He was weak as an administrator and a planner." And yet "he was always ready to receive advice."[82]

Since the departments and agencies had been managing on their own, "it was a little difficult to persuade [them] to coordinate their efforts with the White House."[83] One method was to hold meetings, if for no other reason than to get better acquainted and to reinforce the stylistic change that had occurred. Richard Cheney, who succeeded Rumsfeld as chief of staff, explained: "We started like all administrations do, with a Cabinet meeting every week. Of course, by the end of the term we probably had one a month, because cabinet meetings are basically irrelevant to the function of the government."[84] Meetings were held in connection with specific policy areas, however, and Ford's style was, as one would expect from a former leader of the House, basically consultative.

Just two of Nixon's appointees—Secretary of State Kissinger and Secretary of the Treasury William Simon—stayed through Ford's term. Twelve changes were made in a short period, with two each in Interior, Commerce, and Labor. The numerous changes are explicable more as Ford's attempt to create his own team than as typical for the ending of a term. After all, the president was seeking election in 1976, and prospects were that the new appointees would remain if he won. In making his replacements, Ford drew heavily from those with federal executive experience. Of the twelve appointees, just three came from outside the beltway.

Although conservatives may be thought of as status quo oriented, the Nixon-Ford presidencies were anything but unchanging. Seven of the eleven departments had four or more changes during the eight years, including such blue-chip agencies as Treasury, Defense, and Justice. There were forty-three cabinet secretarial appointments over the period 1969–77, the most for any two-term presidency or presidencies in the twentieth century. It would be difficult to argue that the frequency of turnover resulted in an increasing cycle of effectiveness. And yet it was a time in which a great deal of major legislation was enacted (among the most of any presidency) and a number of foreign policy breakthroughs occurred.[85] At the very least, this remarkable period should arouse curiosity about the roles of organization in a presidency and of the presidency in governing.

Carter

Jimmy Carter's single term in office is the second self-contained presidency in the postwar period. In contrast with the stability of Eisenhower's first term, however, Carter virtually started over, asking for the resignations of his cabinet shortly after the midpoint of his presidency (see figure 3-1) and thereby inviting comparison with Nixon, the president whom he definitely did not want to copy.

WHITE HOUSE STAFF. James P. Pfiffner relates this story, learned in an interview with Richard Cheney:

At a White House staff party Cheney was presented with a bicycle wheel mounted on a large board with all of the spokes of the wheel mangled and tangled except for one that was all that held the structure together. A plaque mounted on the board read: "The spokes of the wheel: a rare form of management artistry as conceived by Don Rumsfeld and modified by Dick Cheney." When the Ford administration left office on January 20, 1977, Cheney left the present on his desk and appended a note reading "Dear Ham [Hamilton Jordan], beware the spokes of the wheel."[86]

Cheney's advice was supplemented by that of Jack Watson, who served as head of Carter's transition team, and Stephen Hess, whom Carter asked to provide recommendations. In a private memorandum Watson warned the new president that one of his strengths—an interest in "the pros and the cons and the ins and the outs of every issue"—could become a weakness. It could result in "overinvolvement," of "pulling too many things into the White House." This strength as weakness, along with a determination to avoid a Haldeman-style staff system, naturally led Carter away from a chief of staff, hierarchical organization and toward the spokes of the wheel, with the president at the hub. Later, Watson reflected that this had been a "fatal mistake."[87]

By the time Hess was asked for advice, it had already been decided not to have a chief of staff. Hess proposed a model that permitted "wide access . . . in a structured setting," thus allowing more screening than is typical of the spokes of the wheel.[88] He advocated a middle ground between the other models, advising that a president need not have a chief of staff, but that he should also avoid giving open access to all his assistants.

As it was, however, Jimmy Carter's problems related to who he was, how he thought he had won, and who his friends were. Most of the organizational subtleties of Washington politics were unfamiliar to him. Carter was a true outsider. In his judgment it was that out-of-town identity that put him in office. More than most, therefore, he was likely to bring a trusted team of advisers who, like him, were new to national politics and policy-making. Circumstances denied him the help he needed. In his memoirs, Carter acknowledges the criticism other presidents had received "for installing their 'cronies' in the White House." Yet he was wary "about bringing new people into our most intimate circle." That intimacy itself made it difficult to opt for a hierarchical organization. The obvious choice for a chief of staff, if there were to be one, was Hamilton Jordan, who had "devised and managed" the presidential campaign. But Jordan resisted being put in charge of his friends, although Carter turned to him later when the president finally "acquiesced to the requests of other staff members" in appointing a chief of staff.[89] Carter's concern about not "bringing new people into our most intimate circle" resulted in an extraordinarily parochial group of close advisers, inexperienced in Washington ways. Among his top aides, only the national security adviser, Zbigniew Brzezinski, was not from Georgia. The new president was heavily criticized for essentially bringing his campaign staff and former gubernatorial appointees into the White House.

One of the more successful organizational features of the Carter White House was the use of Vice President Walter Mondale. Carter's and Mondale's staffs worked well together during the campaign and meshed effectively in the White House. Carter insisted that Mondale be kept informed on major policy matters. The new president was heavily criticized for proposing too much and for lacking priorities. To help with this problem, Mondale headed a group whose purpose was to "unclog a glut of issues that could otherwise immobilize the White House."[90]

Erwin C. Hargrove identifies three major influences that guided Carter's thinking about how to organize his presidency. First was his experience as governor of Georgia: Carter used his personal assistants to "work with the legislature and the public" and his department heads to "develop programs and administer them." Second was Carter's negative reaction to the centralization in the Nixon White House: "During the campaign he promised that no White House staff person would ever be permitted to come between him and the cabinet officers, who were to be his principal advisers." Third was his preference for getting involved in selected policy issues and a low tolerance for "layering of advisory levels between himself and any of his key associates."[91]

Hargrove notes that Carter stressed a decisionmaking process that was "collegial rather than competitive, with the president at the center."[92] The system would definitely include the cabinet, as the president explained in a meeting with members of Congress. "He was going to use [the cabinet] as a collegial body and had asked them to contact the appropriate congressional committee leaders to work directly in the drafting of legislation. That's the way he had operated in Georgia."[93] This system of "centralized collegiality," as Hargrove terms it, worked best in foreign policy, not as well in economic policy, and poorly in domestic policy. In fact, Carter relied heavily on Stuart Eizenstat, head of the Domestic Policy Staff, as a kind of chief of staff for coordinating domestic policy.

In a study of Carter's White House staff operations, John H. Kessel's findings complement those of Hargrove. Kessel found a lack of congruence among the various staff structures, not untypical of the spokes-of-the-wheel organization. Like the Kennedy organization, much depended on the president's own "intellectual capacity to absorb and structure all the information that is available to him."[94] No one questioned Carter's capacity to absorb and even integrate independent streams of information. However, integration in the Oval Office did not automatically encourage coordination among the various units.

One additional preference had a very important influence on how Carter organized his presidency: he wished to be viewed as governing in the public interest, as doing the right thing. However, many analysts and even some of Carter's closest associates interpreted this public interest orientation as antipolitical, even apolitical. Closer examination suggests that he simply preferred a different type of politics to that which was dominant in Washington. As I have written elsewhere: "'Doing what's right, not what's political' is . . . *doing the political in the right way,* based on the president's estimate of his personal advantages and how they contribute to his being in the White House."[95] This basic approach meant that "Carter wanted policy objectives to drive politics. The higher the objective the better the quality of the politics; he hoped to evoke the best in his lieutenants and in the public."[96]

In July 1979 President Carter led what surely stands as one of the most unusual and introspective exercises in White House history—a ten-day retreat. After returning from Japan and seeing that the nation faced further gasoline shortages, Carter canceled a major energy speech. He was at Camp David over the Fourth of July and decided not to return to Washington but rather "have some people come in whom we trusted to give me advice on where we should go from here."[97]

One of the most "extensive and helpful sessions" was with a group of political advisers. By the president's own account, much of the talk was about organizational matters and personal decisionmaking style. The cabinet was reviewed person by person, with recommendations that some resign. The group judged the White House staff to be "competent, but . . . most . . . had an air of immaturity about them." The "strong advice" was that the staff be strengthened. The discussion then turned to the president himself. I give many illustrations in this book of how organizational issues are traceable to presidential characteristics, preferences, and style. Seldom, however, can I use a president's own summary. Here is Carter's:

> Their criticisms of me were the most severe, questioning my ability to deal
> with the existing problems of the nation without bringing about some change
> in public perceptions. They told me that I seemed bogged down in the details

of administration, and that the public was disillusioned in having to face intractable problems like energy shortages and growing inflation. . . . On the one hand, I was involved in too many things simultaneously, but, in some cases, I had delegated too much authority to my Cabinet members. The consensus was that the public acknowledged my intelligence and integrity, my ability to articulate problems and to devise good solutions to them, but doubted my capacity to follow through with a strong enough thrust to succeed.[98]

One can appreciate why those working in the Carter presidency as well as those observing it from the outside were often perplexed by the president's methods. There did not appear to be a formula for separating the presidential from that which was to be delegated to others. Therefore a Sherman-Adams-as-deputy-president model would have failed. Carter would not have tolerated such an arrangement.

Two actions followed the Camp David retreat. Both had organizational overtones. The first was a speech by the president on what he had learned; the second was the reorganization of the cabinet and the White House staff. The debate over what was to be included in the speech triggered a conflict within the Carter White House staff and between his staff and that of Vice President Mondale. The personnel changes resulted in a major shake-up in the cabinet. Carter accepted the resignations of six cabinet secretaries. He also asked that the cabinet secretaries fill out personnel evaluation forms on each of the key departmental staff members so that the president could make judgments about competence and loyalty. According to Health, Education, and Welfare Secretary Joseph A. Califano, the meeting evidenced considerable tension between cabinet members and White House staff.[99]

Within the White House staff, Carter decided at long last to appoint Hamilton Jordan as chief of staff. He announced his decision during the cabinet meeting at which he asked for the resignations of his cabinet. The president was seeking to correct the earlier organizational course that gave cabinet departments and many on his own staff a substantial degree of autonomy. Jordan later left the White House to head up the 1980 reelection campaign, and Jack Watson took over as chief of staff.

Jimmy Carter was his own close adviser. He was actively involved in the large agenda he set for himself and the nation. He had wide interests in both domestic and foreign policy issues, if limited experience and expertise in the latter. He had confidence in his capacity to remain centrally involved in many policy areas and to make the right choices among the options provided by a working cabinet and a supportive staff. Thus an organization permitting substantial access to the Oval Office suited him

well, even if it had unfortunate effects on his image as an effective leader
outside the White House. "Doing the right thing" is generally instructive to
staff and others in government once priorities are set; it is not, itself, a pri-
ority-setting process. As Kessel explains: "Given . . . the staff disagreement
about issues and President Carter's own cognitive style—it was all but
inevitable that the Carter White House would not be seen as standing for
clear political goals."[100]

CABINET SECRETARIES. Jimmy Carter's relationship to the cabinet grew
out of his more general conception of a working government.

> He had a broad conception of what he loosely called cabinet government, by
> which he meant policy development in the departments, rather than in the
> White House. White House staffs were to assist him in making decisions, but
> beyond that he did not have in mind a well-developed model for the relation
> of these staffs to the departments should the need for central coordination of
> policy development appear.[101]

Disagreements within the cabinet and between the cabinet and White
House staff did not bother Carter, because he had confidence in his ability
to profit from the varying points of view. In this process of centralized collegiality, Carter assumed goodwill on the part of those upon whom he relied
for advice and expressed personal confidence that he could manage con-
flicting views on policy issues.

Carter records that "at the beginning, I decided to meet frequently with
my entire Cabinet, and scheduled two-hour sessions every Monday morning."[102] These "get-acquainted" meetings also served the purpose of clari-
fying jurisdictions and responsibilities. Predictably, the number of meetings
lessened each year. There were thirty-six such meetings in the first year,
twenty-three in the second year, nine in the third year, and just six in the
fourth and final year.

Like Nixon, and indeed all other presidents, Carter expected loyalty. But
Carter's brand of loyalty was very different from that of Nixon. It was influenced by a collegialism that provided opportunities for face-to-face communication, even appeals, neither of which suited Nixon. In Carter's view,
his highly disciplined style invited imitation by those in his team. Loyalty,
then, included a devotion to excellence and hard work on the part of department heads. Communication was also serious business for the president,
since it involved time commitments on his part.

Making cabinet appointments was a very deliberative process for Carter,
though he discovered that it was not always possible to attract talented people to Washington. It is true, as Hess points out, that "those filling the top

slots would likely have been included in any Democrat's administration," and that "most of the heavyweights were best known for their accomplishments in Washington."[103] Still, Carter's cabinet secretaries, like Kennedy's, were drawn mostly from the private sphere (but in contrast to Kennedy's, they did include three women, including one African American).

Although he was a one-term president, there were two Carter presidencies. As the first elected post-Watergate president, Carter was determined to distinguish his presidency from that of Nixon. Yet one result of his unprecedented exercise in self-examination in early July 1979 was to ask, Nixon style, for the resignations of his cabinet. Carter quite startled his own appointees with this action. Califano's account of that cabinet meeting is reminiscent of Kissinger's account of the Nixon firings:

> The President began softly. "I have deliberately excluded most of you from my life for the past couple of weeks." He said he had "wanted to get away from you and from Washington." He felt an obligation to reassess his presidency. . . . His words were pessimistic, his voice somber. It was as close to quiet desperation as I had ever seen him.

By Califano's report, Carter then explained what he had been told about his administration by his many visitors to Camp David: that "the people had lost confidence . . . that there was disloyalty 'among some Cabinet members,' and that many had been the source of leaks that had hurt him."

> Scanning the table, he added, "I want each of you to assess your subordinates, their loyalty to us, whether they are team players, whether they will speak with one voice. . . ." Then he said that he wanted us all to submit "pro forma resignations" [in writing]. He was evaluating each of us and he would decide whether to accept the resignations or not. . . .
> [Secretary of State Cyrus] Vance immediately opposed the idea, and was supported by [Secretary of Defense Harold] Brown, and then most of the Cabinet. It would be "too much like Nixon in 1972," we said like a Greek chorus.[104]

It was no doubt perplexing to the cabinet to be brought to heel on the criterion of the Nixon brand of loyalty when that concept had not previously been set forth as central to the management of the Carter presidency, and the president himself had placed a premium on independent thought.

In the end, Carter did not insist on written resignations, nor did he fire the whole cabinet. Still, the damage had been done and there were a number of changes: six new secretaries were appointed (one shifting from one department to another). Two other changes were made later, when Juanita Kreps resigned for personal reasons and Cyrus Vance resigned in protest over the Iran hostage crisis. Also, a thirteenth cabinet department was created, and Shirley Hufstedler was appointed the first secretary of education. In replacing cabinet secretaries, Carter drew less from those inside the government than did other presidents in such circumstances. In all, a total of twenty-one cabinet secretarial appointments were made for the thirteen departments in Carter's single term.

It is likely that Carter did achieve more control over the government with the changes that he made in 1979, perhaps for some of the same reasons as Richard Nixon. The restructuring also reflected revisions in Carter's concept of his place in the government, resulting from the extraordinary retreat at Camp David. But it was done so clumsily that it was not likely to enhance Carter's standing as a leader—the very goal he was seeking to achieve. Carter is the only president in this set to renew his organization substantially in the first term, a change made even more dramatic because of the stability that characterized the early months of the administration (see figure 3-1).

Reagan to Bush

The final postwar transitional presidency also has special characteristics. A vice president assumed the office, as with the other three during this period, but he was elected on his own. Nevertheless, the successor, George H. W. Bush, had to accommodate expectations borne from the legacy of his predecessor, Ronald Reagan (see figure 3-1).

REAGAN WHITE HOUSE STAFF. Of the presidents reviewed here, Reagan was least directly interested in White House organization, even in regard to critical appointments. He had strong and clearly articulated, if quite general, ideas about what his administration should accomplish in terms of policy. But he did not come to the White House with well-formed notions about how to set up an organization to reach these goals. According to Neustadt, the Reagan management style, if it can be called that, was to "choose targets and men, leave the details to them—except that he was evidently careless in his choice of words and distinctly casual in his choice of men."[105] It was a loose style, to say the least, but, again, by the Polsby test, it was revealing of the person for whom it was designed to work.

Whereas most presidents discuss organizational matters in their memoirs—particularly those affecting the White House and cabinet—Reagan wrote virtually nothing about this topic in his. In fact, one chapter ends with his having gotten out of the shower to receive the concession call from Jimmy Carter; the next chapter begins with his inauguration as president.

There is no mention in his memoirs of the eleven-week transition period in which the foundations of an administration must be laid.[106]

This lack of strong direction from the president naturally left it to others to frame the Reagan government. The responsibility lay primarily with an unusual troika of James Baker, Michael Deaver, and Edwin Meese. According to Lou Cannon's biography of Reagan, an understanding of his organizational team and strategy begins with the removal of John Sears as campaign manager early in the 1980 campaign. William Casey was then made campaign manager and Edwin Meese chief of staff (a position he had held with Governor Reagan in California). Their lack of experience in managing a national campaign worried Reagan's wife, Nancy, among others, so a rival team was created: Stuart Spencer, an experienced political consultant, and Michael Deaver, a long-time Reagan loyalist. "The rival teams managed to work together in uneasy coexistence."[107]

Spencer and Deaver looked ahead to organizing the White House and were determined that James Baker, not Meese, should be the chief of staff. Given that Baker was not from California and that he had managed George H. W. Bush's nomination campaign, the proposal had to be presented tactfully to Reagan. However, Reagan reportedly realized that Meese was not suited to the job, and he readily accepted the idea of appointing Baker.[108] Even so, it was inconceivable that Baker could perform the chief of staff role in the manner of Sherman Adams or Bob Haldeman. Thus the troika was created, with Meese serving as counselor and Deaver as deputy chief of staff; all three had equal access to the president. A Legislative Strategy Group (LSG) proposed by Richard Darman, deputy chief of staff, "expanded the troika to include other players key to the enactment of the President's agenda" (including all of the top staff persons).[109]

Colin Campbell labeled the Reagan organization a "modified spokes-in-a-wheel format" that was "a middle ground between a hierarchical White House and one attempting to offer equal access for all senior assistants."[110] The principal difference between the Reagan operation and other multiple-access systems was that it emerged more from the preferences and positioning of his aides than those of the president. When a hierarchical system was set in place later, it too was less Reagan's choice than that of his aides.

Reagan had one chief of staff, James Baker, during his first four years and three during his second four years: Donald Regan, Howard Baker, and Kenneth Duberstein. A review of the changes in that position reveals how the president related to his staff. The first change was a consequence of an independent decision by Secretary of the Treasury Donald Regan and Baker to switch jobs. According to Regan, the idea was born out of a confrontation that resulted in a "chat" between the two men.

Baker and Regan then met with the president, with Deaver also present. Deaver was let in on the proposal and first got Nancy Reagan's approval. Having been briefed by his wife, Reagan "listened without any sign of surprise" to the planned switch. Regan wrote: "He seemed equable, relaxed—almost incurious. This seemed odd under the circumstances."[111] Indeed, both men had considered leaving the White House. Yet the president had confidence in both men and no strong preference as to their respective positions, only that they serve.

Regan's assumption of the chief of staff post led to important changes in White House staff organization. The multiple-access troika was no more. Baker went to Treasury, Meese was appointed attorney general, and Deaver returned to private life. Regan assumed a role much more like that of Sherman Adams and Bob Haldeman (minus the close, personal association with a president aware of why he wanted a functioning chief of staff). Cannon concludes correctly that no modern presidency "has ever undergone such a thoroughgoing transformation in management style as Reagan's did under his new chief of staff." Most postwar presidencies experienced adaptive or evolutionary development of their staffs. The Baker-Regan shift was breathtakingly abrupt, if alarmingly casual. As Cannon observes: "Because of Reagan's passivity, his presidency easily assumed the coloration of whoever was running the White House."[112]

In the classic hierarchical, chief of staff system, responsibility is clearly set. Thus, when investigators looked to see who was in charge of the White House following the Iran-contra revelations, Donald Regan was naturally at the top of the list. The report of the President's Special Review Board (the Tower Commission, named for its chair, John Tower, R-Tex.) concluded: "More than any other Chief of Staff in recent memory, [Regan] asserted personal control over the White House staff and sought to extend this control to the National Security Advisor. . . . He must bear primary responsibility for the chaos that descended upon the White House."[113] Regan strongly rejected this assessment; as he saw it, he did not have personal control over the national security adviser. Whether that was so or not, Regan was inevitably held responsible, for the reasons cited in the report, and he was removed.

President Reagan wrote that "Iran-contra had nothing to do with his [Regan's] replacement." His analysis reveals something of the president's style in regard to organizational matters, as well as his reliance on his wife for advice:

> I learned from Nancy and then from others that many people—staff members, cabinet members, and congressional leaders—felt that Don had an oversized ego that made him difficult to deal with. . . . According to some, Don thought of himself as a kind of "deputy president" empowered to make important decisions involving the administration. . . . In short, he wanted to be the *only* conduit to the Oval Office, in effect making that presidential isolation I just complained about even more complete.[114]

Reagan's description of Regan's role as deputy president is not unlike other presidents' conception of a chief of staff position. But to be effective, such a relationship has to be based on mutual understanding and communication—not delegation by inadvertence. It also requires of the chief of staff self-effacement, sensitivity to and appreciation of politics, an understanding of who else is close to the president and why, and a staff to assist in realizing the first three goals. According to Cannon, and as corroborated by the president's own final assessment, Regan lacked all four requisites.

Reagan's choice for a new chief of staff was former senator Paul Laxalt (R-Nev.), but he declined. Laxalt instead suggested former senator Howard W. Baker (R-Tenn.). Baker accepted, the news was leaked before Regan had been told (though Regan had informed the president that he would resign), and the parting between Reagan and Regan was bitter.[115]

Once more there was an abrupt change in White House staff organizational style. Along with the new chief of staff in the wake of the Iran-contra scandal, there was also a new team at the National Security Council: Frank Carlucci and Lieutenant General Colin Powell. When Carlucci later became secretary of defense, General Powell was appointed national security adviser. Wholesale changes also occurred in other vital White House staff positions. The atmosphere changed dramatically, primarily because of Baker's experience and personal style. "The low-profile Baker, skilled at accommodating Congress, pursued no agenda of his own; rather, he returned the chief of staff's role to that of mediator, while opening access to the president and broadening the decisionmaking process."[116]

The new style could not prevent organizational problems. The Reagan presidency was completing its last two years. The Iran-contra scandal was unfolding as a possible fatal threat to its legacy. Under the circumstances, Baker gets credit for restoring a stable operating system. Among those whom he brought to the White House was the former director of congressional liaison, Kenneth Duberstein, a knowledgeable and professional staff person. "At Baker's behest, Duberstein accepted the responsibility of dealing with Nancy Reagan, who was once more openly welcomed as a political adviser."[117] When Baker stepped down as chief of staff in 1988, Duberstein took over—a change that barely produced a ripple in White House staff operations.

No précis of the Reagan White House staff operations would be complete without citing the role of Nancy Reagan. David Gergen, who served as communications chief, aptly referred to her as "First Friend." "No other president I have known has had such a singular relationship with the First Lady, shutting out almost everyone else from his inner thoughts."[118] Gergen explained that whereas the president was reluctant to fire anyone, Nancy was not. Communicating primarily through Michael Deaver, she let her strong preferences be known, motivated always by her estimate of the president's best interests.

Neustadt observed that Eleanor Roosevelt "was a substitute for legs, hence eyes and ears, outside her husband's physical confines" and a "hair-shirt on social issues. But she was not an intimate." In striking contrast, Nancy Reagan was her husband's intimate. "The President's closest, perhaps only, friend, she was utterly devoted to his person, his prestige, and his eventual renown in history. As such, she evidently could and did police his policies and personnel, alert to the threats against his personal public standing."[119] What Neustadt describes is that rarity for a president: someone interested only in preserving his reputation and status, whose personal agenda matched that of the president, and who was willing to serve as a backroom enforcer.

BUSH WHITE HOUSE STAFF. Like other takeover presidents in this group, it is unlikely that George H. W. Bush could have won the presidency on his own. He tried and failed in 1980, winning primaries in only four states and the District of Columbia. Accordingly, he lacked the political experience of having won a major campaign. Bush's advantage in 1988 was clearly that he was the sitting vice president for a popular president. He was the heir apparent, or as Walter Dean Burnham labels him, a third-term understudy selected as a "promising conservator of the 'revolution' carried out by others."[120]

One might reasonably question whether Bush was an understudy of Reagan as president or of the presidency more generally. His career represented what many think is the model required for the presidency: service in the

House of Representatives, in several executive posts, and as national party chairman. This vast governmental experience even before Reagan chose him as vice president, as well as his opportunity to observe White House organization closely, meant that Bush arrived in the Oval Office with definite ideas as to how to structure his presidency—a conception based more, however, on his role as chief executive than as topmost politician.

One special feature of the Bush presidency that had important organizational implications was his close, long-term friendship with his fellow Texan James Baker, his campaign manager whom he appointed secretary of state. Their association sent signals as to how the White House would likely be organized. After all, Baker had served as chief of staff for Reagan and thus was familiar with the problems of internal staff structure. No member of the White House staff could ever expect to be as close to the new president as was Baker.

It was a foregone conclusion that Bush would opt for a chief of staff. He had used such a position when serving as vice president. But many were surprised when Bush chose John Sununu, the acerbic governor of New Hampshire who had supported him strongly in his crucial battle for the nomination against Robert Dole in that state's primary. The reasons for this choice reveal yet another variation in structuring the White House. Sununu was not part of the Bush inner circle, nor had he previously served in Washington. He was an engineer, educator, and businessman with a reputation for offending those who disagreed with him. The most popular explanation was that Sununu was willing to be the person Bush did not want to be but judged he needed. Since Bush had selected so many staff aides with White House experience, Sununu would be the one "to kick the administration out of its almost certain 'we know best' complacency," and to run the White House "with an iron fist."[121]

Sununu's strong role as the White House bully did not prevent others from gaining access to the president. In fact, Bush was unwilling to be isolated from the many close associates he had come to know in his many years of service in the national government. Thus geometric models once again fail as representations of White House organization. The relationship with Baker cut across and through any pyramid that might have been imposed, especially given the president's strong interest in foreign policy. And Baker was not the only cabinet secretary with whom Bush had a prior close association. Consequently it was less likely that the White House staff would "interpose themselves between president and cabinet or have major fights with cabinet departments."[122] Within the White House itself, Bush's acquaintance with Brent Scowcroft, the national security adviser; C. Boyden Gray, counsel to the president; and Richard G. Darman, director of the Office of Management and Budget, among others, was unlikely to be altered or interrupted by a chief of staff. But this did not prevent Sununu from trying to control access and creating resentments within the staff.[123]

Sununu met his downfall when it was revealed that he had taken many personal and political trips on U.S. Air Force jets at taxpayer expense and he refused to apologize for his behavior. Since any chief of staff who is headline news has lost effectiveness, Sununu resigned in early December 1991. He was replaced by Samuel Skinner, then serving as secretary of transportation. Skinner reorganized the White House staff, bringing in new people and attempting to prepare for the ensuing campaign. No reorganization was likely to have a measurable impact on two crippling developments: the steady decline in the president's approval ratings, and the increase in conflicts with congressional Democrats.

In the end, Bush turned to his close friend James Baker to take charge of his campaign and his White House in August 1992. Skinner was moved to the Republican National Committee. There was, at this point, very little to manage in the White House itself, and as it happened Baker's arrival was too late to help his friend's campaign very much. His steady hand did assist the transition to the new president, however.[124]

REAGAN-BUSH CABINET SECRETARIES. Cannon explains that Reagan had been devoted "to the grail of cabinet government" as governor of California. However, cabinet meetings were less "instruments of decisionmaking" than "convenient forums for keeping 'citizen-governor' Reagan roughly familiar with issues and for ratifying decisions that had been made before the cabinet assembled." Cannon observes that the symbolic value of the cabinet-as-government was not lost on the president: "Reagan hugely enjoyed the spectacle of cabinet meetings, even if he did not always stay awake at them."[125]

However, Reagan was quite disengaged from the task of building his presidential cabinet. He had set the course; now it was the job of others to form a presidency that would reach his goals. This detachment apparently prompted Reagan's staff to organize for that purpose. William E. Walker and Michael R. Reopel conclude that "the Reagan transition was the most carefully planned and effective in American political history."[126] Clearly the concept of Ronald Reagan as leader had sufficient meaning in and of itself as to be a force for organization.

Reagan's domestic policy chief, Martin Anderson, outlined the complex tasks involved in ensuring that the message was conveyed to those appointees who were not a part of the campaign. Cabinet members often were persons of stature and were unlikely to have been a part of the hurly-burly of campaigning. "The problem every winning campaign faces is how to ensure that those with more distinguished public reputations who will be chosen for the cabinet posts do not betray the policies the campaign was fought on. . . . The president-elect placed Ed Meese in charge of all transition activities." Meese developed an "indoctrination course for cabinet members [on] ideas and people." Cabinet secretaries were consulted in making subcabinet appointments, but they were also informed "that they could not freely choose the people who would work for them."[127]

The Reagan team wished to avoid the mistake that Nixon and Carter made of allowing cabinet secretaries to appoint their subordinates. Therefore, months before the election, Meese enlisted the help of E. Pendleton James, a corporate headhunter, to create a personnel selection system that would guarantee fidelity to the political and policy aims of the new president. By all accounts, James was notably successful. No administration before had attempted such an elaborate clearance system. "Each nomination had to run a formidable gauntlet running from the cabinet secretary and the personnel office to Lyn Nofziger (political clearance), to White House counsel Fred Fielding (conflict of interest), to either Martin Anderson (domestic) or Richard Allen (national security), to the triad (James Baker, Michael Deaver, Edwin Meese), to the congressional liaison office and finally to the president himself."[128]

This elaborate process took time, and the administration was criticized for the delay in filling certain positions. This criticism did not appear to bother Reagan, who was not greatly involved, and he certainly agreed with the results. For while "publicly extolling the virtues of cabinet government, steps were being taken to ensure that ultimate control over subcabinet appointments—indeed, over all lower-level political appointments—would remain firmly in the hands of the White House."[129] Further, as John Kessel has shown, the structure resulted in substantial issue agreement among staff, as well as a clear sense of who was in charge.[130]

Control through personnel appointments could work only if there was clear policy direction and a system for implementing it. The Reagan administration developed a network of cabinet councils, cross-departmental units to control and coordinate policy. These councils met at the White House, close to the Oval Office. This meant that the president could attend (he chaired approximately one-fifth of the meetings in the first year). Just as important, however, it meant that departmental secretaries or their representatives were brought to the White House for policy discussion. Thus the councils provided an excellent counterforce to the tendency to "go native" within the departments. Anderson explains:

> Just the act of having to leave their fiefdoms, get into a car, and be driven to the White House was a powerful reminder to every member of the cabinet that it was the president's business they were about, not theirs or their department's constituents. . . . It simply is easier to elevate the national interest above special interests in that building. It does not always happen, but it is easier.[131]

There were three identifiable cabinets during the Reagan years: the initial group with several early changes, a second-term cabinet that included a number of holdovers, and a most interesting third group that acted almost as a transition cabinet for George Bush. In the initial set of appointments, Reagan followed the standard pattern of drawing primarily from outside Washington. Still, he included as many or more with executive and congressional or court experience as had other presidents, and substantially more than his Republican predecessors.

The second cabinet was well seasoned in federal government experience. The combination of carryover appointments and new appointments drawn from within the government meant that all cabinet secretaries had executive experience. There was no mass firing following the 1984 reelection, yet the break offered a natural point for turnover and renewal. There were five changes among the cabinet secretaries; one involved a switch in departments, and two involved moving White House staff to cabinet departments.

It is not uncommon to have high turnover in the cabinet toward the end of an administration. Often, cabinet secretaries resign and a deputy or under secretary assumes the position for the last few months. In the last months of the Reagan administration, however, the appointments appeared to be more than temporary and terminal replacements. Three members of the third cabinet carried over to the new Bush presidency. In addition, Bush appointed two other persons who had served earlier in Reagan cabinets.

Bush's cabinet secretarial appointments "were widely praised for their experience and competence," as were his son's twelve years later.[132] One appointee, former senator John Tower (R-Tex.), was rejected for secretary of defense by a majority of his former Senate colleagues, which was an embarrassment for the new administration. This position was then filled by Representative Richard Cheney (R-Wyo.) (who later served as vice president to Bush's son). It was a "friends and neighbors" kind of cabinet: many were Bush's long-time associates, most of whom had impressive political and administrative experience. As a result, the president was comfortable with giving them a fair amount of discretion. Still, this characteristic has to be evaluated in the context of the lack of strong programmatic direction from the White House.

Following the transition, there were relatively few adjustments and no wholesale firings in the Bush cabinet. A high proportion of the secretaries— six of fourteen—served through the four years, and four of those who left did so to take other jobs in the administration. The president hinted during the 1992 campaign that he might make changes if he were to be reelected, but this announcement appeared to be motivated more by a desire to show that a second term would differ from a first than by dissatisfaction with specific individuals or the announcement of a new policy direction.

In summary, the Reagan-to-Bush transfer was the least dramatic of those examined in this chapter. George H. W. Bush was the inheritor of the Reagan legacy, and there was no reason to make major organizational changes. The difference was in the person occupying the Oval Office. Whereas Reagan set a general policy direction and expected his aides and secretaries to move the government toward it, Bush actively presided over and interacted with an organization designed primarily to carry on as before.

Clinton

The last presidency of the twentieth century can be counted with those of Eisenhower and Carter as self-contained, that is, it was not followed by a takeover. (It should be noted, however, that if Vice President Al Gore had not lost Florida by just a few hundred votes, the 2000 election would have resulted in the fifth takeover—a Democratic version of the transition from Reagan to Bush.) More broadly, the organizational challenge facing Clinton can be compared to those of other freshly elected presidents (Eisenhower, 1952; Kennedy, 1960; Nixon, 1968; Carter, 1976; Reagan, 1980; and George W. Bush, 2000) and to those serving two full terms (Eisenhower and Reagan). As will become evident, the Clinton case is a superior illustration of the impact of contemporary events and the personal preferences of presidents.

WHITE HOUSE STAFF. The White House staff organization during the Clinton years is perhaps the least describable by any of the geometrical models—pyramid, circle, or isosceles trapezoid. If one were to scale the postwar presidents by the clarity of their organizational thinking, Eisenhower would rank highest, Clinton lowest. What developed at first was a rather free-form, flat, and interactive organization, with a perfunctory chief of staff and several interdependent centers. Gaining influence with the president was a competitive exercise, one seemingly acceptable to Clinton. This pattern fostered continuous adjustments as staff jockeyed for position or were relocated and as events, mishaps, and scandal encouraged organizational adaptations. As it happened, this fluidity in White House staff operations contrasted with the stability in the cabinet (see table 3-1).

Clinton's approach to organizing the White House was signaled during the transition. He ignored the advice of Neustadt, the acknowledged expert on how to form a presidency, by postponing senior staff appointments until January. In a memo to Robert B. Reich (later appointed secretary of labor), Neustadt advised Clinton to "organize the core of the White House staff by or before Thanksgiving." Neustadt's rationale was clear: "They desperately need to gain experience before January 20 in working with him and with each other in the new roles they are assuming."[133] This delay prevented many senior staff from gaining experience or in some cases knowledge of what their responsibilities were upon being appointed. Clinton's priority after the election was to make cabinet appointments, a sequence he later regretted because the staff "turned out to play a much more critical role than he expected."[134]

Another mark of Clinton's preferences occurred with the appointment of Thomas ("Mack") McLarty as chief of staff. According to Hess, Clinton intended "to act as his own chief of staff."[135] A close friend of the president from their school days in Arkansas, McLarty was selected along with the first cabinet appointments, but at that time had no other senior staff with whom to interact on a formal basis in organizing the work of the White House staff. Clinton explained it this way in his memoirs: "I pressed Mack to accept the position, because I was convinced he could organize the White House staff to function smoothly and create the kind of team atmosphere in which I wanted to work."[136]

McLarty's lack of experience in Washington limited his capacity to take charge or to organize the White House as Clinton wanted. Additionally, it meant that colleagues who did have such experience, for example, Leon Panetta (director of the Office of Management and Budget), John Podesta (staff secretary), and George Stephanopoulos (director of communications), were able to shape their roles with little or no direction from the chief of staff. This arrangement facilitated the senior staff's access to Clinton, which suited his face-to-face, interactive decisionmaking style. It was estimated that as many "as ten different advisers had direct access to Clinton."[137] Shirley Anne Warshaw characterizes the Clinton White House organization as "spokes of the wheel."[138] But as distinct from such organization under both Kennedy and Carter, there was a chief of staff, however weak. Even more important, the senior staff were not career-long intimates of the president. Many had been active in the campaign, but had not had a working relationship with Clinton earlier. Accordingly, access developed as the more aggressive staff defined their roles rather than being based on previous close association with the president.

One power center that emerged during the early months was that of the National Economic Council (NEC), headed by Robert Rubin. Created by Clinton by executive order, the NEC was to do for the economy what the National Security Council did for security. Given that the campaign quip "the economy, stupid" became identified as the initial priority, Rubin's role was critical. He was generally given high marks for assembling an able team and pursuing deficit reduction rather than a promised middle-class tax cut.[139]

It did not take long for important personnel changes to be made. Stephanopoulos was not effective as director of communications and Clinton took the unusual step of replacing him within the first five months in office with David Gergen, a Republican who had worked for Presidents Nixon, Ford, and Reagan. Gergen wrote, "When Bill Clinton is in trouble, he looks for a quick fix. I know. I was one of them."[140] Clinton believed that Gergen "was a bona fide member of the Washington establishment who thought and kept score the way they did; and for the sake of the country, he wanted us to succeed. . . . David had a calming influence on the White House."[141]

During the summer of 1994, it became evident to Clinton that he needed a more effective chief of staff. He replaced McLarty with Leon Panetta, director of the Office of Management and Budget and former House Budget Committee chair—a person as rich in Washington experience as McLarty had been poor. Panetta brought as much order as was possible in a Clinton presidency. Notably, he cleared staff work, routed decision memorandums through his office, demanded that presentations to the president be rehearsed, reduced the size of and set agendas for senior staff meetings, limited so-called walk-in privileges to the Oval Office by "free floating advisers," and took control of staff hiring.[142]

Panetta left at the end of the first term and his deputy, Erskine Bowles, took over. A former Small Business Administration director, Bowles brought a businesslike organizational demeanor to the White House, often focusing on the identification and achievement of goals. When he left in 1998, his deputy, John Podesta, took over to serve out the second term. Legal battles, including the president's impeachment, complicated the management of the White House during Podesta's service. One important consequence was the inability to act on an elaborate domestic agenda that had been prepared in late 1997 to be introduced in the State of the Union address on January 27, 1998. In the week prior to the address, the president was alleged to have had an affair with White House intern Monica Lewinsky. Thenceforth scandal dominated Clinton's presidency.

CABINET SECRETARIES. An adviser pointed out that Governor Clinton "knew about cabinets. But he didn't know very much about White House staff."[143] Whatever the reason, Clinton decided that appointing his cabinet took precedence during the transition. In accordance with making the economy a priority, Clinton's initial appointments included the secretaries of the Treasury, labor, and commerce, along with the director of the Office of Management and Budget and the chairman of the Council of Economic Advisers. Other appointments usually judged to be crucial early appointments, notably the secretaries of state and defense, were among the last to be named.

Clinton also announced that diversity would be a criterion in making appointments to a cabinet that "looks like America." He was successful in achieving "my goal of naming the most diverse administration in history."[144] The cabinet secretaries included three women, four African Americans, and two Hispanics; making Caucasian men a minority in the cabinet for the first time in history. One nominee, Zoë Baird, withdrew her name for the position of attorney general in the face of questions about hiring an illegal alien for household help. A second nominee also withdrew her name, and Janet Reno was finally confirmed to the position.

As discussed earlier, the Clinton cabinet was among the more stable in recent history for two-term administrations (see table 3-1). First-term turnover among cabinet secretaries was relatively low, the fewest since Eisenhower's first term. Just two left voluntarily, both at the end of the second year: Secretary of the Treasury Lloyd Bentsen and Secretary of Agriculture Mike Espy (who was the subject of an independent counsel investigation). One was replaced, Secretary of Defense Les Aspin; and Secretary of Commerce Ron Brown was killed in an airplane accident.

Changes were made after the president was reelected. A second term is often a time for renewal, sometimes to suit the president's wishes, sometimes because cabinet secretaries want to leave. Five secretaries resigned at the end of the first term: the secretaries of state, labor, housing and urban development, transportation, and energy. Along with the untimely death of Ron Brown, these resignations gave the president a chance to change nearly half of the department heads (though one involved a switch, Federico Peña from Transportation to Energy). There were just four changes during the rest of the second term.

The Clinton experience is one of the best illustrations of the dynamics of interaction between person and institution. The early White House organization reflected the president's preference for a loose, nonhierarchical structure, featuring open access and disregard of flow charts and other administrative standards. Discovering that the rest of government was much more tightly structured, the president accepted changes suited to the institutional world within which he and his staff worked and sought to have influence. His personal style remained less structured, but the staff organization adapted to how the permanent executive was organized. Meanwhile those appointed to cabinet-level departments and other major agencies joined the permanent bureaucracy, where institutional practices are ingrained. As a result, the White House organization at the start was not well integrated with that of the departments and agencies, which makes it more difficult to provide an overall summary of organizational development for purposes of figure 3-1.

George W. Bush

Organizing a presidency after the 2000 election was bound to be challenging. Delay in declaring a winner, from election day to the U.S. Supreme Court's decision in *Bush* v. *Gore,* reduced the formal transition period by half. Resentment and bitterness were inevitable. Democrats had net gains in both houses of Congress, but the Republicans retained a narrow margin in the House and the vice president's vote broke a tie in the Senate. As it happened, however, the Bush presidency's passages from campaign to transition to governing were among the smoothest in the postwar era.

The Bush organization was as tight as the Clinton organization was loose. In fact, David Frum, a speechwriter for Bush 43 in the early months of the first term, described the Bush White House as the "un-Clinton." "The Bush team lived clean. . . . I did my best to live up to the upright and hygienic local norms." The cabinet was "able, solid, and reliable," according to Frum. But "conspicuous intelligence seemed actively unwelcome in the Bush White House."[145]

Clearly George W. Bush himself was no Bill Clinton. He brought business-honed organizational principles to the task at hand. One might likewise observe that his White House was "un-Bush 41," for the son appeared determined to avoid the mistakes of the father, for example, in hiring an unpredictable chief of staff (John Sununu) or a brilliant but manipulative budget director (Richard Darman). The larger point is simply that White Houses are ordinarily organized to suit the personal preferences and styles of presidents. George W. Bush had the most well-formed organizational model upon entering of any president since Eisenhower.

WHITE HOUSE STAFF. Hierarchy, discipline, punctuality, planning, purposefulness, control—these were the operational features of the new presidency. These principles were clear even before Bush was declared the winner. Shortly after the election, Bush assumed the role of president-elect, inviting the press into a meeting with his running mate and transition chief, Dick Cheney; Condoleezza Rice, expected to be his national security adviser; and Andrew Card, his chief of staff designate. In justifying this initiative, Bush stated: "I think . . . that the country needs to know—that this administration will be ready to assume office and be prepared to lead. I think it is up to us to prepare the groundwork for an administration that will be ready to function on Day One."[146] The meeting was criticized as presumptuous, even arrogant; the election outcome was not final. Yet Bush's action was in keeping with his concept of position, which came to be his principal source of power. As discussed in chapter 1, position, in this context, refers to the status of being president. The concept incorporates Neustadt's objective "vantage points in government" along with the more subjective, but very real, qualities normally associated with the presidency.

Capitalizing on position required creating a White House staff of the type Frum identified, a characterization confirmed by Donald F. Kettl in what he labeled the "teamwork imperative." According to Kettl, "Team Bush" was formed from loyalists who signed on to an orderly Bush style incorporating these principles: Don't start without a plan. Make the organization fit the personality of the president. Keep focused on the task at hand. Develop your own leadership style.[147] The White House staff insiders all had experience in government and with the new president. They included Card as chief of staff, Rice as national security adviser, Ari Fleischer as press secretary, Karen Hughes as counselor, Karl Rove as political adviser, and Alberto Gonzalez as counsel. The team concept for Bush meant access to him for his loyalists: "I want a flat structure where my key senior staff members report directly to me. I don't want opinions filtered through one individual."[148] The result was an organization less strictly pyramidal than Eisenhower's and yet more articulated than Kennedy's. There were but two changes among top advisers during the first term: Fleischer and Hughes left (but Hughes returned to work in the 2004 campaign).

A notable facet of the Bush White House organization and decision-making style was the elevated role for Vice President Cheney. It was apparent from the time of his selection as Bush's running mate that Cheney would have major responsibilities. His vast and varied experiences in Washington compensated for the president's lack thereof. His first task was to head the transition, and he then settled into a full partnership with the president in both national security and domestic policy. While Cheney's role was criticized, even lampooned as that of a virtual puppeteer, all recent presidents, at least from Carter forward, have assigned their vice presidents real and important work, consistent with the adage that "the president needs help." Why let one position, with staff, go unutilized?

In her review of the Bush 43 White House, Karen M. Hult establishes the importance and effects of the continuities of the institutionalized presidency. In acknowledging the special features of the Bush organization, for example, the major role played by the vice president, creation of new units, discipline and control of leaks, efforts at greater management of the bureaucracy, she observes: "his White House is defined far more by continuity than disconti-nuity. Moreover, many of the changes that have appeared . . . are consistent with longer-term trends, with the efforts of past Republican presidents, and with expected responses to crisis." Hult reminds one that the differences more generally among presidents' organization of the White House vary from an institutional trend line that is steady and identifiable, one associated with "the impact of environmental and organizational factors."[149]

CABINET SECRETARIES.   In keeping with an early emphasis on position, Bush used the period of the Florida recount to process potential appointees to the cabinet. Two separate teams were at work. One, led by James Baker, dealt with the legal issues of the disputed ballots in Florida. The other, led by Dick Cheney and Clay Johnson, worked on building a Bush presidency. Consequently, once Bush was certified as the president-elect, cabinet sec-retarial appointments could be announced in a timely fashion.

For the most part, in making appointments Bush followed the prescrip-tions set out by Neustadt in a series of memos prepared for John F. Kennedy in 1960 and later modified and adapted for other presidents-elect or candidates. Among the more important suggestions were these: to appoint personal staff shortly after the election, to be sensitive to the rank order of cabinet departments (State, Defense, and Treasury being the most important), to set priorities but avoid policy statements prior to inauguration, and to arrange the physical takeover.[150] The first cabinet appointments came just days after the Supreme Court's decision: Colin Powell was named as secretary of state on December 16, followed by the secretaries of agriculture, commerce, housing and urban development, and the Treasury on December 20. Just thirteen days later, on January 2, the last names were announced. It had taken seventeen days to announce the entire cabinet. Later, the nominee for secretary of labor, Linda Chavez, had to be withdrawn because of her failure to disclose that she had sheltered an illegal alien from Guatemala. Elaine Lan Chao was subsequently appointed.[151]

The secretary-designates were unusually qualified by reason of their executive experience: seven had served in federal government, five in state, and three in local; five were lawyers; five were from business; five had served in Congress, and four had experience in educational or charitable institutions or think tanks. There were three ex-governors, three former chief executive officers, a former chairman of the Joint Chiefs of Staff, a former White House chief of staff, two former state attorneys general, and two former cabinet secretaries. Most were high-profile national figures or familiar to the Washington community. Colin Powell had an approval rating exceeding all others, including the president. Additionally, the group was one of the most ethnically diverse ever appointed: two Asian Americans, one Arab American, and one Hispanic American. It also included four women.

The first-term cabinet was the most stable in the postwar era. Just one secretary was replaced, Secretary of the Treasury Paul O'Neill; and one resigned, Secretary of Housing and Urban Development Mel Martinez, who left to run successfully for the U.S. Senate from Florida. The period before the first change was the longest of any postwar presidency, and the number of changes the smallest. In fact, Bush 43's initial cabinet had the lowest percentage of turnover of any president's from 1896 to 2004 (Taft and FDR also had two secretaries leave, but with fewer total cabinet secretarial posts). No doubt this continuity was encouraged and justified by the war on terrorism.

Low turnover among White House staff and cabinet secretarial posts has been complemented by fidelity to the team concept. The president declared, "I like clarity." He explained his position in an interview:

I know it is hard for you to believe but I have not doubted what we were doing. . . . A president has got to be the calcium in the backbone. If I weaken, the whole team weakens. If I'm doubtful, I can assure you there will be a lot of doubt. If my confidence level in our ability declines, it will send ripples throughout the whole organization.[152]

This organizational perspective was bolstered by the terrorist attacks on 9/11, which led the president to declare: "I am the commander . . . I do not need to explain why I say things. That's the interesting thing about being the president. Maybe somebody needs to explain to me why they say something but I don't feel like I owe anybody an explanation."[153] Based on such statements, few could doubt that Bush had a clear working concept of presidential leadership, one likely to prompt discontent among his adversaries, and charges of arrogance.

As noted, the cabinet secretaries of Bush's first term had the lowest turnover 1896–2004. They then set another record for the highest number of resignations at the end of that first term. Nine chose not to stay for the second term, thus giving the president the opportunity to renew his cabinet. Changes were made in the Departments of State, Justice, Energy, Homeland Security, Agriculture, Veterans Affairs, Health and Human Services, Commerce, and Education. A second-term president has the advantage of being able to draw on a pool of people with whom he and his aides have had a working relationship. Bush followed the pattern of other second-term presidents in his new appointments, mostly selecting those with experience in the first Bush term. Three of his appointees were drawn from the White House: Condoleezza Rice, national security adviser, was appointed secretary of state; Alberto Gonzalez, White House counsel, was appointed attorney general; and Margaret Spellings, domestic policy adviser, was appointed secretary of education. Just two of the nine were brought to Washington from outside: Mike Johannes, governor of Nebraska, was brought in to head the Department of Agriculture; and Carlos Gutierrez, chief executive officer of the Kellogg Company, was brought in to head the Department of Commerce.

Controlling the bureaucracy and the regulatory process is one strong motivation to appoint those who are tried and true. Paul C. Light, who advised Bush about bureaucracy reforms prior to his election in 2000, observes that the Bush 43 White House has worked with some success to manage the bureaucracy. He expects that these efforts will continue, but that there will be "no interest" in a major restructuring, as this would not be feasible.[154]

Organizing and Adapting

Presidents face the distinctive problem in a separated system of developing an organization that will suit their personal style, policy goals, and temporary custody of a continuous government. There is no one formula for accomplishing these ends, and even if there were, most presidents are not prepared to make such a formula work well for them. Much of what has been described above appears to be trial-and-error experimentation, in which presidents often appoint large numbers of persons with little or no background or training in the organization and management of the federal government. A White House staff of close advisers and a presidential branch have emerged over the postwar period to enhance the president's control, but these developments have created as many organizational problems as they have solved.

I have concentrated on three features of a president's effort to attach himself to the government for which he will be held responsible: the individual president's operating style, the White House staff, and the cabinet secretaries. Three points merit attention. First, four presidents in the postwar period (the three vice presidents taking over—Truman, Johnson, Ford—and, to a lesser extent, Bush 41) had a limited opportunity in the crucial early stages to fashion an organization suited to their styles and goals. Second, the standard models for White House organization do not adequately account for the variations in how presidents structure their staffs. Third, there is no formula for appointing and effectively interacting with cabinet secretaries.

I have little to add to the first conclusion, except to remind the reader that takeover presidents are faced with the formidable task of restructuring an organization already in place while determining the goals for guiding change. The degree of latitude they have in reshaping the administration will vary, circumscribed by their predecessor's organizational preferences, staff still in place, and legacy. Trained only to watch and wait for an assignment by the president, they were then thrust by circumstance, without the legitimatization of being elected president, into the premier leadership post in national government and politics.

Regarding the second conclusion, the review of White House staffs indicates that the dominant models—the hierarchy or chief of staff and the circle or spokes of the wheel—vastly oversimplify the many differences among presidents' interactions with their staffs, and their staffs', in turn, with the cabinet. The key variables are the president's preferences and practices for fulfilling his responsibilities, along with the weight of what is already there and how it has come to work. Changes in the president's interpretations of the job will typically be followed by organizational adjustments, if not always fidelity to his intentions.

Several characteristics of White House organization are shown in table 3-2, noting the variation for each president in the postwar period. No two staff organizations look exactly alike. Even when a president lacks a well-formed organizational concept, the staff normally tries to form one that suits their understanding of what works best in the Oval Office. As it happens, presidents seeking reelection face yet another organizational challenge, that of managing the side-by-side White House and reelection campaign staffs. As Kathryn Dunn Tenpas has shown, these two staffs may be at odds; indeed, they may even follow different organizational models.[155]

There is an astonishing lack of accepted wisdom as to how the White House should be organized. It is true that there have been developments within each presidency that have then been carried over to form a predictable set of the organizational units now labeled presidential branch.[156] I am referring, rather, to how the people within those units work with each other and with the president. Presidents and their aides often rely on quaint maxims such as "Don't do it like your predecessor" or "Don't trust those in Washington to know how to manage." And so the variation shown in table 3-2 may be expected to continue in future presidencies.

My third conclusion directs attention to the president's relations with the cabinet secretaries. These appointments receive the most attention from the media and the public, particularly in the recent monitoring of representativeness. I have stressed that cabinet secretaries are unlikely to form a policymaking unit, although presidents often enter office believing that the group can perform that role. They serve primarily as emissaries to their departments and the clienteles they serve, as spokespersons on Capitol Hill and sometimes to the public, and variably as policy advisers to the president, singly or in teams for related issues. Those types of interactions are consistent with the nature of a separated system, lacking as it does a structure or motivation for appointing persons with similar political backgrounds or habits of teamwork in governing as "the" government.

All postwar presidents except Kennedy had more than one distinct cabinet, as measured by turnover. Often these changes were the result of a transition from an elected president to a vice president taking over, or the expected adjustments during an administration and following a reelection. There were, however, several cases of renewal: Nixon, Carter, Reagan, and

Table 3-2. Characteristics of White House Staff Organization, Truman to Bush 43

| President | | All presidents | | | | Takeover presidents only | |
	Access	President's concept	President's interaction	Change in personnel	Staff relations	Transition	Tenor of interim arrangements
Truman	Multiple	Unformed	Occasional	High	Conflicted	Continuance	Cordial
Eisenhower	Controlled	Well formed	Occasional	Low	Harmonious	...	...
Kennedy	Open	Well formed	Frequent	Low	Harmonious	...	...
Johnson	Multiple	Unformed	Frequent	Moderate	Conflicted	Continuance	Conflicted
Nixon	Controlled	Changeable	Occasional	High	Conflicted	...	...
Ford	Open to controlled	Changeable	Frequent	High	Conflicted	Change	Conflicted
Carter	Open to multiple	Well formed	Frequent	Moderate	Variable	...	...
Reagan	Multiple to controlled to multiple	Unformed	Passive	High	Variable	...	...
Bush 41	Multiple	Well formed	Frequent	Moderate	Variable	Change	Cordial
Clinton	Multiple	Unformed	Frequent	Low to Moderate	Variable	...	...
Bush 43	Multiple	Well formed	Frequent	Low	Harmonious	...	...

to a somewhat lesser extent, Clinton and Bush 43. Given these patterns of change (see figure 3-1), the process of connecting presidents with the departments through cabinet secretaries is a constant. A secretary's tenure rarely extends even to that of the relatively short term of the president himself. Only ten secretaries served through two full terms—for eight years—in the postwar period, four of them with Clinton. Many others served through one term with a president (see table 3-2), but just thirty served as long as the president, and nineteen of these were with presidents who were in office four or fewer years.

It is difficult to imagine how a cabinet secretary can be an effective emissary with this amount of turnover. Accordingly, evaluating a presidency by a collective one-on-one test—that is, as a composite of the president interacting with individual cabinet secretaries—will prove challenging. There are cases—the first Eisenhower, Clinton, and Bush 43 presidencies or the first years of the Kennedy, Carter, and Bush 41 presidencies—that would permit development of such a composite. But for most presidencies, the pictures would have to be drawn, redrawn, then redrawn again. Such an undertaking is to be recommended, but, not surprisingly, has not been done.

The U.S. executive branch is managed by political appointees hardly in place long enough to learn their immediate responsibilities, let alone the intricacies of participating meaningfully in the policymaking and politics of a separated system. It is understandable that representativeness has come to be an important criterion for appointment, but the transient quality of departmental leadership suggests that allegiance to a president over time is equally, if not more, important. The permanent government has enough reasons to be reluctant to conform to an impermanent leadership.

There are a number of potential positive effects of meeting the organizational demands of the presidency. Those presidents who are successful in establishing a compatible organization are likely to enjoy more positive public standing, to have a greater capacity for designating priorities, and to participate more actively in lawmaking. In fact, one can envisage a continuum from the presidencies with clearly etched organizational images (Eisenhower, Kennedy, Bush 43) to those with images substantially less fixed (Truman, Reagan, Clinton). In some cases that imagery changed significantly during the president's term in office (most notably in the case of Nixon). Organization cannot save a presidency from failure, but it can surely aid in preventing disaster in the first place.

CHAPTER 4

Public Standing of the President

The public standing of the president is receiving much greater attention than in the past. Pollsters and analysts are not content to await the next presidential election for a test of public approval of presidential performance. Nor need they do so. Americans are polled regularly on this question: "Do you approve or disapprove of the way [president's name] is doing his job?" George C. Edwards III observes that the data produced are likely "the largest set of public responses to a single question asked over an extended period of time."[1] The results are treated as news, often as a lead story. The Gallup Organization initiated polling on this question and therefore has the largest set of historical data. There has been an exponential increase in polling on presidential performance.[2] Gallup alone has taken ten times as many job performance measurements for George W. Bush as were taken during the Truman presidency. And Gallup is no longer alone. A total of seventeen news and polling organizations measured presidential job approval in 2001–04.

Media and commentators frequently use job approval scores as a basis for evaluating a president's record, sometimes using them to advise him on how to govern. High ratings are viewed as a source of power, the "prestige" element in Richard E. Neustadt's formulation, and therefore the president is advised to take advantage of them to enact programs. Low ratings suggest failure, and should encourage a president to reorient his leadership practices.

I propose that presidents pay little heed to counsel of this type. They should not ignore public approval ratings, but neither should they or others take them as the primary basis for decisionmaking. And, as Edwards has shown, even if presidents are motivated to boost their own numbers, the record shows limited results. "Although sometimes they are able to maintain public support for themselves and their policies, presidents typically do not succeed in their efforts to change public opinion."[3] Poll results should be considered in the context of a president's overall status in the separated system. The same ratings simply cannot be interpreted in the same way for every president or for every decision a president makes. The work of evaluating presidential performance is not made less taxing by asking questions of a sample of otherwise engaged people going about their daily routines. To clarify, I begin with the tale of two Bushes who were, by these generated numbers, the most popular presidents of modern times, at least for a time.

The Most Popular Presidents

Only once before in the postwar period had a president exceeded 85 percent approval. Truman had an 87 percent rating shortly after assuming office upon Roosevelt's death (see figure 4-1, page 147). George H. W. Bush reached a high of 89 percent approval at the end of February 1991.[4] This record stood until September 2001, when Bush's son, George W., received a 90 percent rating. Both scores were associated with war and exceeded those of any other war president, including Franklin D. Roosevelt. As one would expect with such high ratings, support was strongly positive among all groups, including Democrats, across race, gender, age, and income.

These results were all the more remarkable considering that expectations following the elections of father and son were not encouraging. The *Economist* was certain that the elder Bush could never match Ronald Reagan's popular approval. "After eight years in the shadows, he has his own presidency. But George Bush will never enjoy the popularity of Ronald Reagan . . . nor will he have the same opportunity to shine."[5] If anything, predictions were even more dire for Bush the son. Serious questions remained as to whether he had even legitimately won election, the poll provided for in the Constitution. "So now . . . he would have to begin all over again: He would have to win the political majority that had eluded him in November. . . . It was difficult to be optimistic about his chances."[6] As it happened, both met the challenge—the father besting Reagan's early third-year approval score by nearly 50 points; the son setting the all-time best score just eight months into his presidency.

Bush 41's high ratings were naturally attributed to the successful conduct of the Persian Gulf War. With the end of the war, attention turned to how the president would use these favorable numbers to get bills passed on Capitol Hill, preferably those favored by the evaluators. At the conclusion of the Gulf War, *Washington Post* columnist Haynes Johnson wrote: "Bush now has an opportunity to take advantage of the public glow and summon the nation to tackle unfinished agendas at home. If he does, Americans will have far more sound reason to cheer."[7] Both the tone and substance of Johnson's comment suggested that the true test is not gaining the approval itself, but whether it is then used for specific policy purposes.

Johnson was not alone. A *Wall Street Journal* headline read: "Bush's Surging Across-the-Board Popularity May Translate into Greater 'Clout' in Congress."[8] These appraisals suit what Mark J. Rozell refers to as the "activist-visionary leadership model" that is used to test the president.

> Journalists view as "successful" those presidents who articulate a leadership "vision" and a set of broad-ranging government policies to achieve the public good. The press view of presidential leadership entails an activist policy agenda framed by the White House. The president is expected to use the White House "bully pulpit" to "sell" his proposals to the public and Congress.[9]

Expectations of presidential activism were not limited to the press. Senator Trent Lott (R-Miss.) was quoted as saying, "This is a golden opportunity. It's a matter now of focusing on some of these domestic issues and pushing them through."[10] Congressional Democrats joined in this call for domestic policy action. Senate Majority Leader George Mitchell (D-Maine) did not disappoint: "In the wake of the war, the President says he seeks a new world order. We say, Join us in putting our own house in order. Our first priority must be the American people and economic growth and jobs in the United States."[11]

George W. Bush's dramatic increase in job approval was likewise a consequence of his leadership in a national security crisis, one substantially more compelling than that of his father. The tragedy of September 11, 2001, fixed attention on the president and generated high expectations of leadership. Seemingly, he met those demands. In the aftermath of 9/11, Bush the son adopted a more aggressive legislative program than did Bush the father following the Gulf War. There was an important difference. A successful war had ended for the senior Bush; a "war on terrorism" was just beginning for the younger Bush.

Two patterns of presidential-congressional relations developed after 9/11. Bipartisanship in both forms (competitive bipartisanship and bipartisanship; see chapter 1) was featured in regard to legislation directly related to the war on terrorism and homeland security. John C. Fortier and Norman J. Ornstein refer to it as a time of "hyperbipartisanship."[12] Members from both parties worked on proposals primarily initiated by the president but materially altered in the lawmaking process. Accordingly, Congress' job approval ratings increased along with those of the president. Realizing these successes, the president attempted to associate several items that had originated before September 11 with the war on terrorism, for example, energy resources, economic stimulus, and trade protection authority. His record job approval provided little aid in getting these bills enacted into law. "Congressional Democratic leaders interpreted this support [the president's approval ratings] as applying to the president as commander-in-chief, not as domestic czar."[13] With the coming of the new year, "politics began to return to normal—acrimonious and partisan."[14] The president's job approval rating at the start of 2002 was at 84 percent—the eighth highest score recorded by Gallup (with Bush 43 having held five higher scores, Bush 41 two, and Truman one).

The logic of using increases in approval ratings to get Congress to act when it would not do so otherwise is somewhat unclear. The reasoning seems to derive from an activist, presidency-centered model in which the system awaits an expression of preferences from the White House. An alternative view imagines a government working continuously on a mostly stable and predictable agenda that carries over from one year to the next, much of it generated from programs already on the books, and as such, subject to pressures from affected interests. In this scenario, a president regularly judges when, where, and how his popularity might be a factor in regard to enacting a specific policy. High ratings would not be thought to translate automatically into legislative breakthroughs. In fact, the president might be moved in some cases to rely on that popularity as a potential source of power to thwart action, as well as to promote it.

In the case of Bush 41, he had reasons to doubt that success in Congress was in any way related to high approval ratings. He had the highest approval rating of any postwar president at the end of his first year in office (71 percent in December 1989) and the lowest presidential support score on legislation in Congress, eleven points below that of Richard Nixon in 1969 (who had a job approval rating of 59 percent).[15] While such a record would not in itself dissuade any president from seeking congressional approval of important legislative proposals, neither would it encourage extraordinary efforts to clear the domestic agenda at the point of high approval.

There are other reasons besides his previous record in Congress why Bush 41 might not have interpreted his high approval rating in the early months of 1991 as bearing instructions for Capitol Hill. Most obvious, perhaps, was the fact that Democratic congressional leaders did not even support his decision on the action that appeared to contribute to his popularity, the use of military force to make Iraq withdraw from Kuwait. Further, he had asked in a speech marking the end of the Persian Gulf War that Congress "move forward aggressively" on the domestic front, and requested that transportation and crime legislation be passed in one hundred days.[16] It did not happen. The day after his speech, the House rejected funding for a housing program favored by the president: in a strongly partisan vote, the House, with a Democratic majority, said no, 177-240.

Conditions were very different for Bush 43. Congressional Democratic leaders did back the president's actions in Afghanistan following his well-received speech to the Congress and the nation on September 20, 2001. The president's popularity as marked by job approval scores was rightly interpreted as a barometer reading of the rally-around-the-flag effect. But presidential support among Democrats in Congress was confined mostly to the declared war on terrorism. The terrorist acts did not revoke the competitive partisanship inherent in a narrowly split-party Congress on the bulk of the domestic agenda. Consequently, even though Bush 43's job approval rating was sustained at a higher level than for any president since such polling began (it was March 2002 before it dropped below 80 percent, July 2002 before it dropped below 70 percent), intense competitive partisanship returned on issues not directly related to the war on terrorism.

Finally, one must question what the strategic advantage is at the point of maximum popularity, particularly if it is explained primarily by a dramatic increase in popularity and associated with an event. Surely the likelihood that the advantage will decrease is greater as approval approaches 100 percent. The probability of decline in approval with the passing of the event is extremely high. Jon R. Bond and Richard Fleisher argue that they have "analyzed popularity and success every way you can think of, and, basically, popular presidents don't win that much more than unpopular presidents."[17] However sensible, that finding is unlikely to reduce the pundits' expectations that presidents with high job approval scores will succeed on Capitol Hill if they just try.

These stories of Presidents Bush and Bush illustrate the common misconceptions associated with translating popularity into undifferentiated policy success, as well as misunderstandings about how the American system works. Public approval of presidential performance is sometimes a recognition of or reward for an action deemed successful, an acknowledgment that things are going well, or an expression of comfort with a president's style. George H. W. Bush's highest approval rating, in early March 1991, was more than halved by March 1992. With the Gulf War long forgotten and a stubborn economic recession at hand, many felt the president lacked the leadership required to make things better. It took longer for President George W. Bush's job approval to drop below 50 percent (twenty-eight months). Entering an election year in 2004, Bush had the lowest ratings of his presidency and was still fighting for several legislative initiatives that had been stalled in Congress during his long period of record-setting scores.

Approval Ratings and the Diffusion of Responsibility

In a system of separated elections, the presidential contest does not necessarily convey political dominance. This is particularly true when voters send mixed signals by producing split-party government. Even when a Republican president is declared to have a mandate, as was Reagan in 1980, doubts remain in the minds of analysts. After all, Reagan's 91 percent "landslide" Electoral College win (doubling Ford's percentage four years earlier) was gained with less than 51 percent of the popular vote (just 2.7 percent more than that received by Ford in 1976). Further, the Republicans' majority in the Senate in 1980 was won through their successes in close races: fifteen won by 54 percent or less, nine by 51 percent or less. The Democrats actually garnered a majority of the national two-party Senate vote in 1980, even though they had a net loss of twelve seats and lost control of the Senate.

It is reasonable to expect more polls, more analysis, and frequent revisiting of presidential power and its purposes. Public standing has always been of interest because of the inherent limitations of the president's formal powers. Every White House is organized to seek, maintain, and exercise power. As Neustadt explains: "Power is the capacity of the President to have his way."[18] Split-party governments intensify the search for influence because the president is still held responsible, whether or not he is able to have his way.

Polls increase the number of data points for testing public acceptance of the president. Thus analysts will pay them greater attention even though polls do not change the basic structure or partisan arrangements within which presidents govern. Increasing the number of approval ratings from one to a dozen does not greatly alter the capacity of the president to effect legislation or other governmental actions. In a system of separated institutions, participants in each unit (congressional committees, bureaucratic agencies, state and local governments) typically are cognizant of the function and role of the other units, yet retain a substantial degree of autonomy and purpose. Popular approval may improve a president's capacity to bargain if he is resourceful enough to know how to use it to that end. But even then it is likely to have only a marginal effect, that is, taken in the context of other advantages and dependent on the commitments already made by him and other vested participants. No president can expect the ongoing policy process to be held in place to absorb an increment in his popularity. Any increase in approval will be fitted in to the extent that it improves the president's persuasiveness or that other participants judge the improved ratings to be relevant to their political status.

James W. Ceaser points out that presidencies should not be built around approval ratings. Presumably most presidents are shrewd enough not to try to do so, nor even to raise expectations with increases in approval.

> It is worth emphasizing how little approval ratings have to do with any lasting judgment of presidential performance. A President's legacy derives from his accomplishments or failures, and no President will be long remembered for having an average approval rating of more than 60 percent, nor quickly forgotten for having an average lower than 45 percent. As an instrument of presidential power, a high approval rating has some value as a reminder to others of the potential "cost" they might have to pay in opposing a popular President. Yet it is important to remember that an approval rating is a lag, rather than a lead, indicator. What determines the score will be the public's assessment of conditions, performance, and persona. An astute President should accordingly be prepared in most cases to sacrifice his standing today, if by doing so he can affect positively the future assessment of these factors.[19]

Thus the fascination, almost fixation, with approval ratings is curious. This near-obsession is partially due, I argue, to a devotion to the dominant perspective of party government and the disappointment that it seldom, if ever, exists. Given the failure of elections to clearly define a government and entrust it to act, approval ratings become periodic tests of public support. Richard A. Brody explains it this way:

> In a nation as large and politically complex as the United States, opinion polls become the only practicable means for one leader to find out how another leader is viewed by the public. The president is the figure about whom other national leaders regularly need information, and the polls on the

division of opinion in the public, on the way the president is doing his job, regularly provide this information.[20]

While I agree in general, I suggest one important caveat. The public responds to a directed question offering four choices: approve, disapprove, no opinion, or don't know. The results supply limited information on the "way the president is doing his job."

The Permanent Campaign

"We live in the era of the permanent campaign."[21] Most likely, constant campaigning, involving as it does greater travel and more direct communication with the public, is part and parcel of a growing publicness of the policy process, a development featuring more participation, greater use of communication by all officials and interested groups, increased opinion polling, and intensified public debate and partisanship. Of most relevance for public standing is the quantum increase in polling on presidential job approval, which acts as a stimulus for a campaigning style of governing.

Knowing of the media's interest in approval ratings, presidents naturally try to project the most favorable image of their performance. Few White House organizational units have grown as much as those of the Office of Communication and the Office of the Press Secretary. Although all presidents are concerned to maintain a favorable public standing, those in split-party governments have a special incentive because their political status is compromised by having to manage with Congresses controlled by the opposition party. Therefore they are moved to secure high approval ratings as a potential source of influence.

The extent to which the president and his aides can improve public standing is uncertain. According to Ron Nessen, former press secretary to President Ford,

> The ability of the White House to manage the image of a president, to manipulate the press, is wildly exaggerated. . . . A President who is doing the right things in a substantive way and is popular because of what he is doing or for what he stands for is not going to have to worry about his image in the press. A president who is doing things that are unpopular, or the economy is bad, or his views are not fully accepted—he's going to have problems with the press. There's only a marginal, small impact that any sort of media management or image making can have on this relationship.[22]

Richard A. Brody and Benjamin I. Page provide evidence in support of Nessen's views. In studying the effect of events on presidential popularity, they conclude: "In general, people seem to cast a broad net of responsibility, blaming the President (or giving him credit) for bad or good news even in matters we might consider beyond his control. . . . If the news was good, the President's popularity rose; if bad, it fell. . . . A popularity-maximizing President, then, would do well to produce good results."[23]

Thus it is that presidents will be held responsible for events over which they have relatively little or no control. Because job approval ratings are taken to indicate liability, the White House is tempted to manipulate the findings, whether or not these efforts can be demonstrated to have a positive effect. Was it President Clinton's dramatic increase in travel related to campaigning that sustained his relatively high approval ratings through periods of personal scandal? Or was it the strong economy and lack of major crises? Put otherwise, could he have won reelection in 1996 or later survived impeachment had there been double-digit inflation, unemployment, and interest rates, as were experienced by Carter in 1980? Likewise, was it because Bush 43 matched Clinton in travel that his approval scores rose dramatically and remained high, or because of his management of the 9/11 crisis and its aftermath?

Truman was tested on job approval by the Gallup Organization a total of twelve times in the first three years of his presidency, whereas Bush 43 was tested 115 times in his first three years. By 2004, however, seventeen polling organizations and outlets provided measures of presidential job approval, including major national newspapers, news magazines, the Associated Press, and network and cable television outlets, often working cooperatively. (And this count does not include the many polls administered at the state level, many sponsored by newspapers or television and radio stations.) These seventeen polling operations presented 630 measures of Bush's job approval rating during the first three years of his presidency; 210 per year, 17.5 per month, or just over four per week (Truman had four per year). Additionally, nine of the seventeen asked respondents whether they had a "favorable or unfavorable opinion" of George W. Bush, in an attempt to measure public reactions to the president as a person. For this question, a total of 255 measurements were presented in the first three years—eighty-five per year, seven per month, or 1.6 per week. Combining the two sets of scores, Bush 43's job performance and favorability were measured 885 times in his first three years in office.[24] Whether or not he could positively influence these numbers, it is not surprising that he would try.

A significant problem for the president and his team in influencing performance and favorability ratings is how to interpret their meaning. If an event is crucial, then its passing or transcendence can result in changes in public reactions. Perhaps the "approve or disapprove?" question is interpreted as "how are things going?" In all likelihood, an aggregated response obscures distinctions between types of issues or the importance assigned by respondents to one over another at any one time. For example, at the height of his approval for conducting the war, President George H. W. Bush had relatively low ratings for his handling of the economy. However, the Gulf War came to be the salient issue in the early months of 1991, and his performance was primarily rated by his handling of that crisis. The ailing economy emerged as the salient issue after the war's end, and Bush 41's approval scores dropped significantly (from 89 percent in early March to the low 50s by the end of the year).

One measure of the president's effort to influence his performance ratings is the amount and type of his travel. Clinton was the consummate campaigner as president, setting records for travel. During his first two years in office, he traveled to 228 places—194 domestic, thirty-four abroad, making 268 appearances in the United States and 62 in other countries. The huge majority of these appearances were policy related, with health care and the economy topping the list of domestic concerns.[25]

As noted earlier, George W. Bush, was viewed by many as the "un-Clinton," who set out to manage the presidency very differently from his predecessor. Undoubtedly many changes were made. But as Corey Cook has shown, Bush matched Clinton in his use of travel to promote his agenda. In volume, his travel in the first year of his presidency was nearly the same as Clinton's. However, they differed in the places they visited (Clinton went more to the Northeast and the Pacific; Bush, more to the South and the Midwest), the issues discussed (Clinton talked more about health care; Bush, more about education and much more about foreign policy and defense), and the volume of international travel (Bush spent over twice as many days abroad). Cook concluded that:

> The evidence offered . . . strongly suggests that the permanent campaign has become a permanent feature of the contemporary presidency. Attributable not to certain political styles or personalities, the permanent campaign model of governance relies on modern technological advantages to overcome uniquely modern political disadvantages facing contemporary presidents, including the growing individualism of members of Congress, the increasing

partisan polarization of Congress, and the demands of a twenty-four-hour news cycle.[26]

Cook's analysis suggests that presidents now have little choice but to take their message directly to the people. This strategy was well expressed by a Clinton aide, Mandy Grunwald: "The president's popularity first had to be improved, then Congress could be moved by a popular president." She used a basketball analogy: "It's a bank shot, what you say to the American people bounces back to Congress."[27] There was little evidence that the bank shot worked in Clinton's first years in office. His policy campaign stressed health care, yet his plan was never voted on in either house of Congress.

Is defeat in Congress a reason to abandon permanent campaigning? Clearly not, for exactly the reasons identified by Cook, as well as some others associated with the growing publicness of lawmaking. Adaptations to technological developments in communication and information flow are not limited to the White House. Members of Congress, interested and affected groups in the private sphere, government departments and agencies, and the media engage in campaigning styles of governing to pursue major policy issues. No one of these participants can expect to score consistently on bank shots. But that they try is stimulus enough for the president to join in, particularly given the advantages of "position"—the vantage points plus the qualities of the presidency. No president can forgo participation in an ever-changing lawmaking process on account of stylistic preferences.

Congressional Calculations

Charles W. Ostrom Jr. and Dennis M. Simon find that a president's relations with Congress contribute to the public's evaluations of his performance.[28] Much less clear, however, is the extent to which high public approval ratings help a president to buy influence with Congress. If a high approval rating is the result of things going well in the country, why should this cause a member of Congress to follow the lead of the president? A member might logically be cautious about opposing the president on an issue of major importance and yet not be prepared to support him on all issues, especially those of direct interest to the member's own constituency. "When [a member is] confronted by a choice between supporting a popular president and the clear interests of his constituents, the president's public prestige is a poor match for his or her constituents' interests."[29]

Ceaser's observation would seem to be the correct one: that a high approval rating is a reminder of the potential costs in opposing the president.

Members of Congress will vary considerably in their individual calculations of the costs within their own states and districts of opposing a popular president. Further, according to Edwards, approval is "an important
background resource for leadership" that helps a president determine
"whether or not an opportunity for change exists" and makes "other
resources more efficacious."[30] Presidents will vary in the extent to which
this resource is available to them and their personal capacities to use it
effectively. In brief, the president's prestige may be important on issues for
which members of Congress sense they share a "common fate" among
themselves and with the president.

This is not to suggest that members of Congress ignore a president's
high approval rating. Members naturally interpret what these numbers
mean for their states or districts. A former House Republican member
explains:

> Among Republicans, there is a greater willingness to support the president
> . . . if, by golly, the president is so popular that I'd be nuts not to support
> him. Democrats tend to move the same way, but less markedly. We are talk-
> ing about more moderate and centrist Democrats who tend to vote with the
> president if they think he is powerful. That won't necessarily help them but
> it could hurt them.
>
> I don't think you have to say that the president is at 90 percent. Everybody
> has noticed it and calculated whatever odds one places on one's own conduct.
> How much of a political risk is it for me to oppose President [G. W. H.] Bush
> given where he is? For instance, [suppose] I decided not to give him the right
> to risk the lives of my sons and daughters in the Persian Gulf. Do I have the
> guts to turn around and not let him sit down and negotiate with our partners
> on this vote on the extension of negotiating for the Uruguay Round [trade
> talks], when he is so popular? Maybe I can get away with voting against him
> once, but with two, I'm dead meat.[31]

This discussion provides an example of how an individual member might
assess the costs of voting against a popular president—very much as
Neustadt interpreted public prestige as an asset or liability as perceived by
others. It also illustrates the personal nature of the calculation, which will
unquestionably take the constituency into account. After all, members of
Congress are, first and foremost, representatives, and they must regularly
run unsystematic tests of the public mood.

Harvey G. Zeidenstein sought to identify the effect of presidential
approval ratings at the aggregated level of congressional roll call votes on
key issues. He found a strong relationship between popularity (as measured by the approval question) and success on congressional roll call votes

in three-fourths of the correlations. In nearly half of these cases, however, the relationships were inverse: high popularity was correlated with low legislative success, and vice versa.[32] Zeidenstein then reversed the analysis to determine whether high legislative success might explain increases in presidential popularity. He discovered differences among policy areas, but concluded that "whether a president is an able legislative leader does not directly affect his popularity."[33]

Perhaps the most telling comment on studies that correlate approval ratings with key votes in Congress is that they are "theoretically irrelevant." According to Edwards, "there is no theoretical reason to expect such close associations. The impact of public approval is at once broader and more subtle."[34] Bond and Fleisher agree:

> The proposition that the president's popularity systematically alters congressional support is based on a rather naive theory of democracy and representation that assumes levels of citizen knowledge and interest that rarely exist. Most members of Congress know that very few voters are likely to have information about their votes on specific roll calls or about their support for the president. . . . Incumbents seldom lose because they support a popular president too little or support an unpopular president too much; they are more likely to lose because they are too liberal or conservative for their constituencies.[35]

Exactly so. This conclusion follows from what has been learned about why approval ratings rise and fall, as well as the logic of how individual members of Congress are likely to interpret the effects of the ratings for themselves and their constituencies. Some members of Congress will make personal judgments about the effects of going against a popular president, whether or not those judgments can empirically be demonstrated to be sound.

The Larger Context

Put together, these studies and observations advise one to pay attention to presidential approval but to set it in the context of what else is happening in the policy and political life of the president and Congress. This book is about the president's role in the national policy process of a separated system. It is a process that has life before and after any one president—and any one president's approval scores. For pressing issues, legislation will get passed in some form no matter who is in the Oval Office. This is not to suggest that presidents are unimportant; rather, they are part of a large and complex working government, one in which they struggle to exercise influence in some measure equal to their accountability.

Going Public

In an influential book, Samuel Kernell draws attention to the growing tendency "whereby a president promotes himself and his policies in Washington by appealing to the American public for support." While acknowledging that such a strategy is not new, Kernell argues that it has increased substantially. He points out that presidents give more speeches, travel more, appear more frequently on television, and have expanded their press operations. These developments have coincided with "the continuous technological advances in transportation and mass communications during the past half century."[36] It would be odd in the extreme, therefore, if presidents were to hunker down in the White House—"go private," as it were. Indeed, President Carter elicited strong media critcism when he decided not to campaign for reelection until the American hostages held in Iran were released, a decision he later reversed.

The fact that presidents are heard and seen more is not in the least surprising. What is of particular interest is Kernell's argument that "going public violates" and threatens "to displace" bargaining. Instead of "benefits for compliance," the strategy of going public "imposes costs for noncompliance." It also involves "public posturing" and may undermine "the legitimacy of other politicians." Kernell seems not to like this development, and yet he acknowledges that a president has a strong incentive to go public because of important changes that have occurred in Washington politics. "Individualized pluralism" (a sort of atomistic politics) has replaced "institutionalized pluralism" (characterized by bargaining among large coalitions). "As Washington comes to depend on looser, more individualistic political relations, presidents searching for strategies that work will increasingly go public."[37]

It is important for the purposes of this book to clarify the developments that Kernell has identified. He believes that the stimulus to go public creates a different politics from that of bargaining. Another interpretation might be that bargaining conditions have changed because of the many developments Kernell cites. I would add yet another development: the frequent election of split-party national governments and, very recently, narrow-margin congresses. An option available to a president for improving his position at the bargaining table is to go public. When he does, the effect then is less a case of freely imposing "costs for noncompliance" than, in Ceaser's words, a reminder of the potential costs of opposing the president. Bargaining does not disappear in a system of diffused responsibility and competitively partisan politics. But the process may well look very different from that in a system of focused responsibility and noncompetitive partisan politics.

In a system of diffused responsibility a president may also go public to prevent legislation from passing; he may not wish to bargain at all. It might be that technological developments make going public a more rational strategy to achieve this goal than in the past, but the goal itself has been common enough throughout history. And, in fact, the veto power exists precisely to permit the president to stop a bill from becoming law either because he failed to win through bargaining or because he refused to participate in the bargaining process from the start. Ford and Bush 41, in particular, chose to employ a veto strategy, sometimes going public with their objections to provide a rationale for congressional Republicans to sustain the veto. Each president had serious weaknesses for classic bargaining: Ford had not been elected even as a vice president, and Bush 41 had a smaller proportion of his party in the House of Representatives than any newly elected president in the twentieth century.

Kernell's argument places the politics of split-party government in sharp relief. The juxtaposition of going public and bargaining suits the party responsibility perspective quite well. Lyndon Johnson, who had huge Democratic majorities in Congress, explained that he "preferred to work from within, knowing that good legislation is the product not of public rhetoric but of private negotiations and compromise." He was not anxious to go to the public because to do so typically involved "picking a fight with the Congress" in order to satisfy the press.[38] Nor did he have any illusion that he would always win. His successors have been less reticent about taking this route, in part because they have had many fewer resources. This "new breed of presidents," as Kernell refers to them, not only has lacked the two-thirds congressional majorities that Johnson enjoyed, most did not even have simple majorities in Congress. These political realities reinforce the viability of the diffused-responsibility perspective by directing attention to the variation in political resources and strategic advantages of different presidents.

Is going public effective in building support for the president's proposals? In a systematic, empirically based analysis of the messenger, the message, and the audience (is anyone listening?), Edwards finds that most such efforts fall "on deaf ears."[39] His findings raise serious doubts as to whether a president much improves his bargaining position by attempting to get his message across to a mostly inattentive public.

So, why do they bother? Edwards proposes three reasons. First is the habit of seeking support. "Presidents *become* president by going public." They are campaigners, and as such are predisposed to seek public support. The second and third reasons are audience considerations. Presidents may not be going to the *general* public. In fact, they may not be seeking to change opinion but to reinforce opinion among loyalists—essentially, "preaching to the converted." Additionally, the audience may consist of elites, those active in the policy debates. So the president will try to ensure that his preferences are in the mix of reporting, commenting, and committee and floor action (and perhaps even department or agency development of proposals).[40]

There are other reasons compatible with those cited by Edwards. Split-party government and narrow margins in Congress encourage a more public approach. Further technological development in communications provides more and varied opportunities. Political consultants are now institutionalized within the White House staff, there to urge and analyze public contact. And, as mentioned above, the greater publicness of lawmaking has become the contemporary political context. Which raises the "compared to what" question: how effective are other messengers with different messages?

The Public Standing of Postwar Presidents

There is a substantial literature dealing with the public approval of presidents as measured by various polls. Much of this work concentrates on why approval ratings change over a presidential term. Typically the overall trend is down, with numerous upticks or spikes along the way. Various explanations are given for both the overall trend and the jagged nature of the downhill slide. John E. Mueller attributes the decline to a "coalition of minorities," that is, a growing number of interests displeased with presidential decisions. Short-term boosts can be realized by a "rally round the flag" effect in international crises.[41] Kernell finds that changes in the president's popularity are related to events and government actions for which he is held accountable. "Fluctuations in his prestige can be located in observable events and conditions. . . . His decisions on policy do not affect his popularity so much as their results."[42] He may be held as responsible for inaction as for action. Other studies show that presidential speechmaking can improve approval ratings.[43] Some presidents seem principally to have lost support among the other party: Eisenhower, Nixon, Reagan, and Bush 43 lost among Democrats; Kennedy and Clinton, among Republicans. Each of these presidents retained steady support within his own party (except Nixon in his final year in office).[44]

In his review and summation of much of this literature, Dean Keith Simonton observed that "a president's approval rating seems to be a partial consequence of an early term effect. A honeymoon occurs at the onset of a presidential term in which the president receives high, and usually his highest, ratings."[45] The initial measure is apparently less one of approval than of public willingness to encourage a new president. If so, that may not be the best point from which to measure subsequent standing. Simonton's observation requires modification to this extent: Events can have dramatic effects on popularity, as was the case with both Bush presidencies (the Gulf War and 9/11). And prolonged economic well-being can sustain moderately high ratings through an otherwise troubled presidency, as during the Clinton years.

My purpose here, however, is to evaluate the effects of these changes in job approval ratings. Do presidents care about them? A check of presidential memoirs revealed that before Nixon, only Truman had much to say about public opinion polls—understandably, since the polls were wrong in predicting the outcome of the 1948 election. In classic Truman style, he explained: "A man who is influenced by the polls or is afraid to make decisions which may make him unpopular is not a man to represent the welfare of the country."[46] Eisenhower and Johnson made only brief mention of polls. Nixon, Ford, and Carter commented frequently, noting that their approval ratings were associated with particular decisions. Reagan made no reference to them. Clinton, likewise, does not discuss polls as a discrete subject, though he frequently cites poll results. His political consultant Dick Morris reported that he once told the president: "You're better at reading polls than any pollster I know." According to Morris, Clinton used polls "as a tool for governing" and "polling for him was not a onetime test of opinion" but "an extensive dialogue with the public."[47]

Is there reason to nurture public approval ratings in order to establish one's place in history? Table 4-1 ranks the postwar presidents by their average approval ratings for their full term in office and their last quarter. It also presents rankings of these presidents by historians (as surveyed by C-SPAN in 1999), first among themselves, and then in relation to all presidents, Washington through Clinton. Several findings deserve comment. Most dramatic are the numbers for Truman. Dead last in average job approval overall (second to last in the last quarter of his term), he has the highest score

Table 4-1. *Rankings of Public Approval and Historians' Assessments, Truman to Clinton*

President	By average approval rating		Historians' assessments	
	Over entire presidency	Last quarter of presidency	Among postwar presidents	Among all presidents
Kennedy	1	3	2	8
Eisenhower	2	2	3	9
Bush 41	3	6	6	20
Clinton	4	1	7	21
Johnson	5	7	4	10
Reagan	6	4	5	11
Nixon	7	10	10	25
Carter	8	8	8	22
Ford	9	5	9	23
Truman	10	9	1	5

Sources: Rankings based on quarterly average approval ratings, as calculated from *Gallup Report,* various issues. The Historian Survey was conducted by C-SPAN, 1999 (www.americanpresidents.org/survey/historians/overall.asp).

from historians among the postwar presidents, fifth all time (behind Lincoln, the two Roosevelts, and Washington; ahead of Wilson and Jefferson). Being in that company would no doubt please Truman, without elevating his own estimates of his service. Kennedy's high ratings across entries are noteworthy, but it is difficult to draw any definitive conclusions, given his limited tenure and the emotions associated with his death. Eisenhower's outstanding approval ratings at the time of his presidency were not at the time matched by strongly positive evaluations of his presidency by analysts. These judgments have since been revised and he is now ranked by historians among the top ten presidents, third among those in the postwar period. Bush 41 and Johnson both carry relatively high overall job approval scores, but these averages are due primarily to high initial scores that subsequently deteriorated—for Bush, because of a poor economy; for Johnson, a prolonged and unpopular war. Historians appear to give Johnson more credit for his active domestic agenda than they do Bush 41 for his Gulf War record.

Reagan's reputation may also be undergoing revision. Thought by analysts at the time to be protected by Teflon, in fact, his average job approval ratings were just that: average. And contemporary judgments of his presidency were not laudatory. Yet historians now place him eleventh all time, very nearly in the top quarter of presidents. Of the rest, only Clinton's numbers are of special note. Despite being the subject of constant scandal, his job approval scores were strong during the last six years in office, and highest of all postwar presidents in the last quarter of their presidencies. Historians have not been as positive but that may change with the passage of time (he was still in office when the C-SPAN survey was conducted). The scores of Nixon, Carter, and Ford are mostly consistent across the columns of table 4-1. Perhaps the active post-presidential lives of Nixon and Carter will encourage stronger evaluations by historians in time. But ranking Ford will always be problematic, given his short tenure and the fact that he was not elected, even as vice president.

Commenting specifically on the so-called honeymoon period, Brody emphasizes that the policy outcomes of an administration are important. "In the end, opinion on President Reagan . . . depends less upon the public's response to him as a person than on the success or failure of his policies to achieve the outcomes he has led the American people to expect. After the honeymoon is over, it is by this standard that the president will be judged."[48] Brody's standard is also relevant after the presidency is over. In other words, a presidency is ultimately judged more by its legacy than by how people at the time react to events and associate them with the person in the White House. Ceaser's admonition might well be recast to state that "an astute president should . . . be prepared in most cases to sacrifice his standing today, if by doing so he can affect positively the future assessment of his presidency." If it is correct that the ultimate historical judgment, like that of the post-honeymoon period, is based on the policy outcomes, then a president's preoccupation with job approval ratings is a distraction and may ultimately be self-defeating.

I focus on two outcomes in discussing the public standing of presidents from Truman through the first term of George W. Bush: midterm and presidential elections and the passage of important legislation. For elections, it should be noted that whatever a president's approval rating, the critical factor in the end is what choice the voters have. They may think less of a president than before, but be unwilling to choose someone else. They may also decide not to vote. For the passage of legislation, one must look beyond the president and his popularity to the legislative product during his term in office. As before, the stimulus for this inquiry is a conception of government as engaging in policymaking regardless of whether presidents have high or low approval ratings. Major legislation is commonly associated with the president who was in office when it was enacted. As will be shown, however, often it may be more properly credited to congressional initiative or

Figure 4-1. *Presidential Approval Ratings, Truman Administration*[a]

Quarterly average (percent)

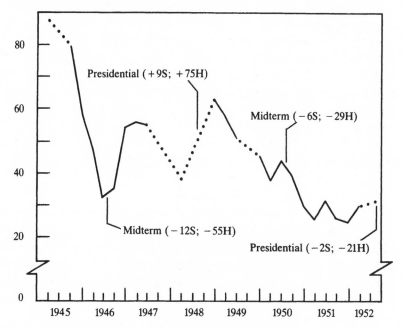

Source: Calculated from Gallup Poll data in the *Gallup Report*, various issues.
a. Legends denote net electoral gains or losses for the president's party in the Senate (S) and House (H). Dotted lines indicate lack of data.

joint presidential-congressional participation (see chapters 6–7). The separated system provides for lawmaking beyond polls and alongside presidents.

Truman

Truman's presidential approval scores plummeted during his initial months in office, as the nation was plagued by strikes and inflation in the immediate postwar period (see figure 4-1). By the third quarter of 1946—just before the midterm elections—his rating had fallen from an initial 87 percent to 32 percent. No other president experienced such a steep drop in so short a time (though Bush 41 came close to matching that record). At this low point, the Republicans captured control of both houses of Congress for the first time since 1928.

Truman's public standing was measured only twice in 1948, and both readings were low: 36 percent in April, 39 percent in May–June. His election in November remains one of the greatest upsets ever recorded, primarily because of the widely held perception that the public was dissatisfied with his performance and voters would surely turn him out of office. The candidacy of Dixiecrat Strom Thurmond (D-S.C.) in the South fed this perception, as did polls showing Dewey comfortably ahead in the fall. Truman's surprise win was complemented by congressional Democrats' recapturing control of both houses of Congress. Once Truman had been elected on his own, his approval score climbed to 69 percent, only to suffer substantial decline the following January, to 45 percent. During his last three years in office, his score averaged 33 percent, never reaching 50 percent. In the 1950 midterm elections, Democrats retained their House and Senate majorities but suffered substantial net losses.

Superficially, it would seem that the midterm results were related to Truman's approval ratings. Congressional Democrats did poorly in 1946 and 1950, when Truman's approval scores were low. The small number of scores in 1948 makes it difficult to draw any firm conclusions about that election. Truman did, however, make the "terrible 80th Congress" an issue in the campaign, and the Democrats realized very substantial gains in both houses (see figure 4-1).

A review of major legislation passed during the Truman presidency does not lend much credence to the contention that presidential approval ratings are a barometer of achievement (see table 4-2).[49] In fact, much of the major legislation identified with Truman was enacted in a period of split-party government during that terrible 80th Congress. The Taft-Hartley Labor-Management Relations Act (passed over Truman's veto), the Truman Doctrine, legislation to unify the military services in one department, and the Marshall Plan were all passed in 1947–48.

Other major legislation was enacted during the precipitous decline in Truman's popularity following his inauguration. The following are especially notable:

—1949: Housing Act of 1949, NATO ratification, Mutual Defense Assistance Act.

—1950: Point Four aid program, Social Security expansion, creation of the National Science Foundation, McCarran Act (over Truman's veto), Defense Production Act, Excess Profits Tax.

—1951: Mutual Security Act, Reciprocal Trade Act.

Table 4-2. *Number of Important Laws Enacted, by Presidential Administration, 1947–2003*

Administration	Year in office								Total	Annual average (rank)
	1	2	3	4	5	6	7	8		
Truman (1945–53)	n.a.	n.a.	6	4	5	7	3	3	28	4.7 (7)
Eisenhower (1953–61)	1	8	2	4	2	9	3	2	31	3.9 (10)
Kennedy (1961–63)	9	6	6	...	...	...	...	...	21	7.0 (4)
Johnson (1963–69)	...	...	...	7	15	7	6	10	45	9.0 (2)
Nixon (1969–74)	6	16	5	11	11	5	...	...	54	9.5 (1)[a]
Ford (1974–77)	...	...	...	...	...	6	6	8	20	8.6 (3)[a]
Carter (1977–81)	7	5	3	7	...	...	...	...	22	5.5 (5)
Reagan (1981–89)	2	7	3	4	2	7	5	7	37	4.6 (8)
Bush 41 (1989–93)	2	7	3.	5	...	...	...	...	17	4.3 (9)
Clinton (1993–2001)	7	4	4	11	4	4	3	3	40	5.0 (6)
Bush 43 (2001–09)	7	10	n.a.	n.a.	n.a.	n.a.	n.a.	n.a.	17	8.5
Total									332	

Source: Calculated from David R. Mayhew, *Divided We Govern: Party Control, Lawmaking, and Investigations, 1946-1990* (Yale University Press, 1991), pp. 52-73, and Mayhew's updates at http://pantheon.yale.edu/~dmayhew/.

n.a. Not available. Mayhew does not provide a listing of important laws for the first two years of the Truman administration.

a. Nixon's total is divided by 5.67 years; Ford's, by 2.33 years.

—1952: McCarran-Walter Act (over Truman's veto), Japanese peace treaty ratification.

The fact that three of these acts (Taft-Hartley, McCarran, and McCarran-Walter) were passed over Truman's veto is a reminder that legislation is often more attributable to Congress than to the presidency with which it is associated. It is also worth noting that revisionist views of a presidency may well take into account the full measure of government activity, not just that initiated or favored by the president. Equally relevant is the fact that historians are not asked to rank Congresses, thus obviating any revisionist perspective on that branch.

Figure 4-2. *Presidential Approval Ratings, Eisenhower Administration*[a]

Quarterly average (percent)

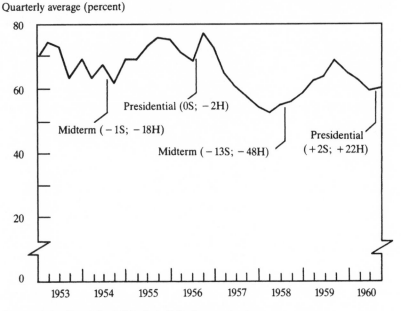

Source: Calculated from Gallup Poll data in the *Gallup Report*, various issues.
a. Legends denote net electoral gains or losses for the president's party in the Senate (S) and House (H).

Eisenhower

President Eisenhower's public approval ratings are legendary. His quarterly average never fell below 50 percent, and his individual scores fell below that figure just once (March–April 1958), to 48 percent (see figure 4-2). His approval score always exceeded his disapproval score. He experienced one period of sustained erosion in public approval, between his reelection in 1956 and the midterm election of 1958, which was disastrous for congressional Republicans. But his personal popularity increased steadily during the next year, then declined somewhat following the U-2 incident (the downing of a surveillance plane in the Soviet Union) and the collapse of the summit talks with the Soviets. It is difficult to determine his effect on the congressional elections, but it seems that his popularity was not transferable. The Republicans narrowly lost their thin congressional majority margins in 1954, experienced little change in 1956, but then in 1958 fell back to the low numbers experienced during the Roosevelt years. This pattern was to be repeated frequently: a winning Republican president unable to convey his electoral or popular support to his party sufficiently for it to win majorities in Congress.

Eisenhower's popularity was also not a good barometer for the passage of major legislation. His presidency had the lowest annual production of major legislation, at 4.1, of the postwar period (see table 4-2). During his first year in office, the only major law passed was the Tidelands Oil Act. In the second and sixth years of his presidency, 1954 and 1958, more important legislation was passed than in the other six combined. Legislation enacted in 1954 included a major tax schedule revision, Social Security expansion, approval of the St. Lawrence Seaway, the Communist Control Act, the Atomic Energy Act, agricultural and housing acts, and the food for peace program. During this time, Eisenhower's approval ratings were a bit jagged but remained high.

In 1955 and 1956, Eisenhower realized his highest sustained approval readings, yet very little major legislation was enacted. Only the Federal Aid Highway Act is ordinarily remembered as a great achievement. Substantially more notable legislation was enacted in 1957 and 1958, during the most sustained decrease in Eisenhower's popularity:

—1957: Civil Rights Act, Price-Anderson Nuclear Industry Indemnity Act.

—1958: Alaska statehood, National Aeronautics and Space Administration established, National Defense Education Act, Department of Defense reorganization.

The solid recovery in Eisenhower's job approval ratings during his last Congress was not matched by an increase in legislative productivity. Congressional Democrats were actively preparing alternatives that would form an election platform for the 1960 presidential contest. Mayhew lists only five important legislative enactments during the two years, of which four were typically associated with the Eisenhower presidency:

—1959: Landrum-Griffin Labor Reform Act, Hawaii statehood.

—1960: Civil Rights Act, Kerr-Mills aid for the medically needy aged.

As Neustadt has observed, public prestige is a source of influence if it is perceived and interpreted by other elected officials as such, notably by the members of Congress.[50] But for high popularity to produce a large volume of legislation there must be presidential interest and intent, as well as a substantial agenda. The president's performance is expected to fit the activist model so admired by many observers of the White House. The Eisenhower presidency confirms, however, that a less aggressive president can, over time, stimulate greater congressional participation in the policy process. Agendas are created by the accumulation of issues. For example, many of the Great Society programs of the Johnson presidency can be traced to the identification of issues by congressional Democrats in the later, rather passive, years of the Eisenhower presidency.

Kennedy-Johnson

I treat the Kennedy-Johnson presidencies together, as I do the Nixon-Ford presidencies. A good case can be made for policy continuity in each instance. Further, they had equally dramatic interruptions: an assassination and the first-ever presidential resignation. The patterns of popular approval are fascinating, particularly in juxtaposition to the production of important legislation. As shown in table 4-2, these four presidencies account for 42 percent (140 of 332) of the major laws, 1947–2003.

Kennedy had a very good first year at the polls: his final reading for the year exceeded his first (see figure 4-3). His ratings dropped in the second year but were on the rebound by the midterm elections, when congressional Democrats did exceptionally well, gaining Senate seats and losing well below the average number of House seats for a first midterm. Kennedy's approval ratings fell steadily during his third year, though they remained higher than the ratings of most other presidents at that point in their presidencies.

With Johnson's accession to the White House, his presidential approval scores rose once again to the mid- to high 70s and remained there through June 1964. No readings were taken before the election that fall, but Johnson's overwhelming victory showed strong public approval, at least in the choice between him and Barry Goldwater. As noted earlier, the 1964 election was interpreted as one of the most policy oriented in contemporary times, as close to the "good election," as defined by the party responsibility advocates, as those in the 1930s. It was followed by a steady decline in Johnson's job approval (figure 4-3). There were increases from time to time, but they were followed soon after by decreases, and subsequent improvements tended not to recapture the earlier high ground. By the midterm elections in 1966, Johnson's approval rating had fallen to 44 percent from 80 percent in January 1964. Democrats suffered huge losses in the midterms. However, since they had achieved very wide margins in the 1964 election, they retained their congressional majorities. When Nixon was elected to the White House in 1968 (by a very narrow margin), congressional Democrats endured further losses while retaining their House and Senate majorities.

Figure 4-3. *Presidential Approval Ratings, Kennedy-Johnson Administration*[a]

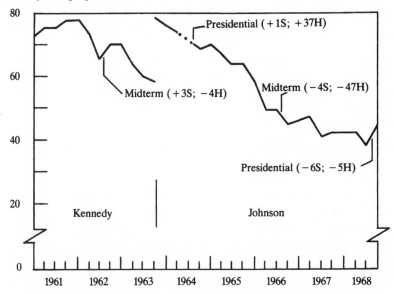

Quarterly average (percent)

Source: Calculated from Gallup Poll data in the *Gallup Report*, various issues.
a. Legends denote net electoral gains or losses for the president's party in the Senate (S) and House (H). Dotted lines indicate lack of data.

A significant number of major laws were enacted in Kennedy's first year, countering the conventional wisdom that he failed to move more legislation early in his presidency. Despite his narrow margin in the popular vote and a questionable mandate, more major bills were passed than in the first year of any other first-term postwar president. James L. Sundquist explains that although the election could not be counted as an endorsement of all of the specific proposals developed by the congressional Democrats in the late 1950s, "it was a clear endorsement of an approach to domestic problems, of a governing temper—and tempo."[51] Thus while Kennedy's popularity remained high several pieces of legislation that had been in the works were enacted: a housing act, increases in the minimum wage and Social Security, the Area Redevelopment Act, and the establishment of the Peace Corps, the Arms Control and Development Agency, and the Alliance for Progress.

During the next two years other important legislation was passed, although so much was in the pipeline that Kennedy was criticized for not producing more. Here is a sample of important measures, some of which were new initiatives:

—1962: Trade Expansion Act, Manpower Development and Training Act, Communications Satellite Act, Revenue Act, public welfare amendments.

—1963: Nuclear Test Ban Treaty ratification, Higher Education Facilities Act, Clean Air Act, Equal Pay Act.

Major legislation takes on an entirely new dimension as one turns to the Johnson presidency. The steady slide downward in the president's approval while major legislation flowed from Congress is of particular relevance to this discussion of public standing and legislative products. Johnson's average quarterly approval scores increased in only five of the more than twenty quarters of his presidency. The events in Vietnam and riots in major cities contributed substantially to this decline in public endorsement, supporting the view that public approval is subject to forces beyond Washington. Here is a sample of the Johnson presidency's remarkable record of landmark legislation, much of it representing new initiatives.

—1964: Civil Rights Act, Economic Opportunity Act, tax cut, Urban Mass Transportation Act, Wilderness Act, Food Stamp Act.

—1965: Medical Care for the Aged, Voting Rights Act, Elementary and Secondary Education Act, Department of Housing and Urban Development established, Appalachian Regional Development Act, immigration reform, Higher Education Act, Housing and Urban Development Act, Water Quality Act.

—1966: Department of Transportation established, Clean Waters Restoration Act, Traffic Safety Act, Fair Packaging and Labeling Act, Demonstration Cities Act, Social Security increase.

—1967: Public Broadcasting Act, Air Quality Act, Age Discrimination Act.

—1968: Open Housing Act, Housing and Urban Development Act, Gun Control Act, Omnibus Crime Control and Safe Streets Act, Truth-in-Lending Act.

The Johnson presidency produced a domestic policy legacy that continues to dominate the agenda and budget politics today. Yet the president could not in any significant way reverse the downward spiral of his job approval. The story of this extraordinary legislative production is complicated and can be fully told only by turning back to developments in the 1950s, but it confirms that analysis of public standing is peripheral in the study of national policymaking. High approval ratings do not transform a president's program into law; declining approval ratings do not suspend a policy momentum that has been building for months or years. In fact, one can make a case that much of the Great Society was part of a 1930s, New Deal agenda interrupted by World War II and postwar reorientation during the Eisenhower years.

Nixon-Ford

During his first three years, Nixon experienced a gradual decline in job approval, starting in the low 60s and bottoming out in 1971 around the 50 percent mark, primarily because of the continued conflict in Vietnam and the poor economy. In the 1970 midterm election, congressional Republicans experienced little change. Going into the 1972 general election, foreign policy initiatives with China and the Soviet Union balanced the continuing bad news from Vietnam, giving Nixon mostly positive job approval ratings. However, this recovery and his stupendous victory in 1972 did not transfer to his party in Congress. The congressional Republicans were in no better position in 1972 with Nixon's forty-nine-state landslide than they had been with his narrow victory in 1968.

Following the inauguration, Nixon's job approval ratings began to plummet—a drop of 40 points in 1973 between the Vietnam peace agreement and the firing of Archibald Cox as special prosecutor (see figure 4-4). They fell even further in 1974, to 24 percent just before his resignation. As shown in table 4-1, his last quarter average prior to his resignation was the lowest of the postwar presidents.

Ford entered the White House to a collective sigh of approval. His pardon of Nixon, however, cost him dearly in public support: his rating dropped 21 points in just over a month. Then came the disaster of the 1974 midterm elections. Congressional Republicans were back to their numbers in the Johnson and Roosevelt eras (144 House members, 37 senators), yet with a Republican president. It seemed that they could lose when there were dramatic decreases in presidential approval but could not realize substantial gains when approval was high. Their position still did not improve in 1976 (143 House members, 38 senators), even though Ford came very close to winning the presidential election.

Was the production of legislation at all associated with the president's approval ratings? There was an outpouring of major laws, but presidential approval appeared unrelated. These eight years were the most productive of major legislation for the period 1947–2003 and included the single most productive year, 1970 (see table 4-2). Equally remarkable, there were three consecutive productive years—1972, 1973, and 1974—while the political

Figure 4-4. *Presidential Approval Ratings, Nixon-Ford Administration*[a]

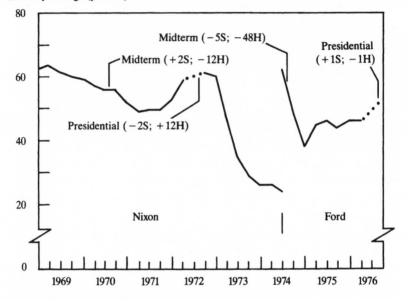

Quarterly average (percent)

Source: Calculated from Gallup Poll data in the *Gallup Report*, various issues.
a. Legends denote net electoral gains or losses for the president's party in the Senate (S) and House (H). Dotted lines indicate lack of data.

system was presumably disintegrating. The pipeline was full of legislative proposals, and much of the system operated in spite of weakened Democratic presidential politics (a forty-nine-state loss in 1972), the Watergate scandal, and the threat of impeachment. Apparently the nation has a government, not just a president.

Paul C. Light points out that Nixon made few legislative requests during his first three months in office and also had fewer first-year requests than Kennedy, Johnson, or Carter.[52] Still, the first-year production was impressive: the Coal Mine Safety Act, Social Security increase, Tax Reform Act, Nuclear Nonproliferation Treaty ratification, and National Environmental Policy Act. Nixon made even fewer new requests in his second year but, as noted above, legislative production was outstanding. And none was enacted over the president's veto.

—1970: Organized Crime Control Act, postal reorganization, Voting Rights Act extension, Clean Air Act, Water Quality Improvement Act, ban on cigarette advertising, Occupational Safety and Health Act, Rail Passenger Service Act (Amtrak), Narcotics Control Act, Economic Stabilization Act.

In 1971 and 1972 Nixon's new requests were relatively few, but a number of issues carried over from the previous Congress. There were five major laws enacted in 1971, the most notable being an increase in Social Security, the Emergency Employment Act, and a constitutional amendment lowering the voting age to eighteen. The agenda remained full in 1972, and once more an impressive variety of programs was enacted by the Democratic Congress with presidential approval. The pending election was clearly a major factor; for example, Social Security benefits were increased. Of the eleven major pieces of legislation, only one was passed over the president's veto, although Nixon had begun to use this tactic much more frequently in 1972 to check congressional spending.

—1972: Federal Election Campaign Act, Water Pollution Control Act (over Nixon's veto), State and Local Fiscal Assistance Act (revenue sharing), Social Security increase (cost-of-living allowances, or COLAs), Equal Rights Amendment, Pesticide Control Act, Anti-Ballistic Missile (ABM) Treaty ratification, Consumer Product Safety Act, Equal Employment Opportunity Act, Supplementary Security Income, Higher Education Act.

The next two years represent the most serious challenge to the traditional understanding of how the political system works. The White House and many members of Congress became absorbed by the Watergate scandal that was to force many resignations, and ultimately that of the president. Yet the 93rd Congress (1973–75) matched the 89th Congress (1965–67) as among the most productive of major legislation in the postwar period. Clearly both the executive and legislative branches were doing work other than investigating the president. Only two bills were passed over the president's veto, although both Nixon and Ford used that tool frequently as a threat to get amendments adopted or to kill legislation. A sample of legislation again illustrates the manifold issues treated during this tense period in the history of the two institutions.

—1973: War Powers Resolution (over Nixon's veto), Federal Aid Highway Act, Comprehensive Employment and Training Act, Social Security increase, trans-Alaska pipeline, Foreign Assistance Act, Regional Rail Reorganization Act (Conrail), Aid for Health Maintenance Organizations, Emergency Petroleum Allocation Act.

—1974: Trade Act, Employment Retirement Income Security Act, Federal Election Campaign Act, Budget and Impoundment Control Act, Freedom of Information Act (over Ford's veto), creation of Nuclear Regulatory

Commission and Energy Research and Development Administration, National Health Planning and Resources Development Act.

Ford's presidency was presumably one of the least favorable arrangements possible for a working government: a takeover by an unelected vice president. His one advantage, that he was untainted by the Watergate scandal, was dissipated when he pardoned the former president; his job approval declined significantly, and the Democrats gained overwhelming majorities in both houses of Congress in the 1974 elections. Not surprisingly, Ford relied heavily on the threat and practice of the veto (most were sustained). Public approval of Ford's performance improved marginally in 1975 and 1976. It was not a factor in the work done by Congress during that time, as members continued to act on proposals in the pipeline.

—1975: Energy Policy and Conservation Act, Voting Rights Act extension, New York City bailout, Tax Reduction Act, Securities Act Amendments.

—1976: Unemployment compensation overhaul, copyright law revision, Toxic Substances Control Act, Tax Reform Act, Railroad Vitalization and Regulatory Reform Act, National Forest Management Act, Federal Land Policy and Management Act, Resource Conservation and Recovery Act.

What explains the failure of analysts to take note of legislative accomplishments during the Nixon-Ford era? Mayhew argues that what occurred did not fit the "script," and in addition there was a great deal of captivating political theater going on in Washington. "Legislation moved along not all that visibly under a canopy of verbal shellfire about Vietnam, Nixon's and Agnew's 'social issues,' the 'imperial presidency,' and Watergate." And so nobody much noticed, nor was anyone much moved to attribute the passage of this legislation to the public prestige of Nixon or Ford.

> Probably most of us, for evidence that vigorous lawmaking is taking place, tend to rely on the familiar narrative in which a presidential candidate presents a program, wins an election, claims a mandate, and then stages a well-publicized "hundred days" of passing laws. . . .
> But no such familiar or engaging script fit the Nixon and Ford experience. Nixon entered office without much of a program. . . . There was never a "hundred days." In 1969 and later, statutes tended to pass in a jumble at the close of a Congress rather than according to someone's plan at the start of one.[53]

Related to Mayhew's explanation are three facts: the pipeline of post–Great Society issues was full, the Democratic Congress was well prepared, by reason of reforms in the 1970s, to participate actively in the policy process, and the deficit had not yet come to constrain all decisionmak-

Figure 4-5. *Presidential Approval Ratings, Carter Administration*[a]

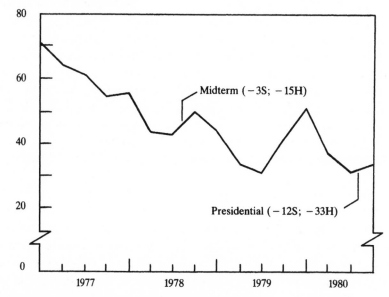

Quarterly average (percent)

Source: Calculated from Gallup Poll data in the *Gallup Report*, various issues.
a. Legends denote net electoral gains or losses for the president's party in the Senate (S) and House (H).

ing. Consequently there are few better illustrations in history of the workings of the separated system than the legislative product of these troubled times.

Carter

The 1976 election returned one-party government to Washington. Superficially, the results looked very much like those in 1960: a narrow win for the Democratic president and the return of large Democratic House and Senate majorities elected in 1974. In terms of public standing, however, the two presidencies look very different. Carter's approval ratings dropped dramatically during the first year. The overall pattern for his four years looks more like that of Truman for his first five years, with almost the same rises and falls. The drop in the first two years is also like that of Reagan (see figure 4-5).

The Democrats had modest net losses in the 1978 midterm elections. They retained a 119-seat edge in the House, a seventeen-seat edge in the Senate. Carter experienced two peaks after his first year: one associated with the Camp David peace accords and the other with the taking of the hostages in Iran. In 1980, with his popularity at a low point, Carter lost overwhelmingly to Reagan, the Republicans captured the Senate, and the Democrats' margin in the House was reduced to fifty-one.

Upon entering office, Jimmy Carter acted in accordance with the script described by Mayhew. Believing he had a mandate to do the right thing, he was determined to effect large change in the tradition of Roosevelt and Johnson. A number of important laws were, in fact, passed in that first year, most of which revised those already on the books: a minimum wage hike, an agriculture program, a Social Security tax increase, and amendments to the clean air and clean water programs. The principal new initiative was the Surface Mining Control and Reclamation Act. A major energy policy proposal, prepared behind closed doors, carried over to 1978.

The remaining three years of the Carter presidency produced less important legislation than the second year of the Nixon presidency (see table 4-2). Many proposals were organizational and regulatory (or deregulatory) in nature. Carter's reduced public standing appeared to be less significant for this limited production than the changing nature of the national agenda, including the rise of major fiscal and economic issues associated with government spending and the deficit.

—1978: comprehensive energy package, Panama Canal treaties ratified, Civil Service Reform Act, airline deregulation.

—1979: Chrysler Corporation bailout, Foreign Trade Act extension, creation of Department of Education.

—1980: Depository Institutions and Monetary Control Act, trucking deregulation, Staggers Rail Act (deregulation), windfall profits tax on oil, synthetic fuels program, Alaska Lands Preservation, Toxic Wastes Superfund.

There is very little to say about the one-party government of Jimmy Carter. Clearly the agenda itself was shifting. Carter's public standing never fully recovered from its decline in the first eighteen months. His standing within his own party was questionable and he was never moved to improve it. His renomination was challenged by Senator Edward M. Kennedy (D-Mass.). But other presidents too suffered similar reductions in public and party standing, even as many major laws were passed. Quite simply, times had changed and so had the work of the government. By 1980 economic issues at home and a seemingly intractable hostage crisis in Iran contributed to Carter's defeat.

Figure 4-6. *Presidential Approval Ratings, Reagan Administration*[a]

Quarterly average (percent)

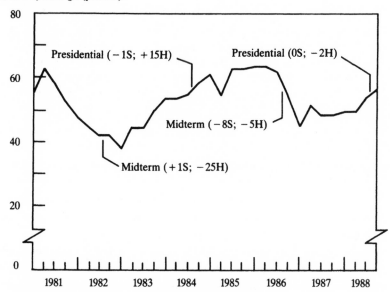

Source: Calculated from Gallup Poll data in the *Gallup Report*, various issues.
a. Legends denote net electoral gains or losses for the president's party in the Senate (S) and House (H).

Reagan

There is an extraordinary myth about the public popularity of Ronald Reagan, said to be the Teflon president. In fact, his early record is more like that of Truman and Carter than of the other postwar presidents. He had a lower approval rating upon entering office than any of his postwar predecessors (later matched by his successor, George H. W. Bush). After the assassination attempt in late March 1981, the reading rose to 68 percent. At the first midterm election in 1982, Reagan's approval rating was 42 percent (see figure 4-6). House Republicans' hopes of finally attaining majority status were dashed; once again, the Democrats had a one-hundred-seat majority.

Where Reagan does compare favorably with other presidents is in his recovery following the low point in his popularity in late January 1983. Although his ratings never achieved extremely high levels, they steadily improved until the Iran-contra scandal in 1986. In part, this improvement appeared to be a consequence of his persona. He projected optimism, a mood seemingly in favor with most of the public. As Ceaser observed:

> In the style of monarchies, while one may attack the ministers and the policies of the government, the person of the king remains inviolate. This "rule" was respected even more by Reagan's detractors than his defenders. Detractors discovered that the best way to neutralize Reagan's influence was not to dispute his benevolence. People might love Ronald Reagan, but that implied nothing about his policies.[54]

As it happened, just before the 1984 election Reagan's approval rating (at 58 percent) was at its highest point in over three years. However, his overwhelming victory in the election was accompanied by his party's net loss of one Senate seat and modest net gains in the House. Given the lack of issues during the campaign and the coronation-style reelection, it was difficult for Reagan to claim a strong policy mandate as he had in 1980. Nor did he have a substantial agenda for the nation.

Reagan's approval rating before the 1986 midterm election was higher than it was before his landslide reelection in 1984. That positive standing did not prevent the Senate from returning to Democratic control, however (though Republican losses in the House were the smallest for any Republican presidency in the twentieth century). In the 1988 election Reagan's heir apparent, George H. W. Bush, won easily, but there was virtually no change in party margins in Congress. Meanwhile, Reagan's approval rating had recovered modestly from the Iran-contra debacle.

As a leading authority on postwar lawmaking, Mayhew would be the first to concede that major laws vary in their importance; some are more major than others. There are few better illustrations of this point than the legislative product of Reagan's first year. By Mayhew's tests, only two major pieces of legislation passed in 1981, making it the least productive first year since that of Eisenhower (see table 4-2). But the impacts of the Economic Recovery Tax Act and the Omnibus Budget Reconciliation Act were greater than those of a dozen other major pieces of legislation. Just as the Great Society programs reset the agenda for the 1970s and beyond, these two acts shaped policy choices for the 1980s and beyond.

Although Reagan's approval ratings had declined after the high mark associated with the assassination attempt, many members of Congress, including many Democrats, believed that Reagan was strong in their states and districts. House Speaker Thomas P. O'Neill recalled it this way:

I was afraid that the voters would repudiate the Democrats if we didn't give the President a chance to pass his program. After all, the nation was still in an economic crisis and people wanted immediate action. . . .

I was less concerned about losing the legislative battle in the spring and summer of 1981 than I was with losing at the polls in the fall of 1982. I was convinced that if the Democrats were perceived as stalling in the midst of a national economic crisis, there would be hell to pay in the midterm elections.[55]

In regard to Reagan's unprecedented tax cut proposal, O'Neill had explained at the time that "we will ultimately send a bill to the president that he will be satisfied with."[56] What was going to satisfy the president was a tax cut to trigger the supply-side economic experiment. He got most of what he wanted from Congress, but the supply-side theory did not work as expected and previously unimaginable deficits mounted to produce a very different policy politics.

During Reagan's second year in office—when his approval rating never exceeded 50 percent—a rather eclectic bundle of laws was enacted. As his public standing improved approaching the 1984 election, the most important piece of legislation to pass was a substantial revision of Social Security. Here is a sample of the limited production after 1981:

—1982: Transportation Assistance Act, Tax Equity and Fiscal Responsibility Act, voting rights extension, Nuclear Waste Repository Act, Depository Institutions Act, Job Training Partnership Act.

—1983: Martin Luther King Jr. holiday, Social Security Act Amendments, antirecession jobs program.

—1984: anticrime package, deficit reduction package, Trade and Tariff Act, Cable Communications Policy Act.

Reagan sustained his longest period of high approval ratings during the first twenty-three months of his second term. Mayhew records just two pieces of major legislation during 1985: the Food Security Act (agriculture subsidies) and the Gramm-Rudman-Hollings Anti-Deficit Act. The latter was primarily a congressionally inspired move. The 1986 record was quite different. Two major reform measures passed: the Tax Reform Act and the Immigration Reform and Control Act. Both were enormous undertakings that had been under way for many months. Those measures alone would have marked this session as productive, but also enacted were South African sanctions (over Reagan's veto), an antinarcotics measure, Superfund expansion, the Omnibus Water Projects Act, and another reorganization of the Department of Defense.

The final Congress of the Reagan presidency is particularly interesting: it was the most productive of the four, and yet Reagan's approval hovered near the 50 percent mark. Several pieces of legislation were attributable to congressional initiative (two were passed over the president's veto). But that is precisely the point: the president's public standing is only one factor—and often a marginal one—in the workings of the system. The record of the 100th Congress (1987–89) not only disproved the notion that one-party government is necessary for major legislative production; it also showed that split-party control may actually be favorable for the development of competitive and cross-partisan coalitions to deal with controversial reform packages. Here is the record:

—1987: Water Quality Act (over Reagan's veto; a carryover from 1986), Surface Transportation Act (same), deficit reduction package, Housing and Community Development Act, Homeless Assistance Act.

—1988: Catastrophic Health Insurance for the Aged, Family Support Act (welfare reform), Omnibus Foreign Trade Act, Anti-Drug Abuse Act, Grove City civil rights measure, Intermediate Range Nuclear-Force Treaty ratification.

Perhaps part of the explanation for the myth that Reagan was the most popular postwar president is the fact that his job approval score when he left the White House was higher than his score on entry. But this was also true for George H. W. Bush, who is unlikely to be remembered as a popular president, even though his average job approval rating was higher than Reagan's (see table 4-1). Unquestionably there was a reservoir of public support for Ronald Reagan. Over the period of his presidency, however, members of Congress apparently came to realize that this support did not necessarily extend to his program, and that it need not interfere with their own policy initiatives or prevent them from going far beyond what the president had proposed. Whatever was proposed, however, had to account for mounting deficits incurred as a consequence of the initial perception that Reagan had won a mandate in 1980 and that he deserved to execute his program even in the face of steadily declining public support. This experience confirms Neustadt's emphasis that the key variable is the perception of public prestige, rather than the approval ratings. Additionally, the Reagan presidency exemplifies the importance of personality in politics. Reagan was well liked, even if not always supported.

Bush 41

I began the chapter with the intriguing story of George H. W. Bush and public approval, and there is little more to write. He experienced impressive

Figure 4-7. *Presidential Approval Ratings, Bush 41 Administration*[a]

Quarterly average (percent)

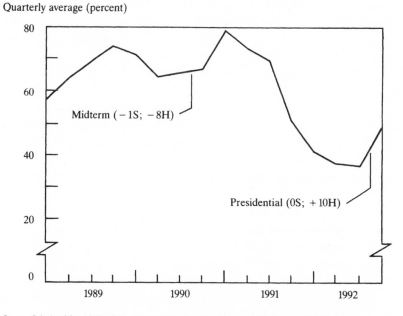

Source: Calculated from Gallup Poll data reported in *American Enterprise* 4 (March–April 1993): 94.
a. Legends denote net electoral gains or losses for the president's party in the Senate (S) and House (H).

increases in quarterly averages during his first year in office (figure 4-7). Following a dip to averages that matched Reagan's best showing, Bush's approval rating then broke records during the popular Gulf War. Its descent then nearly matched Truman's.

This remarkable record is all the more fascinating because, apart from the Gulf War, the source of Bush's popularity was not exactly clear. He was regularly criticized in the press for lacking a comprehensive program. In my view, although poll respondents had no special, deep-seated reason to think that Bush was doing a good job, neither did they have reason to believe he was doing a poor job. Not all that much went wrong during the first months of his presidency. And when one thing went well—the Gulf War—poll respondents reacted positively. It is very likely that if an election had been held in spring 1991, Bush would have won handily. In this system, however, presidents cannot choose the date for their reelection.

During that first year of steadily rising approval scores, just two major pieces of legislation were enacted—more evidence that approval is not tied to legislative productivity. These were a minimum wage increase for teenagers and authorization for $50 billion to assist with the savings and loan disaster—notable but hardly Earth-moving initiatives. The second year saw Bush break his "no new taxes" pledge. Several of the acts most associated with his presidency were passed in this second year:

—1990: Americans with Disabilities Act; Clean Air Act; deficit reduction package.

Bush's conflicts with Congress were almost certain to intensify following the 1990 election, when the Democrats had net gains in the House and Senate. The partisan gridlock predicted for split-party government was very much in evidence during the last two years of the Bush presidency. If the president proposed a program, congressional Democrats typically criticized or ignored it. If congressional Democrats were successful in passing a program, the president often vetoed it. Competitive partisanship gave way to intense partisanship and stalemate. The president's support score on Capitol Hill dropped from 54 percent in 1991 to 43 percent in 1992, the lowest ever recorded by *Congressional Quarterly*.

Congress's support score with the president, as measured by successful vetoes, was also low. He vetoed four bills in 1991 and twenty-one in 1992. Just one of the forty-six vetoes in his four-year presidency was overridden. The success of the president's strategy of checkmating with the veto was no doubt in part the result of problems in Congress in 1992. Several scandals and a vigorous movement to limit terms contributed to low approval ratings for Congress (down to 18 percent in March 1992).[57] Democratic congressional leaders found it difficult to appeal for public support to override a veto.

Mayhew's update of major legislation for the 102nd Congress includes just seven acts—two (later three) in 1991, five in 1992.

—1991: Intermodal Surface Transportation Efficiency Act and Civil Rights Act amendments (first vetoed by Bush). Mayhew later added the Persian Gulf Resolution.

—1992: Omnibus Energy Act, ratification of Strategic Arms Reduction Treaty, Soviet Economic Aid package, cable television regulation, and California water policy reform.

Most Americans apparently approved of George Bush as a president for good times. They even viewed him more favorably than not when he left office. But it is hard to know what to make of public approval as a resource when a passive president is both rewarded and punished for inaction.

Figure 4-8. *Presidential Approval Ratings, Clinton Administration*[a]

Quarterly averages (percent)

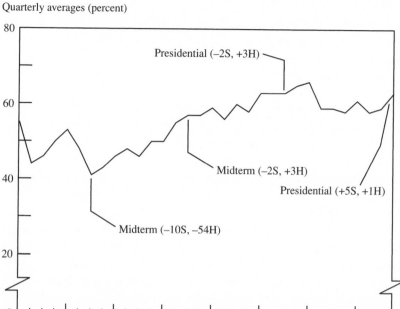

Source: Calculated from Gallup Poll data in the *Gallup Report*, various issues.
a. Legends denote net electoral gains or losses for the president's party in the Senate (S) and House (H).

Clinton

The relationships between approval ratings and election returns, legislative output, and the personal status of the president during the eight years of the Clinton presidency are of particular interest. There are few better examples of Brody and Page's analysis that good news encourages a positive public appraisal of the president's performance. The strength of the economy prior to and during Clinton's second term trumped personal scandal and impeachment. Note in figure 4-8 that Clinton first exceeded a 60 percent quarterly approval rating in the early months of 1998, when the Monica Lewinsky affair first came to light. And his numbers increased slightly during the impeachment proceedings, and again during the Senate trial. This record contrasts sharply with that of Nixon during the Watergate scandal (see figure 4-4). Nixon's approval ratings reached their low points during spring and summer 1974, just preceding his resignation under the threat of impeachment.

Interestingly, Clinton's job approval began to improve in 1995, after the Republicans had won majority status in both houses of Congress. His mean quarterly approval score was 47 percent for the 103rd Congress, which was controlled by the Democrats; it increased to 51 percent in the Republican 104th Congress, then jumped to 61 percent in the 105th and settled at 60 percent in the 106th Congress. Accordingly his mean approval score for the second term was significantly higher than that for the first term. Of the other two-term postwar presidents, Reagan also had a higher average approval rating in his second term; Eisenhower's score was lower.

It is certainly plausible that Clinton's low approval scores in his first two years contributed to the loss of the Democrats' congressional majorities in 1994. As it happened, Clinton's lowest quarterly score (41 percent) was recorded in the third quarter of that year. These numbers were no doubt associated with the defeats he had suffered on Capitol Hill, notably on his national health care plan. Clinton campaigned vigorously for congressional and gubernatorial candidates, most of whom lost. One postelection study concluded: "The more the Democratic incumbent voted to support the president's policies, the more likely he or she was to be defeated."[58]

Subsequent improvements in Clinton's public standing did not produce a marked improvement in the Democrats' numbers in Congress. Clinton's comfortable reelection in 1996 was accompanied by a slight net gain of three House seats and a net loss of two Senate seats. The results in 1998, at the height of the impeachment battle, were minimally more favorable to Democrats—no change in the Senate and a net gain of four House seats (see figure 4-8). Good times may have contributed to relatively high job approval scores for Clinton, and even perhaps saved him from being removed from office. But this support was not transferable to his party. Clinton was the first Democratic president to govern with three consecutive opposition-party Congresses (and just the second of either party—Eisenhower being the first).

The Clinton presidency was moderately productive of major legislation, ranking third among the two-term presidencies (including Kennedy-Johnson) in table 4-2. The totals are as follows: Nixon-Ford (seventy-four pieces), Kennedy-Johnson (fifty-six), Clinton (forty), Reagan (thirty-seven), and Eisenhower (thirty-one). Perhaps surprisingly, more than a quarter of the Clinton-era bills in Mayhew's list were passed in 1996 alone. In 1994 the Republicans had won a majority in the House for the first time in forty years. Led by Speaker Newt Gingrich (R-Ga.), they aggressively pursued an agenda that had been formed as a campaign document for the 1994 midterm elections. The budget confrontation with the president during fall 1995 was so intense that portions of the government were shut down. Prospects for the passage of major legislation in 1996 were judged to be slight. Yet eleven major bills were passed, tying with three other years for the third most pieces of major legislation enacted in a single year.

To some degree this outpouring might be attributed to increases in public standing of the president. In the aftermath of the 1994 elections, Clinton's status had declined to such a point (40 percent) that he was moved to declare his "relevance" in a public speech—just prior to the bombing of the Alfred P. Murrah Federal Office Building in Oklahoma City on April 19, 1995. National tragedies typically highlight the president's symbolic role as leader. As with Bush 43 after the 9/11 disaster, Clinton became the national symbol of leadership. In such instances, public desires make it so.

Clinton's approval ratings did not improve dramatically in April 1995—a five-point increase to 51 percent in the week following the tragedy—but the recovery had begun. Furthermore, he personally gained confidence as his public status improved, and with the assistance of political consultant Dick Morris began to develop a strategy for winning reelection in 1996. The 1995 budget battle with congressional Republicans was the test of Clinton's recovery. Speaker Gingrich expressed doubt that the president could resist the will of the country, as he interpreted it. Asked in the spring of 1995 whether congressional Republicans would press to have their way even "to the point of shutting down the government," Gingrich responded, "If that's what it takes . . . I'm not sure the President will want to be in the position of shutting down the government in order to block something that most of the people in the country want."[59] This early judgment could not account for a political recovery that would alter the president's "position," making his interpretation of the country's mood significantly more competitive. In the event, Clinton, not Gingrich, won the budget battle.

As regards the specifics of Clinton's legislative record, his first year in office was the second most productive of important legislation (seven pieces) in his presidency and a most respectable first-year record (tied in second place for a newly elected president). The legislation fell into three groups. The first was a set of bills passed by the Democratic 102nd Congress but vetoed by President Bush, including a Family and Medical Leave Act, the so-called motor voter act to facilitate voter registration, and the Brady bill, which required a waiting period for the purchase of handguns.

Campaign finance reform legislation, also passed by the 102nd Congress and vetoed by Bush, was not sent to Clinton. The second group included two big-ticket items that were the most significant actions taken in 1993. The Omnibus Deficit Reduction Act, especially controversial because it contained tax hikes, passed in the Senate with the tie-breaking vote of the vice president, and in the House by just two votes (see chapter 7). The North American Free Trade Agreement, initially negotiated by the previous administration, divided the Democrats and passed only with the support of Republicans. The third group included Clinton initiatives, the most notable of which was an AmeriCorps program offering college education grants for community service.

The second year of the Clinton presidency produced just four major pieces of legislation, by Mayhew's count. Of the four, the most notable were an Omnibus Crime Act (which nearly lost in the House when the rule for debating it was defeated) and the General Agreement on Tariffs and Trade (GATT). But these successes were overshadowed by a more telling defeat—that of the president's national health care plan. It failed to get a vote in either house.

The 104th Congress had Republican majorities, and its first session featured the budget battles discussed above. Only four major pieces of legislation passed, one over Clinton's veto. No one of these—a curb on unfunded mandates to the states, lobbying reform, a congressional accountability act, and curbs on stockholder lawsuits—matched the significance of bills enacted either in the 103rd Congress or the second session of the 104th.

The second session, in 1996, was a remarkable demonstration of the workings of the separated system. The president's political status had been restored, the Republican Congress appeared anxious to recover after losing the budget fight, and an election was pending. The effect was a classic case of competitive partisanship producing agreement. Nearly a dozen pieces of major legislation were enacted, many including reforms that had been in the works for a long time, notably, welfare reform, immigration reform, farm support deregulation, telecommunications regulation, health insurance portability, overhaul of safe drinking water regulation, and the line-item veto. No one predicted the president's demonstration of his checkmating capability in 1995 would provide the incentive for such an outpouring of legislation in 1996. Yet, as discussed above, his success was the result of improved status during the summer and fall of 1995. As shown in figure 4-8, voters rewarded both parties: President Clinton was easily reelected, and the Republicans maintained their majority status in both houses of Congress.

Production of major legislation during Clinton's second term was the lowest among two-term postwar presidents. The Kennedy-Johnson and Nixon-Ford years produced over twice as much major legislation, but even Eisenhower's and Reagan's second terms were more productive (see table 4-2). Of the fourteen major actions under Clinton, clearly the most important was the historic balanced budget agreement with Congress in 1997. Mayhew's year-by-year summary of Clinton's second term is as follows:

—1997: Omnibus balanced budget agreement, chemical weapons treaty, Food and Drug Administration reform, facilitation of the adoption of abused children.

—1998: Omnibus transportation construction act, Internal Revenue Service reform, NATO expansion, public housing program reform.

—1999: Banking system reform, limit liability for shifting to 2000 calendar, greater flexibility for states' use of federal education funds.

—2000: Trading relations with China, Florida Everglades restoration, community renewal and development.

As shown in figure 4-8, President Clinton's approval ratings rose markedly during the second term. Why, then, was there not a greater production of major legislation? With occasional exceptions, the incentives for agreements between the president and Congress were many fewer. In particular, the Lewinsky scandal, the report to the House of Representatives by independent counsel Kenneth Starr, and the impeachment and Senate trial that ensued prevented the type of cooperation that characterized 1996 and 1997. Competitive partisanship was distorted by these unsettling developments. One result was the refinement of the agenda, which then came to influence the 2000 election.

Bush 43

The George W. Bush presidency is an equally interesting case of public standing in a separated system as the Clinton presidency, but for different reasons. Data are incomplete at this writing, but enough of interest has occurred to make comparisons with other postwar presidents. Figure 4-9 provides the quarterly averages of Bush's Gallup Poll approval ratings during his first term. As is evident, Bush began with modest averages, perhaps somewhat higher than might have been expected given his narrow win and early assessments of his competence. There was little improvement during the spring and summer of 2001. Scores ranged from a high of 62 in April to a low of 51 in early September. Typically, the raw

Figure 4-9. *Presidential Approval Ratings, Bush 43 Administration (First Term)*[a]

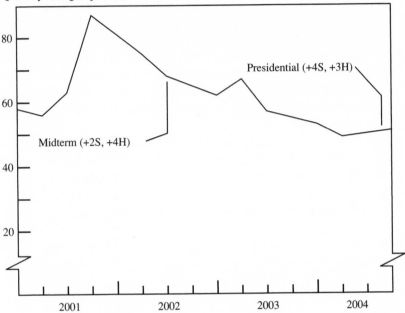

Quarterly averages (percent)

Source: Calculated from Gallup Poll data in the *Gallup Report*, various issues.
a. Legends denote net electoral gains or losses for the president's party in the Senate (S) and House (H).

ratings were close to the means; only four fell below 55 percent from the first test to September 10.

Bush's job approval ratings increased dramatically immediately after September 11: 51 percent positive in a poll taken September 7–10; 86 percent in a poll taken September 14–15, and 90 percent in a September 21–22 poll. Subsequently, his scores did not drop below 85 percent until January 2002, 80 percent until March, or 75 percent until June. No president had ever sustained support of this magnitude over such a long period.

The 2002 midterm election results defied historical trends. Republicans had a net gain of two Senate seats, and as a result recaptured majority status. They also had a net gain of four seats in the House. It was the first time since 1934 that the president's party realized a midterm net increase in both houses of Congress (though it hardly matched the Democrats' gains in that year—eleven Senate seats and fourteen House seats). President Bush campaigned actively in 2002. He was credited with positively affecting the result but criticized for capitalizing on the war on terrorism. As it happened, however, the Senate races in 2002 were overwhelmingly in states that had been won by Bush in 2000—primarily in the South, the Midwest, and the mountain states. It is conceivable that these seats would have been won by Republicans without the president's campaigning.

The record of major legislation enacted in the 107th Congress (2001–03) was impressive: seven pieces in the first session, ten in the second. Bush's first year tied with Clinton's for the second highest number of major enactments for a newly elected president in the postwar period. The number enacted in Bush's second year tally was also the second highest for that year, less than the sixteen enacted under Nixon but greater than all others. This record can be attributed to Bush's high approval ratings, but only in the context of the many urgent issues associated with the national security crisis that had enhanced his status. These same issues account for Bush's dramatic increase in job approval ratings, and so a positive correlation is apparent. However, it was a time during which Congress's job approval ratings also increased, as classic bipartisanship was featured in lawmaking. Strong support for both the president and Congress tends to result in legislative production.

A review of the seventeen major pieces of legislation shows the dominance of the war on terrorism (those items directly related are marked with an asterisk):

—2001: Tax cut, education reform, use of force resolution*, USA Patriot Act*, emergency spending*, airline bailout*, airport security*

—2002: campaign finance reform, bioterrorism defense*, agricultural subsidies, Corporate Accountability Act, trade authority, election reform, Iraq war resolution*, Homeland Security Department established*, terrorism insurance*, independent September 11 Commission established*

In all, ten of the seventeen items were directly related to the war on terrorism. Without them, the record for the first Congress of the Bush presidency would have been the lowest in the postwar period. Two comments are relevant. First, September 11 supplanted the agenda being worked on at the time (for example, immigration reform, patients' bill of rights, energy reform). Other bills might well have passed had Congress continued with the regular order. Second, one measure of the success of any political system is its capacity to respond to crises. The aftermath of 9/11 demonstrated the responsiveness of the separated system to a challenge of historic proportions.

The limitations of presidential influence were illustrated during the fall of 2001. At a time when he was receiving better than 85 percent approval scores, Bush sought to have Congress enact several pieces of domestic legislation. The administration argued that energy reform, an economic stimulus package, and trade authority were associated with the war on terrorism. Democrats disagreed. These measures passed in the Republican House, but were then either defeated or stalled in the Senate.

The legislative production of the 1996 reelection year was not to be replicated in 2004. The similarities included strong competitive partisanship, a senior senator as presidential challenger (Bob Dole in 1996, John Kerry in 2004), and a full agenda of issues. But they were far outweighed by the differences: the president's party had House and Senate majorities, a controversial war was under way, the president's status was eroding rather than improving, and economic recovery was sluggish. As shown in figure 4-9, President Bush could no longer claim impressive public approval of his job performance, thus encouraging the type of opposition to his proposals that his father had experienced in his 1992 reelection bid. The Republican margin in the Senate was so narrow that bills continued to be passed in the House and then stalled by filibuster threats in the Senate.

The 2004 election returned an all-Republican government. It did not dramatically change the numbers, however. The marginal public standing of the president, as measured by the first job approval rating taken after the election (53 percent), essentially confirmed his narrow win in the popular vote (51 percent). The largest difference from the first term was the notably larger Republican margin in the Senate. A net increase of four seats meant that the Republicans were within five votes of being able to thwart a filibuster and thus making it possible to enact more of the president's program. Yet although the election did not bring much change, President Bush moved confidently to reshape his presidency and announce a substantial agenda of reform for his second term.

Public Approval and the Work of Government

The greater attention to public approval of the president's performance can be explained in part by the desire to have interim readings for presidents whose party is either not in the majority in Congress or has the narrowest of margins. The diffusion of responsibility that is characteristic of split-party government is unsatisfying to those who are eager to assign liability. The reasoning appears to be that a president with a high approval rating should use it to get legislation enacted. There is a presumption that members of Congress will fall into line and support him on the basis of his public standing. This same reasoning would indicate that presidents with low ratings should not actively press their policy preferences, but rather allow the majority party in Congress to shape the agenda.

In fact, testing the president's job performance has come to be a process with a life of its own. Presidents are tested more often, the media treat the results as relevant to policy and politics, and the White House, in turn, worries about the ratings and seeks to manage them. Presidents are said to "go public" more often, but of course presidents *are* public. They cannot fail to be the major political figure, given their treatment by the modern media.

Trying to read policy consequences from the public's reaction to presidential job performance is even more difficult than interpreting elections for the same purposes. Therefore, going public is unlikely to be a very productive or coercive strategy for a president who is weak on Capitol Hill. Still, a president may not have a choice, either because of media demands or because he has so few other advantages. Thus it may come to be a factor in bargaining, although the experience of the two Bushes suggests that it does not carry much weight.

How important are the ratings for electoral and legislative outcomes? Congressional candidates from the president's party surely prefer to have positive approval scores, for the good reason that low scores indicate that things are not going well. But the evidence suggests that high scores are no guarantee of net increases for the president's party in Congress, nor, as Gary C. Jacobson has shown, do they automatically overcome divisiveness on policy issues.[60] Further, the lawmaking process is clearly not held hostage to the president's popular appeal. Legislative production does not turn on the popularity of the president. The Eisenhower years produced the fewest major laws on an annual basis; and the Nixon-Ford years, the most. Some presidents want little, others want a lot; and some who want little find they have to respond to congressional initiatives. Meager production in one era may spawn significant output later. The work of government hinges more on the nature of the agenda than on periodic tests of presidential job performance.

Although the public standing of the president is a part of how the system works, it is not a very important part. It provides a spot reading from a sample of respondents as to how things are going. But Harry Truman had it right: a president who seeks to govern by maintaining high approval ratings has been distracted from his main duties. Presidencies are neither destroyed nor saved by these ratings, and lawmaking does not await tests of presidential job performance.

CHAPTER 5

Presidents, Mandates, and Agendas

Presidents are expected to govern: to know about, perhaps to manage, the workload of government. Personal and political advantages, organization and appointments, and public backing are resources directed to this purpose. Proponents of the perspective of a responsible party government and an activist chief executive expect presidents to enter office with policy proposals, perhaps even a vision. By this view, good elections grant mandates, and mandates imply agendas and a will to see them acted on. The good and effective president is one who brings work to the government and aggressively manages the work that is already under way. He is a firm and productive leader of the national policy process and therefore can justifiably be held accountable by the voters at election time.

However appealing this formulation might be, there are numerous barriers to its realization in a separated system. Some are constitutional in nature; others are political or related to an annual budget now exceeding two trillion dollars. I begin with the constitutional impediments. The Founders were not ignorant of the potential advantages of accountability or classically responsible government, but they found greater advantages in a system of diffused responsibility.

Elections and Agendas in the Constitution

The Constitution clearly specifies the terms of office for the president and members of Congress, providing for elections by the calendar, not in response to the emergence of issues or crises. The president "shall hold his office during the term of four years; The House of Representatives shall be composed of members chosen every second year; The Senate of the United States shall be composed of two senators from each state . . . for six years." For much of the nineteenth century, presidential and congressional elections occurred at different times, further confounding any direct or unified policy message. It was not until the latter years of that century that the elections for the three institutions occurred on the same day every four years.

Although longer presidential terms were proposed and discussed at the Constitutional Convention, a four-year term was approved, with no limit on the number of terms. A one-term president serves the equivalent of two House terms, or two-thirds of a Senate term. Presidents were limited to two terms by precedent until Franklin D. Roosevelt broke with tradition and ran and was elected four times. Following Roosevelt's record, the Twenty-Second Amendment was ratified in 1951, limiting a president to two terms.

Before the 1930s, any ardor for specific issues or policies realized from the campaign and the election cooled off during the long period between the election and the inauguration. By precedent, the terms of the president and members of Congress ended on March 4. At that time the new president was inaugurated, but Congress typically did not meet until the following December (as provided in article I, section 2, of the Constitution). For most members of Congress, therefore, this first meeting was more than a year after their election. The Twentieth Amendment, ratified in 1933, corrected this oddity, moving forward inauguration to January 20 and the meeting of the new Congress to January 3.

Nowhere does the Constitution even hint at the possibility of holding elections as a result of a crisis or some issue configuration. Constitutional provisions for removing a president from office could conceivably have led to issue-based elections. That is, had an early president resigned for failure to have key elements of his program enacted, or had the "inability to discharge the powers and duties of the . . . office" been interpreted as failing to command majorities in Congress, then a precedent for issue-based elections would have been established. This did not happen. And, in any event, the provision for succession was that the vice president would assume the duties of the president. Should both be removed, Congress would then provide for succession.

Elections legitimate the government and therefore are highly relevant to agenda setting. An election should not ordinarily be treated as a national policy test. Yet most elections are interpreted as such: the presidential election for whether and how voters endorse proposals made by the winning

Figure 5-1. *Electoral Time Line: President, Representatives, Senators*

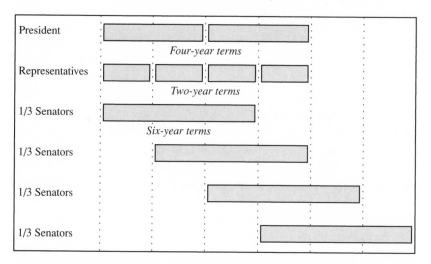

Source: Charles O. Jones, "Separating to Govern: The American Way," in Byron E. Shafer, ed., *Present Discontents: American Politics in the Very Late Twentieth Century* (Chatham, N.J.: Chatham House, 1997), p. 54.

candidate, and the midterm elections for what they reveal about how the president is managing his job. In fact, when the issue content is obscure, as in 1984 or 1988, most analysts are critical of the candidates, the political parties, and even the system. They often call for reform. But interpreting American elections as issue events that invest presidents and members of Congress with a mandate distorts constitutional intent and political practice.

Figure 5-1 depicts the electoral time lines of a two-term president, the House, and the Senate. Consider an election in which certain House members from the president's party believe that they won because of a landslide victory by the president, as perhaps with Johnson's win in 1964. These members may logically feel beholden to the president and provide support for his program. In two years, however, they are on their own. The president is not on the ballot and voter turnout will be lower. In other words they must prepare for a very different election at the midterm. The record shows that a huge proportion of incumbents get very good at winning both with and without presidents on the ballot, more evidence in support of the separation they see between their elections and those for presidents.

Then consider that same landslide election as viewed by senators from the president's party. Again, some may interpret their victories as related to that of the president and be moved to support his program. But their six-year term means that they will be up for reelection in the middle of the president's second term, if he has a second term. Senators elected in the first midterm will seek reelection at the end of the president's second term; those elected with his reelection are up at the midterm of his successor; and those elected at his second midterm, at the end of his successor's first term. The lesson is obvious: senators' electoral fates are seldom linked to those of the president. Ordinarily, those elected with a president will never again run with him. Therefore, presidents must continually work for support in the Senate, even within their party.

Yet the concept of the "mandate" lives in spite of these constitutional barriers to its realization. It is an essential element of the party responsibility perspective, because of its agenda-laden implications. Therefore I discuss it first. I then consider what the agenda is at any one time and how presidential preferences about issues can be and are folded into agenda politics. As commonly used, the term *agenda* refers to several different policy-related matters: a set of continuing problems more or less unaffected by elections; an orientation or a dominant policy preference—sometimes liberal, sometimes conservative; a crisis that overrides or displaces current policy problems; and presidential initiatives, variably interpreted as emanating from a mandate. I attempt to distinguish among these uses of the term, incorporating the findings of scholars who view the agenda in dynamic terms.

Finally, I addresss the differences observed among the postwar presidents and place each president's policy or programmatic efforts in the context of the ongoing agenda. This latter exercise identifies the opportunities presidents have for influencing and altering the agenda, as well as the limitations that may force them to work "at the margins," as George C. Edwards III puts it.

The Mandate

Given the separation of elections and variable term lengths for elected officials, why are mandates discussed at all? Why should one expect that an election would convey a mandate for policy action? What is it that leads analysts to expect, want, and demand that issue definition be the central purpose of elections? A number of distinguished scholars have thought about these questions, arguing persuasively that the concept is not useful in the American political setting. Of these, Raymond E. Wolfinger is most blunt: "Mandates are inherently implausible. . . . As Chairman Mao might have said, 'Many issues, one vote.'"[1] Henry Jones Ford would have added "several elections" to Wolfinger's paraphrasing of Chairman Mao. He stated this principle: "The greater the number of elections the less is their effect on public policy!"[2]

In *A Preface to Democratic Theory,* Robert A. Dahl severely challenges the idea of a policy mandate. Here is a sample of relevant propositions:

> On matters of specific policy the majority rarely rules. . . .
>
> Strictly speaking, all an election reveals is the first preferences of some citizens among the candidates standing for office. . . .
>
> We can rarely interpret a majority of first choices among candidates in a national election as being equivalent to a majority of first choices for a specific policy. . . .
>
> Most interelection policy seems to be determined by the efforts of relatively small but relatively active minorities. . . . If you examine carefully any policy decision . . . you will always discover, I believe, that only a quite tiny proportion of the electorate is actively bringing its influence to bear upon politicians.[3]

In an extended review of the mandate concept, Dahl concluded that the Framers had no such notion in mind in designing an elected executive. "The theory of the presidential mandate not only cannot be found in the Framers' conception of the Constitution; almost certainly it violates that conception." He concludes that the mandate was not accepted in practice during the nineteenth century by presidents themselves, most having espoused the Whig perspective that Congress was the representative institution. The president's power was that of an executive. "Even Abraham Lincoln, in justifying the unprecedented scope of presidential power he believed he needed in order to meet secession and civil war, rested his case on constitutional grounds, and not as a mandate from the people."[4]

Yet one renowned political scientist, Woodrow Wilson, did articulate a theory of presidential mandate, motivated by his concern that congressional government was not working well. "By 1908, when *Constitutional Government in the United States* was published, Wilson had arrived at strong presidential leadership as a feasible solution" to the problem of congressional government.[5] It is worth quoting at length to convey both the logic and the verve of Wilson's argument in favor of the contemporary presidency. Clearly the prospect of the mandated president, as leader of his party and the nation, excited him. In the passage below he establishes the public legitimacy of a president's leadership as a basis for his obligation to take charge. If he fails, the responsibility is his: "His capacity will set the limit."

He cannot escape being the leader of his party except by incapacity and lack of personal force, because he is at once the choice of the party and of the nation. . . . Members of the House and Senate are representatives of localities, are voted for only by sections of voters, or by local bodies of electors like the members of the state legislatures. There is no national party choice except that of President. No one else represents the people as a whole, exercising a national choice; and inasmuch as his strictly executive duties are in fact subordinated . . . the President represents not so much the party's governing efficiency as its controlling ideals and principles. He is not so much part of its organization as its vital link of connection with the thinking nation. He can dominate his party by being spokesman for the real sentiment and purpose of the country, by giving direction to opinion, by giving the country at once the information and the statements of policy that will enable it to form its judgments alike of parties and of men.[6]

Having established the president's legitimacy as a representative and a policy spokesman, Wilson turned directly to the matter of the president's obligation to exercise leadership and the obligation to others to follow. "The President is at liberty, both in law and conscience, to be as big a man as he can." And how might that happen in a system of separated elections?

Let him once win the admiration and confidence of the country, and no other single force can withstand him, no combination of forces will easily overpower him. . . . He is the representative of no constituency, but of the whole people. When he speaks in his true character, he speaks for no special interest. If he rightly interpret the national thought and boldly insist upon it, he is irresistible; and the country never feels the zest of action so much as when its President is of such insight and calibre. Its instinct is for unified action, and it craves a single leader. It is for this reason that it will often prefer to choose a man rather than a party. A President whom it trusts can not only lead it, but form it to his own views.[7]

Wilson's argument is close to that of a more contemporary president, likened to Wilson by some. Jimmy Carter described the president's role before winning in 1976: "Congress is inherently incapable of unified leadership. That leadership has got to come from the White House. . . . There's no one in any congressional district in the nation that won't be my constituent if I become President."[8] Later, upon completing his service in the White House, Carter explained in Wilsonian style: "Members of Congress, buffeted from all sides, are much more vulnerable to these groups [powerful lobbies] than is the President. One branch of government must stand fast on a particular issue to prevent the triumph of self-interest at the expense of the public."[9]

Wilson and Carter outline a trusteeship of the public interest, by which the president is invested with the responsibility of overcoming the natural tendency of members of Congress to accede to the pressures of special interests. Their view is, however, very much in the tradition of strong presidential leadership of party government (with Wilson more willing than Carter to lead through his party, though insistent on defining what his party will support).

How can presidents know that they have been invested with custody of a national purpose? Voter intentions at election time are often not clear, whatever is said on the day after. And as Dahl notes, "The systematic analysis of survey evidence that is necessary (though perhaps not sufficient) to interpret what a presidential election means always comes well after presidents and commentators have already told the world, on wholly inadequate evidence, what the election means."[10]

The 1980 election is illustrative. Analysis of survey data following that election cast serious doubt on the proposition that voters were consciously awarding Ronald Reagan a mandate for his conservative, antigovernment proposals. Many voters were rejecting Carter, but not necessarily approving Reagan. And yet under the circumstances of a postelection rush to judgment, it was unlikely that the new president would urge caution. In fact, had he stated that he did not plan to press for his program until he heard from the professional analysts of voting behavior, he would have been criticized for betraying the voters' trust.

There is a problem, however. The implausibility of the mandate seemingly cannot prevent its use. As Dahl points out, it is "now too deeply rooted in American political life and too useful a part of the political arsenal of presidents to be abandoned."[11] It is just plain handy during those frantic hours following an election when commentators want a simple explanation of what happened in a complex series of elections. Here is how one prominent journalist put it: "Elections should be a mandate for something. If elections aren't a mandate for something, then what do they mean?"[12]

Dahl has the answer to this journalist's question: an election "confers the legitimate authority, right, and opportunity on a president to try to gain the adoption by constitutional means of the policies the president supports."[13] This formulation is consistent with the constitutional separation of powers as perpetuated by the separation of elections, precisely the alternative perspective I espouse in this book. In fact, it sounds very much like the analysis offered by Richard E. Neustadt in his definition of presidential power as "persuasion," varying among presidents because of their differences in personal, public, and political sources of power. I suggest a clarification, however. The policies the president supports may not always require expansion of government. Some presidents may propose consolidation, even contraction, of government. Thus analysts need to take account of alternative strategies to those associated with an activist president or one promoting large-scale social programs. Voters sometimes elect—even resoundingly—presidents who have made few policy promises.

Whatever the policy preferences of the president, consideration also must be given to the independent nature of the agenda. As Frank R. Baumgartner and Bryan D. Jones describe it, "Any study of the dynamics of American political institutions must be able to account for both long periods of stability and short, violent periods of change—again, with respect to the processing of issues, not in the basic constitutional framework."[14] These periods do not necessarily coincide with presidential administrations. There is a whole world of policy outside the White House, a world in which presidents seek their place.

The structural implausibility of the mandate, the plausibility of power as persuasion, and the agenda-bending effects of dramatic events are unlikely to overcome the next-day convenience of the idea of a mandate in explaining election outcomes. The mandate is a classic example of an illusion becoming reality in the context of power as persuasion. If others declare that the voters have invested in a president the right to pursue particular policy goals, then he may be expected to rely on that interpretation as a source of power. Indeed, he may well be judged by whether he uses this strength to whatever advantage it has been defined to convey; if he does not, there may be talk of his having "wasted his mandate." Further, even if survey data later show that many voters were saying no to the loser rather than yes to the winner and his program, members of Congress and others in Washington may acknowledge a mandate as a hedge in case the president develops a strongly positive policy standing within their constituencies or among their clienteles. Thus the preposterous can become genuine and may contribute to expectations that cannot, perhaps should not, be met. Still, presidents are well advised to be cautious in accepting a mandate or in declaring one on their own.

Judgments about Mandates

A review of postelection analyses in the postwar era suggests several uses of the mandate concept: the perceived mandate for change, the status quo mandate, the mixed or nonmandate, and the unmandate. These categories direct attention to how analysts read elections for issue messages.

Mandate for Change

The preferred outcome for party government advocates is a mandate for change. This is how an election meets the ideal conditions discussed in chapter 1: publicly visible issues, clear differences between the candidates, a substantial victory for the winner and his party in Congress, and a post-election declaration of party unity. Whatever the survey results show later by way of voter intentions, an election meeting these conditions will be perceived to have conveyed a mandate to the president as leader of his party.

The postwar elections that come closest to meeting these conditions are those in 1964 and 1980. A third possibility is the 1952 election, though it did not match the others in regard to differences between the candidates on issues or substantial gains for the president's party in Congress (due primarily to the narrow Republican majorities in each house). If all elections are placed on a continuum, there is little doubt that these three elections fall nearer to the "mandate for change" point. In all three cases, there were those who raised questions about whether the vote was for the new president or against his opponent (particularly in 1980). No analyst doubted, however, that these elections served as a major source of power for the new presidents, with varying legitimacy, clarity, and strength of their mandates.

The 1964 election presented postelection analysts with the most unambiguous case of a mandate for change. Some acknowledged that many voters were rejecting Goldwater, however, and that fact had an effect on how the returns were read for purposes of declaring a mandate. A *Washington Post* columnist wrote, "It is evident that the President's victory could best be interpreted as one either for him personally or against Sen. Goldwater personally, rather than a massive victory for the Democratic Party." *Time* magazine agreed: "As far as figures are concerned, the mandate could hardly have been written more clearly. But since the figures meant anti-Goldwater as much as pro-Johnson, carrying out the mandate will not follow automatically."[15]

But the main emphasis was on the strong policy message of the election, and, following Woodrow Wilson, the attendant responsibility of the president to convert this message into government action. Arthur Krock exemplified this point of view in the *New York Times*: "President Johnson has four years in which to supply the answer to the great question created by the most emphatic vote of preference ever given to a national candidate: How will he use the mandate to lead and govern that has been so overwhelmingly tendered by the American people?" An editorial in that paper proclaimed that the "overwhelming vote for the Johnson-Humphrey ticket reflects popular attachment to the policies of moderate liberalism." And a *Washington Post* editorial described the mandate as "clear and unmistakable" and "essentially, a mandate to pursue a national consensus at home and abroad with restraint and common sense."[16]

The 1980 election raised even more questions as to exactly what message was being sent by the voters. After all, Jimmy Carter was the first Democratic incumbent to be defeated since Grover Cleveland in 1888. *Time*'s commentary was typical:

> Though the conservative trend of the country was obvious from the results, Reagan's mandate was a good deal less than indicated by his 489 electoral votes. . . . His victory was surely not so much an endorsement of his philosophy as an overwhelming rejection of Jimmy Carter, a President who could not convince the nation that he had mastered his job.[17]

For James Reston, the election did not convey a policy mandate for Reagan: "Obviously there has been a conservative sweep of opinion in the nation. . . . But it does not follow that a Reagan administration can impose a dramatic, conservative set of policies on a Congress still dominated by Democrats."[18]

Much of the commentary was muted. This was surprising, given that a party declared virtually dead after Watergate had ousted an incumbent president and won a majority in the Senate for the first time in twenty-eight years (casting doubt on Reston's analysis that Congress was still dominated by Democrats). Could it be that a new era was dawning? Or did the results merely represent voter dissatisfaction with President Carter? The results both stunned and perplexed the analysts, and they were cautious in their responses. According to David Broder, "Victorious Republicans and decimated Democrats looked back yesterday at an election that gave the national government its sharpest turn to the right in a generation and wondered if 1980 would go into the history books as the start of a new era of conservative and Republican dominance." A *Washington Post* editorial agreed that "Governor Reagan surely has both a strong public mandate and strong personal inclination to do something. . . . But we have no doubt that some large part of Tuesday's Democratic liberal defeat must have been owing to dissatisfaction with [Carter] and his economic and foreign policy handiwork."[19]

It is interesting that even the purest cases of the mandate, by their own criteria, do not satisfy the demands of party government advocates. Commentators express caution because of the weakness of the opponent, the

lack of clarity of policy positions, lack of knowledge of the precise intentions of the voters, or the failure to win full control of Congress. Yet they
acknowledge that something unusual has happened and are willing to use
the term freely, sometimes with the implication that a president will be
tested subsequently by whether he satisfies it, and them.

In the third election in this group, in 1952, a military hero viewed as a
political outsider won a substantial victory and his party won majorities,
albeit narrowly, in both houses of Congress for the first time since 1928.
But reading the returns for policy messages was not simple. General Eisenhower had defeated the true conservative, Senator Robert A. Taft (Ohio), for
the Republican nomination. Thus there was no nice, clean choice between
conservatism and liberalism. A common interpretation was that the election
was a "personal" victory for Eisenhower, not a real win for the Republican
Party. The mandate was for a "fresh start" or for "leadership," typically
without any specified goal (presumably a goal would have been apparent
had the win been for the party rather than personal). These characteristics
naturally cast doubt on the victory as a party government mandate and no
doubt encouraged analysts to predict problems for the outsider president as
he worked with his own party in Congress.

The following selections reflect the analytical themes in the immediate
postelection period. Arthur Krock of the *New York Times* spoke for the view
that it was a personal, not party, victory: "That General Eisenhower, and not
the Republican Party, was the principal reason for the termination of the
Democratic tenure in the White House . . . was made evident by the result
of the contests for Congress." *Time* agreed: "Ike generally ran well ahead of
G.O.P. Congressmen. . . . Hence his victory was clearly more of a personal
victory than a party victory." Yet *Time* used the term "mandate for leadership," and *Newsweek* also supported the notion of a generalized mandate:
"The voters chose the future. And they chose Eisenhower and the Republican Party as its custodians. . . . Congress . . . will honor Eisenhower's fresh
mandate from the people by giving him almost anything he requests."[20] And
pundit Walter Lippmann carried the theme to new heights:

> The mighty majority which the people have given him is conclusive. He is
> the captive of no man and no faction. He is free, as few men in so high an
> office have ever been, to be the servant of his own conscience. For his man-
> date from the people is one of the greatest given in modern times and it is
> beyond dispute.[21]

The mandate for change carries with it expectations for policy action by
the White House. Paul C. Light's recommendation to "move it or lose it" is

clearly most appropriate for presidents under these circumstances, assuming, of course, that they have a program to move.[22] However, the act of perceiving a mandate does not annul or overcome the continuing set of issues on the national agenda or the lack of uniform term lengths for the president, representatives, and senators. Rather, the widespread perception of a license to make change becomes a potential resource that can strengthen the president's hand in setting priorities and identifying alternatives. And it is transitory for all of the reasons identified by Dahl and Wolfinger: it was never that presumptive in the first place.

Mandate for the Status Quo

The persistence of the mandate concept in the lexicon of political analysis is amply illustrated by elections in which the president is reelected by a landslide but his political party fails to garner majorities in Congress. The postwar cases are 1956, 1972, and 1984. (In 1984 the Republicans did have a majority in one house of Congress, the Senate, though with a net loss of one seat.) A fourth case, 1996, is a variation on this pattern: a Democrat, Clinton, was reelected by a significant but not a landslide margin and the Democrats remained the minority in Congress. Working from the party government model, analysts insist on employing the term *mandate* when a president is overwhelmingly reelected. In the first three elections, that was definitely the case: the combined electoral vote split was Republican candidates, 1,502 (winning 139 states); Democratic candidates, 103 (winning just 9 states).

A standard conclusion about the status quo mandate is that the president has won, not his party. Typically the analysis is cast in disapproving terms. In spite of an electoral system and campaigning practices that permit, even facilitate, split-ticket voting, the president is expected to deliver Congress and the state offices for his party. Failure to do so is judged a weakness for him and for the system. In 1956 a typical assessment was that "the Eisenhower victory was a personal endorsement and not a victory for the Republican Party." In 1972 Republican National Party Chairman Bob Dole explained that "this is a personal triumph for Mr. Nixon, and not a party triumph." And in 1984 Haynes Johnson attributed "the great landslide" to "personal affection for Reagan and better feelings about the country" rather than "a strong national tide leading to some great ideological realignment of the two political parties."[23] In 1996 poll data provided an explanation for the split results: Clinton and the Republicans drew from very different segments of the population, with only one in seven voters in both coalitions—a "two majorities" argument.[24]

There were differences in how postelection analysts viewed these results and their effects. Although there was general agreement that voters supported continuance, what was to be continued varied among the four presidents. For Eisenhower, the landslide was said to represent "an opportunity to consolidate his domestic program of moderate social advance in a stable economy, while living up to his pledges to do everything possible to preserve peace in the world."[25] Also reiterated was the voters' "confidence" in his leadership. There was no effort to suggest that Eisenhower voters were really voting against Adlai Stevenson.

For Nixon, however, it was suggested that the size of his victory could be attributed to the weakness of his opponent. Arthur Krock wrote: "The huge popular majority was merely registering its judgment that his opponent was not of Presidential caliber." Thus questions were raised about the extent to which the sweeping victory conveyed added authority. One editorial put it this way: "There is no evidence from the election at the Congressional level that the country is either seething with discontent or carried away by the glories of the Nixon Administration."[26]

In 1984 there was little suggestion that a vote for Reagan was a vote against Walter Mondale; in fact, one comment was that "for the first time in at least a dozen years, Americans were voting for rather than against."[27] But there was an ideological cast to the interpretations of this election. For some, to continue, or to maintain the status quo, meant accepting a conservative approach to public policy, and there was even talk of a "mandate for continuation of [Reagan's] conservative policies." Others questioned the extent to which the results endorsed Reagan's ideology: "Tuesday's mandate, as in most Presidential elections when times are good, is a broad instruction to keep them good."[28]

Commentary on the 1996 election expressed concern that President Clinton had worked with the Republican Congress, thus making a less clear policy choice for voters. One seasoned observer explained that Clinton "adopted Republican programs, even changing previous positions on many issues" during the 104th Congress. "He won reelection, but at the cost of the loss of policy initiatives."[29] As a consequence, expectations favored the status quo in presidential-congressional relations, but the presidency had been diminished.

It might be argued that a fifth postwar election also fits into this category of the "status quo mandate": the interesting and unusual election of 1988.

It has many of the characteristics of an approval election. For the first time since 1836, a vice president directly succeeded the president he had served, and for the first time since 1928 a party was returned to the White House (not including reelections or vice presidents who served as president and then won election, such as Truman).

George H. W. Bush did not win by the same overwhelming margin as did Eisenhower, Nixon, and Reagan in their reelections. Still, he won handily, exceeding Nixon's first-term margin, coming close to Eisenhower's, and exceeding Clinton's reelection margin in the Electoral College (though not his share of the two-party vote). But Republicans had small net losses in the House and the Senate, thus encouraging analysts to downplay any talk of a Bush mandate. According to Broder, "If the voters meant that either as a personal accolade or a policy mandate, they muffled the signal by giving Democrats a renewed vote of confidence in congressional and state elections." The election was described as one "that affirmed the status quo and the reluctance of the American electorate to give either party a real vote of confidence." Thus Bush was said to have won "a decisive victory and a personal vindication, but no clear mandate." And in a frank expression of the perceived importance of political analysts, the *New York Times* editorialized: "Thus it remains for partisans, pundits and, above all, for Mr. Bush to sculpt the mandate. The President-elect can do so only by fashioning ends and means and costs into policies that make sense."[30]

It is fascinating that elections returning an incumbent split-party government are interpreted within the context of a mandate. The search for issue instructions from an election continues in spite of evidence that such instructions can seldom be clearly identified.

The Mixed or Nonmandate

The 1988 election provides a perfect transition to the third category of mandates. It was truly on the borderline between status quo mandate and no discernible mandate. What encourages one to include it with the status quo mandates is simply the size of the victory for Bush. The four main candidates for the nonmandate category—1948, 1960, 1968, and 1976—feature extremely close presidential elections, among the closest in history. I also include the 1992, 2000, and 2004 elections in this group, although, as discussed below, they have a number of special characteristics.

The 1948 election is the most perplexing for analysts because of Truman's surprise victory. Most pollsters had predicted that Dewey would win. Yet Truman pulled it off in a three-way race, garnering less than 50 percent of the popular vote. At the same time, congressional Democrats pulled off an impressive triumph. They recaptured control of both houses, with a net gain of nine Senate seats and seventy-five House seats. What did it all mean? Interpretations varied.

On the one hand, there was Arthur Krock's classical party responsibility interpretation:

> Once more in our history, and at an essential time, a party is in power at both the White House and Congress with definite responsibility for the conduct of the government.
>   The voters of the nation have told the Democratic party to discharge this responsibility. The President's task as the party leader and the party's popular mandate are to compose Democratic differences to the degree required to govern.[31]

On the other hand, Raymond Moley warned, "President Truman should not consider this result a real popular endorsement of his own policies and methods of administration. . . . This election can hardly be taken as a mandate for the repeal of the Taft-Hartley Act or for a continuous increase in the rate of Federal expenditures."[32]

Commentators paid little attention to the discontinuity between the president's narrow win and the huge net gains for House and Senate Democrats. It was not easy for Truman to claim coattails. Further, J. Strom Thurmond, the Dixiecrat Democrat from South Carolina, won thirty-nine electoral votes, capturing four southern states. All these factors contributed to making the 1948 election one of the most difficult to interpret for those devoted to the mandate concept of American government.

Analyses of the 1960, 1968, and 1976 election outcomes were largely interchangeable. Fill in the blanks with John F. Kennedy, Richard M. Nixon, or Jimmy Carter:

> In the end, _____ won the election but not the mandate. . . .
> But an electorate that proved to be more cautious than apathetic, more unimpressed than dispirited, turned out in substantial numbers to produce a collectively narrow judgment. . . .

> It is a good thing that the election was so close. It should serve as a restraining force and as a reminder to the _____ Administration that it should proceed with caution and that it has no mandate to embark on drastic changes of policy, either foreign or domestic. . . .

> There is not much of a mandate here for anything, except a new face in the White House and that "New Leadership" in the Executive Branch which _____ was promising all along the campaign trail. . . .[33]

The correct matches are Jimmy Carter (1976) for the first statement, John Kennedy (1960) for the second, and Richard Nixon (1968) for the third.

The Carter and Kennedy elections were remarkably alike. The two men won with a similar combination of electoral votes from the South and the Northeast and sufficient pivotal wins in midwestern industrial states to ensure victory. The popular and electoral votes were also very similar: 49.7 percent and 56.3 percent, respectively, for Kennedy; and 50.1 percent and 55.2 percent, respectively, for Carter. In addition, both ran behind most Democratic House and Senate winners. House Democrats won 54.4 percent of the popular vote in 1960—almost 5 points ahead of Kennedy—and they ran 6 points ahead of Carter in 1976. These statistics are not encouraging for presidents seeking automatic support for their programs from Congress. Congressional Democrats would not ignore the White House, but their support had to be won on a basis other than the electoral success of the president in their districts.

Kennedy and Carter at least had Democratic majorities in Congress. In fact, Walter Lippmann even found a mandate for Kennedy: "Although the popular vote was very close . . . there is nothing ambiguous about Kennedy's majority. . . . He has a clear mandate to undertake what he promised to do."[34] In the case of Nixon, however, there was no Republican majority in either house of Congress. The judgment was uniform: no mandate "for any particular policy direction," and therefore the president was advised to proceed with caution.[35]

Nixon's win in 1968 was special. No newly elected president since the founding of the modern two-party system had entered office with his party in the minority in both houses of Congress. (Bush 41 was to suffer the same circumstances twenty years later.) There is ample reason to expect different behavior from presidents under these conditions. The election results violate several of the basic requirements of party government, yet they are wholly constitutional. Thus it seems only reasonable to search for another model to describe and evaluate presidential-congressional interaction in this type of split-party government. The party government model is of no more value to the analyst in this case than it is to a president who must meet the challenges of governing.

The 1992 election had several characteristics of the other mixed or non-mandate elections and yet was special in many ways. Clinton won comfortably in the Electoral College (69 percent of the vote, compared with 57 percent for Truman in 1948, and 56 percent each for Kennedy in 1960 and Nixon in 1968). Because Ross Perot's candidacy split the vote three ways, Clinton garnered a lower proportion of the popular vote than Michael Dukakis had in a losing cause in 1988. Yet Clinton's margin over Bush was substantially greater than that of the other nonmandate winners over their opponents. Although the House Democrats had a net loss of a few seats, the Democrats controlled both branches of government for the first time in twelve years and for just the second time in twenty-four years. Thus there was a strong temptation to declare an end to "gridlock," with the attendant expectations of a strong policy record for the new presidency.

For the most part, analysts doubted that the results constituted a mandate. They did marvel at Clinton's accomplishment, however, since many of them had declared his candidacy to be in deep difficulty during the campaign.

> The truth is that Bill Clinton deserves congratulation not just for prevailing in the contest but for having waged a strong, smart and civil campaign. It is certainly the case that neither the size of his victory nor the nature of his campaign rhetoric provides a clear and specific mandate or 1-2-3 agenda for action that all can agree on.[36]

Michael Kramer believed it was up to the president to define a mandate because "a majority of Americans voted for someone else," and "there is a vast difference between being an instrument *of* change and being a catalyst *for* change."[37] The notions that a president should quickly declare a mandate before anyone notices that there is none or because most people voted for someone else surely raise doubts about the meaningfulness, if not the popularity, of the concept.

Meanwhile, journalists covering Capitol Hill advised the new president that the end of political gridlock did not mean that there was "a compliant legislature ready to respond to [Clinton's] every command. Instead, Clinton is likely to be confronted by . . . a largely Democratic but freewheeling group of legislators who hunger for results but chafe at discipline, unaccustomed to dealing with a president of their own party and used to calling the shots for the party themselves."[38] This analysis by a veteran congressional reporter comes as bad news for those who expect smooth sailing under a unified party government. It is not in the least surprising to those attuned to the nature and workings of a separated system.

The 2000 election offered even more unusual features. Robert J. Samuelson wrote: "No self-respecting screenwriter would have submitted this election script. It is too contrived."[39] The results produced near perfect conditions for competitive partisanship. Both parties could point to wins; neither could claim a complete victory. Democrats had net increases in both houses of Congress, but failed to get majorities. Republicans reclaimed the White House but by the narrowest of margins in the Electoral College and a slim loss in the popular vote. James W. Ceaser and Andrew Busch, in their appropriately titled book *The Perfect Tie*, expected "governing without a mandate."

> The election of 2000 . . . delivered an unambiguous and unmistakable message: that there is no popular mandate of any kind. George W. Bush received nothing more than a key to his office. Neither party could make a plausible claim to be unambiguously in power. The reaction to the election on the part of party leaders was remarkable. Spokespersons of the two parties were strangely subdued. . . . All they laid claim to were the races they had actually won—nothing less, yet also nothing more.[40]

The lack of a mandate cannot halt governance. Bush 43 and the evenly divided Congress had to press forward, seeking to develop processes for setting the agenda and determining the sequence of issues. As it happened, there was an unusual agreement on the agenda during the 2000 presidential campaign, although Gore and Bush put forward very different proposals on the issues. Accordingly the president, as chief designator of issue sequence, pressed forward, and congressional Democrats responded with counterproposals (and when the defection of James Jeffords (R-Vt.) resulted in a Democratic majority in the Senate, they even designated the agenda in that body).

In 2004 President Bush was reelected by the smallest margins in eighty-eight years (that is, since Woodrow Wilson in 1916). His share of the two-party popular vote was just over 51 percent, and of the Electoral College vote just over 53 percent. The mean share of the two-party popular vote for other reelected presidents in the postwar era (Eisenhower, Nixon, Reagan, and Clinton) was 59 percent; of the Electoral College vote, 88 percent. Not surprisingly, therefore, the White House emphasized the raw vote totals. The president received more votes than any candidate in history, 61.1 million, and whereas he lost the popular vote in 2000, he won it in 2004 by more than three million votes. He also received the first outright majority in the popular vote since his father in 1988 (Clinton had been denied a majority by a third candidate, Ross Perot). Congressional Republicans had net gains of three House seats and four Senate seats.

Relying on the raw vote would surely introduce a new consideration for declaring a mandate. The second highest total in history was received by John Kerry, the third by Bush's opponent in 2000, Al Gore. At the time of their reelection, Eisenhower, Nixon, and Reagan each received the highest raw vote to date; Clinton received the third highest ever in his reelection bid in1996, with a third candidate in the race.

Bush's numbers were indeed impressive, reflecting not just the increase in population but a significantly higher turnout. But the case for a mandate would be a hard sell, given that none of the other postwar reelected presidents were judged to have had one. Yet, the term was once again freely used in describing what had happened. The Republican party was described as having "a rare monopoly of power in all three branches of government and a mandate, however slim, that did not exist four years ago."[41] Columnists disagreed on whether to award a mandate, mostly reflecting their political views. For Charles Krauthammer, "George Bush got his mandate." E. J. Dionne concluded that "a 51-48 percent victory is *not* a mandate."[42] The *Financial Times* expressed an internationalist perspective: "Bush Gets Mandate to Be Strong Abroad." In its view, "hard-nosed nationalism . . . in the perceived defence of US interests has now been democratically endorsed."[43]

Why, then, was the term *mandate* used in connection with Bush's second victory? Several points appear to be relevant. Many commentators and editorial writers did not expect him to win, as he had had many setbacks during the year, making the outcome of the election seem all the more striking. His goals were clearly set forth, thus lending a substantive basis for interpreting a mandate. His win in 2000 had been disputed, whereas the results in 2004 were clear. And, as distinct from other reelected postwar presidents, his party was also victorious in Congress (even defeating the Democratic leader of the Senate). The *Washington Post* found his win "remarkable" for many of these reasons, asserting that there was "no question as to his legitimacy." Mandate or no, "it would be odd if he did not now do everything within his power to realize his goals."[44]

The president himself explained in a news conference two days after he declared victory that he had "earned capital in the campaign, political capital, and now I intend to spend it."[45] He then mentioned the agenda on which he had campaigned. He did not use the term *mandate*. This formulation is suited to Dahl's explanation of an election as settling who has the legitimate right "to try to gain the adoption by constitutional means of the policies the president supports." The right to spend political capital in this endeavor is no guarantee of success or of public support for the effort in regard to any one proposal. The conferral of legitimacy was, in Bush's case, a confirmation of the status quo, in the sense that he promised to continue a nationalist foreign policy and to pursue many of the domestic proposals that had been stalled in the Senate in his first term. Yet Bush 43's impact on the subsequent agenda could be significant to potentially massive (see table 5-1, p. 208). President Bush declared that he intended to work for reforms of Social Security, Medicare, litigation (especially medical malpractice suits), immigration, and the tax code, and continue to fight a war on terrorism. Success in any one of these areas could profoundly affect future agendas.

The Unmandate

So far I have stressed how the mandate concept—a staple of the responsible party model of governing—is used by analysts to explain the policy effects of an election. Two points are evident from this review: despite its popularity, the concept has limited value for understanding the conditions under which the government works; and most elections turn out not to suit the demanding tests for declaring a mandate. In other words, devotion to the mandate in explaining elections often results in exactly the kind of contorted analysis I have cited above. My journalist friend has put the question: "If elections aren't a mandate for something, then what do they mean?" That is precisely the problem for party government advocates in postelection analysis.

This conundrum typically shows up in analysis of midterm elections. Again, the Constitution is perfectly clear: "The House of Representatives shall be composed of members chosen every second year," and the Senate "shall be divided as equally as may be into three classes . . . so that one third may be chosen every second year." There is no language accompanying to suggest that these elections every second year will be tests either of the president's personal popularity or of a mandate he did not receive in the first place. The president, in fact, is not even mentioned in these clauses. Yet the mandate-based analysis persists.

"The nation has, in effect, flashed a 'Caution—Go Slow' signal to the Johnson Administration."[46] This reaction was not uncommon following the large Republican gains in the 1966 midterm elections. The voters giveth and they taketh away, according to the theory of the mandate. Seldom are midterm elections interpreted as what they are: state and local contests, not tests of a presidential administration. The shifts in House seats can usually be explained by the extent to which the president's party, in the presidential election, won seats normally held by the other party. If many such seats were won, then the president's party enters the midterm election in a vulnerable position and losses may be heavy. Bruce I. Oppenheimer, James A.

Stimson, and Richard W. Waterman refer to the "exposure" of the president's party in congressional elections: "the degree to which a party has more or fewer than its normal complement of seats going into the election." They conclude that "the proportions of strong or vulnerable candidates [are] likely to be very much a function of party exposure levels."[47]

Still it is common to read the midterm results for the political and policy messages they may hold for the president. A sample from analyses of various postwar midterm elections shows that this popular interpretation has persisted throughout the period. After the 1950 midterm elections, the *New York Times* proclaimed, "No good reason remains . . . for the President to insist upon his oft-repeated claim that he has a 'mandate from the people.' . . . There is no evidence in Tuesday's elections of such a 'mandate.'" Four years later, William S. White wrote: "The people of the country clearly have registered some anxiety at the course of a Republican Congress that never has exactly typified the president himself. They have not given the Democrats any clear mandate in the Legislative Branch. . . . They have only set the Democrats to watch . . . certain tendencies of the Republicans in Congress."[48]

In one of the most candid acknowledgments of the role played by the mandate in election commentary, the *Washington Post* stated in 1974:

> When it comes to extracting "mandates" from elections results we can be as arbitrary as the next person. . . . The voters seem to be saying that they want the President to be more like a President. Their message does not include, of course, an explanation of how he is now supposed to deal, presidentially, with an overwhelmingly Democratic Congress; that's how it often is with "mandates."[49]

It continued: "A certain subjective arbitrariness is inherent in the traditional post-election game of figuring out who has been 'mandated' to do what." In other words, an election is often an occasion for analysts to comment on the president's performance. And since the midterm results normally show a net loss for the president's party in Congress, the mandate concept works well as a device for instructing a president what to do next. That the exercise itself is both arbitrary and illogical seldom stands in its way.

As a last example, in 2002 Republicans had historic gains in the House and the Senate—the first for a president's party at midterm since 1934. Bush was said to have gained a mandate because he had campaigned vigorously on behalf of the Republican candidates. Thus he had no mandate when he was on the ballot in 2000, yet gained one when he was not, in 2002.

The Persistent Concept

The preceding review illustrates how entrenched the mandate concept is as a crutch for postelection commentary. I have shown how it can vary and thus illustrates yet again how presidencies differ, even when analyzed by inappropriate concepts. There is no escaping the complexity caused when opposite party forces are frequently installed in positions of power. Even if analysts try to stuff an election into a standard mandate container, it pops out again. It seems too much to hope that the concept will be abandoned; as Dahl notes, it is "too deeply rooted in American political life and too useful a part of the political arsenal of presidents." But it may be used well or badly, depending on whether the analyst acknowledges the parts that spill out of the container and modifies the analysis accordingly.

The Continuing Agenda

So the mandate lives. But is it necessary to rely on it so heavily in judging how an election affects a president's capacity to govern? Is there a better way to comprehend the set of policy and political constraints within which a president tries to do his job? I believe there is, and that better way begins with an understanding of the policy agenda that serves as the context for campaigning, voting, and making choices once the winner takes office.

The national government has an agenda that is continuous because much of it is generated from existing programs. In his masterful review of policy development during the 1950s and 1960s, James L. Sundquist identified the following six issues as "those that appeared to reflect the most pressing concerns of the people": jobs for the unemployed, opportunity for the poor, schools for the young, civil rights for minorities, health care for the aged, and protection and enhancement of the outdoor environment.[50] It is striking that as I write some fifty years later, all six issues continue to find an important place on the agenda, though not in the same form. Many of the issues of the 1990s and early 2000s have been related either to the cost of programs enacted during this earlier period or to the new problems that have emerged as those programs are implemented.

Presidents are not actively involved in most of what government does. There is a momentum and rhythm to a working government that cannot be stopped or easily redirected. It is useful to remind oneself of this fact as a corrective to the tendency to overstate the role of the president as an agenda setter. Neustadt, who has stressed the important agenda-setting function of the White House, acknowledges that the president's choices occur within the limits of ongoing policies. Commenting on the decade before the publication of the first edition of his book *Presidential Power*, Neustadt observed:

> To sense the continuity from Truman's time through Eisenhower's one need only place the newspapers of 1959 alongside those of 1949. Save for the issue of domestic communists, the subject matter of our policy and politics remains almost unchanged. We deal as we have done in terms of cold war, of an arms race, of a competition overseas, of danger from inflation, and of damage from recession. We skirmish on the frontiers of the welfare state and in the borderlands of race relations. Aspects change, but labels stay the same. So do dilemmas. Everything remains unfinished business.[51]

The notion of cycles places the president in a larger social, political, and policy context, since the cycles are not typically coterminous with presidential administrations. Bert A. Rockman explains:

> The president usually is assumed to be the chief director of goals. As time wears on, however, presidential agendas become susceptible to alteration. The unforeseen consequences of past policies—those of previous occupants of the White House and those of the incumbents—conspire along with unprogrammed events and with changes in the composition of political majorities to provide new problems requiring reaction. Some of these will not be consistent with earlier elements of the presidential agenda.[52]

One obvious conclusion is that the president's agenda—his list of priorities—is influenced by, and has to be fitted into, a larger set of ongoing issues.

Erwin C. Hargrove and Michael Nelson categorize individual presidents as presidents of preparation, achievement, and consolidation. They acknowledge that each type is subject to the policy or political conditions of the time. Presidents of preparation "generate, distill, and present new ideas. The political situation calls on [them] to attempt to build a rising tide of support for such ideas." Presidents of achievement "get an ambitious legislative program passed. [Their] political situation is one of strong but temporary empowerment, and the president must seize the day by mobilizing the public in favor of action." Presidents of consolidation "have the task of rationalizing existing programs."[53] Again, the president's role in the agenda is not at all of his own making. In fact, one measure of leadership is the capacity of a president to comprehend the policy environment accurately. Baumgartner and Jones explain it this way:

> Sometimes skillful leaders can foresee an onrushing tide and use their energies to channel it in a particular direction. Others fail to see the tide or attempt to oppose it, virtually always unsuccessfully. Successful political leaders,

then, are often those who recognize the power of political ideas sweeping through the system and who take advantage of them to favor particular policy proposals. Leaders can influence the ways in which the broad tides of politics are channeled, but they cannot reverse the tides themselves.[54]

Light offers the most extensive analysis of the president's role in regard to the agenda. He finds that the president is "constrained by the level of both internal and external resources." Presidents naturally vary in their capacity to set and control the agenda.

> It is important to recognize that the agenda changes substantively from administration to administration. However, the President's domestic agenda does have several stable characteristics. . . . The President's domestic agenda is set very early in the term; . . . the timing of agenda requests affects ultimate legislative success; and . . . the size of the domestic agenda varies directly with what I will call presidential "capital."[55]

However much one speaks of context, it is seemingly tempting to overstate the president's role in agenda setting. In the first place, it suits the common preference for an activist president playing out his role in party government. There is also the related view that a system of separated institutions sharing powers can work only if the president sets the agenda. "Congressmen need an agenda from outside, something with high status to respond to or react against. What provides it better than the program of the President?"[56] This observation by Neustadt also implies that there is a convenience to having an agenda set by the most prominent player in a system of distributed powers. John W. Kingdon found confirmation in his interviews with national officials "that the president can single-handedly set the agendas, not only of people in the executive branch, but also of people in Congress and outside of government."[57]

The White House surely does serve to orient others to policy priorities. The president's involvement can be absolutely crucial, given media and public attention to the White House. As Baumgartner and Jones see it:

> The personal involvement of the president can play a key role in further strengthening the positive feedback processes. No other single actor can focus attention as clearly, or change the motivations of such a great number of other actors, as the president. . . . We conclude that the president is not a necessary actor in all cases, but when he decides to become involved, his influence can be decisive indeed.[58]

Reasonable as these views may be, one should not lose sight of the context within which the president makes choices. Normally he chooses from among a set of issues that are familiar because they are ongoing. The president's alternatives are also increasingly structured by the deficit, which has in recent years come to be recognized as an overarching issue itself. It is also useful to remember that a conscious decision not to act represents a policy preference every bit as much as a decision to act, even though it may prompt criticism that the president has failed his obligations as an agenda setter.

The fact that the agenda is continuous does not preclude shocks to the system. Wars, disasters, and severe economic dislocations compel exclusive attention by policymakers, often in a bipartisan manner. The most recent example was the terrorist attacks on the World Trade Center and the Pentagon. A primarily domestic agenda was supplanted by a set of national and homeland security issues, which then reshaped the domestic agenda. On these occasions, the president's role as certifier is mostly formal, given the broad recognition of the issues at hand. But his responsibility for designating where and how to begin is greatly enhanced over that of a two-house legislature.

Agenda-Related Concepts

Various scholars have sought to clarify the agenda-setting process by distinguishing between types of agendas. I borrow heavily from them in formulating the following concepts.

Agenda Orientation or Context

The concept of agenda orientation simply refers to the policy setting within which a president must try to govern. Some people use the labels "conservative" and "liberal" to denote different eras. What they typically mean, in the American setting, is support for more or less national government involvement in solving social and economic problems. There are several problems with these labels. Most Americans resist being so classified, conclusions about public support for conservatism or liberalism are often based on weak evidence, and policy preferences may have different meanings for government action in different eras or on issues within the same era (for example, conservatives supporting government action to curb abortion or liberal efforts to prevent government from acting to tap phone lines).

Any effort at labeling is subject to exceptions, but it is possible to identify agenda orientations related to issue priorities. For example, in social welfare there are periods when conditions support expanding the role of the national government; these are often followed by periods of consolidation.

Baumgartner and Jones speak of "lurches and lulls" in policymaking.[59] Expansion is characterized by new programs, consolidation by reorganization and occasional retrenchment. The two notable periods of expansion were during the Roosevelt and Johnson presidencies: the New Deal and the Great Society. These were followed, respectively, by efforts to consolidate during the Truman and Eisenhower presidencies and the Nixon, Ford, and Carter presidencies.

Until 1980 there had not been a contractive orientation. The cutbacks during consolidative periods were normally intended to make government programs more effective, not to eliminate them altogether. In 1980, however, a president was elected who not only doubted government's capacity to solve social welfare problems but believed that government contributed to these problems. In 1981 President Reagan was successful in enacting policies that definitely established the contractive agenda orientation. Tax cuts, increases in defense spending, and limited cuts in domestic programs created huge deficits. Even liberals had to consider how to cut back in order to go forward with proposals to expand government or increase existing programs.

Once it was no longer politically feasible to cut back further, and as deficits mounted, attention turned to taxes—a fiscal orientation. George H. W. Bush campaigned on the slogan "read my lips, no new taxes," but he reneged on that promise because of the continued failure to control the growth of government spending. In 1992 Congress seriously considered a constitutional amendment to balance the budget, a measure acknowledged by many to be an admission of incapacity to deal with increasing deficits. The amendment failed in the House, just nine votes short of the required two-thirds majority.

The terrorist attacks on 9/11 launched a new agenda orientation—that of security. The events on that day enveloped much of the existing agenda within two broad dimensions: national security (aggressively, even preemptively, protecting national interests) and homeland security (sensitizing the public to threats, improving security in public places, border control, and screening for terrorists). It is too soon to judge the full effects of this orientation on the presidency. The expectation is that the president has an early advantage but that Congress will then assert its prerogatives as the costs of proposals affect other priorities. A national security orientation almost certainly ensures larger deficits, given existing commitments to entitlement programs and, in Bush 43's case, substantial tax reductions.

In summary, I have identified five agenda orientations within which presidents prepare programs: expansion, consolidation, contraction, fiscal, and security. None of these categories is pure. Consolidative, contractive, and security efforts, for example, can expand government through regulation. The point is simply to characterize the policy and political conditions that serve to constrain or define the president's program.

Proposals and Programs

John Kingdon finds it useful to distinguish between an agenda and alternatives. The first is "the list of subjects or problems to which governmental officials, and people outside of government closely associated with those officials, are paying some serious attention at any given time." He identifies a governmental agenda ("the list of subjects that are getting attention") and a decision agenda ("the list of subjects within the governmental agenda that are up for an active decision").[60]

Alternatives, for Kingdon, are the various proposals under consideration to address a problem on the agenda. Proposals may be generated in many places in and out of government: within agencies with responsibility for the issue, within the Office of Management and Budget, among White House aides, within think tanks, within congressional committees, or among clienteles for existing programs. Kingdon's point is that presidents do not control the production of alternatives. In fact, for most major issues there are many alternatives available, readily offered by support groups or bureaucratic agencies. The election of a new president is an occasion for policy advocates to reach down into that bottom desk drawer (or the "to do" computer file) and pull out the great idea whose time has finally come. Baumgartner and Jones broaden Kingdon's point by adding federalism and committee jurisdictional overlaps to the separation of powers as affecting the production of alternatives. They observe that many commentators view the multiple sources of policy proposals as "inhibitors of change." But in their view the opposite may be true: "Federalism, separation of powers, and jurisdictional overlaps are opportunities for change as much as inhibitors of change."[61]

The president may select among proposals; he may also ignore them. He may select one from many or create a blend. At the beginning of each year he is expected to offer his alternatives in a State of the Union address, preferably as part of a larger program that lends itself to labeling (New Deal, Fair Deal, New Frontier, Great Society). It is usually easier to name a program that expands government than one that is more consolidative or contractive. Perhaps it is not surprising to observe a progovernment bent to governing. A president who prefers limited government is often said not to have a program. Put otherwise, choosing not to act, encouraging others to act, or thwarting an action judged inadequate or even harmful is typically not considered to be a presidential program, however internally consistent these choices may be. Bush 43 may be an exception. He offered "compassionate conservatism," and later the "ownership society," as descriptive labels for his intentions. However, the adjective "compassionate" was meant to define a role for government in promoting both conservatism and ownership.

As used here, *proposals* refer to the various alternatives that are available for acting on a problem; *program* refers to the set of presidential choices among proposals, including not to act or to defer government action. Note that *program* is used to refer to the president's choices. Because Congress is a two-house legislature with no single leader, it is not normally thought of as having a program, though certain leaders, such as House Speakers James Wright (D-Tex.) in 1987 and, even more, Newt Gingrich (R-Ga.) in 1995 have sought to offer one in competition with the White House.

Consensus

The concept of consensus directs attention to the level of agreement between members of Congress and the president in regard to the agenda orientation and a program for acting on problems on the agenda. Elections naturally can have a major influence on the level of agreement. For example, as previously discussed, the 1964 and 1980 elections resulted in a high level of agreement on the agenda and substantial concurrence that the president had the approval of the public to proceed with his program. There was no such agreement following the 1960, 1968, 1988, or 2000 elections. Thus consensus is characteristic of elections that are perceived as conveying a mandate for change. It is built on superficial evidence of congruity between the policy messages of presidential and congressional elections. That is, it is assumed that the public was sending strong policy signals, whether or not that conclusion can be sustained by a survey of voter intentions.

A second type of consensus may be the result of a disaster like that on 9/11. In this case the broad agreement regarding the agenda is more clearly demonstrable to reflect the intentions of the public and government officials. Still, as with that following a landslide election, the consensus may be short-lived, especially if the president interprets the original agreement as sanctioning actions that turn out to be controversial, such as the war in Iraq.

Leeway

The separated system provides leeway, a novel feature that can contribute to successful agenda certification. Here is how it works. Certifying agendas, designating priorities and their sequence, and offering proposals are speculative enterprises. No president can know in advance how they will turn out. Yet it is essential that he and his aides engage in conjecture, even if the costs of failure may be high. In a one-person or one-party government, there is no escaping responsibility for the results of what is an uncertain process. By contrast, the separated system guarantees multiple sources of certification, designation, and preparation of alternatives, just as Kingdon and Baumgartner and Jones describe. Others besides the president exercise their legitimate right to speculate too, and to compete in the lawmaking process, generally producing an amalgam for which they share responsibility or creating deadlock when no such compromise is possible.

Presidents who acknowledge and become accustomed to leeway are likely to be rewarded with success on Capitol Hill. The case of President Clinton and House Speaker Newt Gingrich in 1996 is illustrative. Following difficult and contentious budget negotiations in 1995, the two leaders adapted to each other's political status and capitalized on the contributions each could make in managing the agenda. As a consequence, the two adversaries could both claim credit for the enactment of a large volume of major legislation.[62] This case also illustrates costs along the way to discovering the advantages of leeway, especially in a partisan era of split-party government. In fact, President Clinton found that leeway was simply not available two years later, during his impeachment.

Taking advantage of leeway typically requires working in cross-partisan fashion and thus is more or less mandatory in split-party government. However rational it may be to implicate the other party in lawmaking in one-party government, conditions may work against capitalizing on leeway. If the president's party has large congressional majorities (as with Johnson, 1965–67), cross-partisan agreements may be viewed as unnecessary, except on issues that divide the majority party. And if the president's party has narrow congressional majorities (as with Bush 43, 2003–07), the need for partisan discipline may overcome efforts to work across the aisle. The latter case is well illustrated by the Republican House during the George W. Bush's first term. As shown in chapter 7, many House Republicans objected to and were critical of the president's bipartisan push for education reform in 2001. Conversely, a highly disciplined House Republican leadership passed most of the rest of Bush's program in a partisan and disciplined manner, making it difficult for the president to rely on leeway in the Senate.

Postwar Presidents and the Agenda

In his final State of the Union message, in 1960, President Eisenhower observed that "progress implies both new and continuing problems and, unlike Presidential administrations, problems rarely have terminal dates."[63] Thus when he departed the White House in 1961, Eisenhower left to Kennedy a set of new and continuing problems as the context within which the new president would ascertain his priorities. How much any one president shapes the agenda is not easy to determine. In his review of the Eisenhower-Kennedy-Johnson period, Sundquist concludes that these presidents "seem as actors, following a script that was written by events."[64]

As in other discussions of the individual presidents here, the distinction between takeover and elected presidents is relevant. The latter have an issue-orienting experience during the campaign. They have an opportunity to test ideas and probe for openings in a crowded calendar of issues. Takeover presidents do not have the same kind of experience, since loyalty to their leader precludes an effort to fit their policy preferences into the ongoing agenda. And in two cases—Truman and Ford—they had little time even to acquaint themselves fully with their predecessor's orientation and style. An overview of each postwar presidency is shown in table 5-1, which characterizes the agenda orientation, the ambitiousness of the president's program, the degree of consensus, major events that influenced the agenda, and the president's impact on later agendas.

Truman

The agenda at the time of Roosevelt's death was clear enough. First, it was necessary to bring the war to a close; then, a substantial set of foreign and domestic issues required attention. The list of issues was not difficult to compile. Whole nations required assistance in rebuilding after World War II, and in the United States a great many domestic problems had been put aside during the war. The orientation, therefore, was consolidative, one of postwar reassembly. The emphasis was not on creating new programs but on making up for lost time in programs enacted during the New Deal. Truman himself was active in proposing legislation to deal with issues of housing, health care, employment, farm support, and public works. His surprise win in 1948 was partially based on the image he propagated of himself as facing a "do-nothing" Republican Congress (in fact, some of the most important legislation of the postwar period was enacted in the 80th Congress, including the Marshall Plan, the National Security Act, and the Taft-Hartley Act). New proposals were introduced as a part of Truman's Fair Deal, and some were enacted. However, the boldest of these—a national health care program—did not pass.

The Truman presidency was characterized by significant policy conflict. His own unexpected election in 1948 did not carry with it a consensus on policy direction, and in 1950 Republicans once again increased their numbers in Congress. The principal events affecting Truman's management of the agenda were the labor disputes immediately following the end of World War II and the Korean conflict in the last years of the administration. Throughout his term, Truman struggled to maintain control of the policy agenda, to prevent events from overtaking him. The mark of his leadership is that despite limited resources, or "political capital" in Light's terms, he remained a major actor throughout, even if he was not always in charge.

Eisenhower

Truman's agenda legacy for Eisenhower was the Korean conflict. As one of his few campaign promises, the new president said that if elected, he would "go to Korea." This was an engrossing issue for the new president and one that he was, by training, well prepared to engage. An armistice was signed July 27, 1953, just six months after Eisenhower's inauguration. As for the domestic agenda, most of the issues were consolidative in nature: extensions and refinements of existing programs, along with a number of reorganizations. Toward the end of the administration new problems began to emerge in the domestic economy, civil rights, and medical care. And, as is well documented by Sundquist, congressional Democrats actively worked to prepare proposals responsive to the emerging agenda.

Eisenhower himself was not particularly active in proposing alternatives to deal with the consolidative issues of the time; his style was more permissive. He was more a manager or commander than an initiator or promoter. Although there appeared to be a moderate degree of consensus in 1952 with the election of Republican House and Senate majorities, the president's own limited program was unlikely to result in major change in the consolidative agenda inherited from Truman. For example, significant cutbacks were unlikely in the New Deal programs that continued to shape much of the work of the national government.

Table 5-1. *Presidents and the Agenda, Truman to Bush 43*

President	Agenda orientation	President's program	Agenda consensus	Major events	Impact on subsequent agenda
Truman	Consolidation	Active	Low	Korean War	Significant
Eisenhower	Consolidation	Permissive	Moderate to low	Little Rock, U-2, recession, McCarthyism	Limited
Kennedy	Expansion	Active	Low	Civil rights, Cuban missile crisis	Significant
Johnson	Expansion	Active	High	Vietnam War, urban riots	Massive
Nixon	Consolidation	Active	Moderate to low	Vietnam War, China initiative, Arab oil embargo, Watergate	Significant
Ford	Maintenance	Permissive/reactive	Low	Nixon pardon	Limited
Carter	Consolidation	Active	Moderate to low	Camp David, Iran hostages, recession	Limited
Reagan	Contraction to fiscal	Active to permissive	High to low	Tax and budget cuts, assassination attempt, Iran-contra	Massive
Bush 41	Fiscal	Permissive/reactive	Low	Gulf War, recession	Limited
Clinton	Reform	Active	Low	Economy, health care, loss of Congress, impeachment	Moderate
Bush 43	Reform, Security	Active	Low	Tax cuts, 9/11, war on terrorism, Iraq war	Significant to potentially massive

Several major events during the period had a definite effect on the agenda. Senator Joseph R. McCarthy (R-Wis.) began an anticommunist crusade that led to many prominent public officials' being charged with conspiracy. His campaign had a chilling effect throughout the government. The confrontation between state and federal officials over desegregating the schools of Little Rock, Arkansas, reflected growing discontent on racial issues and presaged the passage of civil rights legislation in 1957 and 1960, during the Eisenhower presidency, and in 1964 and 1965, during the Johnson presidency. The economic recession brought huge Democratic majorities in Congress in 1958 and encouraged the party to prepare to recapture the White House in 1960. Finally, the U-2 incident created a rift with the Soviet Union that would be exacerbated in the early months of the Kennedy presidency.

President Eisenhower was seemingly content to conform to the agenda as it moved through his years in the White House. Events made a difference, but the president settled for guidance more than innovation, which had the ultimate effect of permitting, perhaps encouraging, congressional Democrats—particularly the liberals—to participate actively in policy development. Legislative production was limited, but the congressional Democrats identified an agenda to take to the voters in 1960.

Kennedy

As a candidate, Kennedy was anxious to convey a sense of command, and therefore he created a group of advisory committees following his nomination. Task forces worked on proposals during the campaign and immediately following the election. The expansionist orientation of the agenda suited the activist president. Kennedy's desire for control was fortified substantively by the work of the Democrats (mostly liberal senators) in the 86th Congress.

However impressive this early effort was, agenda consensus, as defined here, was relatively low. It was not easy for Kennedy to sell the idea that the results of the presidential and congressional elections represented a congruous policy message. He won narrowly, and in both houses the Democrats suffered net losses in the margins of their majorities. Theodore Sorensen believed that the 87th Congress was the most conservative since the Republican-controlled 83rd. "The balance of power appeared to have swung decisively in the direction of the conservative coalition of Republicans and Southern Democrats who had since 1937 effectively blocked much of the progressive legislation of four Presidents."[65]

Events also worked against the president's desire to clear the agenda. In particular, the Bay of Pigs disaster did not sustain an image of effective leadership. Kennedy's presidency was also preoccupied by civil rights demonstrations, the erection of the Berlin wall, a confrontation with the steel industry, and, above all, the Cuban missile crisis. In the meantime, however, a substantial foundation was being laid for the enactment of new programs in many policy areas. The difficulty in making a firm judgment about Kennedy's presidential effectiveness is that no one can know what might have happened had he lived out his term and won a second.

Johnson

Seldom have personal, political, and policy forces converged so positively as in 1964–66. Important factors—the preparation of an agenda by Kennedy, national contrition for the shooting of the former president, the legislative mastery of the new president—were bolstered by an overwhelming Democratic victory at the polls in 1964. The result was the Great Society. The expansionist agenda was fully engaged as Johnson added to the activist Kennedy program and benefited from perhaps the greatest agenda consensus since the 1932 election.

Johnson's triumph in enacting the Great Society led to a shift in agenda orientation. After the expansionist calendar was cleared, a more consolidative set of issues naturally arose. It became time to make these many new programs work. Then, events like the escalation of the Vietnam War and inner-city riots diverted attention from the previous agenda and Johnson's remarkable success on Capitol Hill. What began as the ideal activist party government disintegrated in the face of foreign and domestic policy challenges.

The Kennedy-Johnson years had a massive impact on the national policy agenda. The next president did not have to search for issues. A quantum increase in domestic programs had generated a full calendar of work at the White House. Civil unrest among minority groups and antiwar activists would have to be dealt with. And, like Eisenhower, the next president would be left to close down a war—one even more unpopular, yet more of a political tangle, than that in Korea.

Nixon

The former vice president, long identified as a strong partisan, was narrowly elected to cope with this new and challenging agenda. So as not to make it too easy for him, voters also returned a Democratic Congress. At this critical juncture, the voting public appeared to send mixed signals, making agenda consensus most unlikely apart from ending the Vietnam War.

The national government had become a much larger enterprise as a result of the Great Society program. The Nixon White House was preoccupied with administering, reorganizing, extending, and refining the legislation passed in the Johnson years. This work was not confined to consolidation, however. There were, as well, fresh issues generated by Great Society programs and defined by the clienteles that had been created. In particular, there were new emphases on the environment, energy, and safety. It was not a set of issues that instinctively attracted Nixon, but as president he could not ignore their politics: they were a major part of the agenda during his presidency.

The Vietnam War was nearly as difficult for Nixon to resolve as it had been for Johnson, but there was a promise of settlement by the time of the 1972 election. Nixon's initiatives with China and the Soviet Union were to have a substantial effect on the foreign policy agenda for subsequent presidents. Another significant event was the Arab oil embargo imposed October 18, 1973. The price of imported oil quadrupled, sending reverberations through the domestic economy for several years. Finally, the Watergate scandal diverted executive and congressional attention from the more substantive agenda, an effect replayed in the Clinton White House twenty-four years later.

Clashes between the president and Congress were frequent throughout the period but did not forestall legislative productivity. In many cases members of Congress were not content to await presidential initiatives. They participated more actively in all phases of the policy process and enacted congressional reforms to increase their ability to analyze policy and perform oversight. One major consequence was a Congress prepared psychologically and materially to play the role of an alternative government, adapting itself to split-party control and to the incapacitation of the president as a result of the Watergate affair.

This period, more than almost any other in the postwar era, illustrates the dynamics of the agenda. Even a relatively superficial review suggests that a complex, independent, consolidative agenda had been created as a result of the Great Society programs. This agenda dominated domestic policy politics in the White House and on Capitol Hill and had the force to carry beyond Nixon's service. Much of the puzzle of high legislative productivity during the Nixon-Ford presidencies (see chapter 4) may well be solved by inquiry into the extent to which the agenda guided policy action. In both foreign and domestic policy, a focus on the effects of agenda continuity and change on institutional response contributes materially to understanding the context within which the president and Congress do their work. Such analysis also clarifies institutional adaptation to the variable political conditions encouraged by the separation of elections.

Ford

Of the three modern takeover presidents, Ford clearly was the least able to escape the legacy of his predecessor. Most of what he had to manage had been set in motion by the Nixon administration or by Congress before he entered the White House. The agenda orientation was maintenance of the consolidative efforts already under way. It was extremely difficult for Ford to fashion a program of his own. He had little choice but to be permissive or reactive, allowing a Democratic Congress to work its will and vetoing measures that went too far. "During his brief tenure Ford undoubtedly vetoed more bills raising important substantive issues than any previous president."[66] Unlike the other takeover presidents, Truman and Johnson, he did not have an opportunity to establish or to reset an agenda consensus. The momentum carried through the final years of the truncated Nixon presidency. The environmental and energy agendas remained active through the Ford presidency, accounting for six major pieces of legislation.

The event with the greatest impact on Ford's capacity to influence the agenda was, of course, his pardon of Nixon. Whatever political or policy advantage he may have gained from taking over was lost almost immediately. "In the wake of the Nixon pardon, Congress showed little inclination to respond to Ford's promises of 'communication, conciliation, compromise, and cooperation.'"[67] Already sizable Democratic majorities in the House and Senate grew substantially in 1974, further isolating the president politically. Ford's presidency will be correctly analyzed as filling out the Nixon term, essentially as Nixon's "lame duck." On a continuum of presidential influence and management of the agenda, Ford will forever be placed at the low end. That is not to say that his presidency was a failure, but it acknowledges the context for judging his options as a leader.

Carter

The consolidative agenda orientation of the post–Great Society era and the aftereffects of events like the Arab oil embargo continued to influence policy choices beyond the Nixon and Ford presidencies. The major legislation enacted during the Carter presidency dealt predominantly with environmental, energy, reorganizational, and deregulatory issues (accounting for fourteen of Mayhew's tally of twenty-two important laws passed during Carter's single term).

In this context, Carter himself was an activist, initiating a large number of consolidative proposals. Members of Congress were also actively engaged in dealing with these same issues—not always to the president's liking. They were unwilling to shut down the policy apparatus on Capitol Hill that had been created and honed during the Nixon-Ford years. Thus not only did the agenda look very much like it had in those years, but frequently, so did the politics. Democratic control of both branches made less of a difference than many people had expected. "Congress never did hit it off with Carter . . . who as president remained a stranger to much of official Washington."[68] The Carter presidency demonstrates that when one party manages to win control of Congress and the White House, there is nothing automatic about party government.

None of the three elections in which Carter was involved conveyed a high degree of agenda consensus. Carter won narrowly against a weak Republican opponent in 1976, by choice he was not heavily involved in the 1978 congressional elections, and he suffered a substantial loss in the 1980 presidential race. Again, as in previous, Republican presidencies, there was no obvious evidence that Congress had conceded agenda-setting authority to the president, however much the president may have believed that he had such a prerogative.

The events receiving the most press coverage during Carter's time in office were the Camp David accords and the hostage taking in Iran. Neither had the effect of, say, the Arab oil embargo for restructuring the agenda, however. It was the recession that dominated the 1980 presidential election and provided a favorable agenda orientation for the contractive policy message of Ronald Reagan.

Reagan

Never before 1980 had there been conditions so favorable to a contractive agenda orientation. In the twentieth century, expansion has typically been followed by consolidation or maintenance. In 1980, however, Reagan reiterated his view that government was not the solution; it was, in fact, the problem. Therefore he believed it was essential that programs be cut back, regulation and bureaucracy be reduced substantially, and federal taxes be cut sharply. The 1980 election results were interpreted as affirming this policy approach and representing a consensus for the Reagan program. Public support for the new president was enhanced by an assassination attempt that occurred at the critical point when Reagan had introduced his budget and tax-cutting proposals.

Comparison with the Johnson presidency is informative. As described, conditions in 1964–66 allowed Johnson to have a massive impact on the subsequent agenda. But the repercussions would come later, as succeeding presidents sought to administer the new programs put in place. Reagan also enjoyed high agenda consensus at the beginning of his first term. However, the reordering of priorities in 1981 had significant effects on the agenda during his terms in office. The combination of reduced taxes, significant increases in defense expenditures, and a failure to achieve compensatory decreases in domestic expenditures produced deficits that constrained the choices available to policymakers for the remainder of the Reagan presidency and for many years to follow.

The Iran-contra scheme, which came to light toward the end of Reagan's second term, had the potential, not unlike that of Watergate, to paralyze the White House. The president acted quickly to defuse this plausible result by appointing a commission and by having his administration cooperate with congressional investigations. Even so, the event had important policy effects. Congressional Democrats, led by Speaker Jim Wright (D-Tex.), became more active than they had been in Reagan's first term, defining and acting on the agenda. In order to preserve an active policy role for himself in this atmosphere, the president took these initiatives seriously. The effect was to produce more than the expected amount of important legislation on major issues. As was the case in the last Congress of the Eisenhower era, a capacity for initiative and productivity was displayed under circumstances of split-party government and during the lame-duck months of a two-term presidency.

Once it was no longer possible to significantly reduce major social welfare or entitlement programs, attention naturally turned to fiscal issues. The agenda orientation shifted to how to improve the economy and increase revenues. That orientation persisted into the Bush and Clinton presidencies. New program initiatives were severely constrained by the reality of the deficit. If cuts could not be made, or if additional spending was agreed upon, then taxes had to be raised or more jobs created, or both. These options defined the choices for Reagan's successors.

Bush 41

Many analysts found it difficult to judge what the 1988 election was about. It was said that Bush did not have a mandate, in spite of his impressive personal victory. Expectations were low, and George Bush did what was expected. Given his limited political capital and the limited agenda identified during the 1988 campaign, it would have been surprising had he sought to match the policy initiatives of his predecessors who had won by large margins.

The limited agenda during the first year of the Bush 41 presidency is amply demonstrated by the fact that only two major pieces of legislation were enacted. In Bush's second and subsequent years, the domestic agenda was dominated by a growing realization that the deficit was substantially greater than had been anticipated. Ryan J. Barilleaux and Mark J. Rozell refer to the Bush presidency as "incremental leadership" relying on "prudence."[69] Although Bush worked with the Democratic Congress to enact a number of important laws—rights for the disabled, clean air, child care support, immigration, affordable housing—his second year will be best remembered for the passage of a bipartisan deficit reduction package. A major part of the package sought to respond to the fiscal agenda that was carried over from the last years of the Reagan presidency. An unfortunate political by-product of the agreement was that Bush had to renege on his famous "no new taxes" pledge. However much he was praised in the media for breaking the promise, the act symbolized his loss of even the limited control he had of the domestic agenda. He did not regain even a small edge during his last two years in office.[70]

Capitol Hill took the initiative in agenda setting during the last two years of the Bush presidency. At first the president was triumphant in gaining support for the Persian Gulf War. But congressional Democrats then established a pattern of sending to the president legislation that they believed either was in the best interests of the country or would give them a political edge if the president exercised his veto power (or both). Bush did not disappoint them in regard to the latter strategy. In 1992 alone he vetoed twenty-one bills, including several that fit the "political issue" category: conditional most favored nation status for China (twice), a tax-the-rich bill, campaign finance reform, fetal tissue research, motor voter registration, family leave, family planning, and funding for abortions. All these vetoes were sustained in at least one house. An end-of-term review of Congress had this to say about the last two years of Bush's presidency:

> Scandal, special interests, sagging poll ratings, divided government, presidential election politics. They all share the blame for the 102nd Congress' meager record of legislative accomplishment. But the real culprit may be more fiscal than political, and that problem will remain even if voters change the players Nov. 3.[71]

Much of Bush's agenda was fiscal in nature. But he was constrained by limited political resources and his pledge to forgo one potential solution: higher taxes. Therefore he found it difficult throughout his term to take charge of the crucial certification process in agenda setting and could only act defensively with the veto to thwart Democratic initiatives. The agenda for a complex government remained in place, awaiting a president with sufficient political support to certify particular items for attention.

Clinton

Expectations were unrealistically high for the Clinton presidency. Fueling this optimism was the return of one-party Democratic government after twelve years of Republican presidents serving with at least one house of Congress in Democratic control. At a conference called "Beyond Gridlock," James L. Sundquist expressed this optimism in the context of governance:

> If the government cannot succeed in the present configuration, when can it ever possibly succeed? As Joan Quigley, the former official astrologer [in the Reagan presidency], might have said, the stars are really aligned right for the next four years.
>   The country has finally gotten back to unified government. For the first time in twelve years, somebody is going to be responsible. . . . Now the day of buck passing blame shifting is over. The Democrats asked for complete responsibility for the government and got it. They know they are going to be held accountable, and on Capitol Hill they know they have to stick together and make a record.[72]

Not everyone at the conference was so sanguine about the end of gridlock. Reagan's former chief of staff Kenneth Duberstein was dubious, noting that "most representatives and senators do not feel beholden to any president, let alone one who ran behind them in the last election."[73] In fact, there was as much or more evidence to support Duberstein's view as that of Sundquist. Clinton failed to get a majority of the popular vote; Democrats sustained a net loss of House seats; and an independent candidate, Ross Perot, got nearly a fifth of the popular vote. Discerning a mandate was difficult, though an all-Democratic government did invite responsibility, as Sundquist suggested, and an unrealistic partisan strategy made it difficult for the president to take advantage of leeway (as discussed above).

In contrast to 1989, there was an active agenda orientation. The Clinton campaign team identified it as: "Change vs. more of the same. The economy, stupid. Don't forget health care." The second point was apparently the most relevant to voters. In exit polls, 53 percent of respondents said they were concerned about issues related to the economy (jobs, deficit, taxes); health care was mentioned by 13 percent.[74]

The priorities of the Clinton administration were drawn from different ends of the political spectrum—an economic package that included deficit reduction for those on the right and a national health care proposal for those on the left. The reform of welfare was also favored, but lost out initially to health care. The economic package raised taxes and therefore was opposed by Republicans. It passed by one vote in the House and with the tie-breaking vote of the vice president in the Senate. Health care never even received a floor vote in either chamber.

Agenda setting shifted to Capitol Hill as a result of the stunning 1994 midterm election. Republicans took control of both chambers, gaining a majority in the house for the first time in forty years. The new speaker of the House, Newt Gringrich (R-Ga.), and his associates had proposed a "Contract with America" that offered a rare policy agenda for a midterm election. That document became the new agenda for the 104th Congress. Displaying unprecedented party unity (98 percent), House Republicans passed all but one of the items on the contract in the first one hundred days of the new Congress.

The most important items in the contract were welfare reform and a budget package that Speaker Gingrich predicted the president could not possibly veto. Proving Gingrich very wrong, Clinton twice vetoed the budget proposals, leading to partial shutdowns of the government before an agreement was reached. Likewise, Clinton vetoed welfare reform legislation twice before he finally signed it in 1996. While the first one hundred days were dominated by Gingrich, the 104th Congress thenceforth was a story of the political restoration of the president and the political education of Speaker Gingrich. Most notably, Gingrich learned that the speaker does not command the government. Even so, the second session of the 104th Congress was the third most productive year for major legislation in the postwar period, as congressional Republicans and President Clinton compiled a reelection record that was successful in returning both to power. Leeway, dubbed "triangulation" by Clinton's political adviser Dick Morris, was used to advantage.

Clinton's second term was unusual, to say the least. Again winning without a majority of the popular vote and in a three-candidate race, Clinton had to manage another split-party government. Budget issues carried over into the 105th Congress, and the president and the congressional Republicans reached a historic balanced-budget agreement But once the

Lewinsky scandal erupted and the president was impeached, few major bills were enacted.[75] Clinton continued to specify agenda issues but his loss of personal status and Republican intransigence all but ended prospects for engaging the president's priorities.

Bush 43

The limited production of major legislation during the last three years of the Clinton presidency resulted in a full agenda for the next president. The text for the 2000 campaign was set, and candidates Gore and Bush mostly agreed on what issues were on the agenda: education, prescription drugs, Medicare and Social Security reform, energy, some form of tax cut, a patients' bill of rights, campaign finance reform, and trade authority. Their proposals, of course, differed. As it happened, Congress had also been working on most of these matters.

Having barely won a disputed election, Bush functioned within an agenda orientation that was argumentative, if not downright hostile. It was set as much by partisanship as by policy substance. There was no talk of a mandate. Undeterred, Bush set two priorities: tax cuts and education reform. Both were enacted, the first early in the session, with intense competitive partisanship, the second much later, with bipartisan participation and support.

The switch of Senator James Jeffords (R-Vt.) to independent status, voting with the Democrats for organizational purposes, severely constrained the president's ability to certify the agenda in the Senate. The new majority leader, Tom Daschle (D-S.D.) set a patients' bill of rights as the prime issue, following the passage of the tax cuts, although that was not the sequence desired by Bush. Meanwhile House Republicans continued to pass Bush's favored legislation on to the Senate, where it was stalled by the majority Democrats.

All of this byplay was abruptly halted by 9/11. This historic event created a new and compelling agenda. Issues of national and homeland security took precedence and influenced other issues that were being processed at the time of the attacks. Five of the seven major pieces of legislation in 2001 were enacted in less than four months, in response to 9/11.

The shift in agenda orientation in 2001 was the most dramatic of any in the postwar era. Not even an economic recession could match the dominance of the threat of terrorism during the first Bush term. The Bush team then decided, with pressure from Capitol Hill, to seek authority to go to war against Iraq. Congressional authorization and a United Nations Security Council resolution provided legitimacy, as interpreted by the Bush White House, for an invasion in March 2003. The war on terrorism and the aftermath of the war in Iraq ensured that national and homeland security would continue to influence the agenda orientation through the 2004 campaign and into Bush's second term.

Summary

I have sought to identify how presidents fit into the government's work when they take office. I have raised doubts about their capacity to set the agenda at that point, while they play a critical role in designating the sequence for taking action. Most of the policy issues a president faces upon entering the White House predate him. Indeed, these issues typically were central to the rhetoric and debate of his campaign. Seldom can the president interpret the election results as providing a mandate. However, because others employ the concept in reading election outcomes, the mandate comes to have political and policy consequences for how his record will be evaluated and for the resources available to him in dealing with Congress and taking advantage of leeway.

The president becomes part of a continuous and changing government. He has significant influence in setting priorities, certifying certain issues, proposing policy solutions, and reacting to the policy initiatives of others (such as those offered by the increasingly policy-active members of Congress). These are vital functions for a busy government. Under most circumstances, the agenda is full to overflowing. Since it is not possible to treat all issues at once, members of Congress and others anxiously await the designation of priorities. These presidential choices typically come from a list that is familiar to other policy actors. Nonetheless, a designator is important, even if he is a president who has to work with congressional majorities of the other party. As in any organization with too much to do, there is a need for someone in authority to say, "Let's start here, with this." A president who says, "Let's start here and here and here and here" fails as a designator. Carter erred in this way, as did Clinton, if to a lesser extent. It is critical, too, that the right sequence be set among acknowledged priorities. For example, Clinton was criticized for tackling health care before welfare reform. An accurate estimate of political support is key to making that choice correctly. As 9/11 has shown, events can also designate the agenda sequence. The president's task in such circumstances is to be sensitive to the full range of new issues and provide detailed analyses and credible proposals in the right sequence.

I have also emphasized the fact that presidents vary markedly in their capacity to alter the agenda during their term in office. Occasionally a president has sufficient political resources to reset the agenda: examples are Johnson's quantum expansion in social programs in 1964–65 and Reagan's major contraction in revenues in 1981. September 11 reset the agenda for Bush 43. But most presidents are substantially more constrained in the policy choices available to them. Analysis of the presidential role suitably begins with the continuing agenda and the way each incumbent employs his limited resources to influence outcomes.

CHAPTER 6

Presidents and Lawmaking
in a Separated System

Presidential participation in lawmaking is not formulaic. Presidents vary in the advantages they possess for working with Congress, and forces beyond the president's influence may be the deciding factors in what gets done. Presidents do have programs, which often become the focal point of congressional action. But members of Congress can, and do, prepare proposals on their own initiative or in response to those offered by the president. Few, if any, major policy proposals are likely to pass both houses unchanged. Presidents rarely expect that to happen, and if they do, they are inevitably disappointed.

The very first words of the Constitution are among the more clear and straightforward in that document: "All legislative Powers herein granted shall be vested in a Congress of the United States, which shall consist of a Senate and House of Representatives" (article I, section 1). Knowing no more than these words, and understanding that they were written with a serious purpose, one might expect that those who want laws passed must travel to Capitol Hill. The words bestow upon that institution a legitimacy regarding a fundamental power of government: lawmaking.

To acknowledge that Congress has the ultimate authority to make law is not to dismiss the president's influence in that process. After all, he has both constitutional and political standing to participate. Rather, that acknowledgment offers a way to assess his influence. This discussion is meant to correct a tendency by many analysts to exaggerate the president's strategic position. Many view the president as agenda setter and program initiator and director, rather than as designator, certifier, or sequencer of priorities. A president's record is typically scored by how much of his program is enacted into law and sometimes simply by the number of laws passed, whether or not he initiated the proposals. Should he fail to propose a large and innovative program, or should circumstances not demand such action, the president will score low on what John B. Bader refers to as the "FDR scale"—essentially, the first-one-hundred-days test.¹ This test may even be applied at regular intervals throughout a president's term. There is, therefore, a real need to identify the characteristics of lawmaking as a first step in determining the president's role in the process.

Misinterpreting or oversimplifying the president's role in lawmaking may be a consequence of a failure to account fully for the complex features of lawmaking or the elaborate structure of a bicameral legislature. Lawmaking in a democratic system of separated institutions will be substantially more intricate and variable than in a unified, parliamentary structure. As a Britisher observer once noted, "You replay the match." The many arenas of decisionmaking provide multiple points of access and foster a permeability that makes it difficult to predict either participation or outcomes.

The Nature of Lawmaking

Lawmaking is an effort by society to manage itself. It is "the means by which governments legitimize substantive and procedural actions to reshape public problems, perhaps to resolve them."² Lawmaking in a democratic society can be traced through its many stages and venues: it is a trackable process. Legislators are most commonly thought of as *the* lawmakers, and as noted above, they have a constitutional responsibility to participate meaningfully in the process. But statutes passed by legislatures are not the end of lawmaking. Executives, bureaucrats, judges, and others implement and evaluate statutes through rule and standard setting, administrative and executive interpretations, court decisions, and petitions. At its most effective, lawmaking mirrors social life. J. Willard Hurst believed that "law moves with the main currents of American history."

> First, it is what [people] think: how they size up the universe and their place in it; what things they value, and how much; what they believe to be the relations between cause and effect, and the way these ideas affect their notions about how to go about getting the things they value. Second, it is what [people] do: their habits, their institutions.³

So conceived, no one can doubt the significance of lawmaking, nor question the vital role of those who make laws. T. V. Smith, an academic who served in the House of Representatives, eloquently wrote about legislative life and those who live it.

> The American way is a way of life and of law—and then of life as the final object of government. . . .
>
> Legislatures exist to solve those otherwise insoluble problems. . . .
>
> Blessed is the man who, through patience, sagacity, and co-operation with other men, can take the purely private thing called conscience and turn it into socially acceptable action through law. . . .
>
> Whoever has a genius for legislation has a mission of major importance to mankind.[4]

Jeremy Waldron contributes another major purpose of lawmaking in democracy—that of displaying disagreement. "Legislation is the product of a complex deliberative process that takes disagreement seriously and that claims its authority without attempting to conceal the contention and division that surrounds its enactment."[5] Legislatures are organized precisely to invite disagreement, publicly identify alternative views of an issue, and provide means for reaching an accommodation.

What are the features of lawmaking in Congress, specifically, those attributes of statute making to which presidents must accommodate?[6] The process is speculative, continuous, iterative and alterative, informative, deliberative, sequential, orderly, and declarative. These features are shaped by legislative contexts—those in the House and Senate. For example, representation and partisanship guarantee iteration and alteration. Institutionalism reinforces continuity and often designates sequence, as well as granting the means for securing and maintaining order and declaring agreements. All three—representation, partisanship, and institutionalism—influence what and how information is developed and communicated. Information, its volume and quality, aids in explaining the scope of speculation.

Speculation

"Legislation . . . is an act of the speculative imagination." As understood by Elijah Jordan in this way, enacting law is an exercise in comprehending "the world as fact within the same unity with the world regarded as ideal plan."[7] Election campaigns provide especially rich displays of the speculative imagination, of treating the "now" facts within the ideal plan. Presidential candidates' stump speeches and their platforms are replete with "if→then" propositions nested within ideal plans, articulated as seemingly practical policy moves. They often speak of changes that will happen as though presidents alone make law. As Senator Daniel Patrick

Moynihan (D-N.Y.) once observed, "You get into pretending to know the unknowable."[8]

The speculative feature of lawmaking is a rationale for a separated, representative government with checks and balances. Doubts about the vision and ability of any one decisionmaker encourage multiple sources of speculation. The Founding Fathers' misgivings about placing sole power in one person or institution remain lively today. "Whoever insists that he can state other people's position as well as they can is a dictator at heart; he has the psychological equipment if only he can add to it the necessary power."[9] Accountability might serve as a corrective to single-source speculation. But the costs may be high: economic disruption, human tragedy, war. Multiple sources, by contrast, foster competition and compromise among legitimate participants in different institutional venues. They are therefore justified, even at the cost of failure to assign responsibility and of governing by successive approximations rather than executing the ideal plan.

Lawmaking is ever and always speculative, a reach into the unknowable. Accordingly, lawmakers are risk takers. Yet, the separated system offers both corrections to and protections for the risks involved. Responsibility is diffused as proposals work their way through the elaborate institutional processes. No one lawmaker is typically held solely accountable, and therefore no one has an unbreakable commitment to the outcome. Accordingly, it is easier to make incremental adjustments or even root-and-branch reform, especially when responsibility is diffused across party lines (see the discussions of welfare reform, a balanced budget agreement, and education reform in chapter 7). Further, creativity, the super nova of the speculative imagination, may be nurtured simply because there is a high probability that proposals will be modified. So why not try?

Continuity

Lawmaking is continuous. Most laws create tangible programs, benefits, regulations, organizations, or processes. Funds are authorized and appropriated. Agents are instructed on how to collect taxes. There are behavioral, organizational, and structural effects once statutes are on the books. As a political system matures, much of the agenda is generated from within the programs previously authorized. Most of what a president proposes builds on what is already there, for example, in education, trade, agriculture, health, or housing. There are very few new initiatives, and virtually no new programs originate, live, and die within a single presidency. Presidents do have options, to be sure, but they are typically exercised within the constraints of ongoing commitments.

To say that most programs are continuous does not suggest they are without change. Often programs are expanded, particularly those judged to be politically, organizationally, and substantively successful. Incremental adjustments may be made and coverage extended. Most striking are those cases of full-scale evaluation of a program, leading to reform or reorganization. But root-and-branch reform requires substantial cross- or bipartisan political support. Beneficiaries, clienteles, and bureaucrats typically resist attempts to alter the status quo, except to expand existing provisions. Changes to the tax laws, in general, and welfare reform during the Clinton presidency, are prime examples of the resistance presidents encounter. Clinton's health care reform initiative illustrates the hazards of proposing broad-scale change, as well as inviting sole accountability for speculative creativity and thus losing the protective shield offered by the separated system.

As is amply demonstrated in chapter 7, continuity is a bedrock feature of lawmaking. It is the history that we are advised to acknowledge so as to avoid repeating errors, as well as the roster of interests and actors affected by and involved in a program. Typically, then, the study of any major law will reveal all or most of the politics of the separated system, including the place of the president at that time.

Iteration and Alteration

Lawmaking is iterative and alterative. Iteration is commonly defined as repetition. One dictionary, however, defines it as "a computational procedure in which replication of a cycle of operations produces results which approximate the desired result more and more closely." Alteration is therefore implied in the repeated exercises of exploring problems, developing solutions, and testing options. A substantive element is introduced in this process, making iteration a purposeful rather than a mindless activity. A proposal is worked and reworked to approximate the interests of those participating. This use of the term is familiar to bureaucrats engaged in planning and policymaking.

Iteration is not simply a function of the passage of time. Thus, for example, computation or approximation does not occur automatically just because a problem has been on the agenda for a long period. Conversely, efforts to block lawmaking, as occurred for decades on civil rights and federal aid to education, do not constitute iteration. However, faithful representation of the complex dimensions of an issue can result in significant delay, as efforts are made to compute and recompute formulas that "approximate the desired result more and more closely."

Iteration is not limited to partisan interactions, that is, one party repeating a policy exercise engaged in by its opposite. It can and does occur within one party, one institution, or one committee. It may be politically motivated or inspired solely by substantive policy concerns. Lawmaking is not a one-shot process, and iteration may occur over a period of months or years. Therefore, if the president is interested in a piece of legislation, he will have to be involved in many instances over time in order to exert influence. He cannot simply announce his position when a bill is introduced or when roll call voting begins.

A separated system facilitates iteration. Representation in a bicameral Congress was designed in part to provide assorted perspectives on public issues. Each chamber is organized and structured to encourage access and expression. Congress has a mature and active committee system with sophisticated iterative routines. These committees are formidable policy units, with user-friendly institutional memories, a modified seniority-based structure, and staffs oriented to serve their chairs or ranking members. Presidents ignore the advantages of iteration at their peril, however understandable their impatience with the seemingly interminable processes of the bureaucracy and on Capitol Hill.

Information and Inquiry

Hurst identified three related advantages of the legislature in a democratic political system: "its legitimacy in public opinion"; "its broad authority under the Constitution"; and "its power . . . to inquire into matters of public concern." Regarding the third advantage, Hurst explains:

> Law represents an effort—however short of the ideal—to order men's affairs according to rational weighing of values and the means of achieving them; how the lawmaker learns the facts of the living society in which he intervenes is, therefore, a point of fundamental importance regarding the manner of lawmaking. No agency in our government inherited a fact-gathering authority in any degree comparable to that of the legislature.[10]

Making law requires "the power to look for facts," so that reasonable choices can be made and current laws can be evaluated.

Keith Krehbiel offers a contemporary explication of the informational function of lawmaking. He identifies a "legislative signaling game" that is both sequential and informational. "The committee proposes a bill. The legislature updates its beliefs. The legislature chooses a policy." Krehbiel conceives of congressional committees as having power primarily because of their informational advantages: they signal facts needed by lawmakers. "In instances of informational committee power, a committee credibly transmits private information to get a majority to do what is in the majority's interest."[11]

This purpose of defining society's needs through representational lawmaking is rarely appreciated. In fact, presidents often decry the inevitable fact gathering by lawmakers. But their right to inquire cannot be denied. The manner of writing and enacting laws intimates the strategic relevance of inquiry. As Jordan observed, "the necessity of making law becomes the obligation to know."[12] Various rationales are used to locate the fact-finding function of lawmaking in one or another institution. Legislators have a strong claim because of their legitimacy as elected officials and their representational function. Specialists' claims are based on their expertise. Both justifications are genuine, if sometimes competitive. The legislators' claim is the more likely to be challenged, but no policy subject can legitimately be defined as beyond their purview.

Deciding what information to rely on is crucial for the conclusions it may allow and foster. One can observe the impact of the constituency-based anecdote in most congressional committee hearings, sometimes competing with more systematic evidence drawn from scientific studies. Alternatively, the gathering, analysis, and use of information may be framed by a specific event. The report of the 9/11 Commission, published in 2004, exemplifies an event-stimulated inquiry, prompted by a common urge to act speculatively to prevent a like occurrence in the future. The case also demonstrates that presidents are as much subject to the consequences of inquiry as they are in controlling others through information gathering. President Bush was moved to support the recommendations of a commission whose creation he did not initially favor. That the report was issued in the context of a presidential campaign further affected how the recommendations were received and acted on.

Deliberation

Lawmaking is deliberative. This feature is broadly accepted. Indeed, many observers express concern that lawmaking is *less* deliberative than in the past. Implicit in these worries is a standard of how much discussion, talk, or debate is necessary for effective lawmaking, presumably weighed against the need for timely action on a public problem. It is also assumed that deliberation will invite consideration of alternative perspectives or plans. The separated system offers many venues for deliberation among elected, bureaucratic, and judicial institutions. Often, however, the venues most carefully monitored are within legislatures, as the most publicly visible arenas for discussion.

Elijah Jordan identifies discussion as integral to speculation as a method. "The most elementary general function of the legislative body is to talk." Discussion is the means by which ideas are tested "as to their logical consistency." He promotes "the pressure of critical comparison with other ideas" because it "constitutes the experimentation under logical conditions which we have accepted as the definition of legislative thinking." Discussion may profit from debate and argument but it is more than either of those. It is a "genuine synoptic unity of all the pertinent ideas presented" and can only be achieved by talk, that is to say, communication.[13]

Not all legislative bodies allow discussion in the same form. The time allowed for debate also may differ. Woodrow Wilson wrote, "the Senate . . . enjoys a much greater freedom of discussion than the House can allow itself." Much as the Framers intended, the Senate can scrutinize and sift matters coming from the House. "The Senate's opportunities for open and unrestricted discussion and its simple, comparatively unencumbered forms of procedure, unquestionably enable it to fulfill with very considerable success its high functions as a chamber of revision."[14]

This freedom to discuss in the Senate has concerned advocates of deliberation. In particular, the filibuster is judged an abuse of the privilege and purpose of talk in legislatures as defined by Jordan and Wilson. But, of course, they propose an ideal lawmaking enterprise. Sarah A. Binder has documented the increasing reliance on filibusters, but their present-day use often thwarts rather than facilitates deliberation. The threat to filibuster is now frequently used to prevent legislation from being deliberated and voted on.[15]

Sequence

Lawmaking is sequential: laws are made in a series of stages, and because several institutions are legitimately involved, there are sequences within and between the institutions. The budget process is a notable example of elaborate sequencing. The executive produces a budget document that is then introduced in each house of Congress. The House and Senate have sequences of action leading to a budget resolution, which eventually must be approved by the other chamber. The various sequences by which the two houses act are themselves factors in the development of lawmaking strategies.

There are several types of sequences. Those that are required by the Constitution include the origination of revenue measures in the House and the requirement of action by both houses to enact a law. Some sequences are institutionally created to allow the House, Senate, and White House to do their work, such as legislative clearance in the White House or the movement of bills from subcommittee to committee to scheduling for floor consideration in each house of Congress. And some sequences are cross-institutional between the House and Senate or between the White House and the two houses of Congress, as is the budget process.

Decisions about sequence are typically strategic in nature. Who acts first may make an important difference. Yet before the split-party Congresses of the Reagan presidency, when an effort was made to build momentum by having the Republican Senate act first, little attention had been paid to this matter. The sequence was reversed in the Bush 43 presidency after Senator James Jeffords (R-Vermont) switched to independent status and voted with the Democrats to give them majority control of the Senate. From that time the Republican House passed legislation first, sending it on to the Democratic Senate. Strategic sequencing may also be developed for complex legislation. For example, during the Carter presidency, a special House committee was formed to manage a multijurisdictional energy bill. During the Clinton presidency, a bipartisan group worked with the White House to fashion a balanced budget agreement that was then applied in the budget resolutions and reconciliation bills on Capitol Hill.

Orderliness

Lawmaking is orderly, an attribute much like sequencing but more directly related to issues than to institutional flow. A major function of the executive is to set priorities—"Let's start here, then go there." But legislatures, too, must set an order for legislation to be taken up. Preferences are weighed against those of the president. Major battles may be fought over which legislation will be considered first. Even where there is little or no conflict over status, decisions have to be made simply to facilitate the flow of work in a legislative body, to suit timing demands (for example, for reauthorizations or other legislation subject to deadlines), or to accommodate various interests.

An important function of leadership is to set priorities in scheduling in consultation with the committee chairs. Presidents may participate in these decisions but are by no means in command. Split-party control greatly complicates orderliness. Congressional leaders from the other party will have their own priorities, which, if backed by party members, will prevail. President George W. Bush lost his advantage in setting the order when the Democrats took charge of the Senate after Jeffords switched in 2001 in the first months of the presidency. The new majority leader, Thomas Daschle (D-S.D.), brought up the patients' bill of rights rather than Bush's preferred issues. Order may be an issue too in one-party government. In 1993, with his own party in control of Congress, President Clinton selected health care reform rather than welfare reform as his priority. But many in Congress thought the order should have been reversed. Crises typically have the effect of displacing the expected order. When this happens, the president has the advantage in setting the new order, because of the singularity of his leadership in crises. A bicameral Congress does not have a single leader; indeed, each house may have a different party in the majority, as was the case during the 9/11 crisis.

Declaration

Lawmaking is declarative. An iterative, informational, deliberative, sequential, and orderly process within a two-house, representative legislature requires verbal announcements of agreements or their publication (typically in documents), as they are reached. The declaration of the most recent iteration is crucial. Jordan explains why: "the type of problem involved in practical life necessitates that the speculative process be also a public process, since life posits . . . a wider area for action than the will of the individual can comprehend."[16] Furthermore, declaration keeps track of who wants what of or for whom at various stages. Thus the visions, plans, agreements that represent various versions of the facts and expectations of participants are revealed. Others may then test a proposal by their own rendition of reality, however it is that their story has transpired.

Declaration contributes toward the desired goal of building majority support for a proposal, or revealing that no such coalition is possible. Here is a familiar pattern in Congress: an agreement is reached in a subcommittee; the results are displayed for participants in subsequent stages in the sequence; further changes are made as new interests are represented, an agreement is reached, and the results are published; previously nonparticipating interests try for an advantage in the rules for floor debate; an agreement is reached on how the proposal will be debated, and that is published; and still further interests require representation in the settlement on the floor. The media play an important role by advertising the agreements reached along the way, and this in turn affects the number of interests that participate at each stage. It is important to note that declaring agreements is no guarantee that they will be refined and passed along. Each stage is also an opportunity to obstruct further action.

The president's strategy typically accounts for the probability of greater participation as successive agreements are declared. Estimates are made regarding who is likely to respond and how. Presidents cannot wait to see what happens, nor can they ever trust that agreements will remain confidential. Carter, Reagan, Clinton, and Bush 43 were criticized for preparing major legislative packages—on energy, tax cuts, health care, and energy, respectively—behind closed doors. Such a reaction suggests that there are costs to failing to publicize agreements along the way. Affected interests typically want to offer their own versions of the facts at early stages and in official settings, especially for large-scale programs. They may even resort to the courts to support openness, as in the case of health care for Clinton and energy for Bush 43.

Statute making, then, can be understood as a series of *agree-and-display* exercises, each iteration being declared to a wider audience for its reactions. Publication leaves a record of affected interests and how they define their claims, as well as who won and who lost. Accordingly, when to display what to whom is an important strategic issue. Declaration may also contribute to efficient and timely participation by informing lawmakers of progress, thus permitting them to judge the effects on interests they represent.

Summary

In summary, representation justifies iteration, iteration produces information and occurs in sequence, an iterative-informational-sequential process requires declaration of prior results, and legislative agreements will be taken up in an order that is itself subject to influence. Viewing the lawmaking process in this way has the distinct advantage of directing attention to the role of the many participants who are legitimately involved. The president is often one of the most important participants. But no one who has read the Constitution or watched the government of the United States work expects him to be the sole actor.

This chapter examines a number of topics so as to show how presidents work on Capitol Hill. The first is presidential "success." Part of the problem of governing for presidents is calculating how to manage their participation in an ongoing legislative body with multiple dependencies. As Steven A. Shull points out, for presidents, success may require an understanding of what happens at several stages of the policy process.[17] To assess the role of the president requires study of more than roll call voting; study of compromise and change along the way is also needed.

Next is the production of laws in a separated system. Replacing the presidency-centered, party responsibility mode of analysis with a more system-oriented perspective allows one to accept evidence that production does not cease under split-party control. If a president does not act, perhaps Congress will.

The evidence of legislative productivity also encourages one to consider the continuity of issues. Perhaps the system produces in ways not predicted by party responsibility advocates, because legislative work is prolonged, bearing fruit in its own time rather than in four- or eight-year segments coincident with a president's tenure.

Presidential Success with Congress

There is an understandable interest in judging how well the president is doing on Capitol Hill, for all of the reasons that analysts focus on the president in the first place. If the president is supposed to lead the government, then people naturally want to know what is being accomplished. A standard test is the number of major laws enacted. This concentration both follows from and encourages a presidency-centered framework of analysis, leaving scholars unprepared to view or appreciate the president when he must take a lesser role because of political circumstances, personal policy preferences, or both. Jon R. Bond and Richard Fleisher acknowledge that "the present arrangement between the branches makes it extremely difficult for the president to fulfill promises made during the election period. Yet the public tends to hold the president accountable if he fails to deliver."[18] That the president may not wish to lead by passing legislation is seldom taken into account. Nor are other types of progress frequently scored, for example, progress in problem definition, agenda preparation, and proposal development—all of which may contribute to the passage of legislation at a later time. And until recently little attention has been paid to the effects of unilateral decisionmaking, as in executive orders.[19]

Comparing Two Eras

How determinative is presidential influence? Has it changed over time? Does he command Congress? Studies of both the pre– and post–World War II eras, relying on similar research methods, help to answer these questions.

In the most extensive study of presidential-congressional interaction before World War II, Lawrence H. Chamberlain examined ninety pieces of legislation.[20] His categorization is shown in table 6-1. There are relatively few instances where presidential influence was preponderant, but the number of such cases increased greatly during the New Deal decade of the 1930s, with a concomitant drop in the number of cases where congressional influence was preponderant. Pressure group influence was preponderant mostly on tariff acts. Twelve of the ninety acts (13 percent) were passed during the infrequent split-party governments of the period. By contrast, in David R. Mayhew's study of the postwar period (see futher below), 152 of 267 acts (57 percent) were passed during split-party governments, reflecting their greater frequency in this period.

Although Chamberlain's findings have received little notice in contemporary empirical studies of presidential-congressional interaction on legislation, they deserve attention for two reasons. First, they represent painstaking analysis of an earlier era, and therefore provide a most interesting basis for comparison. Second, many of his findings about the system are relevant today.

Chamberlain concluded that his results "indicate not that the President is less important than generally supposed but that Congress is more important."[21] This role is attributable in large part to the fact that most issues are treated over a period of time. His study demonstrates not only "the joint character of the American legislative process," but also that Congress cultivates proposals.

> One of the points brought out most clearly by the case studies . . . was the depth of the legislative roots of most important statutes. For instance, a law is hailed as something new at the time of passage but further examination reveals that the proposal had been discussed more or less continuously in Congress for several years.

The president's role often is one of designating or certifying an issue or proposal as worthy of further attention, according to Chamberlain.

> Presidential attention had led to [a bill's] elevation from the obscurity of just another bill to the prominence of an administration measure. Administrative experts had participated by drafting a new bill but there was not very much in the new bill that had not been present in one or more earlier drafts. At all events, driven by the power now behind it, the bill becomes law without great difficulty or delay, while in the absence of presidential action years might have gone by without its adoption.[22]

Table 6-1. *Major Legislation, by Institutional Influence, 1873–1940*

Preponderant institutional influence	1873–1900		1901–10		1911–20		1921–30		1931–40		Total	
	Number	Percent	Number	Percent	Number	Percent	Number	Percent	Number	Percent	Number	Percent
Presidential	1	6	4	29	4	20	0	0	10	36	19	21
Congressional	12	75	4	29	10	50	6	50	3	11	35	39
Joint presidential-congressional	1	6	5	36	6	30	3	25	14	50	29	32
Pressure group[a]	2	13	1	7	0	0	3	25	1	4	7	8
Total	16	100	14	101[b]	20	100	12	100	28	101[b]	90	100

Source: Developed from the summary of legislation in Lawrence H. Chamberlain, *The President, Congress and Legislation* (Columbia University Press, 1946). pp. 450–52.
a. Without the pressure group category, the total percentages (far right column) for the other three categories are presidential, 35 percent; congressional, 42 percent; joint president-congressional, 23 percent; (N = 83).
b. Numbers do not add to 100 due to rounding.

Chamberlain estimated that seventy-seven of the ninety acts could be traced to bills previously introduced in Congress by members themselves. He judged this "long germinative period" to be "one of the most valuable contributions that a legislative body can make."[23] I will have reason to return to these important observations later in this chapter.

In the postwar period, many analysts have concluded that Congress is no longer able to perform the active role that it played during the period of Chamberlain's study. Some have alleged that power shifted to the White House: some have even spoken of the "imperial presidency" and of "presidential government."[24] In a particularly critical analysis, Samuel P. Huntington argued that "momentous social changes have confronted Congress with an institutional 'adaptation crisis.'" Huntington asserted that Congress was fighting against itself in trying to preserve autonomy relative to the executive.

> Apparently Congress can defend its autonomy only by refusing to legislate, and it can legislate only by surrendering its autonomy. [When] Congress balks, criticism rises, [and] the clamoring voices of reformers fill the air with demands for the "modernization" of the "antiquated procedures" of an "eighteenth century" Congress so it can deal with "twentieth century realities." The demands for reform serve as counters in the legislative game to get the President's measures through Congress. Independence thus provokes criticism; acquiescence brings approbation. If Congress legislates, it subordinates itself to the President; if it refuses to legislate, it alienates itself from public opinion. Congress can assert its power or it can pass laws; but it cannot do both.[25]

Ronald C. Moe and Steven C. Teel sought to test Huntington's analysis by reviewing legislation passed during 1940–67 (after the period studied by Chamberlain), relying primarily on case histories in twelve categories of legislation. Their review does not support Huntington's observations:

> Our conclusion challenges the conventional wisdom that the president has come to enjoy an increasingly preponderant role in national policymaking. The evidence does not lend support to Huntington and his thesis that Congress ought to recognize its declining state and forego what remains of its legislative function. Quite the contrary, the evidence suggests that Congress continues to be an active innovator and very much in the legislative business.[26]

In seeking to explain the continued importance of Congress in lawmaking, Moe and Teel identify the "decentralized structure of both chambers." They believe that "Congress provides innovation in policy through 'successive limited comparisons.'" Congress, it seems, is well organized to do its job of making law. In the process, and not surprisingly, the members and their staffs come to know a lot about what public policy is and whom it affects.

During the 1970s, after both Huntington's and Moe and Teel's studies had been published, Congress engaged in substantial reform. One main purpose was to enable it to be even more heavily involved in contemporary policy-making. Increased personal and committee staff, new and enhanced policy analytical units, new budget procedures, and committee and party reorganizations all contributed to creating an enormous policy factory on Capitol Hill. Coincident with this development was the start of an era of presidents who, for several reasons, were less likely to propose extensive new programs or were forced by the sheer magnitude of administering the Great Society to offer proposals that were more consolidative than innovative.

These developments—a more policy-active Congress, a less policy-active president—would seem to invite even more contextual analysis of lawmaking to account for the characteristics identified above. Yet analysis of roll call votes came to be the basis for gauging presidential-congressional interaction. Roll calls surely afford a tempting test of presidential success in legislating. And indeed they would be a most convenient and meaningful measure if presidents submitted proposals to be voted up or down in a one-house legislature. Such conditions would satisfy the avid sports fans among analysts, who like to have winners and losers in the game of politics. Alas, the Founders were not engaged in preparing an eighteenth-century version of a contemporary sports contest. One noted congressional scholar, R. Douglas Arnold, wrote about roll calls: "I am struck by how inconsequential many of these decisions really are."[27]

Presidential Support Scores

Congressional Quarterly prepares annual support scores for estimating how well presidents have worked with Congress. When the score is announced each year, it typically gets considerable attention in the press, including comparison with the scores of other presidents. Scores are based on roll call votes on matters on which the president has taken a position or for which a position might reasonably be deduced. While of general interest, they should be used with caution. *Congressional Quarterly* itself advises that the scores "must be interpreted with care." For example, the editors note that the scores do not take into account "matters approved by voice vote or that are killed or bottled up in committee"; the administration sometimes does not take a position on an important issue; equal weight is given to all issues and to all votes (that is, whether they fall narrowly or with a wide margin); and a proliferation of votes on a single issue can skew the composite score for a president.[28]

Many scholars have identified other reasons not to rely too heavily on these scores.[29] The judgment about the president's position may not always square with how those in the White House see a particular vote. The president's position may shift along the way (*Congressional Quarterly* uses his position at the time of the vote). The number of noncontroversial votes that are included in calculating the scores varies across presidents (between 12 and 51 percent, according to Bond and Fleisher).[30]

Additional concerns arise when one reviews the votes that are included in any one year. The House may vote on an issue that is not voted on in the Senate, thus producing different issue sets for each chamber and reducing the potential for comparison between them. The two chambers seldom vote on the same amendments, and the bills subject to conference are, perforce, different. Sometimes the votes that form the basis of the scores are heavily weighted to a few issues. For example, in 1989 eleven of President Bush's fourteen victories and eight of his eleven defeats on domestic policy came on two bills. Also in 1989, twenty-one of Bush's total of seventy-four victories on Senate roll call votes were on nominations, which typically cluster in the first year of a presidency. Had nominations not been included (he suffered one defeat), his Senate support score would have dropped by 6 percent.

Other distortions may occur as a result of the politics of the time. President Clinton had the same high support score in both 1993 and 1994: 86.4 percent. The White House touted these scores as matching those of the Johnson presidency. As it happened, however, Clinton suffered major defeats on procedural moves that were not represented in recorded votes (as was the case with his national health care program). The Bush 43 presidency had even higher support scores in 2001 and 2002, 87.0 and 87.8 percent, respectively. Yet much of Bush's original program was stalled, having been superseded after 9/11 by national and domestic security legislation, which had bipartisan support.

Examination of specific pieces of legislation and how the votes on them were assessed also raises questions about the utility of the scores for interpreting a president's success in getting what he wants from Congress. Consider the Civil Rights Act of 1957. Six Senate and four House votes were selected for purposes of determining presidential support. Four of the Senate votes were counted as victories for the president: rejection of two amendments and adoption of two motions (one was to adopt the House version of the bill). The other two Senate votes, both on amendments, were counted as defeats for the president. The four House votes were counted as presidential victories: the rejection of a motion to recommit and the rule, initial passage, and subsequent approval of a modified bill. So, the president scored eight victories out of the ten roll call votes, a highly respectable batting percentage. Yet Eisenhower signed the bill without comment, and the *New York Times* reported that his silence "reflected in part his dissatisfaction with the drastic revision of the Administration measure as it passed through the Senate."[31] There was, in fact, substantial question as to the strength of the president's commitment in this area (see chapter 7).

President Carter's experience with his proposed Department of Education offers another interesting example of the potential hazards in analysis based on presidential support scores. Carter was credited by *Congressional Quarterly* with seventeen victories and two defeats on this measure, for purposes of calculating his 1979 score. These wins constituted 7 percent of Carter's total roll call victories in 1979. Yet the legislative history of this proposal suggests anything but sure-handed presidential control. In fact, the debate was almost comical at times, especially in the House, where twelve of the seventeen victories were registered (see chapter 7 for details and for further examples of incongruous or misleading results). Study of the substance of decisions and the process of lawmaking raises questions about these scores as indicators of presidential preference and achievement, even in the final stages of action on legislation.

The support scores fail for all the reasons listed above. But more fundamentally, their creation is driven by a faulty premise regarding the operation of the political system—that it should be tested by the extent to which Congress approves of an identifiable White House program or preference. The premise itself is wrong, and therefore so is the test. As discussed, lawmaking in the United States is, by design and practice, iterative and sequential. It is not temporally bound to a Congress or a presidential term. The president plays a role in this process, but equally so does each house of Congress. How all these components work together at any one time depends heavily on the issues and the politics of the time.

Other Indicators

Scholars have sought to overcome the problems inherent in presidential support scores and other indexes. Edwards offers four indexes of presidential support in the House and Senate for 1953–86, from "the comprehensive to the very selective."[32] *Overall support* includes all the votes on which the president has taken a stand (as determined by *Congressional Quarterly*).

Nonunanimous support includes the votes on which the president has taken a stand and the winning side constitutes less than 80 percent of those who voted. *Single-vote support* includes only the most important non-unanimous vote on each bill, thus avoiding the problem of distortion caused by many votes on amendments to a bill. And *key votes* include those on which the president has taken a stand among those selected by *Congressional Quarterly* as being of particular importance. This produces a small number of votes for each Congress.

Each of the four measures permits the calculation of a score for members of Congress as well as for the House and the Senate. There are differences among the indexes, to be sure, but overall one is struck more by the similarities, most notably those between the indexes of nonunanimous and single-vote support. Edwards concludes that "including more than one vote per issue in an index of presidential support has little impact on the index."[33]

However one develops and uses indexes of support, it is important to recall precisely what the data represent: aggregated individual decisions on an unsystematic sample of the questions dealt with in the lawmaking process. To avoid the problems with scores discussed above, Bond and Fleisher simply rely on the underlying roll call votes. They then distinguish between conflictual and nonconflictual votes and between important and less important issues.[34] These refinements enable them to offer a more reliable test of presidential "success." Peterson draws a sample from *Congressional Quarterly*'s list of important issues (updating it to include the Carter and Reagan presidencies) and specifies a wide range of explanatory variables for how Congress responded to presidential initiatives. His approach, the least presidency-centered of the empirical studies of Congress, eschews a search for "success" in favor of several potential outcomes: inaction, opposition dominance, compromise, presidential dominance, and consensus. Peterson accepts, as I do here, that "the president's role in legislative policy making, and the response to the executive's initiatives, depend on the type of policy under consideration, because the structural implications of the tandem-institutions setting differs across policy domains."[35]

It is interesting and relevant that those who rely on floor voting in the House and the Senate typically conclude by challenging the conventional wisdom about presidential command of Congress. For example, Edwards finds that even those presidents who appeared to dominate "were actually facilitators rather than directors of change." And Bond and Fleisher attribute doing well on Capitol Hill more to "Congress-centered" than to "presidency-centered" variables. The implications are clear. As Edwards explains, "By examining the parameters of presidential leadership and not assuming that presidents will succeed in influencing Congress if they are just skillful enough in employing their resources, one is better positioned to understand the consequences of leadership efforts."[36]

However they are interpreted, roll call votes cannot be more than they are: one form of floor action on legislation. If analysts insist on scoring the president, concentrating on this stage of lawmaking can provide no more than a partial tally. But I would question a focus on "presidential success" to the exclusion of other important topics associated with how the government makes law. An emphasis on scoring in this way contributes to a presidency-centered appraisal, often neglecting to account for how the larger system works under the variable conditions permitted by the Constitution.

Legislative Production: What Gets Done and When

A concept of presidential success that is questionable and limited under unified party conditions is bound to be even more so when the two parties settle in at each end of Pennsylvania Avenue. If one believes that the government can only work well when one party is in control of the White House and Congress, then split-party control is a serious problem. Woodrow Wilson believed that "you cannot compound a successful government out of antagonisms."[37] James L. Sundquist concluded that presidents and Congresses of opposite parties will produce stalemate.[38] James MacGregor Burns has held that "the majority party should be the perfect instrument for carrying out a popular mandate." In 1990, when various Eastern European regimes were collapsing, he advised them to pay little heed to the American political system: "Our system of checks and balances, with the resulting fragmentation of power, frustrates leadership, saps efficiency, and erodes responsibility. . . . The governing party is failing to govern and the opposition party is failing to oppose. . . . We can, paradoxically, learn from [Eastern Europe]."[39]

In reading such analyses one would think that the government had ceased to work: that the United States was witnessing the "deadlock of democracy," as Burns once described it; the end of politics, by other accounts.[40] Yet presidents continue to make proposals and Congresses still legislate, even when voters return split-party government to Washington. In fact, studies show little difference in the quantity of major legislation passed under one- and split-party governments.

The Mayhew Study

It is precisely this matter of whether the system passes important laws that is of interest to David R. Mayhew. He originally studied the period from 1947 to 1990 to find out how many major laws were enacted and when. Mayhew acknowledges the importance of ideological differences that may be associated with the parties and their control of one or both branches, "But the basic concern in this work, as regards lawmaking, is not with direction but with motion—whether much gets done at all."[41]

In addition to the usual concerns about presidential support scores, Mayhew asks, "Why should we care whether presidents got what they wanted?" He doubts that is "the appropriate question." He understands that not all laws are a part of a president's program, and indeed, some are exactly contrary to what the White House wants. "But laws are laws. System production should be the final test, not whether presidents happened to get what they wanted."[42] That is exactly the perspective to which I adhere. Presidents are a part of a government, and so is Congress. Both have the right and duty to participate in lawmaking, and both do so. As stressed earlier, those who score the president typically ignore other players with a defensible interest in legislation. The ultimate test is the success of that system in treating public problems. A president whose proposals score well in roll call votes may find that his programs do little to solve problems. Conversely, presidential proposals that are substantially changed by Congress may do the job. If so, then failure to win in the short run may actually result in a respectable record for a president's term in office in the long run.

Mayhew understands that he cannot begin to answer his central question regarding system production without establishing criteria for important legislation. In a meticulous accounting, he "sweeps" twice through the period. First, he draws on contemporary judgments, mostly those by journalists doing an end-of-the-year wrap-up story on Congress. Next, he draws on the retrospective judgments of policy specialists in forty-three policy areas. He uses the second sweep to validate choices from the first sweep and also to identify further important acts. Through this process, he identifies 267 important enactments. Mayhew has provided updates to this original list, relying on his "first sweep" method.

There are two problems with Mayhew's technique, for my purposes. First, it cannot easily account for the prevention of the passage of a law as a form of system production. Sometimes a president does not want a bill to pass and will count it among his achievements if he is able to stop it from being enacted. Presidents may even hope that failure to act at the national level will result in private action or legislation at the state or local level. Second, there is a natural tendency to treat all important legislation as equal, when in fact the enactments listed by Mayhew differed tremendously in their impact. Mayhew would be the first to acknowledge this latter point, yet he does not weight the laws in drawing conclusions about the differences between single- and split-party governments (and nor do I in reviewing specific pieces of legislation in chapter 7). However, aggregating these enactments as though they were equal is misleading in calculating legislative production.

A provocative study typically spawns scholarly reactions and further contributions to the basic issues raised. Mayhew counts what did pass and finds little difference between single- and split-party governments. The matter of what might have passed had there not been a split-party government intrigues scholars. But perhaps presidents don't even try under these circumstances, though they may acknowledge the importance of an issue. Or possibly more attention should be paid to House and Senate differences in explaining what does not get passed. Refinement in what is and is not called major legislation is called for, as well as advanced calibration in the types of single- and split-party conditions. At the very least, Mayhew has stimulated work on how the system functions, even if much of what has been done subsequently has returned to the theme of "gridlock"—why the system doesn't work—rather than elaborating on his theme of governing—how it does work.[43]

Laws and Mandates

I turn now to a highly aggregative exercise. First, I categorize Mayhew's list of important enactments, as he does, by president and by whether the government or Congress was single-party or split-party (table 6-2). The years and circumstances of greatest production are clear. Under single-party control, the number of enactments during a Congress ranges from six during the last two years of the Truman presidency (1951–53) to twenty-two during the first two years of Johnson's full term (1965–67). For split-party control, the range is from five during the last two years of the Eisenhower presidency to twenty-two during each of two Congresses, under Nixon (1969–71) and Nixon-Ford (1973–75). As Mayhew emphasizes, by this gross measure there is very little difference in the production of important legislation between single- and split-party control. If split-party control is divided into two

Table 6-2. *Major Legislation Passed, by Type of Presidential Mandate and Party Control, 1947–2003*[a]

Type of mandate and president	Number of enactments	Party control
Change		
Eisenhower (1953–55)	9	Single
Johnson (1965–67)	22	Single
Reagan (1981–83)	9	Split/Democratic House
Total	40	
Annual mean	6.7	
Status quo		
Eisenhower (1957–59)	11	Split/Democratic Congress
Nixon-Ford (1973–75)	22	Split/Democratic Congress
Reagan (1985–87)	9	Split/Democratic House
Clinton (1997–99)	8	Split/Republican Congress
Clinton (1999–2001)	6	Split/Republican Congress
Total	56	
Annual mean	5.6	
Mixed (presidential year)		
Truman (1949–51)	12	Single
Kennedy (1961–63)	15	Single
Nixon (1969–71)	22	Split/Democratic Congress
Carter (1977–79)	12	Single
Bush 41 (1989–91)	9	Split/Democratic Congress
Clinton (1993–95)	11	Single
Bush 43 (2001–03)	17	Single to Split/Democratic Senate
Total	99	
Annual mean	7.1	
Mixed (midterm)		
Truman (1951–53)	6	Single
Eisenhower (1955–57)	6	Split/Democratic Congress
Kennedy-Johnson (1963–65)	13	Single
Johnson (1967–69)	16	Single
Nixon (1971–73)	15	Split/Democratic Congress
Carter (1979–81)	10	Single
Reagan (1983–85)	7	Split/Democratic House
Bush 41 (1991–93}	8	Split/Democratic Congress
Total	81	
Annual mean	5.1	
Unmandate		
Truman (1947–49)	10	Split/Republican Congress
Eisenhower (1959–61)	5	Split/Democratic Congress
Ford (1975–77)	14	Split/Democratic Congress
Reagan (1987–89)	12	Split/Democratic Congress
Clinton (1995–97)	15	Split/Republican Congress
Total	56	
Annual mean	5.6	

Source: Developed from list in David R. Mayhew, *Divided We Govern: Party Control, Lawmaking, and Investigations, 1946–1990* (Yale University Press, 1991), pp. 52–73, and his subsequent updates.
a. See chapter 4 for types of mandates.

groups—that in which there are opposition party majorities in both houses of Congress and that in which just the House is controlled by the opposition party—the Reagan years show a substantially lower annual production when only the House was under Democratic control (1981–87) and an increase when both houses were won by the Democrats.

Mayhew draws attention to the "bulges in the middle" of the forty-four-year period of his initial study. The sixteen years from the beginning of the Kennedy presidency to the end of the Nixon-Ford presidencies (36 percent of the period) produced 52 percent of the important enactments. A review of the laws themselves suggests an agenda-based explanation like that presented in chapter 5: significant expansion during the 1960s, followed by various consolidative and regulatory actions during the 1970s.

I now add to Mayhew's findings by categorizing presidents by the interpretation of their mandates (see table 6-2). The first category—the perceived mandate for change—illustrates the problems of ideological direction that are raised but not addressed as such by Mayhew. Over half the important enactments were products of the first two years of Johnson's full term. This was the core of the Great Society. By comparison, Eisenhower hardly had a program. As for Reagan, to count either the Economic Recovery Tax Act or the Omnibus Budget Reconciliation Act (both passed in 1981) as one enactment shows clearly the need for a weighting system. These two enactments may not have exactly matched the effect on the subsequent agenda of the twenty-two passed in 1965–67, but their impact was substantial. In Mayhew's defense, however, such weighting would only lend further support to his overall conclusion regarding the lack of independent effect on the volume of lawmaking of single- versus split-party government.

The perceived mandate for the status quo is restricted to the records of reelected presidents at this writing: Eisenhower, Nixon, Reagan, and Clinton. In each case, the voters returned the whole government, which meant a party split (except in 1984, when the Republicans retained their Senate majority). Again, the volume of major legislation enacted within this group varies considerably, ranging from six pieces for Clinton in his final Congress (1999–2001) to twenty-two for Nixon-Ford (1973–75). The Nixon-Ford period is particularly fascinating, as it surely violates every conceivable condition for responsible party government. A Republican president won reelection by one of the widest margins in history, but voters returned a Democratic Congress. The president was then severely handicapped by the resignation of Vice President Agnew and by the Watergate scandal that led to resignations and indictments of many in his government, culminating in his own resignation. And yet, through it all a sizable number of important laws were enacted. Major legislative initiatives were successful in spite of the media and public preoccupation with what was interpreted as a constitutional crisis. How could that be? Possibly because the president is not, and was never intended to be, the whole government: the political system was purposely designed to weather such predicaments.

Two of the reelected presidents, Eisenhower and Reagan, experienced major midterm losses in their sixth year (as discussed below), and Nixon was not even in office at that point. Clinton, on the other hand, survived an impeachment in part because his party defied historical trends in the sixth-year midterm elections and had a slight gain in House seats and stayed even in the Senate. Thus, whereas the other three reelected presidents suit the "unmandate" conditions during their final two years, Clinton remained a "status quo" president, albeit one with little production of major legislation. The first midterm of the Bush 43 presidency, in 2002, is interesting for a different reason. The Republican Party increased its margins in the House and the Senate, the first time the president's party did so since the Democrats'gains in 1934. The results encouraged a strengthened status quo mandate for Bush. Having barely won in a disputed election in 2000, the president was in a stronger position to continue his leadership in the war on terrorism, at least until the aftermath of the war in Iraq. Reelection in 2004, accompanied by Republican increases in Congress, further reinforced the president's status (though, as noted earlier, his win was substantially less than that of other postwar reelected presidents).

The third category, the mixed mandate, is the largest. It includes the cases following a presidential election that produced incongruous results—for Congress in one direction and the president in another, or less strongly in the same direction—thus causing problems for the mandate readers. Also included are cases following midterm elections in which a declared mandate was more muted (1954, 1966, 1982) or a previously mixed result was confirmed (1950, 1962, 1970, 1978). Together, the annual mean production of legislation does not vary greatly from the other categories.

Differences do emerge, however, when the two types of mixed mandate are separated. The first-term mixed-mandate presidents—Truman, Kennedy, Nixon, Carter, Bush 41, Clinton, and Bush 43—have the highest annual average legislative production of any group. Two in this group, Nixon and Bush 41, faced an opposition party Congress. Another, Bush 43, began with Republican control of both houses but lost the Senate when

James Jeffords (R-Vt.) opted for independent status and voted with the Democrats. Perhaps lack of clarity in the policy messages of an election is a good thing for the passage of major legislation (the two-year count of major legislation for these three cases was twenty-two, nine, and seventeen, respectively). If so, there is not much solace for party government advocates. The second group, those following midterm elections, has a significantly lower annual mean production, perhaps because in some cases the first two years had been quite productive.

The "unmandate" refers to those conditions when analysts declared governing capabilities to be seriously jeopardized. Three of the five cases come at the second midterm election of an eight-year administration, when Republicans suffered major losses: 1958 for Eisenhower; 1974 for Ford, who was completing the second Nixon presidency; and 1986 for Reagan, whose party lost its majority in the Senate. The fourth case is that of Truman after the 1946 election, when Republicans won control of both branches for the first time since 1930. These four were not highly productive Congresses, and yet even under these dire political circumstances the system did not cease to operate. In fact, contrary to what most analysts would predict, major legislation was enacted during such periods: the Taft-Hartley Act and the Marshall Plan during the 80th Congress (1947–49); the Landrum-Griffin Labor Reform Act and a civil rights act during the 86th Congress (1959–61); energy and environmental laws and a tax reform act during the 94th Congress (1975–77); and welfare, Medicare, and trade reform in the 100th Congress (1987–89).

The fifth instance of an "unmandate" is the 1994 election. As in 1946, the Republicans recaptured majority status in both houses of Congress after a lengthy period in the minority. In 1994, however, House Republicans had not been in the majority for forty years, compared to sixteen in 1946. Senate Republicans had been in the minority for just eight years in 1994. As shown in table 6-2, both the 80th and the 104th Congresses produced substantial major legislation. Both Truman and Clinton vetoed major bills, but landmark bills were eventually passed.

Mayhew asks this relevant question: Do important laws enacted during unified control pass by large margins, while those enacted during divided control pass by small margins? The answer is that most laws drew either bipartisan or cross-partisan support; more were passed with majorities of two-thirds or more during split-party control than during single-party control. This outcome is actually what Mayhew expects, because under divided government "wider assent is needed to permit action."[44] But, of course, his thinking runs counter to that of the party government advocates, who would predict stalemate. Moreover, Mayhew finds cross-partisan politics in two directions: southern Democrats joining Republicans (the conservative coalition) and moderate Republicans joining northern Democrats (most often on civil rights legislation). That there have been fewer of each type of coalition in Congresses since 1994 shows the effects of party discipline in an era of narrow-margin politics.

Two points bear reiteration. First, neither Mayhew in his work, nor I in my use of it, is suggesting that it makes no difference who is in control of which parts of the national government. The product of Lyndon Johnson's Great Society was very different from that of the great consolidation of the Nixon period and the great deficit of the Reagan period. To show that there are no substantial differences between single- and split-party governments in the quantity of important enactments is not to say that the laws themselves do not differ in substance, kind, and direction. But the system does move under both types of governments, and it appears to move rationally toward an expanded role under some circumstances and toward consolidation, even contraction, under other circumstances. Critics may not like the policy decisions that are made at any one time or under particular circumstances, but such concerns differ from conclusions that the system is deadlocked and cannot act.

Second, nothing in this discussion is meant to suggest that the president is an unimportant player in national lawmaking and politics. I am seeking to illustrate the variable role that a president plays in a system of separated institutions competing for shares of powers. The presumed goal of that competition is the resolution of problems on the government agenda, which has a dynamic all its own.

Legislative Time Lines

Chamberlain stresses that study of legislation reveals that "new" proposals typically have been "discussed more or less continuously in Congress for several years." John W. Kingdon describes a continuous process of policy initiation, testing, and change, often involving a "recombination of already familiar elements." Richard E. Neustadt acknowledges that "everything remains unfinished business." Former senator (and White House chief of staff) Howard Baker (R-Tenn.) observed that "issues are like snakes—they just refuse to die! They keep coming back, time after time." Richard Rose refers to the president as a "policy taster": "When a President goes [to]

Washington, he does not have to bring a new set of policy proposals with him. There are lots of ideas circulating in executive agencies and Congress. . . . From the viewpoint of a President who is a professional campaigner and an amateur in government, it is just as well that a pile of ideas awaits him."[45] Serious students of national policymaking concede that what has gone before helps immeasurably in explaining what will happen next.

A related notion is that of the "idea whose time has come." That was the explanation given by Senator Everett M. Dirksen (R-Ill.) for the passage of the Civil Rights Act of 1964. When told that his colleague Barry M. Goldwater (R-Ariz.), the odds-on favorite to run against President Johnson, refused to support the bill, Dirksen reportedly told Goldwater: "You just can't do it, not only for yourself, but you can't do it for the party. The idea has come!"[46]

One former House member identified a policy cycle for major issues that is independent of the electoral cycle.

> The issue governs. . . . Some things have a shelf-life in Congress and they don't have to fit the quadrennial patterns of elections. Clean air was one of those. After we'd screwed around with it long enough, it was going to come due. Trade Act of 1988. [After] four years [it] eventually came to a point where it suddenly came to life and it was an important policy piece.[47]

Yet there are calendar markings derived from the Constitution that encourage categorizing policy by a presidency, legislative session, or Congress. Those are, indeed, useful dividing points. But they should not deter scholars from inquiring into policy lineages, particularly to better understand how institutions cope with public issues. In other words, the convenience of, say, a presidential term should not blind one to how a particular legislative initiative fits into its policy context or when an issue may suddenly spring to life.

Most of the current studies of presidential-congressional interaction raise serious questions about the extent to which the president controls the agenda and manages Congress. The White House is not a bad place to start in identifying the agenda, to be sure, but one must move on. Nor, as Mayhew has shown, can one rely solely on single-party government to produce policy results.

All of this is by way of justifying the next exercise, which is itself a prelude to more detailed treatment of selected laws in the post–World War II period (see chapter 7). In understanding how a president does his job, how he tries to find his place in government, it is useful to consider the policy setting within which his actions and preferences have force and meaning.

He judges how to place himself and his policy preferences in ongoing institutional, political, and policy processes. I will concentrate here on the latter, drawing specific attention to time lines for the enactment of legislation.

I selected twenty-eight laws from Mayhew's original list to illustrate variation in issues, adding others from those he subsequently identified in the Clinton and Bush 43 presidencies (which I discuss separately). Like Richard F. Fenno in choosing members of the House of Representatives for his analysis of their *Home Style*, I did not know which laws would best serve my goals, since I was not fully certain what I was looking for. Also like Fenno, I did not know the answers in advance, nor was I very clear about the questions.[48] But I did know why I wanted to study laws. I was dissatisfied with my own understanding of the variable role of the president in lawmaking under different types of party control and under varying partisan conditions, as discussed in chapter 1. The number of laws I selected for each presidency is not in proportion to the years involved; I was more intent on choosing cases that represented achievements of the time, those normally associated with a particular president, and that offered a suitable variety of issues. Many policy issues are included: labor, foreign policy and trade, health and welfare, education, taxation and budgeting, transportation and energy, environment, civil rights, regulation, and crime. Defense and agriculture are, perhaps, the principal omissions (although the War Powers Resolution was as much about defense as foreign policy, and the Food Stamp Act, when passed, was as much a farm surplus as welfare program).

The first exercise in regard to these bills is to establish a time line for each (see figure 6-1). I ask, was it a new idea? Was it an extension of a basic law passed earlier? Was there an immediate precursor? Did the legislative history carry over from one presidency to the next? The overwhelming conclusion is that most of these enactments were part of a continuing legislative story within an issue area. Two cases of the twenty-eight were without obvious precursors in either a previously enacted basic law or efforts that trace to previous presidencies. The Marshall Plan and the War Powers Resolution of 1973 were developed within the Truman and Nixon presidencies, respectively. The first was a proposal of the administration, originating within the Department of State, with the approval of the president. The second was a proposal originating in Congress and vehemently opposed by the president, who vetoed the resolution when it reached his desk.

The Budget and Impoundment Control Act of 1974 is somewhat of a special case inasmuch as it proposed substantially new reforms. The Legislative Reorganization Act of 1946 had provided for a legislative budget,

Figure 6-1. *Legislative Time Lines, Twenty-Eight Selected Enactments, 1947–90*

Truman (1945–53)
Taft-Hartley (T-H)
Marshall Plan (MP)
National Housing Act (NHA)
Excess Profits Tax (EPT)

Tenure

Labor Act → Bill → T-H (1947)
Truman Doctrine → MP (1948)
Housing Act → Bills → Act → NHA (1949)
Revenue Act → Act → EPT (1950)

Eisenhower (1953–61)
Atomic Energy Act (AEA)
Highway Act (HA)
Civil Rights Act (CRA)
Landrum-Griffin Act (LGA)

Tenure

Atomic Energy Act → Hngs → AEA (1954)
Highway Act → Amdts → Proposal → HA (1956)
Proposal → Proposal → CRA (1957)
Labor Act → T-H → Bill → LGA (1959)

Kennedy (1961–63)
Manpower Dev. & Tng. Act (MDTA)
Revenue Act (RA)
Clean Air Act (CAA)

Tenure

Voc. Ed. Act → Amdts → NDEA → Amdts → MDTA (1962)
Revenue Acts → Int. Rev. Code → RA (1962)
Air Pollution Act → Amdt → Amdt → CAA (1963)

Johnson (1963–69)
Food Stamps (FS)
ESEA
Medicare (MD)

Tenure

AAA → Amdts → Food Stamps → Bills → Pilot → FS (1964)
Lanham Act → NDEA → Bills → ESEA (1965)
SSA → Proposals → Bills → Kerr-Mills → Bills → MD (1965)

Nixon (1969–74)
OSHA
COLAs
War Powers Resolution (WPR)
Budget Reform Act (BRA)

Ford (1974–77)
Energy Act (EA)
Toxic Substances (TS)

Carter (1977–81)
Airline Deregulation (AD)
Dept. of Education (DOE)
Synfuels (SYN)

Reagan (1981–89)
Econ. Recovery Tax Act (CUT)
Social Security Reform (SSR)
Anticrime (AC)
Trade Act (TA)

Bush (1989–93)
Deficit Reduction (DR)

Tenure

Walsh-Healey Act → Bill → OSHA (1970)
SSA → Increases and expansion → Amdts → COLAs (1972)
Legis. Reorg. Act → Proposals → WPR (1973)
→ Hngs → BRA (1974)

Tenure

Emer. Act → Reorg → EA (1975)
FIFRA → Amdts → Bills → FIFRA Ex → TS (1976)

Tenure

Federal Aviation Act → Hngs → AD (1978)
Office of Education → FSA → Department of HEW → DOE (1979)
Defense Production Act → Bills → SYN (1980)

Tenure

Revenue Acts → Int. Rev. Code → Acts → Bills → CUT (1981)
SSA → Increases and expansion → COLAs → Tax Inc → Cmsn → SSR (1983)
Crime Control Act → Bills → AC (1984)
Tariff Act → Amdts → Tariff Class. → Act → Act → TA (1988)

Tenure

Gramm-Rudman → DR (1990)

1930s 1940s 1950s 1960s 1970s 1980s 1990

Sources: Developed from information on legislation in *Congressional Quarterly Almanac*, various vols.; and Congressional Quarterly, *Congress and the Nation*, various vols.

but the experiment did not work. It could hardly be considered a precursor to the 1974 act. This was a reorganizational effort conceived on Capitol Hill as a response to congressional inadequacies and fear of presidential usurpation of a fundamental legislative power.

There are five other cases of relatively short legislative heritages, even though they carry through from one presidency to the next. The Energy Policy and Conservation Act of 1975 and the Toxic Substances Control Act of 1976 had relatively short histories (although in the latter case, the legislative history bears some relation to the Federal Insecticide, Fungicide, and Rodenticide Act of 1947). Had it not been for Watergate, action on both bills presumably would have been completed during Nixon's presidency. That both were passed following Watergate is itself evidence of the continuity of the legislative process in the face of institutional crisis. Airline deregulation in 1978 and the synthetic fuels program of 1980 also had relatively short legislative histories, carrying over as proposals from the Ford presidency to Carter's—from a split- to a single-party government. The one case from Bush 41 also had a relatively short lineage and can be directly traced to the congressionally initiated Gramm-Rudman-Hollings deficit control efforts of Reagan's second term.

The rest of the twenty-eight each had a substantial legislative heritage traceable to a basic law. Battle lines are already drawn on most important pieces of legislation: committee and subcommittee members and staff are familiar with the issue, other members have participated in previous debates, agency personnel know the administrative and legislative history, and interest group representatives are aware of who did what and how members of Congress voted. The problem, then, for presidents and their advisers is to find a place in this network in order to enact their proposals, modify the proposals of others, or kill a bill they oppose.

Summary

This chapter has moved from the organizational, public, and agenda contexts discussed in earlier chapters into the president's direct workings with Congress. A review of the nature of lawmaking has shown the complexity of decision points beyond roll call voting. These features—speculation, continuity, iteration, information, deliberation, sequence, order, and declaration—provide a basis for comparative analysis across issues, over time, and between political systems.

Some scholars judge that split-party government produces stalemate. or worse, bad decisions. Mayhew has shown that in regard to the quantity of major laws enacted, "it does not seem to make all that much difference whether party control of the American government happens to be unified or divided."[49] Mayhew's study takes a step further from presidency-centered analysis than do studies of roll call voting. The message is: understanding the production of laws requires analysis of lawmaking. The system is now, and always has been, one of "separated institutions sharing powers," as Neustadt puts it.[50] In a lengthy period of split-party government, Neustadt's formulation might better be cast as separated institutions *competing* for shares of powers. Either way, efforts to comprehend presidential power in lawmaking require study of congressional power, even if the president acts "with the stroke of a pen," as with executive orders. Those who are separated must agree or acquiesce if there is to be law.

I have identified the legislative lineage of selected enactments in the postwar period to confirm the continuous nature of lawmaking. This exercise moves the analysis from abstract formulations of presidential-congressional interaction to the concrete setting that awaits a president or member of Congress who wants to make change, and it introduces a set of important enactments that will serve in the next chapter as the basis for an in-depth examination of the lawmaking process of a representative legislature.

CHAPTER 7

Making Laws

Making laws in a separated system is a task as varied as the problems to which the laws are directed and the status of existing statutes. Incentives and prerogatives are widely distributed across governmental institutions, and this allocation ensures differing patterns in presidential-congressional relations. To illustrate the mix and variance, I have developed legislative histories for twenty-eight laws chosen from David R. Mayhew's list of important enactments in the postwar era.[1] I gathered information on the principal stages of the statute-making process and, where available, reactions by the press, elected officials, and other relevant actors. These legislative histories allow me to identify the lawmaking sequence, speculative nature of the proposal, extent of iteration, and nature of partisan interaction. Continuity has been shown in table 6-1. The other features identified in that chapter—inquiry, deliberation, orderliness, and declaration—are variably relevant and noted where appropriate. These features either require refinement in order to compare one lawmaking experience with another (declaration) or are general characteristics related to a set of like proposals (inquiry and deliberation) or a program (setting the order).

The twenty-eight laws are sorted into four categories: preponderant presidential influence in enacting a bill into law; preponderant congressional influence; and two forms of joint presidential-congressional influence, strong presidential involvement and a true balance between the branches.[2] I do not have a direct measure of influence as such. Rather, I rely on the apparent involvement and activity of each branch in the specific pieces of legislation. I am less interested in influence than in identifying presidential and congressional participation at different action points in the lawmaking process. One major purpose is to direct attention to the developmental nature of lawmaking, so as to better place the president in his relationship to Congress.

In some cases it was difficult to estimate which institution was preponderant, even after several reviews of the legislative history. That is not unexpected in a system of separated institutions competing for shares of powers. Both houses of Congress and the president have a legitimate right to participate actively at any number of decision points. It is unreasonable to expect that such a system will be tightly managed and controlled at either end of Pennsylvania Avenue, especially under conditions of split-party government. However, the chosen categories provide a convenient means for identifying patterns and discussing the legislation. My purpose is to clarify the challenge facing the president in leading Congress and adjusting to a moving process of legislative action.

There are fewer cases in the presidential preponderance category than in the congressional preponderance category, and those combined are fewer than the cases of institutional balance (see table 7-1). Here is confirmation that presidency-centered analysis of lawmaking is misleading to the extent that it conveys an impression of presidential dominance or direction, either as an empirical fact or as a normative conclusion growing out of the principles upon which the system is built. These findings do not take into account the more purely presidential actions of executive orders. Two recent books stress the extent to which these law-like orders are examples of presidential "power without persuasion," or the president's acting "with the stroke of a pen."[3] Both books highlight the importance of the political environment, including institutional constraints, in determining the quantity and quality of executive orders.

As noted in chapter 6, of Mayhew's 267 bills, 152 became laws during split-party governments. As would be expected, my sample reflects Mayhew's findings: sixteen of the twenty-eight laws were enacted under those same conditions. I also show in table 7-1 the sequence of decisionmaking for each enactment. As expected, most of the proposals emanated from the president. But a surprising number came from other sources: the House or Senate, a congressional directive, a joint committee, or a commission. Further, in several cases when the president initiated a proposal, members of Congress were preparing an alternative at the same time (for example, the

Table 7-1. *Institutional Interactions, Party Control, and Sequences for Twenty-Eight Selected Enactments, 1947–90*

Legislation and institutional interaction	Congress	President	Party control	Lawmaking sequence[a]
President preponderant				
European Recovery Act (1948)	80th	Truman	Split	Pres.→Sen.→House→Conf.
Federal Aid Highway Act (1956)	84th	Eisenhower	Split	Pres.→House→Sen.→Conf.
Airline Deregulation (1978)	95th	Carter	Single	Pres.→Sen.→House→Conf.
Food Stamp Act (1964)	88th	Johnson	Single	Pres.→House→Sen.→House
Elementary and Secondary Education Act (1965)	89th	Johnson	Single	Pres.→House→Sen.
Economic Recovery Tax Act (1981)	97th	Reagan	Split	Pres.→Sen.→House→Conf.
Congress preponderant				
Labor-Management Relations Act (1947)	80th	Truman	Split	Pres.→House→Sen.→Conf.→Veto→Override
Labor Reform Act (1959)	86th	Eisenhower	Split	Pres.→Sen.→House→Conf.
Social Security Benefit Increases (1972)	92d	Nixon	Split	Pres.→Sen.→Conf.→House
Toxic Substances Control Act (1976)	94th	Ford	Split	Sen.→House→Conf.
Omnibus Trade Act (1988)	100th	Reagan	Split	Congress→House→Sen.→Conf.→Veto→House→Sen.

War Powers Resolution (1973)	93d	Nixon	Split	Sen.→House→Sen.→Conf.→Veto→Override
Budget and Impoundment Control Act (1974)	93d	Nixon	Split	Joint comm.→House→Sen.→Conf.
Balance with president active				
Medicare (1965)	89th	Johnson	Single	Pres.→House→Sen.→Conf.
Department of Education (1979)	96th	Carter	Single	Pres.→Sen.→House→Conf.
Synthetic Fuels (1980)	96th	Carter	Single	House→Pres.→Sen.→Conf.
Energy Act (1975)	94th	Ford	Split	Pres.→Sen.→House→Conf.→House→Sen.
Anticrime Package (1984)	98th	Reagan	Split	Pres.→Sen.→House→Conf.
True balance				
National Housing Act (1949)	81st	Truman	Single	Pres.→Sen.→House→Conf.
Excess Profits Tax (1950)	81st	Truman	Single	Congress→House→Sen.→Conf.
Civil Rights Act (1957)	85th	Eisenhower	Split	Pres.→House→Sen.→Neg.→House→Sen.
Revenue Act (1962)	88th	Kennedy	Single	Pres.→House→Sen.→Conf.
Atomic Energy Act (1954)	83d	Eisenhower	Single	Pres.→Joint comm.→House→Sen.→Conf.→Conf.
Manpower Development (1962)	88th	Kennedy	Single	Pres.→Sen.→House→Conf.
Clean Air Act (1963)	89th	Kennedy	Single	Pres.→House→Sen.→Conf.
Occupational Safety and Health Act (1970)	91st	Nixon	Split	Pres.→Sen.→House→Conf.
Social Security Reform (1983)	98th	Reagan	Split	Cmsn.→Pres.→House→Sen.→Conf.
Deficit Reduction (1990)	101st	Bush	Split	Pres.→House→Sen.→Conf.→Neg.→House→Neg.→House→Sen.

a. Pres. = president; Sen. = Senate; Conf. = conference; Joint comm. = Joint committee; Cmsn. = commission; Neg. = negotiation outside conference.

Taft-Hartley labor-management relations legislation), or the president borrowed substantially from a proposal emanating from the Hill (such as the Reagan tax package in 1981 and the Kemp-Roth tax proposals offered earlier). The lawmaking sequences vary substantially: measures moved from the Senate to the House to conference in ten instances, from the House to the Senate to conference in six instances, and in twelve instances they followed other paths. Most, but not all, important bills go to a conference between the two houses. Three in this sample did not, and one (the anticrime package of 1984) went to an appropriations conference rather than a conference between the House and Senate judiciary committees.

For each piece of legislation I made a number of judgments about the degree of iteration, partisan interaction, sequence of lawmaking, closeness of the final enactment to earlier versions, and number of presidential victories and losses as measured by *Congressional Quarterly*. The exercise of rating bills by degree of iteration and nature of partisanship was repeated several times to increase the likelihood that the same criteria were used throughout. The process is qualitative and judgmental, to be sure. Given the nature of the search, however, it proved difficult to devise shortcuts. No doubt someone else engaging in the same exercise would produce somewhat different results, and thus the advantages of replication are reduced. On the other hand, anyone making these judgments would also find variations in iteration and partisanship, even if not exactly those I offer. And it is these differences in sequence, iteration, and partisan interaction that encourage one to search for an alternative perspective for understanding and explaining national policy politics.

A review and analysis of the sample of twenty-eight laws follows. I then add a selection of laws enacted during the Clinton and Bush 43 presidencies. I decided against incorporating the newer cases into the core sample for two reasons. First, Mayhew's additional selections are the result of his "sweep one" procedure; since these may be altered in "sweep two," they therefore are not strictly comparable with the earlier set. Second, I make use of the earlier analysis in treating the Clinton and Bush 43 presidencies. The two presidencies offer novel variations in party splits: the first ever Democrat to be reelected with a Republican Congress (1996) and the first tie in the Senate since 1880, as well as the first switch during a session to an opposition party Senate majority (2000 and 2001). Narrow-margin politics developed alongside split-party government during the decade, 1994–2004.

Presidential Preponderance

The six laws in this category are of two types. The first three had bipartisan support, either due to the vital nature of the issues involved (European recovery and building an interstate highway system) or a general acceptance that it was time to act (deregulating the airlines). Neither Congress nor the opposition party abandoned its prerogatives, but all had reasons to work with the administration. Split-party government did not appear to be a major roadblock. The remaining three are examples of a presumed presidential mandate. Accordingly, normal presidential-congressional politics, if there is such, was suspended.

Bipartisan Support

The first two entries in the first set show similar characteristics. In both instances, presidential or executive influence was significant, despite split-party government. A consensus developed in favor of the proposals, with bipartisan support at crucial stages in the process. Airline deregulation had broad support but did not experience the smooth sailing of the other bills, even though it was enacted during single-party government.

EUROPEAN RECOVERY. The Marshall Plan is a prime example of the benefits of bipartisanship in foreign policy. Secretary of State George Marshall visited Moscow in April 1947 and returned to Washington "gravely worried and upset" that the leaders of the Soviet Union "were quite content to see uncertainty and chaos prevail in Europe." Marshall instructed George Kennan to prepare a report that could serve as a basis for a recovery plan. Meanwhile, President Truman asked Under Secretary of State Dean Acheson to give a speech for him at a small college in Mississippi. Acheson used the occasion to stress the importance of rebuilding Europe. "The speech . . . was the alarm bell that Truman wanted sounded."[4]

Kennan's report was issued in late May 1947. When Marshall received an honorary degree at Harvard University in early June, he used the occasion, with Truman's approval, to announce the plan. Marshall emphasized that the Europeans themselves had to agree on a plan for recovery, which would then receive support from the United States.

A positive response from Europe was immediate and a meeting took place in July 1947. The Soviet Union sent a delegation, then withdrew and refused to allow its satellite nations to participate (Czechoslovakia and Poland were particularly eager to be included). "By refusing to take part in the Marshall Plan, Stalin had virtually guaranteed its success. Sooner or later congressional support was bound to follow, whatever the volume of grumbling on the Hill."[5]

A report to Marshall on September 22 triggered action by the White House and Congress. The situation in Europe was critical, particularly in France and Italy. President Truman called a special session of Congress on November 17, 1947, to provide for stop-gap aid until a long-range program could be put in place. On December 19, 1947, he outlined a comprehensive plan and called on Congress to act quickly.

The president had to manage the politics skillfully. After all, the Republicans had majorities in both houses of Congress and expected to win the White House in 1948. In the face of a split-party government, his strategy was to identify the plan more with Marshall than himself. "Although Truman's firm backing of the plan was never in doubt, . . . he subordinated his own role and emphasized that of the general. Because his domestic programs were unpopular and Marshall's prestige was high, this stance helped gain supporters for the plan."[6] Truman also relied on outside support from citizen committees, including business leaders, bankers, and foreign affairs specialists like Dean Acheson (then in private life). This was an early example of building outside support for an important foreign policy move, not unlike the strategy used by President Carter in his effort to get the Panama Canal treaties ratified in 1977 and 1978.

Leading the bipartisan effort on the Republican side was Senator Arthur Vandenberg of Michigan. The president, in his memoirs, credited Vandenberg and his counterpart chairman in the House, Charles A. Eaton (R-N.J.): "In a Congress dedicated to tax reduction and the pruning of governmental expenditures, they championed this program in a truly bi-partisan manner."[7] The issue for most members of Congress was not whether to support the proposal, but whether such a large aid program might harm the U.S. economy. The plan was highly speculative in terms of its effects at home and its prospects for success in Europe.

Committee and floor action was moderately iterative, with floor amendments adopted in each house. Members of Congress were interested in who would be aided, how much aid would be authorized, where the money would be spent, the duration of the program, whether it would act as a potential curb against communism, and the loyalty to the United States of those administering the program. Bipartisanship characterized committee and floor action, thanks to the leadership of the committee chairs. But there were holdouts on the floor, and the final vote was cross-partisan. Senate and House Republicans voted in favor of the plan by over 70 percent; Senate and House Democrats, by over 90 percent. Given the partisan balance in each house, neither party's support was sufficient to ensure victory; thus the vote in both houses met the conditions of classic cross-partisanship. Passage of the Marshall Plan was a remarkable achievement under the circumstances: an election year in which a Republican Congress anxious to win the White House worked with a Democratic president eager to win a full term on his own and get a Democratic Congress.

INTERSTATE HIGHWAYS. In 1956 an aid program of a very different, and much less speculative, nature was enacted into law. The Federal Aid Highway Act was correctly described by President Eisenhower as "the biggest peacetime construction project of any description ever undertaken by the United States or any other country."[8] A marvelously distributive program, it would bring money, roads, and jobs to every state in the nation. Following a report by a presidential advisory commission headed by General Lucius Clay, Eisenhower recommended enactment of the program in his 1956 State of the Union message. Like Truman with the Marshall Plan, he faced a Congress controlled by the other party and it was a presidential election year. But here was a program bound to warm the political hearts of members of both parties in Congress. And governments at all levels know how to build roads.

The only important dispute between the White House and Congress was over the financing of the project. General Clay's group recommended the issuance of $20 billion worth of government bonds. Eisenhower preferred self-financing toll highways. Many members of Congress thought that the system should be paid for out of appropriations. In the end, it was agreed to finance the project through increased taxes on gasoline, diesel oil, tires, trucks, buses, and trailers.

The bill was considered by two committees in each chamber: the public works and taxing committees. Committee action was moderately iterative, mostly regarding the financing provisions and the apportionment of funds among the states. Further changes were made on the Senate floor and only minor changes were made on the House floor. The bill had bipartisan support throughout the process. It passed 388-19 in the House and by a voice vote in the Senate. In its support score for 1956, *Congressional Quarterly* credited the president with two wins for this measure.

AIRLINE DEREGULATION. In 1978 airline deregulation was seemingly an idea whose time had come. President Ford was the original champion of deregulation, but he was defeated in 1976, before action on the bill could be completed. With broad support, the proposal was carried forward by the

Carter administration. Even the agency responsible for regulation, the Civil Aeronautics Board (CAB), lobbied for change.

Deregulating an entire industry was no small step: this was a speculative reform with major economic implications, not to mention significant opportunities within the highly competitive airline industry. According to Martha Derthick and Paul J. Quirk, "reform advocacy" of this type has "to neutralize or overcome [the] potential sources of resistance inherent in a congressional perspective." They concluded that a combination of forces had exactly this effect. For example, it is unusual to get agreement, let alone unanimity, among economists on any major issue, and yet "deregulation was, in effect, a recommendation of the economics profession as such." Endorsements also came from government agencies, congressional support units (the General Accounting Office and the Congressional Budget Office), and a coalition of interest groups. The result was that "widely shared interests and values converged in support of reform."[9] Other developments contributed to the momentum for change. President Carter appointed a proponent of deregulation, Alfred Kahn, a Cornell University economist, to chair the Civil Aeronautics Board. United Airlines broke with its competitors and supported deregulation. And the predictions of dire economic consequences were belied when CAB policies to encourage competition before the deregulation appeared to increase business.[10]

This momentum was naturally reflected in Congress. Early conflicts that delayed approval of Carter's proposals were resolved. The president did not get the "quick hit" he wanted, but he did get a bill that was close to what had been proposed. Much of the delay occurred in the House, where a member of the Aviation Subcommittee of the Committee on Public Works, Democrat Elliott Levitas from Carter's home state of Georgia, was successful in substituting a watered-down bill for Carter's plan. This action led to a lengthy and complex markup of the legislation. Meanwhile, the Senate passed a bill more to the president's liking, and the conference agreement favored the Senate version.

Iteration in Congress on this legislation was in the moderate range (somewhat higher in the House), and there were very few changes on the House and Senate floors. The fact that a piece of legislation develops the kind of momentum described above certainly does not preclude congressional involvement, particularly for a regulatory measure with widespread constituency effects. The final votes in both houses were overwhelmingly in favor of airline deregulation, suggesting bipartisanship. However, the pattern was more cross-partisan than bipartisan in the earlier, crucial stages of preparing the legislation. *Congressional Quarterly* awarded Carter six victories and no defeats for this legislation.

Presidential Mandates

The other three pieces of legislation are the most representative products of classic responsible party government in the sample of twenty-eight. They were passed relatively quickly, during periods when it was widely perceived that the president had a mandate to act. Two of the bills did not even go to conference. In the cases of food stamps and the Elementary and Secondary Education Act, President Johnson initially had the self-designated responsibility of enacting Kennedy's uncompleted program, and then the advantage of his own landslide victory in 1964, which was widely interpreted as an endorsement of an activist domestic agenda. In the case of the Economic Recovery Tax Act of 1981, Ronald Reagan capitalized on his perceived mandate to alter the government's role in the economy.

FOOD STAMPS. The idea of food stamps was not new in 1964. It had been tried in 1939, for the same dual purpose identified later: distributing surplus food and improving the diets of the poor. Several problems with the program ended the experiment in 1943. Still, the idea was attractive to many in Congress, and bills were introduced in every subsequent session until one passed in 1964. In 1956, Eisenhower's secretary of agriculture, Ezra Taft Benson, was directed to study the idea, but he recommended against it. Representative Leonor Sullivan (D-Mo.), a particularly strong advocate of the plan during the 1950s, finally won congressional approval in 1959 to authorize the secretary of agriculture to conduct a two-year program. Since he was not actually directed to implement the plan, Secretary Benson simply did not act.

Thus when John Kennedy became president, "the program's political history before 1961 made it ideally suited for adoption by an administration that deplored its predecessor's resistance to innovation and preoccupation with economy."[11] Kennedy had been a supporter of food stamps while in the Senate. Upon assuming the presidency, he initiated a pilot program under existing executive authority. Republicans strongly criticized the program because it was tested only in Democratic congressional districts. Kennedy requested a permanent program in 1963. After Johnson assumed office, he endorsed Kennedy's plan and meant to see it enacted in 1964, once the civil rights legislation passed.

Getting the food stamp bill passed proved to be no simple matter, however. Republicans were strongly opposed and had not yet suffered the devastating losses of the 1964 election. Thus cross-partisan voting, with southern Democrats joining Republicans, could potentially defeat the bill. Republicans questioned why a welfare bill should be assigned to the Committee on Agriculture. Further, they sought to define the food stamp program as a wedge for forcing desegregation in the South by denying food stamps to areas that did not meet federal standards on racial integration.[12] "It took overt, almost crude logrolling . . . to get the 1964 food stamp legislation out of the Agriculture Committee and then passed on the floor of the House."[13] The program was coupled with a cotton and wheat bill to get it passed in committee (by a narrow vote of 18-16). The logrolling to hold southern Democratic support also worked on the floor, where 89 percent of Democrats voted for the bill, against 92 percent of Republicans opposing it. The president actively lobbied for the bill.

Senate action was much less contentious. The bill was reported out of committee with some changes, passed by voice vote, and returned to the House. A conference was avoided when the House accepted the Senate version. Passage of the program was hailed as a victory for President Johnson's broader antipoverty program, a conclusion Johnson himself confirmed in signing the bill.

The lawmaking process in Congress was moderately iterative within and between the House and Senate committees. No important changes were made subsequently. However, one cannot ignore the history of this measure: the program had been tested in the past and most of the arguments on both sides were fully developed, thus making it a less speculative venture. Likewise, the partisan nature of this issue was not invented in 1964. Republicans and northern Democrats had established their positions, making the southern Democrats the critical bloc. Johnson's old-fashioned horse trading ultimately secured the support of 75 percent of the southern Democrats. Since most of the deliberation and all of the roll call votes occurred in the House, the president's three victories for his support score came there.

ELEMENTARY AND SECONDARY EDUCATION ACT. Few pieces of legislation in modern times have a lineage to match that of the Elementary and Secondary Education Act of 1965. How, to what extent, and indeed whether to provide federal aid to education were unresolved issues dating back at least to the 1930s, when President Roosevelt asked his Advisory Committee on Education to report on educational needs. The committee documented significant inequalities among the states in 1938, stimulating introduction of a Senate bill to provide federal aid to the states in proportion to needs. Hearings were held, but the bill went no further. General school aid bills were introduced in every subsequent session of Congress. These bills sometimes reached the floor; seldom did they pass even one house. In 1960 bills passed both houses, but the House Committee on Rules prevented a conference.

By 1961, after more than two decades of effort to pass a bill, the full dimensions of the issues were apparent to all policymakers, if not how these issues were to be resolved or what would be the effects of federal involvement in a historically state-local matter. In their review of the history of federal aid to education before 1965, two scholars concluded that "the struggle over federal aid has not been a single conflict, but rather a multiplicity of controversies only loosely related to one another. The situation might be compared to a better-than-three-ring circus, although, in view of the tactics at times employed, a multiple barroom brawl might make a more apt analogy."[14]

One account of the efforts to pass legislation during this period was entitled "Race, Religion, and the Rules Committee."[15] The racial issues were paramount, centering on whether federal aid would be provided to segregated schools in the South. The Powell amendment (named for Adam Clayton Powell, D-N.Y., who chaired the House Committee on Education and Labor) specifically prohibited any such allocation. Passage of a House bill with the Powell amendment would face a potential filibuster by southern Democrats in the Senate. Southern Democrats also had a lock on the House Committee on Rules.

The religious dimensions were also troublesome. Catholics were well represented on the House Committee on Education and Labor as well as in the Democratic leadership, and in 1961 they held the balance of power in a House Committee on Rules that had been expanded to give President Kennedy a majority. Catholics were bound to ensure that parochial schools were included in the first, precedent-setting federal aid bill.

The political landscape changed dramatically in 1964. The Civil Rights Act prohibited the use of federal funds for segregated public facilities, thus eliminating the racial hurdle to federal aid for education. The Economic Opportunity Act of 1964 provided a method for avoiding the constitutional issue of church-state relations by linking education aid with poverty. School districts would receive aid based on the number of low-income families, for children in both parochial and public schools. The Republicans in 1965 were in no position to block much of anything, having been left with less than a third of the seats in each chamber.

Thus passage of the Elementary and Secondary Education Act in 1965 was almost an anticlimax. It passed virtually as introduced. Amendments by Republicans and southern Democrats were turned back in the House Committee on Education and Labor, and several Republican amendments were defeated in the Senate. A conference was avoided by resisting all amendments in the Senate, much to the chagrin of Republicans. In the House committee, changes favorable to northern Democrats were made in the formula for allocating aid, but overall the process was less iterative than for any bill of the twenty-eight included in the sample. That fact should not mask the efforts over the years to fashion a bill that would win a majority of votes, however. Nor should it convey the impression either that the process had produced the perfect formula for federal aid or that the solution had reduced the speculative nature of the program as regards its substantive effect for educating young people. One member of Congress made this point: "The 1965 bill, in all candor, does not make much sense educationally; but it makes a hell of a lot of sense legally, politically, and constitutionally."[16]

In each chamber, a number of Republicans voted in favor of the bill and a number of southern Democrats voted against it. Ordinarily one might label this a case of classic cross partisanship. However, the Republican votes were not needed in either chamber because a sufficient number of southern Democrats voted with their party. House Republican leaders decided to let their members vote their districts, and 27 percent of them voted in favor of the bill.

The president scored well with this legislation. His fourteen victories came mostly from the defeat of eleven amendments in the Senate (all but one put forward by Republicans). In this case the support score was influenced by procedural differences between the two chambers. The president's House wins came mostly in committee and were then ratified by two roll call votes on the floor. His Senate wins came on the floor, with many recorded votes on amendments. The results in each chamber were similar, but this support score measure cannot distinguish similar outcomes resulting from different processes.

ECONOMIC RECOVERY. One does not normally expect large policy change from the American political system. The constitutional structure itself encourages incremental moves, partly—sometimes wholly—as a hedge against speculation going very wrong. Incremental testing is especially used for economic issues, where the high probability of unanticipated ripple effects induces caution among those likely to be held responsible for adverse consequences of bold decisions. Thus the passage of a multiyear tax cut in 1981 seemed a remarkable exception. The bold "supply-side" plan had its antecedents in proposals by Senator William Roth (R-Del.), and Representative Jack Kemp (R-N.Y.). President Reagan endorsed this approach during the 1980 campaign, in conjunction with proposed budget cuts. Reagan's overwhelming victory over an incumbent president, combined with sizable Republican gains in the House and the Senate, led to expectations that the Reagan program would be put into effect.

Of course, no matter how successful the Republicans had been in the election, the House of Representative still had a majority of Democrats and it is in that chamber that tax bills originate. Thus serious negotiations could be expected among the new chair of the Committee on Ways and Means, Daniel Rostenkowski (D-Ill.), the new Senate Republican leaders, and the White House. At the urging of Speaker Thomas P. O'Neill (D-Mass.), Rostenkowski made a serious attempt at competitive partisan politics by fashioning an alternative to the Reagan tax cut proposal, but he was forced to rely on partisan support at the committee stage. All the Republicans signed the minority report and were prepared to support a Reagan substitute plan on the floor. In order to hold southern Democrats, a tax break for oil-producing states was included in Rostenkowski's plan. Republicans countered with other sweeteners. "The Republican cosponsor of the administration bill, Barber Conable [New York], publicly expressed dismay over the bidding contest that had developed, but stated that it had become unavoidable under the circumstances in order to ensure adoption of the president's basic economic program."[17]

In an extraordinary move, the Republican-controlled Senate Committee on Finance acted first, attaching the Reagan program to a debt-limit measure that had been passed by the House, so as not to violate the constitutional provision requiring that revenue measures originate in the House. The strategy was clearly to put pressure on that chamber by building momentum for the Reagan proposal. A vigorous lobbying effort by the White House supplemented the sequencing strategy of having the Senate act first.

Meanwhile, in the House, the president gained the support of a group of southern Democrats, the "boll weevils," and thus had a working majority to reject the Rostenkowski plan and substitute his own proposal (a modified version of the Kemp-Roth plan). Although each point in the sequence of legislative action in the House was highly iterative, the changes made in the committee were actually negated on the floor and much of the president's original plan was restored. A cross-partisan coalition thwarted the competitive partisan strategy of House Democratic leaders, who no longer had a working majority. Near-perfect Republican unity in the House was compounded by Democratic defections to produce a cross-partisan win. Similar levels of Republican unity in the Senate made Democratic support superfluous, but huge numbers of Democrats crossed over anyway.

Press reaction to the passage of the Economic Recovery Tax Act emphasized Reagan's mastery over Congress, the Democrats' disarray, and the uncertainty of the act's economic effects. On the one hand, columnists, editorial writers, and others in Washington were impressed with the exercise of power as an expression of the presumed mandate; on the other hand, they worried about the boldness of proposals designed to produce real change, given the potential of unintended effects. The Economic Recovery Tax Act resulted in thirteen victories for President Reagan in his support score calculations. Most of these victories came in the Senate, where the highly cohesive Republicans rejected amendments by Democrats.

Congressional Preponderance

All the laws listed in this section in table 7-1 were enacted in split-party governments. In four instances, the initiative for the legislation came primarily from Capitol Hill, not the White House. The president was essentially an observer for much of this legislation—an active observer and monitor, to be sure, but hardly the leader or manager of the lawmaking process. Whereas the sequences for the president-preponderant bills were more or less standard (varying only in which house acted first and whether a conference was required), the Congress-preponderant sequences show considerable variety. Only one (Landrum-Griffin in 1959) followed what is thought of as a standard pattern.

This group of laws also contains the only cases of presidential veto in the sample of twenty-eight: three in total, two of which were overridden. With the exception of the Budget and Impoundment Control Act of 1974, lawmaking for these bills was highly iterative and typically cross-partisan (sometimes competitively partisan within the committees). Again, I have identified two sets. The first five laws demonstrate variable conditions under which Congress was preponderant. Those in the second set involve congressional reforms to limit presidential powers.

Variable Cases

In the first set, the Taft-Hartley Act of 1947 and the Landrum-Griffin Act of 1959 illustrate the making of labor law under obverse conditions of split-party government: a Democratic president (Truman) and a Republican Congress for the first, a Republican president (Eisenhower) and a Democratic

Congress for the second. Social Security benefit increases (1972), Toxic Substances Control (1976), and Omnibus Trade (1988) provide interesting examples of presidential-congressional interaction when the president has an interest but is more reactive than active. These latter cases all occurred in presidential election years: the first two when an incumbent president was seeking reelection (Nixon) or election (Ford), the third when an incumbent vice president was seeking election (Bush 41).

LABOR-MANAGEMENT RELATIONS ACT. Labor-management relations following World War II were bound to be contentious. Labor unions were anxious to improve the status of workers, strikes were frequent, and industry was concerned that unions were already too strong as a result of the protections provided by the National Labor Relations Act of 1935 (the Wagner Act). "Anti-labor sentiment, inflamed by John L. Lewis's defiance of the government in the fall of 1946, was gaining new strength, and labor legislation became a prime issue in 1947."[18] Legislation to curb strikes and provide for bargaining was introduced and passed in the 79th Congress, but President Truman vetoed what he called "that repressive measure." Congress was not able to override the veto.

In the 1946 midterm elections, the Republicans won majorities in both the House and the Senate for the first time since 1930. They looked forward to recapturing the White House in 1948. Therefore, when Truman requested a revision of the Wagner Act, one could expect a highly iterative lawmaking process, featuring competitive partisan and cross-partisan politics. Certainly the congressional Republicans, who had supported the bill Truman vetoed, were unlikely simply to endorse the president's moderate proposals. And some southern Democrats were as eager as the Republicans to go beyond the president's recommendations. On opening day of the 80th Congress, seventeen labor bills were "dropped into the hopper" of the House; more than a hundred eventually were introduced into the House and the Senate.

Republicans on the House Committee on Education and Labor (chaired by Fred Hartley, R-N.J.) prepared a bill that Democrats claimed was "aimed at the heart of industrial democracy."[19] They won the support of southern Democrats on the committee, presaging what was to follow on the House floor. Confirmation of the strength of cross-partisan support came on the rule, which passed 319-47. Northern Democrats tried unsuccessfully to soften the bill; southern Democrats succeeded in making it tougher. The bill passed by a cross-partisan margin greater than that needed to override a presidential veto, 308-107. Support by southern Democrats was not needed for passage, but it would be required for a veto override.

Robert A. Taft (R-Ohio), chair of the Committee on Labor and Public Welfare, led efforts in the Senate. As a prospective presidential candidate himself in 1948, Taft crafted a bill that was less objectionable to the president than the House bill but designed more to win support within the committee than to win Truman's signature. Republicans had an 8-5 edge in the committee, but on this issue Taft had to work with the far right, represented by Joseph Ball (R-Minn.), and a more moderate position, represented by Irving Ives (R-N.Y.). Ives reflected the views of Governor Thomas E. Dewey (R-N.Y.), Taft's likely opponent for the presidential nomination. In a demonstration of legislative mastery, Taft succeeded in building a winning coalition. The committee supported the bill 11-2. After three weeks of intense debate, Taft's omnibus bill passed by a veto-proof margin of 68-24, again with substantial support from southern Democrats. The more moderate, but still tough, Taft version dominated the conference deliberations. "Taft's stubbornness irritated the House conferees, but Hartley knew that he had to give in—or risk a presidential veto that the Senate would fail to override."[20]

The rhetoric in the aftermath of final passage was predictable on both sides. Labor leaders denounced the bill and, along with several congressional Democrats, called for a veto. The volume of mail, over 750,000 letters overwhelmingly supporting a veto, "was the greatest ever received in the White House on any issue."[21] A labor rally was held in Madison Square Garden, with 35,000 in attendance. Few were neutral about the legislation. The scope and shrillness of the public debate were extraordinary.

Editorial reaction to the campaign for a veto was critical of the labor unions. Both the *New York Times* and the *Washington Post* expressed the view that labor leaders were misrepresenting the bill.[22] History tends to confirm these judgments. As James T. Patterson has concluded: "In retrospect, it is clear that the unions grossly exaggerated the adverse effects of the law."[23] It seems that on occasion speculation can be used as a political weapon.

Still, the pressure was on for Truman to say no. And in the end politics dictated his decision.

If he approved the bill one year after his proposal for drafting rail strikers and seventeen months before the 1948 election, his standing with labor would have been destroyed. . . . If he vetoed the bill, his previous sins in the eyes of labor would be absolved. At the same time he might counteract certain liberal support still building for a possible third party under Wallace. Moreover it was evident from the voting on the bill in both houses that Congress probably would override a veto. What did Truman have to lose, therefore, by vetoing it and winning labor's acclaim, if the bill was going to become law anyhow?[24]

The House overrode Truman's veto the same day it was received. A majority of Democrats (60 percent) voted with 95 percent of the Republicans. The Senate override came three days later, following a filibuster. The Senate Republicans were as unified as their House colleagues. They were joined by just less than half of the Senate Democrats.

LABOR-MANAGEMENT REPORTING AND DISCLOSURE ACT. Enacting labor-management relations legislation in 1959 was not as contentious as in 1947, but neither was it a simple matter. As before, there was a stimulus for action. The Senate Select Committee on Improper Activities in the Labor or Management Fields (the McClellan committee, named for its chair, John McClellan, D-Ark.) was established in 1957 to investigate corruption in labor unions, "focusing its attention primarily on unsavory activities of leaders in the Teamsters' union." Hearings were televised, which produced considerable public support for cleaning up the unions. "Many liberal and pro-labor spokesmen were dismayed and astonished at the impressive bill of particulars accumulated by the committee."[25] Yet the political situation was not apparently conducive to getting a bill passed. The Democrats won huge majorities in both the House and Senate in 1958, and President Eisenhower was about to leave office. Further, as had been true in 1947, it was not an issue that Democrats wanted to manage, since it must inevitably lead to conflict with their labor constituency.

Conditions favored a highly iterative and competitively partisan process between the president and Congress as well as within Congress. Early in 1958, President Eisenhower called for anticorruption legislation and for amendments to the Taft-Hartley Act. Meanwhile, the McClellan committee offered an interim report that proposed controls over union management that were not in the least popular with organized labor. Senator John F. Kennedy (D-Mass.) chaired the Subcommittee on Labor of the Committee on Labor and Public Welfare and therefore could be expected to propose his own bill. Kennedy sponsored a wages and pension disclosure act in 1958, successfully shepherding it through both houses. Working with Senator Irving Ives (R-N.Y.), he also succeeded in getting Senate approval of an anticorruption act, but it failed in the House amidst recriminations on both sides of the aisle.

This hostility and anxiety, along with a Democratic triumph at the polls in the 1958 midterm elections, constituted the setting for high politics in

1959. The president repeated his requests (including changes in the Taft-Hartley Act), Kennedy reintroduced a modified version of his bill (excluding Taft-Hartley amendments), and McClellan was prepared to strengthen whatever bill reached the floor. Kennedy's bill passed in committee, with compromises on Taft-Hartley changes to pick up Republican votes. On the Senate floor, McClellan introduced his "bill of rights" amendment to protect union members. According to Samuel C. Patterson, "McClellan now clearly had charge of the debate," taking over from Kennedy.[26] The McClellan amendment split the Democrats and passed by the narrowest of margins (47-46), supported by 94 percent of the Republicans and 25 percent of the Democrats. After acrimonious debate and the approval of a substitute bill of rights, the bill had been sufficiently modified to gain cross-partisan support and passed by a wide margin (90-1). Only Senator Barry Goldwater (R-Ariz.), who had introduced the administration's bill, voted no. He revealed, however, that Eisenhower told him: "Had I been in the Senate, I would have voted with you."[27]

The same contending forces were at work in the House, but conservative southern Democrats were in key positions on the critical committees. Further, "there was a good deal of personal jealousy and ill-feeling among some committee members, especially on the Democratic side." Yet by the time of House action the Democrats were under substantial pressure to overcome these divisions and produce legislation. The Kennedy bill, with many amendments, passed the House committee by a narrow, cross-partisan majority of 16-14. But that result alone hardly revealed the complex and varied views on this issue. The committee report, which included separate statements and "supplementary views" from at least seven subsets of members, was "among the strangest that has ever come from the Congress."[28]

What happened next confirmed the signals sent by the report. Carl Elliott (D-Ky.) managed the modified Kennedy bill on the House floor, rather than committee chair Graham Barden (D-N.C.), who favored a much tougher bill. It was debated under an open rule. Before the debate, both AFL-CIO president George Meany and President Eisenhower addressed the nation to generate support for their positions.

Two members of the House Education and Labor Committee, Phil Landrum (D-Ga.) and Robert Griffin (R-Mich.), introduced a substitute for the Elliott bill on the floor that included the Taft-Hartley changes Eisenhower favored. After two further amendments were rejected, the Landrum-Griffin substitute passed with cross-partisan support, 229-201; 89 percent of the House Republicans and 34 percent of the Democrats voted in favor. The

House bill was somewhat modified in conference; it then passed both houses and was signed by the president on September 14, 1959. George Meany claimed that it was "the most damaging anti-labor bill since the Taft-Hartley Act," but President Eisenhower was reportedly "very pleased" with the bill, as was Secretary of Labor James Mitchell.[29]

The president's pleasure does not qualify this act for the category of "president preponderant." Eisenhower was more active on this than on most legislation, but the action was primarily in Congress, with the president as one of the important players. That he got much of what he wanted in the end was a consequence of the legislative drama in Congress. The president's support scores for this piece of legislation show its importance for his record in 1959: four wins and no losses in the House, two wins and four losses in the Senate. The Senate losses include several amendments for changes that eventually made their way into the legislation in the House, but do not include the crucial vote on the McClellan bill of rights. Given the political dynamics of this legislation, so much of it occurring within Congress, it is misleading for political analysts to characterize this battle in terms of presidential wins and losses.

The Taft-Hartley and Landrum-Griffin Acts illustrate an interesting point regarding speculation as a feature of lawmaking. These pieces of legislation were less exploratory than many others included in this sample. Both sides took confidence from knowing the effects of the bills, even if they were occasionally prone to exaggeration. That this knowledge served to intensify, not moderate, the conflict, suggests that uncertainty may on occasion actually facilitate passage of legislation, especially in the context of a crisis.

SOCIAL SECURITY BENEFIT INCREASES. The increases in Social Security benefits in 1972 illustrate the crucial importance of context in lawmaking. Martha Derthick describes the policy context:

> The interest in antipoverty legislation during the Johnson years, which carried over during the Nixon administration into the campaign for the family assistance plan (FAP), encouraged the expansion of the social security plan in two ways. It lent momentum to welfare legislation generally, and because social security was the most popular and feasible form of such legislation, it won support when more controversial forms were stymied. . . . Incremental changes in well-established programs do not attract attention.[30]

The political context for increases in Social Security benefits is easy to spot. Nixon was seeking reelection, he wanted to win big, and Congress was populated with prospective Democratic opponents. The result was a lawmaking process seemingly out of control, a policy escalation unchecked by the controls that normally contribute to incrementalism. This race to satisfy the Social Security clienteles occurred not in a single-party government, free to work its will or to fulfill its mandate, but in a split-party government with a strongly partisan president and ambitious Democratic congressional leaders. Derthick describes what happened as "the disintegration of policymaking."[31] It is an amazing story.

In his budget message to Congress in 1972, President Nixon proposed increased spending for the aged. He initially proposed a 5 percent increase, on top of a 10 percent increase that had been approved by Congress in 1971. The response on Capitol Hill was in favor of an increase, but Nixon's proposal was criticized as inadequate. Several Democrats proposed increases ranging from 12 to 25 percent.

The principal legislative action occurred within the Senate, in spite of the constitutional provision that revenue measures must originate in the House. A debt-limit increase passed by the House was to act as a vehicle for the Social Security benefit increases (as it had in 1971). The Senate Committee on Finance approved a 10 percent increase, double that wanted by the president. Everyone expected that a larger increase would be proposed on the Senate floor, and it was. Frank Church (D-Idaho) introduced an amendment that increased benefits by 20 percent, raised Social Security taxes, and set in place automatic cost-of-living adjustments (COLAs), a mechanism favored by Nixon. The Church amendment passed overwhelmingly. And so it was that COLAs came into being.

The increases in benefits and taxes and the new indexation procedure were attached to the debt-limit increase passed earlier by the House. Thus the conference agreement now included the Church proposals as nongermane amendments, which had to be approved in the House. They were, by a large, cross-partisan margin. No one could stop this bandwagon as it rolled toward the 1972 elections. John Byrnes (R-Wis.), ranking Republican on the House Committee on Ways and Means, was aghast at the acquiescence of the committee chair, Wilbur Mills (D-Ark.). He expressed his disappointment on the House floor and warned of the consequences: "We are contemplating taking steps that can lead us into very serious problems as far as this system and the many people involved in it are concerned."[32]

COLAs were one more contribution to what R. Kent Weaver calls "automatic government." President Nixon reportedly considered a veto, "but he was in a politically impossible situation."[33] The bill had passed both houses by more than the two-thirds majorities required to override a veto, the national conventions were about to take place, the election was just four months away, and the popular increases were attached to a debt-ceiling bill that had to be approved to keep the government running. And so Nixon satisfied himself by warning of the effects of inflation and of attaching "seemingly attractive, politically popular but fiscally irresponsible riders" to future debt-ceiling increases.[34] These warnings proved prescient. It seems that knowledge of bad consequences does not necessarily act as a check on legislation.

Congressional Quarterly did not include any roll call votes from this legislation in its calculation of the president's support score for 1972. An absolutely crucial piece of social welfare legislation, with major budget implications, is not accounted for in evaluating Nixon. The case illustrates yet again the perils of relying on roll call votes for this purpose. The political dynamics also show the fallacy of testing the system from a presidency-centered perspective. Nixon was a major player in this legislative contest, but he did not manage it—nor, it seems, did anyone else.

TOXIC SUBSTANCES CONTROL. Many have labeled the 1970s as the environmental decade, a deserved title given the number of major enactments during the period. The Council on Environmental Quality (CEQ) issued a report in 1971 drawing attention to the many new untested chemicals that enter the market each year. That same year, the Nixon administration submitted a proposal regulating untested chemicals to Congress that was changed substantially as it worked its way through Congress. A bill passed both houses, but because the House failed to agree to the revised Senate version, the bill died in 1972. Another effort was made in 1973. Again, both houses passed a bill, but conferees could not reach an agreement.

By 1975, this issue was primarily being treated within Congress. While the original initiative had come from the CEQ and Nixon's early proposals, subsequent action was on Capitol Hill, with the Ford White House mainly playing the role of monitor. The issue had strong public appeal. The term *toxic* attracts attention. Not all the effects of emitting chemicals into the air and spilling them into water are known, but this uncertainty alone is cause for concern. As one specialist has observed: "Latency and uncertainty make chronic toxic substances difficult to recognize and control."[35] These characteristics did, however, encourage efforts to try to do so, to take a chance with an exploratory effort.

A renewed initiative began in 1975, with the Senate acting first. Vance Hartke (D-Ind.), John Tunney (D-Calif.), and Philip Hart (D-Mich.) sponsored a bill in the Senate Committee on Commerce. The principal conflict concerned premarket testing of chemicals, with the administration apprehensive about having the Environmental Protection Agency (EPA) regulate the chemical industry. By now the committee had ample practice in building floor support for the bill; it was approved 60-13, gaining majority support among Republicans and nearly unanimous support among Democrats. The question was: what would happen in the House?

The administration's reaction to the Senate-passed bill was not altogether clear. In a letter, the White House stated its opposition because the bill "unnecessarily overburdens both the regulatory agency and the regulated industry." It was reported that EPA administrator Russell Train believed that "this legislation requires the industry to test chemicals in the lab rather than in the marketplace. They should test mice rather than people."[36]

The House Committee on Interstate and Foreign Commerce reported a less stringent bill, more acceptable to the White House. An effort was made to win Republican support, perhaps to avoid a veto. The bill then passed the House with moderate but important changes (one of which banned PCBs). There was uncertainty over the possibility of a veto by Ford and also whether the House and Senate could reach an agreement.

The conference was highly iterative as House and Senate conferees worked out an agreement on the EPA's role regarding the marketing of tested chemicals. The agreement was approved by large majorities in both houses and signed by President Ford, who identified it as "one of the most important pieces of environmental legislation that has been enacted by Congress."[37] In the House, 84 percent of Republicans voted for the conference report; in the Senate, 80 percent of Republicans voted for the report.

Only one roll call vote was included in President Ford's support score for 1976: the early Senate passage of the Hartke-Tunney-Hart bill, which was counted as a defeat for the president. The subsequent modification of the bill to suit the president's concerns was therefore not reflected, in spite of the overwhelming support given to the final bill by House and Senate Republicans and the president's own endorsement of the legislation as an important achievement.

OMNIBUS TRADE. Few policy issues have a longer history than that of trade, making it a less speculative issue than many others. Dramatically worsening trade and investment deficits in the 1980s encouraged many in Congress to fashion a comprehensive policy to stabilize and improve the American position. Many Democrats identified this as an issue with potentially major political appeal, perhaps enough to recapture the White House in 1988. But developing a strategy that will maintain America's competitive position without downgrading the domestic economy has never been a simple matter. This was an issue requiring analysis of enormous scope, since trading problems involve the nation's economic, political, and social structures. No one would recommend that such sensitive and comprehensive policy be developed primarily in Congress. And yet that is what happened during the second Reagan presidency.

As with so many of the bills examined here, the Omnibus Trade Bill was several years in the making. A congressional Democratic task force began work in 1985. In 1986 a bill "was stitched together from individual bills drafted by six committees."[38] The bill invited veto because of its heavily punitive nature. It never reached the president's desk, however, because while it passed the Democratic House, it did not reach the floor in the Republican Senate.

The Democrats gained ten seats in the Senate in 1986, giving them a 55-45 majority. Party leaders announced that Democrats would make trade a priority issue in the 100th Congress. The continuing trade deficit and concern about unfair trade practices ensured that there would be Republican support for a bill, unless the Reagan administration strongly objected. The White House sent clear signals in 1986 that a strongly punitive, highly protectionist bill would be vetoed. Thus party leaders on both sides could hardly fail to understand the terms for reaching an agreement.

Action within the House Committee on Ways and Means was managed by the chair, Daniel Rostenkowski (D-Ill.), and Sam Gibbons (D-Fla.), chair of the Subcommittee on Trade. Together they revised the 1986 trade bill by removing many of the features objectionable to the White House. As a result, the bill attracted cross-partisan support from committee Republicans.

Richard Gephardt (D-Mo.), a Democratic member of the Committee on Ways and Means, was planning to run for president in 1988, primarily on the basis of a tough trade policy. He proposed severe penalties for countries that failed to eliminate unfair trade practices. Gephardt decided not to press for his amendment at the committee stage, primarily because of opposition from Rostenkowski and Gibbons. When offered on the floor, the Gephardt amendment passed by a narrow margin, 218-214. The victory was supplied by seventeen Republicans; fifty-five Democrats voted against. Thus on final passage the bill included the Gephardt amendment. The Democrats were nearly unanimous in supporting the bill, as amended, providing enough votes for passage even without Republican support. In the event, sufficient Republicans voted in favor to override a potential veto.

Senate action closely paralleled that in the House. The bill was reported out of the Senate Committee on Finance by a wide margin. The debate on the Senate floor, which took four weeks, included the adoption of 120 amendments (most uncontroversial). The president warned that the bill contained too many objectionable features, but it passed with cross-partisan support, 71-27. As in the House, Democrats in the Senate supplied sufficient votes for passage, and Republican support meant that a veto override in the Senate was also a possibility.

The sheer size of the bill, its legislative origins in several committees, the significant differences between the two versions, and the pressure from the White House to make modifications all led to one of the largest and most complex conferences in history. In effect, the two houses created a new legislative body, with 199 members and seventeen committees (or subconferences). The conference worked intermittently over a period of months, finally producing a bill that removed the Gephardt amendment and modified other provisions, so as to avoid a veto. It was the most highly and continuously iterative process of any bill of the twenty-eight in this sample and surely one of the most iterative in history.

President Reagan still opposed certain provisions in the bill, however, and he vetoed it. He particularly objected to a requirment to give notice of plant closings. At the same time, he indicated that he would sign a "responsible" bill, virtually inviting Congress to try him again. "By this time, the Administration's negotiators, especially [the Trade Representative], had a vested interest in the compromise, and quietly worked to make it more acceptable to the White House." The House voted to override, with even more Republicans joining Democrats than on the earlier vote. The Senate, however, sustained the veto. Further changes were made, including removal of the plant-closing provision, and the bill was signed into law "in the pre-election atmosphere . . . that makes prompt action possible."[39] The Democrats passed a separate plant-closing bill immediately and held up action on the trade bill until Reagan agreed to allow the plant-closing bill to become law without his signature. Forcing the president's hand in this way substantially compromised the president's rationale for vetoing the original trade bill.

It was an extraordinary achievement for a bicameral Congress: a 1,128-page law that "changed the face of U.S. relations with its trading partners for the rest of this century."[40] Once again, a split-party government acted on a major issue as a presidential election neared. In fact, the Senate cleared the bill for the president's signature just before the Republican convention, and Reagan signed the measure the week after the convention.

Even this brief description raises doubts about the reliability of selected roll call votes to characterize the complex politics of the issue. A total of twelve votes were included in the president's support score for the two years. In 1987 Reagan was credited with two wins and three defeats in the Senate, and two defeats in the House. The Senate votes were on various amendments favored by the president. The House losses were on the Gephardt amendment and on passage of the bill with that amendment. Even though the Gephardt amendment was later removed in conference, there was no way to record that action as a win for the president, since there was not a roll call vote on that specific conference decision.

In 1988 Reagan was credited with one win and four losses on this legislation. The scoring for that year is even more distorted. Two of the losses were the result of House and Senate approval of the conference report that omitted the Gephardt amendment but included the plant-closing notification. A third loss was the result of the House's overriding the president's veto. But sustaining a veto requires only a one-third plus one vote in one house, which the president got in the Senate (and was recorded as his only win). Logically, therefore, this was not a loss, since the Senate sustained the veto.

Finally, the president's fourth loss in 1988 came on a cross-partisan Senate vote favoring the plant-closing notification bill. The House roll call vote on the same legislation was not included among those used to calculate the president's 1988 support score. Just as puzzling is the fact that the vote on final passage of the trade bill, which the president had announced in advance he would sign, was not included as a victory for the president. The legislative tangle that characterized the enactment of the Omnibus Trade Act of 1988 cannot be unsnarled simply by creating scores. To conclude that Reagan won 25 percent of the votes selected for inclusion on this issue reveals nothing of importance about the lawmaking that occurred.

Institutional Reform

The second set in this group of "Congress-preponderant" laws includes two instances of reform: one primarily directed at the executive (the War Powers Resolution of 1973) and one directed at both the executive and Congress (the Budget and Impoundment Control Act of 1974). Both were enacted during the first Nixon presidency. Many members viewed the president as a threat to Congress because of his personal interest and expertise in foreign policy and a style of decisionmaking that was more exclusive than inclusive. In both of these cases, therefore, the initiative came from Congress, not the White House.

The issues involved were at the very core of executive-legislative inter-action on national policy. Had the Vietnam War continued under a Democratic president, it is equally likely that there would have been a War Powers Resolution. The case for budget reform was strong no matter who served in the White House, because of the sheer magnitude and complexity of government spending and the chaotic congressional methods for dealing with it. Impoundment control, however, represented a more strictly partisan response to a Republican president by congressional Democrats. The organizational and procedural changes were not, in and of themselves, in doubt. The sponsors were more or less certain about what would happen by way of changes in structure and process. More questionable were the extent to which form would be followed and the effects on foreign and domestic policies if it were.

WAR POWERS. According to Robert A. Katzmann, "few issues so graphically illustrate the problems of allocating responsibility between Congress and the executive as the power to make war." The War Powers Resolution of 1973 was an effort to define and refine that allocation and illustrates "the difficulties of defining the balance of authority."[41] No one could expect a president to favor efforts to expand the congressional role in foreign and defense policymaking. President Nixon judged any such action unconstitutional.

This issue was not created de novo. The resolution passed in 1973 reflected a legacy of congressional concern about the erosion of authority during the post–World War II period. A major difficulty was that the constitutional authority of Congress to declare war had become passé in a world of alliances, United Nations resolutions, and fast-strike military capability. Congress found itself having to support military commitments in Korea and Vietnam without ever having had an opportunity to declare war. In 1969 a "sense of the Senate" resolution was passed that the president acting alone should not be able to make a national military commitment. This resolution was a second effort by J. William Fulbright (D-Ark.), chair of the Senate Committee on Foreign Relations, to define presidential-congressional responsibilities and was "only an admonition to the President to consult with Congress; he still was not bound to do so." It had the support of many Republicans, despite its characterization by Senate Minority Leader Everett Dirksen (R-Ill.) as "a bundle of mischief."[42]

The incursion of American forces into Cambodia in 1970 again raised the issue of the extent of the president's independent authority to commit military forces. The House passed joint resolutions in 1970 and 1971 defining Congress's role, but the Senate did not act beyond holding hearings in 1971. In 1972 the Senate took the initiative and passed the precursor to the 1973 resolution. The House passed its less restrictive 1970 and 1971 versions in 1972. Nixon endorsed the House action as the lesser evil. The differences between the two chambers were not resolved in conference, so no resolution was enacted.

The House Committee on Foreign Affairs made significant changes to the resolution in 1973. This high degree of iteration was the result of an effort to toughen the measure as earlier passed by the House. The Senate more or less endorsed its work of 1972. The Senate Committee on Foreign Relations unanimously approved and reported a resolution jointly sponsored by Jacob Javits (R-N.Y.) and John Stennis (D-Miss.). This cross-partisan action in the committee virtually ensured floor approval.

Minor changes were made on the House floor, but no changes were made on the Senate floor, as opponents of the resolution counted on a presidential veto. In both chambers, passage was obtained with cross-partisan support: 40 percent of House Republicans joining 74 percent of Democrats; 61 percent of Senate Republicans joining 93 percent of Democrats. The Senate margin was more than was needed to override a veto, but the House margin fell substantially short of the required two-thirds. The conference was active in reaching a compromise between the two versions of the resolution, and in each house the conference report was agreed to by margins similar to those for the original bill.

Editorial reaction urged the president to sign the resolution. Nixon ignored this advice and vetoed it as posing a serious threat to presidential prerogatives in foreign policy. The great concern, of course, was what would happen in the House of Representatives, given the previous votes in that chamber. Certainly it was within the power of House Republicans to sustain the veto, because they held 44 percent of the seats. In the final tally, however, nearly half the Republicans (46 percent) voted to override—more than had voted for the resolution in either of the previous votes. And so the veto was overridden by a slim four-vote margin in the House. The question naturally arose as to why Republicans would switch their votes. *Congressional Quarterly* found that most did so "to assert more independence."[43] Another reason was that Nixon's veto raised the prospect that there would be no clarification of institutional responsibilities in this important area.

Other events occurring at this time were highly damaging to the Nixon presidency. During the month in which both houses voted on the conference report and the override of the veto, Vice President Spiro Agnew resigned, Gerald R. Ford was nominated by Nixon to be vice president, Nixon ordered the dismissal of the special Watergate prosecutor, House Democratic leaders tentatively agreed to begin an inquiry into impeachment proceedings, and Leon Jaworski was appointed as the new special Watergate prosecutor. It was, to say the very least, a time of confrontation between the two branches.

The president suffered seven defeats on this issue for his presidential support score: one in 1972, the other six in 1973. The three votes in the Senate in 1973 hardly varied in the vote split, raising the question of why three votes were included in the score.

BUDGET REFORM. By the 1970s, members of Congress had become just as frustrated with their budget-making role as with their foreign policy-making role. The Nixon administration sought to streamline the process by reorganizing the administrative apparatus and introducing new budgeting procedures. In 1973 Nixon proposed serious reductions in domestic programs, most of which were to be achieved administratively in programs that had strong congressional support. The president also charged that congressional budget making contributed to spending that was out of control. He wanted a cap on expenditures and the authority to make cuts if Congress exceeded the statutory limit. Finally, he threatened to impound funds if Congress failed to set a limit and appropriated funds for programs the administration did not want.

Congressional leaders essentially agreed that their procedures needed to be overhauled, in part for the reasons Nixon outlined and in part for fear that failure to act would result in a significant loss of institutional powers. A Joint Study Committee on Budget Control, made up mostly of members from the House and Senate appropriations and tax-writing committees, was created in 1972 to propose changes in congressional organization and procedures. Al Ullman (D-Ore.), chair of the House Committee on Ways and Means, chaired the joint committee. He observed that "timing in the political arena is of utmost importance. This is the time for Congress to accomplish a purpose which it has not been willing to face up to for 100 years."[44]

A major overhaul of the budget process was proposed, including the creation of budget committees, a congressional budget office, budget resolutions, a change in the fiscal year, and limits on impoundments by the president. The action in both houses was most iterative at the committee stage.

Substantial bipartisanship characterized the legislation throughout (less so at early stages in the House). Liberal House Democrats, concerned that the new Committee on the Budget might lock in a conservative majority, insisted on changes in the committee's makeup. Once an agreement was worked out, by which all legislative committees would be represented on the new panel, the bill, as reported by the Committee on Rules, passed handily.

In the Senate there was a jurisdictional tug-of-war between two committees: Government Operations and Rules and Administration. Following an agreement, the Rules and Administration Committee "conducted unprecedented negotiations among staff representatives from 10 Senate committees, four joint committees and the House Appropriations Committee."[45] Both committees then managed the bill to an 80-0 approval on the Senate floor. The conference negotiations also included input from staff representatives. The final product was agreed to overwhelmingly in both houses.

The passage of the Budget and Impoundment Control Act of 1974 provoked warnings about the workability of the timetable and the possibility of escape hatches, but most reaction was positive. Nixon signed the bill in "an air of joviality," in spite of the new controls on his power to impound funds. At the signing ceremony he observed: "This bill is the most significant reform of budget procedures since Congress began."[46] This was less than a month before his resignation.

Several years later, Nixon expressed quite different views: "I used impoundment to restrain some of the willy-nilly spending of the massive, and now largely discredited, Great Society programs I inherited. . . . In 1974 Congress took the impoundment power away, thus reserving to itself the right to spend irresponsibly without constraint."[47] *Congressional Quarterly*'s calculation of Nixon's 1974 presidential support score included a single vote on an amendment in the House to delete the impoundment control sections of the bill, which was registered as a defeat for the president. None of the final votes on the budget reform act was included.

Joint Participation

The fifteen enactments categorized as involving joint participation are of two types: those in which the president was particularly active and those that demonstrate genuine balance, arguably, even greater congressional involvement. Three variations among the second set are noted: familiar issues, new issues, and unusual procedures. The total number of cases of joint participation is itself noteworthy, being more than in any other category. Try as I might, I found it difficult to assign clear preponderance of involvement by one branch over the other in more than one-third of the laws, a conclusion that would not likely be drawn about any other national political system.

Substantial Presidential Activity: Single-Party Government

Three of the laws in this first category, substantial presidential activity, were passed under single-party government: Medicare in 1965 (Johnson), creation of the Department of Education in 1979 (Carter), and the synthetic fuels program in 1980 (Carter).

MEDICARE. As can be seen from figure 6-1, medical care for the aged was a familiar issue for public policymakers. That fact did not greatly reduce the highly speculative nature of broad-scale health care reform. The issue was also extremely contentious because it pitted a powerful professional group, the American Medical Association, against what was then a sleeping giant of political pressure, senior citizens. "Socialized medicine" was a frequent slogan of the opposition whenever proposals were made. President Truman proposed a comprehensive national health care program in 1949, but no action was taken in Congress. In 1957 Representative Aime Forand (D-R.I.) introduced a health care program for those eligible for old age and survivors insurance, to be funded by an increase in Social Security taxes. The Forand bill had its roots in a plan devised by the AFL-CIO.

President Eisenhower had earlier proposed reinsuring private insurance companies against heavy losses for health claims. Growing interest in the Forand bill prompted the Eisenhower administration to study the problem, and then secretary of health, education, and welfare Arthur Flemming proposed a state-administered, voluntary, means-tested program for those over sixty-five. He called it "Medicare." It was not even introduced in the House. "Although scarcely anyone but its authors liked" the Flemming plan, there had been movement in both parties toward acceptance of the issue's importance and devising a solution.[48] Under the pressure of election-year politics, a mild version of the Flemming plan was enacted, limiting coverage to the indigent. Authored by Senator Robert Kerr (D-Okla.) and Representative Wilbur D. Mills (D-Ark.), it was known as the Kerr-Mills Act.

A highly iterative, developmental phase ensued with the election of a new president in 1960. President Kennedy favored a plan financed through

Social Security, and there was some cross-partisan support led by Senator Jacob Javits (R-N.Y.). But Ways and Means chair Wilbur Mills remained opposed, and thus this proposal (named for its sponsors, Representative Cecil King, D-Calif., and Senator Clinton Anderson, D-N.M.) did not pass.

The 1964 election was, in part, about Medicare. Johnson was for it and his opponent, Barry Goldwater, was against it. Johnson's overwhelming victory, combined with a significant increase in the House Democratic majority, practically all of whom were "committed to medicare," virtually ensured passage of the King-Anderson bill.[49]

Still, it was essential that Wilbur Mills be persuaded to support the Social Security approach. A key player in this effort within the administration was Wilbur Cohen, then assistant secretary of health, education, and welfare for legislation. Cohen believed that winning over Mills required "the adaptation of the legislative proposal to satisfy Mills' prestige and his own personal creativity."[50] Others in the administration believed that pressure on his fellow members would eventually force Mills to support King-Anderson, but Cohen did not favor humiliating him with a defeat or making him into a messenger for the administration. Mills was as capable as others in Washington of reading the 1964 election returns. If there was a mood to act on this issue, then Mills was eager to "put his own stamp upon the program, rather than merely accepting the Administration's proposal as it was submitted to Congress."[51] A contemporary portrayal of Mills pointed out: "The decisions of the Committee are shaped and articulated by Mills, but his word comes close to being law in the Committee because he has listened to others, particularly to the ranking Republican, John Byrnes."[52]

Meanwhile, Republicans countered with a proposal of their own, sponsored by Representative Byrnes (R-Wis.), that provided for a voluntary health insurance program financed by premiums, state contributions, and federal appropriations. A third plan was offered by the American Medical Association; called "Eldercare," it was an extension of the existing Kerr-Mills program. Representatives of the Department of Health, Education, and Welfare (HEW) viewed these proposals "as mutually exclusive alternatives," but Mills instead "suggested that the committee consider a 'medielder-Byrnes bill' . . . [to] combine the three programs." The HEW representatives "were stunned by Mills' combination of the several programs."[53]

Mills now wanted Johnson's support for his incorporative strategy, which was designed to provide maximum cross-partisan support on the House floor. The key vote came on the recommittal motion by Byrnes, which would have sent the compromise package back to the committee with instructions to report the Republican plan back to the floor. Byrnes's motion was defeated by a vote of 191-236. The closeness of the vote, given the large Democratic majority, confirmed the need for Mills's incorporative strategy. Sixty-three Democrats sided with Byrnes. The House Republican Policy Committee endorsed Byrnes's motion but took no position on the final passage of Mills's bill. Nearly half of the Republicans voted in favor of the bill, and forty-two Democrats voted against it.

Although an advance count in the Senate showed a ten-vote margin for the bill, including three Republicans, the immediate problem was getting the bill reported out of the Committee on Finance, chaired by Harry F. Byrd (D-Va.), a declared opponent of Medicare. In a celebrated televised meeting, President Johnson got a public commitment from Byrd to hold hearings on the bill. The committee voted it out by a 12-5 count. The bill passed the Senate by a substantial, cross-partisan margin, 68-21 (48 percent of the Republicans joined 89 percent of the Democrats in favor). A number of liberalizing amendments were passed on the Senate floor. The conference agreement greatly favored the House version of the bill. President Johnson went to Independence, Missouri, to sign the bill in the presence of former president Harry S Truman, whose early efforts at promoting a national health plan had failed.

The legislation contributed fourteen victories and no defeats to Johnson's 1965 presidential support score. Eleven of the fourteen wins were in the Senate; nine of these were on amendments offered by Republicans or on procedural motions. The one successful amendment that was opposed by the floor managers of the bill was not counted. All of the liberalizing amendments passed by voice vote, and many of these changes were then removed in the conference.

Support scores were not calculated for Wilbur Mills, but no one doubted that he had performed well in what began as a difficult political situation for him. It is relevant that Mills joined the effort in his own way, substantially altering the administration's proposal and essentially taking charge of lawmaking for this issue. Accepting the bold changes fashioned by Mills made it possible for the president to claim victory in the House roll call votes.

Medicare was judged to be an outstanding achievement of the Johnson administration. It is no diminution of that accolade to point to the major contribution made by members of Congress or to the progression of this issue over time.

DEPARTMENT OF EDUCATION. One test of responsible party government is whether the president fulfills his promises. In the 1976 presidential campaign, Jimmy Carter "endorsed the idea of creating a cabinet-level department [of education]" because "for those educators who came to Washington to seek help or resolve a question or dispute, it was almost impossible to locate the federal official who was supposed to be responsible."[54] Yet after Carter became president, his proposal for creating the new department was subjected to considerable criticism, even among Democrats, some in his own cabinet. Being responsible in the classic mode does not always pay off for presidents.

The Republican opponents of the new department hardly had to act, given the nature and source of the conflicts over Carter's proposal. The two principal education lobbies were on opposite sides of this issue. The National Education Association (NEA) favored the proposal and had worked for Carter's nomination in 1976 because of his support for the idea. The American Federation of Teachers (AFT) opposed the proposal. President Carter's principal cabinet representative on education issues, Secretary of Health, Education, and Welfare Joseph A. Califano, strongly opposed rending his department in this way.

A serious effort was made in 1978 to get the plan approved. Both House and Senate committees reported bills, but only the Senate acted, approving the plan, 72-11. Opponents in the House prevented action as the 1978 midterm elections were approaching. The most serious issue was the scope of the new department's jurisdiction. Carter and Senator Abraham Ribicoff (D-Conn.), chair of the Committee on Government Operations and a former secretary of HEW, favored a broad department. But each program had its advocates for special status. Califano's account illustrates how iteration proceeds. "As the Education Department proposal worked its way through the Congress, each special interest moved to carve out its own independent fiefdom, with legislative power and protection. This had the effect of making it virtually impossible for the Education Secretary to run the new department efficiently."[55]

The White House renewed and redoubled its efforts in 1979, with the president actively and personally involved in the lobbying. "The president . . . badly needed a major legislative victory to offset several losses he had encountered on Capitol Hill."[56] As before, the bill passed by a wide margin in the Senate (72-21), with significant support from both parties. Once again the House was a major hurdle. The proposal barely got out of the committee (20-19, with two Republicans providing the winning margin).

The AFT became active in a loose coalition of groups opposing the new department. The coalition sought to delay floor action in order to build opposition to the bill. Floor consideration took on the characteristics of an auction, as opposition forces tried to split liberal and black support. A highly iterative amending process resulted in the approval of amendments against quotas, forced busing, and abortion, along with others favoring voluntary school prayer and limits on departmental growth. Even with all of these changes, or perhaps because of them, the bill passed with cross-partisan support by just four votes, 210-206. Republicans supplied a crucial thirty-five votes; eighty-nine Democrats, most of them from the North, voted against the president.

The conference dropped all of the controversial amendments; thus more liberal votes were gained than conservative votes were lost. The House agreed to the conference report by the cross-partisan vote of 215-201, Republicans again supplying a crucial thirty votes and northerners casting the largest share of the seventy-seven Democratic votes against the report. The nature of the cross-partisan voting between conservatives and liberals remained curious throughout the long consideration of the legislation.

President Carter signed the bill on October 17, 1979. Joseph Califano was not present, since he had been fired as secretary of HEW some months earlier. The NEA expressed satisfaction with the passage of the bill and confirmed its support for Carter in 1980. As discussed in chapter 6, the support scores on this proposal—seventeen wins and two losses—gives the misleading impression that Carter was in full and winning command of this legislative battle. He was not. As with war powers and budget reform, this legislation resulted in predictable organizational change. The longer-term effects on education policymaking, however, were considerably more in doubt.[57]

SYNTHETIC FUELS PROGRAM. No issues frustrated President Carter more than those associated with energy supply and demand. Carter recorded in his diary that he found "the Congress . . . disgusting on this particular subject."[58] It was, in large part, his bafflement about how to solve energy issues that led to the Camp David retreat in the summer of 1979. Once the retreat was under way, more systemic issues were raised about Carter's leadership and the state of the nation more generally. A debate ensued among Carter's staff as to what should be said once the president returned to Washington. Carter's chief domestic policy adviser, Stuart Eizenstat, was adamant that the president's speech should contain a specific energy proposal, since gas lines had made that issue a top priority for the American people. Eizenstat got his way. The transitional sentence in Carter's famous "crisis of confidence" speech reads: "Energy will be the immediate test of our ability to unite this Nation and it can also be the standard around which we rally."[59]

One of Carter's proposed energy initiatives was a long-term program to produce synthetic fuels. This was a new proposal but not a new idea. "During World War II, the federal government had begun a program to develop synthetic fuels, and the Truman administration considered them to be nearly commercially feasible."[60] More recently, President Ford had supported synthetic fuels proposals in 1975 and 1976, but Congress did not follow through. In 1979, spurred by a continuing energy crisis, the House had already passed a bill supporting the synthetic fuels industry when Carter made his proposals.

Thus this was a case of a president enthusiastically endorsing a congressional initiative. The president expanded the House proposal and provided a means for funding and managing government support. A windfall profits tax was to pay for the plan, and an energy security corporation (later named the Synthetic Fuels Corporation) was to administer the funds. Carter asked for an $88 billion program over a period of twelve years. How speculative was this plan? As Walter A. Rosenbaum noted, "This would have been the most expensive technological gamble in U.S. history."[61]

The initial reaction from congressional leaders was favorable. Speaker Thomas P. O'Neill (D-Mass.) predicted that "Congress will pull together in this time of crisis"; House Majority Leader Jim Wright (D-Tex.) said that the president's goals were high "but we can keep them"; and Senate Minority Leader Howard W. Baker (R-Tenn.) pledged that "I am willing to work with the president if he would let me."[62]

The lawmaking sequence was somewhat unusual, given that the House had already passed a synthetic fuels bill when the president's program was introduced. The Senate had both the bill passed by the House and the president's proposal. The House bill was sponsored by William Moorhead (D-Pa.), a member of the Committee on Banking, Finance and Urban Affairs. Therefore the Moorhead bill went to the Senate Committee on Banking, Housing and Urban Affairs. Because the president's program had been introduced in the meantime, the House bill also went to the Senate Committee on Energy and Natural Resources, along with the president's bill. A jurisdictional dispute caused delay in the consideration of both bills.

Decisionmaking in the Senate and the conference was highly iterative and featured cross-partisan support. Two very different bills were reported out of the Senate committees. Carter's program, as revised, emanated from the Energy Committee and was passed by the Senate. Funding was not tied to the windfall profits tax, as Carter had requested, and the program was cut back from $88 billion to a start-up authorization of $20 billion. Following agreements reached in conference, the House was forced to adopt legislation that it had not really fully considered under its regular procedures, although Majority Leader Wright played an important role in framing a compromise. The conference report was agreed to by substantial cross-partisan majorities in both houses.

The president scored six victories and one defeat on this bill toward his 1979 support score. The votes used by *Congressional Quarterly* were taken primarily in the Senate (five of the six votes), because of the peculiar sequence of the legislation. That is, a House bill had already passed when the president made his proposal, and he had not taken a position on a synthetic fuels program at the point of House passage.

Although President Carter identified the program as "the keystone of our national energy policy," President Reagan did not consider the synthetic fuels program a priority. In 1985 the Synthetic Fuels Corporation was dismantled, significantly affecting the longer-range "success" for Carter on this issue.

Substantial Presidential Activity: Split-Party Government

The Energy Policy and Conservation Act of 1975 and the anticrime legislative package of 1984 came close to being free-for-alls in the lawmaking process. Unquestionably in each case the president was active in proposing legislation, but his offering was viewed as a starting point on Capitol Hill. The difference from the three cases above lies in the nature of party control: in these two, Republican presidents were working with Democratic congressional majorities (in the House only for Reagan in 1984).

ENERGY ACT. It is hard to conceive of political circumstances less hospitable to classic responsible government than those in 1975. Gerald Ford was nominated by Nixon in October 1973 to be vice president when Spiro T. Agnew resigned. When Nixon himself was threatened by a possible impeachment, "a handful of Democrats wanted to stall the [Ford] confirmation procedure," since Speaker Carl Albert (D-Okla.) would become the president if Nixon resigned or was impeached.[63] Albert would not agree to any such plan. Thus Gerald Ford became the first unelected vice president, under highly partisan circumstances. Then he took over for a president forced to resign in disgrace and pardoned him. The Democrats realized substantial net increases in both the House and the Senate in the 1974 elections, further separating the two branches on a partisan basis.

This context of partisanship and institutional instability was the political setting for an effort to create a national energy policy. The nation faced serious energy problems in the aftermath of the 1973 Arab oil embargo. This least responsible government, by standard criteria, had to manage one of the most complex policy issues of the postwar period. In January 1975 President Ford sent the Congress a 167-page proposal. Ford also announced that he would remove all controls on domestic oil prices on April 1, a highly controversial action. The partisan nature of these issues was signaled immediately when the Democrats sought to upstage the president by presenting their program two days before the annual State of the Union message. Ford quickly responded with a special address to the nation on the same day as the Democrats presented their program.

These political shenanigans were a prelude to a year-long battle between the White House and Congress. The oil price decontrol issue, in particular, was a running story throughout 1975. This story included postponement of the president's decision to decontrol, an extension of controls by Congress, a presidential veto of the congressional extension, a House veto of a subsequent thirty-month decontrol plan from the president, congressional passage of another price control extension, a second presidential veto, and finally, two temporary extensions of controls agreed to by the president.

No one doubted that some action was required. "The country was in the throes of a veritable economic crisis; unemployment was at its highest level since the Great Depression, and inflation was raging at an annualized rate of 12.2 percent." Rising energy prices contributed substantially to inflation. "To much of Congress the energy problem seemed to be essentially one of exorbitant price. This was not the view of the Ford administration, which regarded high prices as a bitter but necessary antidote for wasteful consumption and sluggish domestic production of energy."[64] The president had to be active on this issue, but any proposal he made would have to compete with solutions proffered by others. This was not stalemate; it was intense competitive partisanship within separated institutions on a critical policy matter.

The Senate acted first. Four bills were produced by two committees: Interior and Insular Affairs, and Commerce. The House produced just one comprehensive bill. Iteration and partisanship in the Senate varied substantially among the bills, both within the committees and on the floor. Two of the bills passed on the floor with no opposing votes. The other two were more controversial, yet they received substantial majorities.

On the House side, the legislation was considered by just one committee: Interstate and Foreign Commerce. Oil price control was the most controversial issue, resulting in a partisan division (with three Democrats joining all Republicans in opposition to the committee report). Floor debate and amendments occurred intermittently over a period of more than two months. James H. Quillen (R-Tenn.) characterized the bill as "bad," "controversial," "inadequate," and "unattractive."[65] Democrats were also not altogether satisfied, and therefore the bill was subjected to many changes on the House floor. It finally passed and was then substituted for one of the four Senate bills.

A conference ensued after each house refused to accept the amendments of the other. After a month of deliberations, an agreement was reached without the support of any Republican (or of three Senate Democrats). The House rejected the report on a cross-partisan vote of 300-103 (96 percent of the Republicans joining 63 percent of the Democrats). The House then made further changes and sent a clean bill to the Senate for approval. Perhaps as much out of exhaustion as genuine approval, the Senate approved the House changes, following a debate that ridiculed the bill. Senator Lowell Weicker (R- Conn.) called it "a political energy cop-out," Senator Henry Bellmon (R-Okla.) referred to it as the "Energy Hash Act," and Senator John Tower (R-Tex.) called it the "Cold Homes and Dark Factories Act."[66] For them, the effects of the bill were not speculative; they were opposite of what was intended.

The Energy Policy and Conservation Act is an example of a competitive partisan effort in the early stages, with separate proposals and independent sources of authority on each side, that did not produce cross-partisan majorities. Although the roll calls show that Republicans voted for the final bills, they faced the same dilemma as did the president in deciding whether to sign or veto the bill. Overall, however, this was a battle in which the large Democratic congressional majorities produced a piece of legislation very different from that which the president had requested.

Ford described himself as caught between his economic advisers, urging him to veto the bill, and his political advisers, urging him to sign it.[67] Senate Republicans reportedly reminded the president that with the election year ahead, western conservatives would leave him for Ronald Reagan if he signed the bill. "Enactment of the Energy Policy and Conservation Act might give Ford New Hampshire, but it would lose him Texas, they prophesied."[68] At the last minute, Secretary of the Treasury William Simon urged him to veto the measure. Ford thanked him for his late-night call and signed the bill the next day. Simon later wrote that the Energy Policy and Conservation Act was "the worst error of the Ford administration."[69]

Constructing a support score for this legislation was no simple task. President Ford was credited with three wins and four losses, perhaps an accurate reflection of the politics of the issue. Yet the final, critical votes on the conference report in the House, the changes made before the conference report was rejected, and the final acceptance of the House changes in the Senate are not included in calculating the support score. It would not be easy to determine the president's position at this stage of action, but that merely makes the larger point that in analyzing and interpreting how laws are made one cannot rely solely on presidential position taking or judgments about his success.

ANTICRIME PACKAGE. Like many presidents, Ronald Reagan called for national action to curb crime. Bills had been introduced in 1973, 1977, 1980, 1981, and 1982, but they either died in Congress or were vetoed. In his 1983 State of the Union message, Reagan called for "an all-out war on big-time organized crime and the drug racketeers who are poisoning our young people."[70]

Since crime occurs in every state and congressional district, legislation relating to it is highly constituency oriented. No president can expect that members of Congress will simply ratify his proposals. Moreover, in 1983 a presidential election was approaching. Therefore several bills were introduced in each house as counterproposals to those offered by the Reagan administration. What happened then exemplifies what discourages those wishing to understand American politics.

The Senate acted first, as was common during 1981–87, when Republicans were in the majority. Action within the Committee on the Judiciary was highly iterative and competitively partisan. Senate Democrats introduced their own proposals. A cross-partisan majority emerged, providing widespread support for several bills on the Senate floor. Taken as a package, the bills met with the approval of the president, who then complained about the House's failure to act. Others were not so persuaded of the correctness of Senate action. A *New York Times* editorial declared that the Senate bill "rode pell-mell over the Constitution."[71]

The House Committee on the Judiciary reported fourteen separate anticrime bills, an action interpreted by the Reagan White House as parliamentary maneuvering to prevent a vote on the whole package. The last of the Judiciary Committee measures was reported in September. In late September, House Republicans moved to attach a bill identical to the Senate anticrime package to a fiscal year 1985 continuing resolution. Their maneuver succeeded with the support of over a third of the House Democrats.

The Democratic leadership then offered an omnibus bill containing most of the Judiciary Committee's proposals, which passed by a wide margin. However, the legislative vehicle for the anticrime program was still the continuing resolution. Therefore the conference was not between the two judiciary committees but rather between the two appropriations committees, and members of the House Judiciary Committee played only a consultative role.

Reaction to the passage of the legislation acknowledged the far-reaching nature of the anticrime package and credited both parties. Yet *Congressional Quarterly* gave the president eight victories and one defeat, a ratio that would surely surprise those members of Congress who managed this legislation.

Institutional Balance on Familiar Issues

The final group of ten bills represents genuine balance between president and Congress. I have divided my discussion of them into three sets. First is a group of old-line issues that were well understood in the White House and Congress, if not easy to resolve in either. The National Housing Act of 1949; two tax measures, the Excess Profits Tax in 1950 and the Revenue Act of 1962; and the Civil Rights Act of 1957 displayed the expected joint participation by the two institutions. Of the four, the Civil Rights Act represented something new—the first such act to be passed in many decades—but the issue itself was certainly not novel.

NATIONAL HOUSING ACT. President Truman wrote in his memoirs that "housing was one of the acute postwar problems with which I had to deal. . . . The immediate demand for new housing was far in excess of the industry's capacity to produce."[72] Work on housing proposals had been proceeding since the end of the war in both the White House and Congress. The effort in the Senate had bipartisan leadership: Robert Wagner (D-N.Y.), Allen Ellender (D-La.), and Robert Taft (R-Ohio). Yet in Congress as a whole, the politics of the issue was more cross-partisan than bipartisan: "Northern Democratic senators and congressmen and some nationally known Southern Democrats have usually combined with the Northeast urban Republican senators and congressmen from urban areas to support housing legislation. Opponents . . . are drawn from Southern Democrats and Midwest and rural Republicans."[73] Therefore it was more a matter of building a majority from both parties than being able to rely on one from the start.

A number of laws had been enacted to give temporary housing relief to returning veterans. A long-range housing policy, however, was more difficult to enact because of intense opposition by the real estate and home-building interests. The most contentious issue was public housing. We now know just how speculative was policymaking on this issue. Many of the projects spawned by the program failed miserably to satisfy housing needs.

All parties involved had ample opportunity between 1945 and 1949 to observe and absorb the politics of this issue. In 1946 the Senate passed a bill by a voice vote, but the House Committee on Banking and Currency did not report a bill. In 1947, when the Republicans were in the majority, a joint committee studied the problem but produced no legislation. In 1948 the Senate passed a bill with a public housing provision, but the House Committee on Rules refused to grant a rule to debate the bill. A limited bill was passed and signed by Truman, even though he judged it inadequate. In 1948 Truman was elected, to everyone's surprise, and congressional Democrats regained their majorities in both houses.

In 1949 the cross-partisan characteristic of earlier action in the Senate was replaced by competitive partisanship: both parties offered serious proposals. Wagner, Ellender, and five other Democrats introduced the president's bill. "Democrats, cavalierly assuming they could enact a public housing bill by themselves, drew up a draft at the start of the session, then gave Taft but one hour to study it before they introduced it. Taken aback, he refused to lend his name to it, and joined [Senators Irving] Ives and [Ralph] Flanders in submitting a plan of his own."[74] Senator Ives doubted that the two versions could be reconciled. However, Wagner, Ellender, and Taft had worked on this issue too long not to try. Cross-partisanship was reestablished. The two proposals were melded, sent to the floor, and passed.

The true test was to come in the House. As in the Senate, the Republicans offered their own bill (essentially the Taft alternative). But there was less compromising, and the bill as reported by the committee was closer to the president's original requests. The Committee on Rules first voted to deny a rule. Speaker Sam Rayburn (D-Tex.) then threatened to invoke the newly adopted twenty-one-day rule, by which the Committee on Rules could be circumvented. The committee then reversed itself and voted a rule.

Floor debate on the rule began with the Rules Committee chair, Adolph Sabath (D-Ill.), denouncing the "unholy alliance and coalition" of Republicans and southern Democrats for blocking public housing legislation in the past. "Representative Eugene Cox, Democrat, of Georgia, sixty-nine years old, called Sabath [eighty-three] a liar and punched him in the mouth. Sabath's glasses flew off, and he swung blindly at Cox until the two men were pulled apart."[75] Amid cries of "socialism" by opponents, the bill passed with cross-partisan support. The key vote came on a motion to eliminate the public housing section of the bill. The Democrats could not win this vote on their own, but twenty-four Republicans voted against the motion and it failed, 209-204. On final passage, Republicans supplied a crucial thirty-four votes, without which the bill would have met defeat.

The conference report, slightly favoring the Senate bill, was approved by voice vote in both houses. The new housing act was hailed as an important achievement. Upon signing it, Truman marked the legislation as a breakthrough in the provision of housing for low-income families. Doubts, however, remain as to Truman's commitment to a liberal housing policy. He made no mention of the act in his memoirs.

EXCESS PROFITS TAX. On June 25, 1950, North Korea launched a full-scale invasion of South Korea. Two days later, President Truman committed U.S. forces to aid South Korea. These events had a significant impact on tax policy in a year that John F. Witte refers to as "one of the most active and confusing . . . in the history of American taxation."[76] One of the issues in the enactment of the Revenue Act of 1950 was an excess profits tax, a levy that was popular during war but politically questionable during a midterm election year. The president favored such a tax but wanted it enacted after the election, preferably in 1951. After much maneuvering, a provision was included in the Revenue Act to direct the two tax committees to prepare an excess profits tax either in a special postelection session or in the next Congress, to be retroactive to 1950.

Congress did reconvene following the 1950 midterm elections and quickly began to work on the legislation. Truman wrote to the chair of the House Committee on Ways and Means: "To preserve the integrity of the government's finances, our revenue system must keep pace with our defense expenditures." Senate Majority Leader Scott Lucas (D-Ill.) explained: "We're going to see that no one gets rich just because he happened to get a defense contract, or because he cornered a market on something which is in short supply."[77]

Predictably, labor groups supported the tax and business groups opposed it. Action in the House was strongly partisan. The opposition was not even allowed to testify before the Committee on Ways and Means, though a Republican plan was introduced that "allowed corporations a choice between increased regular corporate rates of 45 to 55 percent or the excess profits tax."[78] The plan was defeated. After modest changes in the administration's proposal, it was reported out by a party-line vote. The Rules Committee granted a closed rule for debate on the floor. The Republicans sought support for their plan in the motion of recommittal. It was defeated, again on a strongly partisan vote. The bill then passed by a wide margin.

As the bill moved to the Senate, Secretary of the Treasury John Snyder warned that defense costs were escalating and more money would be needed. The Senate Committee on Finance accordingly made a number of changes in the House bill to raise more revenue. Republicans did not seriously object, since President Truman had declared a national emergency on December 16 in response to China's involvement in the war in Korea. The bill passed the Senate on a voice vote. Conferees quickly reached an agreement, followed by voice vote support in both houses. In a statement released at the signing, Truman praised Congress and its committees for acting quickly, but others sharply criticized the legislation for containing too many loopholes and not providing sufficient additional revenue.

The Excess Profits Tax of 1950 is an example of emergency legislation responding to events as they occurred. The procedure of having Congress direct itself to act later was unusual. Normal partisan or competitive partisan behavior over tax policy was suspended in the face of the threat of war with China. The president expressed the need for the legislation and the secretary of the Treasury identified the revenue requirements, but the formula itself was written on Capitol Hill.

CIVIL RIGHTS ACT.   In the case of civil rights lawmaking, for decades an important number was sixty-four—two-thirds of the Senate (which had ninety-six members from 1912 to 1959). A two-thirds vote was required to break a filibuster, and southern and border states nearly had the one-third needed to prevent cloture. A strong cross-partisan alliance was needed to overcome the filibuster, and for years it was not forthcoming. Therefore various attempts by Roosevelt and Truman to pass civil rights measures were rebuffed by a minority in Congress.

The Eisenhower administration in 1953–55 had narrow Republican majorities in Congress and thus "had little interest in spending [its] energy blowing on the embers of [its] predecessors' disasters" in civil rights, since southern Democratic support might well be required to enact the president's program.[79] In his 1953 State of the Union message Eisenhower had committed himself "to use whatever authority exists in the office of the President to end segregation in the District of Columbia, including the federal government, and any segregation in the armed forces." He believed that "much could be done by Executive power alone," thus avoiding the bruising, and losing, battles on Capitol Hill.[80]

Pressured by congressional northern Democrats and events (such as the Montgomery bus boycott), Attorney General Herbert Brownell, with cabinet approval, began formulating a civil rights proposal in 1955. Cabinet reaction was mixed, as was that of the president, who remained skeptical about taking a legislative initiative in this area. Brownell was forced to moderate his proposal in sending it to Congress in 1956, but he nonetheless worked for support of the whole package, virtually against Eisenhower's wishes. It seems evident in retrospect that Eisenhower's cautious approach reflected a sensitivity to the politics of the issue, combined with a hope that equality would come about without a fight. His apparent solution was a combination of hesitant support and toleration of more active involvement by Attorney General Brownell. An encouraging increase in his share of the black vote in 1956 contributed to Eisenhower's endorsement of the full Brownell proposal in his 1957 State of the Union message.

Congressional reactions to Eisenhower's more active support of the Brownell proposal were as expected. The powerful leader of the southern Democratic bloc, Senator Richard B. Russell (D-Ga.), vowed uncompromising opposition, and the leader of the liberal northern Democrats on this issue, Senator Hubert H. Humphrey (D-Minn.), welcomed Eisenhower's support. Senate Majority Leader Lyndon B. Johnson (D-Tex.) announced his opposition to the bill, but explained that he would not block efforts to have it debated on the floor.

The House acted first and passed the Eisenhower program after approving a few weakening amendments. The bill was approved by a greater than two-to-one margin, with 90 percent of the Republicans joining 52 percent of the Democrats in favor.

As predicted, the Senate was the stumbling block, as it had been for decades on this issue. Efforts were made, as they had been in 1953, to have new rules adopted, based on the view that the Senate was not a continuous body (thus providing an opening for changing the cloture rule). Johnson pleaded with the Senate not to take this action, so as to preserve the two-thirds vote on cloture as an important protection for minorities. At the same time he indicated that a civil rights bill could pass the Senate if a majority supported it. In essence he was guaranteeing a vote on the bill, but also promising there would be no filibuster. With the support of Minority Leader William Knowland (R-Calif.), Johnson carried the day. Sundquist explains: "The interest of the South in 1957 was therefore not to filibuster but to accept as weak a civil rights bill as they could get away with."[81]

The first hurdle in the Senate was the Committee on the Judiciary, chaired by James Eastland (D-Miss.). The plan was to avoid the committee altogether. Minority Leader Knowland objected on the floor to sending the House bill to the Judiciary Committee; Senator Russell raised a point of order against the objection; and the Senate, by a vote of 39-45, rejected Russell's point of order. The result was to place the House bill on the Senate calendar, thus allowing it to be taken up by majority vote. Knowland's motion to take up the bill was the subject of eight days of debate, after which the bill itself was debated for twenty-four days.

Two important changes were made on the Senate floor, both weakening the bill by reducing the attorney general's authority and providing for jury trials in criminal contempt cases. Senator Russell led the efforts to cripple the enforcement provisions of the bill. After an impassioned speech foreseeing the forced "commingling of white and Negro children in the state-supported public schools of the South," Sundquist concludes, "Russell had the civil rights forces in full retreat."[82]

Eisenhower was of little help during this period. Asked in a news conference about Senator Russell's charges, he responded that he found such a reaction "rather incomprehensible, but I am always ready to listen to anyone's presentation to me of his views." Asked if the bill should be changed, the president responded that he had been reading the bill but "there were certain phrases I didn't completely understand."[83] His biographer, Stephen E. Ambrose, concludes:

> It was a stunning confession of ignorance. Eisenhower had been pushing the bill for two years, had managed to get it through the House and considered by the Senate, and yet now said he did not know what was in it. Eisenhower's admission was an open invitation to the southern senators to modify, amend, emasculate his bill, and they proceeded to do just that.[84]

Following the passage of the crippling amendments, the Senate passed the bill on August 7 by a substantial cross-partisan margin, 72-18. But the House refused to meet in conference or to accept the Senate amendments. On August 22, Speaker Rayburn agreed to negotiations. A cross-partisan group from both houses met to work out their differences, and on August 23 Lyndon Johnson called the president to announce an agreement. Both houses then adopted the compromise, which had been delayed in the Senate by the longest filibuster in history by J. Strom Thurmond (D-S.C.). The speculative feature of lawmaking in this case was much less important or interesting than the maneuvering just to get something on the books.

Reactions to passage were uniformly unenthusiastic. Those supporting a stronger bill were disappointed, and editorial comment was flat. Eisenhower signed the bill without comment. However, the president was credited with 80 percent support on votes for a bill he did not much like, and he suffered only two defeats. Ambrose believes that "the whole experience was one of the most agonizing of [Eisenhower's] life. . . . He had waged two successful campaigns to become the nation's leader, but he did not want to lead on the issue of civil rights."[85] On September 21, twelve days after signing the Civil Rights Act of 1957, Eisenhower sent federal troops into Little Rock, Arkansas, to enforce the court-ordered integration of the schools.

Not all presidents want to lead on all issues on the agenda. The civil rights policy process in 1956–57 is a good example of presidential reluctance in the face of an issue that was being carried along and framed by others. Eisenhower's certification of the issue was very important, but his passivity in other respects affected the debate and the final result. There are few better illustrations of the human factor in presidential participation in governing.

REVENUE ACT. Presidents who win during periods of recession naturally want to get credit for subsequently improving the economy. The state of the economy had been a major issue during the 1960 campaign, so President Kennedy proposed a tax reform program in 1961 to provide greater investment incentives. He planned a two-phase effort: quick action on his 1961 initiatives, followed by greater deliberation on a more comprehensive tax reform proposal that would be offered in 1962. The first set of proposals included an investment tax credit, restrictions on deductions for business expenses, and the tightening of several loopholes, the most controversial of which was a withholding plan for dividends. Reactions ranged from strong opposition to mild approval. Business, labor, and the financial industry all had criticisms, as did Republicans.

The House Committee on Ways and Means held hearings in 1961, but the lesson from this early action was that the president's proposals were sufficiently controversial that legislation would have to be held over until 1962. Witte describes how the committee took charge: "Ways and Means, under the leadership of Wilbur Mills, broadened the investment credit, dropped repeal of the dividend deduction and credit and then adjourned in August 1961, sending a clear message to the administration that depreciation revision was necessary before passage would be possible."[86] The president's role became that of an accommodator or facilitator. Throughout the next several months, Kennedy accepted whatever was agreed to on Capitol Hill.

Action in the House in 1962 was swift. The bill was reported out of committee on March 16, an action praised by President Kennedy. The Committee on Rules granted a closed rule on March 22. The bill passed the House a week later by a relatively narrow vote of 219-196. Only one Republican voted for the bill.

The Senate Committee on Finance held twenty-nine days of hearings on the bill, then made substantial changes that "further sweetened the pot," according to Witte, and thus guaranteed passage. Only one minor amendment was accepted on the floor. As in the House, bargains were made and they held. In contrast, however, these bargains were cross-partisan rather than partisan, with substantial support among Republicans.

Secretary of the Treasury Douglas Dillon called the Senate bill (now quite far from Kennedy's original proposal) "a significant first step toward the reform of our outmoded tax laws," but Senator Albert Gore (D-Tenn.) criticized the administration, saying that it "had lifted not a finger" to fight the changes made in the Senate.[87] The conference largely accepted the Senate version, and Kennedy signed the bill on October 16, 1962. Many expressed the view that it was "a good start," including the president himself. But the nature of the process in 1961 and 1962 led analysts to be pessimistic about comprehensive reform during the Kennedy presidency. Once again, when it comes to tax policy, it is well to be reminded that decisions are made by two institutions, each with a great deal of interest, experience, and political sensitivity.

Institutional Balance on New Issues

The second set of cases deals with issues that were relatively new and emerging, and in which members of Congress could be expected to be very active because of constituency pressures or other interests. It includes the Atomic Energy Act of 1954, the Manpower Development and Training Act of 1962, the Clean Air Act of 1963, and the Occupational Safety and Health Act of 1970. The manpower training and worker safety proposals related to familiar issues associated with the labor force, but there had been limited experience with these problems at the federal level.

ATOMIC ENERGY ACT. Atomic energy policy following World War II was fraught with a number of serious and difficult problems. To what extent should the United States cooperate with other nations, notably its former ally, the Soviet Union? How much nuclear military power was sufficient? How might peaceful uses of atomic energy be developed? Would civilians or the military manage the development of atomic energy? What role would be played by the private sphere, and what were the implications for the spread of nuclear weapons?

Nelson W. Polsby observed that "the principle of civilian control [of atomic energy] emerged very late in a complicated process of deliberation."[88] Civilian control inevitably introduced the whole set of policy issues to the world of politics. Sensitive to this fact, the designers established an independent regulatory commission, the Atomic Energy Commission (AEC), and a joint congressional committee, the Joint Committee on Atomic Energy (JCAE). The JCAE was "the only body in Congress that could draft and submit its own legislation and then act as a joint House and Senate 'conference committee' to prepare the legislation for final vote. [It] thus was able to practice a take-it-or-leave-it attitude towards the Congress as a whole regarding nuclear legislation."[89] The AEC, charged with the highly defense-related function of developing nuclear weapons, was hardly the typical regulatory commission. Therefore decisionmaking in atomic energy occurred in a special organizational setting, but not one devoid of a politics affecting the speculative nature of this vital issue.

Because the Republicans won majorities in both the House and the Senate in the 1952 elections, it was reasonable to expect greater involvement by private industry in atomic energy. Two conservatives, Representative W. Sterling Cole (R-N.Y.) and Senator Bourke Hickenlooper (R-Iowa), took over as chair and ranking senator, respectively, of the JCAE. President Eisenhower nominated Lewis Strauss, another conservative, to chair the AEC. All three—Cole, Hickenlooper, and Strauss—were anxious to revise the Atomic Energy Act of 1946 so as to permit greater private sector involvement in the development and application of atomic power.

The president set the context for the privatization of atomic power and endorsed the peaceful uses of atomic energy in his "Atoms for Peace" speech to the United Nations on December 8, 1953. However, the executive branch became caught up in controversy over the nomination of Strauss. The JCAE was unwilling to wait. It had held hearings during 1953 to lay the foundation for important changes in atomic energy policy. This anxiety to act on Capitol Hill spurred the AEC to prepare legislative proposals sooner than it might have otherwise. The AEC plan was sent to Congress in February 1954, but was not actually introduced. Instead, in April, Cole and Hickenlooper introduced their own bill, which incorporated much of what the administration asked for. Closed, then open, hearings were held in May.

The issue of public versus private in relation to nuclear power came to be contentious and highly partisan. Representative Chet Holifield (D-Calif.), who later chaired the JCAE, was a strong and active supporter of public power and a vigorous opponent of the Cole-Hickenlooper bill. The partisan nature of the debate within the JCAE carried over to the floors of both the House and the Senate, in part, perhaps, because of members' lack of knowledge of the subject. According to Harold P. Green and Alan Rosenthal, floor debate in the House was "generally superficial." The Senate debate was no more edifying and did not really address the complex and highly speculative issues involved in establishing a national policy for peaceful uses of atomic energy: "In the Senate, too, debate on particular provisions was overshadowed by polemic and partisan maneuvering. . . . Thus, Congressional debate, especially in the Senate, was more a study in political strategy and parliamentary tactics than a close scrutiny of atomic-energy legislation."[90]

The Senate debate, which lasted 181 hours, featured a filibuster by the public power advocates, led by Warren Magnuson (D-Wash.). The debate was fueled in part by criticism of the Dixon-Yates power contract, an AEC-supported agreement with private contractors to supply nuclear power to the Tennessee Valley Authority. When the debate ended, both House and Senate Republicans voted overwhelmingly in favor of the bill (97 percent in each chamber). The Republican vote alone was sufficient to pass the legislation in the House and in the Senate. However, amendments were passed in each chamber, so different versions of the bill were returned to the JCAE, now acting as a conference. Partisanship continued to dominate, and three Democrats refused to sign the conference report (once again, because of disagreement on the public versus private issue). The House accepted the conference report, but the Senate rejected it on a partisan vote (although five Republicans actually provided the necessary margin). After a second conference had removed the most objectionable provisions, the report was approved in both chambers. President Eisenhower signed the bill on August 30.

The peaceful use of atomic energy was a relatively new policy issue and among the most exploratory of those included here. Few of the costs were as yet identified. The federal government had supported the development of this new energy source for military purposes. The crucial decision regarding domestic development of atomic energy was one in which Congress would naturally be heavily involved, given the constituency-related effects and the ideological division between advocates of public and private power. The president's role was relatively small, once he had delivered his Atoms for Peace speech and appointed an AEC chair to his liking. In fact, the 1954 act barely received mention in his memoirs. However disengaged he may have been, though, he did receive credit from *Congressional Quarterly* for seven victories and just two defeats in his presidential support score for 1954.

MANPOWER DEVELOPMENT. During the 1960 presidential campaign, Kennedy had been "shaken by the misery he witnessed first hand in West Virginia."[91] Upon winning the White House, he was determined to effect change. In 1961 an Area Redevelopment Act to assist depressed regions was passed, including authorization for job training programs. On May 25, 1961, the president announced to Congress that he was sending a Manpower Development and Training Program to train workers adversely affected by industrial change. Here was a new type of program, that of training and retraining unemployed workers. Since most members were convinced that it would help, the proposal was less speculative in their own minds. Such a program was likely to find favor on Capitol Hill with Republicans as well as Democrats. As historian James T. Patterson observes, "sold as a way of helping people help themselves and thereby get off welfare, the program was popular with Congress."[92]

The Senate acted first on Kennedy's request. The principal issue came to be whether the "retraining of adults should be organized and administered as a new category within the existing federal-state vocational education program . . . or embody some major new departures."[93] The American Vocational Association (AVA) was represented by a particularly vigorous lobbyist, who was successful in getting changes made. The bill enjoyed significant cross-partisan support and passed 60-31 (with Republicans providing a crucial sixteen votes).

Developments in the House were somewhat more complicated. The House Committee on Education and Labor had studied the general problem of unemployment, as had a House Republican Policy Committee Task Force. The bill that resulted was a compromise between Elmer Holland (D-Pa.), the chair of the subcommittee with responsibility for the measure, and the principal Republican activist on this issue, Charles E. Goodell of New York. The Education and Labor Committee failed to consider the changes desired by the AVA, however, and the bill was stalled in the Committee on Rules at adjournment (with the AVA lobbyist taking credit for the delay). At this point, Goodell essentially took over, using the bill that had been passed in the Senate as a model and eventually forcing Holland to accept the changes. Released by the Rules Committee, the Goodell bill passed the House by a wide margin, 354-62 (with well over 80 percent of each party voting in favor). Here was an unusual case of partisanship at the committee stage, competitive partisanship leading to cross-partisan support in floor maneuvering, and voting.

Though it was later to be the subject of criticism, at the time the new act was hailed as a major accomplishment for the Kennedy administration. Members of Congress were equally active in the development of the program, however. There were relatively few votes to be counted in the presidential support score, primarily because the important changes were made within the committees or between the key actors in floor maneuvering, not in amendments subject to roll call voting.

CLEAN AIR. A federal role in pollution control was also a relatively new issue in the 1960s. Therefore policymakers in both institutions had to familiarize themselves with the nature of a technical and scientific problem, the feasibility of solutions, and the advantages or disadvantages of locating a program in various agencies. An incremental approach was favored, so as to develop greater understanding before designing a larger federal program. A small program enacted in 1955 provided limited federal support for state and local governments to control air pollution. In 1960 the few members of Congress interested in this issue were successful in authorizing the surgeon general to conduct a study of automobile exhaust. But basically it remained an issue for the states and localities, not the federal government.

President Kennedy was interested in expanding the federal role. In February 1961 he asked for "an effective Federal air pollution control program now."[94] His ally in the Senate was Thomas Kuchel (R-Calif.), who succeeded in getting a modest bill passed. However, Representative Kenneth Roberts (D-Ala.), who chaired the relevant subcommittee of the House Committee on Interstate and Foreign Commerce, opposed federal enforcement and thwarted action on Kuchel's bill in the House.

Within the administration, there was conflict between those supporting an enforcement role for the federal government and those in the Public Health Service (with allies in the Bureau of the Budget) who were reluctant to serve as the enforcers. Partly because of these internal battles, those favoring an enforcement role decided to have the president recommend legislation but rely on Congress to prepare the bill. Randall B. Ripley describes what happened:

> Virtually all the supporters of the legislation favored not introducing an administration bill. [They] did not want to become involved in the formal legislative clearance process with the Public Health Service and the Bureau of the Budget. . . .

What legislation would emerge, if any, was now up to the Congress. The executive at this point was speaking timidly and with reservations.[95]

Meanwhile, the situation had changed in the Senate. Kuchel's Democratic colleague from California, Clair Engle, introduced legislation in the fall of 1962. In November, Abraham Ribicoff, formerly Kennedy's secretary of health, education, and welfare, was elected to the Senate from Connecticut. Ribicoff sponsored a clean air bill in 1963 (with nineteen cosponsors). Although he was not appointed to the Committee on Public Works, which had jurisdiction for his bill, it became "a major focus of debate throughout the year."[96] In the House, Roberts changed his mind and introduced a bill, as did Peter Rodino (D-N.J.) and James Fulton (R-Pa.). The Rodino-Fulton proposal was the same as the Ribicoff bill; Dean Coston, a special assistant from HEW, worked with all interested members in promoting the legislation and working out compromises. Roberts was successful, following modifications, in getting unanimous committee endorsement of his bill providing grants to the states and enforcement measures. The bill then passed the House without change by a cross-partisan vote of 273-102 (42 percent of Republicans joining 95 percent of Democrats in support). Republican votes were not crucial to its passage, given the unity of House Democrats.

Senate approval seemed a foregone conclusion, given the broad support for the legislation. The issue was the extent to which the bill would be strengthened. A new champion of the legislation emerged in Senator Edmund S. Muskie (D-Maine), who became chair of a Special Subcommittee on Air and Water Pollution of the Committee on Public Works. Six bills were available: those by Ribicoff and Engle, the House bill, and three others. Following hearings, the Muskie subcommittee strengthened the House bill and reported it to the Senate, which passed it with only minor changes by a voice vote on November 19, three days before Kennedy was assassinated.

Muskie and Roberts communicated frequently in working out the differences between the Senate and House versions. The conference agreed on the changes, most of which favored the Senate version, on December 4. The conference report was agreed to in the House by very much the same vote as the Roberts bill had received, and in the Senate by a voice vote. It was one of the first bills signed by Lyndon Johnson, on December 17.

This law is a fascinating instance of a conscious strategy by the administration—with presidential acquiescence—fully aware of the support available in Congress, to work through that institution rather than to prepare a bill itself. Clearly the principal work on this legislation occurred in the congressional setting, and Ripley concludes that "without Congress, the executive would have produced legislation less far-reaching in its provisions than what was produced with the help of Congress."[97] The legislation received little press attention in light of the death of the president and the succession of Lyndon Johnson. In calculating presidential support for 1963, *Congressional Quarterly* counted only two votes, both as wins for the president and both in the House, since Senate action was by voice vote.

OCCUPATIONAL SAFETY AND HEALTH. In 1968 President Johnson offered an occupational safety and health proposal that would authorize the secretary of labor to set mandatory standards and to close down plants that did not meet these standards. Business and industry lobbied intensely and successfully to kill the proposal. A bill was reported from the House Committee on Education and Labor but was bottled up in the Committee on Rules. The Senate Committee on Labor and Public Welfare held hearings but took no further action. The problem to which this legislation was directed was generally acknowledged to be severe, but little had been done at the federal level to establish regulations. A mine disaster in Farmington, West Virginia, in November 1968 drew more attention to worker safety. It might have been one of those trigger events for lawmaking, but Congress had already gone home without having enacted President Johnson's proposal.

Two years later, President Nixon and the Republicans were receptive to proposals that might attract blue-collar support, and an occupational safety and health program seemed a good prospect. Graham K. Wilson counts the 1970 legislation as an example of congressional influence: "The notion that all important bills are drafted in the Executive Branch dies hard. The OSH Act was indeed sired by President Johnson. . . . The form that his brain-child took was determined much more by its gestation in Congress, however, than by the Executive Branch under Nixon."[98] Nixon proposed that a national occupational safety and health board be established to set standards. Congressional Democrats essentially reintroduced the Johnson proposal. They preferred to have the secretary of labor in charge of regulation, since a regulatory board might well come under the influence of industry. Initial reactions to the Nixon proposal reflected exactly those concerns.

The House acted first. The Committee on Education and Labor reported a bill that adopted the Johnson approach. However, on the floor a cross-partisan coalition supported a substitute amendment introduced by William Steiger (R-Wis.) and Robert Sikes (D-Fla.) that was very close to the original Nixon proposal. The amendment passed with the support of 90 percent of the Republicans, who were joined by sixty southern Democrats to form a majority.

The Senate Committee on Labor and Public Welfare also reported out a bill favoring the Johnson approach of giving the secretary of labor the authority to create and enforce standards. On the Senate floor, Jacob Javits (R-N.Y.) proposed an amendment that split the difference. The secretary of labor would set standards, and a board appointed by the president would enforce them. As in the House, the amendment passed with cross-partisan support, eleven southern Democrats joining all Republicans in favor. Once President Nixon had accepted the compromise, the bill passed by a wide margin. The conference agreement favored the Senate approach, to the chagrin of certain House members.

Both business and labor praised the passage of the bill, surely an unusual outcome for labor legislation. It is a classic case of competitive partisanship leading to a cross-partisan compromise. Only two votes were counted in the presidential support sweepstakes, both in the House, which ultimately did not succeed in having its way in conference. The vote on the Javits substitute was not counted, presumably because the president publicly favored the House bill at that point.

Institutional Balance under Unusual Procedures

The third set of cases in this group of balanced participation between the branches offers two of the most interesting enactments in the whole set of twenty-eight. The Social Security Amendments of 1983 and the Deficit Reduction Package of 1990 represent the use of extraordinary policymaking procedures in response to the political, partisan, and institutional conflicts associated with these issues. It was necessary to go outside the normal lawmaking procedures in order to build cross-partisan majorities.

SOCIAL SECURITY AMENDMENTS. As noted earlier (see discussion of COLAs), reforming the social security system is a highly participatory activity. Certainly no member of Congress can opt out. Each is expected to have an opinion and to be engaged when any change in benefits is proposed. Changing Social Security is a less speculative enterprise than many others, simply because of experience with the program, as well as members' knowledge of the potential effects of changes. And yet Congress is not well designed as a planning body. It is a political body, designed to represent interests in making decisions about plans offered by others. Thus rational reform of large-scale programs is not normally initiated in Congress. In addition, as Martha Derthick concludes, congressional "action is never complete. Constantly changing in composition, torn always between its roles as policymaker for the nation and representative of particular constituencies and constituents, . . . Congress engages endlessly in lawmaking."[99]

Unfortunately, a problem of grand scale had been developing in Social Security financing for some time. It was unlikely to be dealt with solely by Congress, yet any administration proposal that recommended cuts would probably be defeated, if considered at all. It was not even clear that members of Congress could publicly acknowledge a problem, for to do so would invite politically unacceptable solutions.

The triumph of the Republicans in the 1980 elections seemingly provided a stimulus for change. Candidate Reagan campaigned on cutting the budget and reducing taxes. Since the burden of program cuts had to be shared, perhaps it would be possible to reach a bipartisan agreement to include Social Security beneficiaries in an overall package of programmatic cutbacks. The problem of funding future benefits had been studied extensively. According to Paul C. Light, "there was no shortage of potential solutions, but no place to hide. In the two short years before Reagan's inauguration, there had already been three major study reports on the social security crisis."[100] The issue was developing policy momentum. J. J. Pickle (D-Tex.), who chaired the Subcommittee on Social Security of the House Committee on Ways and Means, had prepared a bill. Senator Pete Domenici (R-N.M.) was gathering support in the Senate Committee on the Budget for a cross-partisan plan. And the administration was prepared to act in order to take advantage of its perceived mandate for change. Conditions seemed right for competitive partisan politics, leading to a cross-partisan compromise solution.

However, for this result to be achieved on such a politically sensitive issue, everyone involved had to be protected. Both parties had to share in taking credit and avoiding blame. That goal proved impossible to achieve. Reagan's budget director, David Stockman, was eager to show immediate savings, principally through severe reductions for early retirees, while the Pickle plan projected reductions in the future. Neither Stockman nor Chief of Staff James Baker liked the Domenici initiative, and they worked actively to have the president express his opposition at a meeting on Capitol Hill. Confident that speed was of the essence, Stockman controlled the input and "tightened secrecy around his decisions. . . . The [White House] legislative staff did not see the final proposal until just three days before the formal announcement. . . . Pickle . . . was not informed about the Stockman proposal, nor were key Republicans on the Ways and Means Committee.

There was no warning of what was to come."[101] Stockman did get signals of difficulties from within the White House itself, and House Republicans complained of being blindsided. For his part, the president had little interest in the whole subject.

Partisan or competitive partisan politics begins with support from within one's own party. Stockman did not have that support, and his style antagonized many congressional Republicans. The Democrats, reeling from defeats on other budget-related issues, pulled back from proposing their solution, so as to attack the president's plan. Speaker O'Neill "urged Pickle to hold back from any favorable response."[102] And then Democrats hit the president with both barrels. The plan was called a "breach of contract," "insidious" and "cruel," "despicable."[103] Senator Daniel Patrick Moynihan (D-N.Y.) introduced a "sense of the Senate" resolution condemning the administration's proposal. It was defeated by just one vote. Senator Robert Dole (R-Kans.) then introduced a resolution, without the partisan rhetoric, that simply opposed an unfair cut in benefits for early retirees. It passed 96-0.

After suffering this self-inflicted political defeat, the Reagan White House had to back up and try again. The president accepted a proposal by Senator William Armstrong (R-Colo.) to create a bipartisan National Commission on Social Security Reform, whose members would be appointed by the president, the speaker of the House, and the Senate majority leader. Meanwhile the Democrats continued to pound on the president, carrying their Social Security message into the 1982 elections, when their gains in the House almost made good their losses of 1980.

Thus the national commission became the institutional base for policy development. The commission eventually produced a package that was accepted by President Reagan and Speaker O'Neill, each of whom promised to deliver the necessary votes, so that credit and blame would be shared. Once an agreement had been reached in mid-January 1983, the emphasis was on speedy action in Congress lest the cross-partisan support collapse. The House Committee on Ways and Means immediately scheduled hearings and then approved the plan with amendments. The floor debate centered on whether to manage the fiscal future of the program by adding taxes or by raising the retirement age and reducing benefits for early retirees. In a bitter debate, the latter course was chosen. Representative Claude Pepper (D-Fla.), champion of the aged, proposed the former and was defeated, 132-296. J. J. Pickle proposed the latter and won on a cross-partisan vote, 228-202. The Pickle amendment garnered 92 percent of the

Republican vote, 60 percent of the southern Democratic vote, and 13 percent of the northern Democratic vote.

The Senate Committee on Finance modified the House bill but basically accepted the Pickle approach. One further change was made on the Senate floor, but the bill itself passed by a cross-partisan vote of 88-9. The results of the conference favored the House bill. The resulting report was agreed to by the House (243-102) and the Senate (58-14). In both chambers, a higher proportion of Democrats than Republicans supported the final version. President Reagan and Speaker O'Neill stressed the importance of conciliation and compromise at the signing ceremony.

The president was credited by *Congressional Quarterly* with six victories and one defeat. Although Reagan favored certain amendments and opposed others, one can question how accurate it is to conclude that he won 86 percent of the time on this issue, or, for that matter, what exactly victory meant in the case of a hard-fought compromise agreement. It also stands as an extraordinary case of a political stalemate between the president and Congress being broken. As Light concludes, "Congress and the President had created a new form of government."[104]

DEFICIT REDUCTION.   Officially titled the Omnibus Budget Reconciliation Act of 1990, the deficit reduction package passed at the end of the 101st Congress will surely go down in history as one of the most fascinating lawmaking stories ever. What happened in 1990 cannot be understood without some attention to what had gone on before. Among the more important defining factors were these:

—Passage in 1974 of the Budget and Impoundment Control Act, which provided for a congressional budget process. The act directed Congress to enact budget resolutions, thereby providing a tracking device for congressional action.

—Passage in 1981 of the Economic Recovery Tax Act, which contributed to sizable deficits that kept the pressure on Congress to cut expenditures.

—Passage in 1985 of the Gramm-Rudman-Hollings (GRH) deficit reduction process, by which targets were set and failure to meet them resulted in sequestration.

—A pledge in 1988 by presidential candidate George H. W. Bush not to raise taxes: "Read my lips, no new taxes."

These four realities predictably led to high politics. As with the Social Security issue in 1981, it was not clear how an agreement could be reached within the normal workings of presidential-congressional interaction. Conditions were excellent for a political stalemate. And yet that was not an acceptable outcome, since it would trigger the GRH mechanism, requiring severe cuts in domestic and defense programs. Thus there were competitively partisan incentives to fashion a cross-partisan majority. Doing so proved to be arduous, tense, and fraught with conflict.

As required by the GRH provisions, the president presented a budget in late January 1990 that met the deficit target for fiscal year 1991. As dictated by the political realities, the Democrats heaped scorn on the president's plan but were hard pressed to produce their own. The House acted first, producing a budget resolution that, in spite of the criticism, incorporated much of the president's plan. It even adopted the administration's economic assumptions. Still, the changes that were made, primarily cuts in defense, found disfavor among congressional Republicans, who to a person voted against it in the Budget Committee and on the House floor. By the time the resolution passed the House, both sides were backing away from whatever was on paper, because it appeared that the July budget review from the Office of Management and Budget would show a sizable increase in the projected deficit for the year. Eventually the president's plan was withdrawn from the floor. Earlier the president had ruled out a summit; now it seemed inevitable.

Given what had already happened, it was going to be even more difficult for the Senate to produce a budget resolution. The Republicans signaled their opposition to any Democratic proposal. All participants appeared to be waiting for the right time to meet at a summit. Defense, in particular, divided the Democrats, whose majority was rather slim to start with. A document was produced that met the deficit targets on paper, but no one knew for certain whether they would be met in practice. Meanwhile, the president and congressional leaders agreed to meet. Therefore the Senate, by a voice vote, passed a skeletal, policy-neutral resolution.

Charade now seemed the appropriate word to describe events. The House refused to meet the Senate in conference on its resolution. The prospect of a summit agreement obviated passage of any budget resolution. Yet the appropriations committees required such a triggering mechanism to enact their bills. The solution was for each house to produce a "deeming resolution," by which the appropriations process would be authorized to proceed on the basis of the resolution that each house had passed but not agreed to in conference.

The Democrats wanted Bush to go first and rescind his pledge of no new taxes. The president agreed that the talks would proceed with no preconditions, thereby upsetting many Republicans who had already fixed their anti-tax position for the upcoming 1990 congressional elections. In the initial pre-summit sparring, Democrats pressed for an even stronger statement by the president on increasing taxes. As Barbara Sinclair observed, "Democrats had been tarred as high taxers too often; they were united in their unwillingness to propose increasing taxes."[105] As the jockeying proceeded, both the Office of Management and Budget and the Congressional Budget Office agreed that earlier deficit projections were again too low and that there were troubling signs in the economy. Finally, the president issued a statement backing away from his campaign pledge. He explained that all of the following were required in a budget package: "entitlement and mandatory program reform; tax revenue increases; growth incentives; discretionary spending reductions; orderly reductions in defense expenditures; and budget process reform."[106]

Meetings now began in earnest to prepare a budget package, but they were interrupted by the August recess of Congress. Two days before members left town, Iraq invaded Kuwait, producing a serious Mideast crisis that would affect the economic assumptions so vital to producing a workable plan. When Congress reconvened, the summiteers secluded themselves at Andrews Air Force Base outside Washington. Early optimistic reports gave way to pessimism, and the consultations returned to the Capitol with a smaller group of participants.

Representative Bill Frenzel (R-Minn.) observed: "No one wants to concede anything until the last minute. We have to declare a last minute."[107] The approaching mandatory sequester seemingly was such a last minute, so the president and congressional leaders finally announced an agreement on September 30, and each house passed continuing resolutions to keep the government going. A week later a cross-partisan alliance between liberal Democrats and conservative Republicans rejected the agreement in the House. Both houses then passed a second continuing resolution, which was vetoed by the president, who insisted that a budget resolution be enacted first.

During the next three weeks, Congress passed a skeletal budget resolution, a series of continuing resolutions, and at long last, on October 27, a reconciliation package. The final agreement split both parties. The final House majority was made up of 181 Democrats and forty-seven Republicans; the Senate majority included thirty-five Democrats and nineteen Republicans. The product itself was unquestionably a compromise, but Democrats were pleased with the tax program, in which the rich would bear most of the increases. It included significant new procedures for future budget making and, as a multiyear agreement, promised to avoid a replay of the 1990 exercise for at least two years.

In the end, Sinclair probably is correct in asserting that "because the president needed action, he was eventually forced to capitulate and renege on the major promise of his campaign. The decision was clearly necessary to get an agreement, yet it eventually led to a reframing of the debate so as to disadvantage the president."[108] In this case, the president was credited by *Congressional Quarterly* with three victories and four defeats. But among the defeats was the early House budget resolution that was no more than a negotiating position, as stated by the speaker himself, and among the victories was the final agreement, which was judged at the time to be a victory more for Democrats than for the president.

Sequence, Speculation, Iteration, and Partisanship

I began this discussion by stressing that the American representative system makes laws through a mostly public process that, among other characteristics, is variably sequential, speculative, iterative, and partisan. I also raised questions, as have others, about the utility of roll call votes as reliable measures of a president's success with Congress, and challenged the concept of "success," given the complexity of major issues as they are acted on over time on Capitol Hill. Presidents have important roles to play in lawmaking, but most of the time they deal with issues that are familiar on Capitol Hill. Legislative proposals are typically designed to alter programs already on the books. There are relatively few new proposals for new problems. In order to make change, presidents must determine how to manage interested and affected groups, most of whom have established access on Capitol Hill and within the bureaucracy. It is in order now to identify what has been learned.

Sequence is clearly part of the strategic environment. Presidents do often initiate the proposals that form the basis of legislative action, but they may rely on ideas that have been around for some time. When presidents are reluctant to act, Congress is a source of legislative initiative, even for highly significant issues like trade and energy. Further, as has been frequently illustrated, presidential initiative by no means guarantees presidential dominance in lawmaking. Members of Congress rightfully believe they are charged to make laws, and they act on this understanding of their authority.

The matter of which house acts first may be a result of other work that is scheduled, strategic considerations, constitutional mandates (as with revenue legislation), or the issue preferences of the majority. In the cases studied here, the House acted first fifteen times, the Senate, thirteen times. There were sixteen cases of what might be called a "pure or expected sequence"; that is, presidential initiative followed by action in the two houses and either a conference or acceptance by one house of the bill passed by the other (one of the sixteen resulted in a veto). The other twelve cases were extraordinary in that no two were alike. It is intriguing that this simple distinction among these major laws displays significant variations in the president's role and a rich assortment of legislative sequences.

The speculative feature is universal for all the reasons discussed in chapter 6. How much lawmakers do and can know will vary, however, depending on whether the proposal is for a new venture or a change in a program on the books. The cases also illustrate differences between organizational or procedural reform packages and more substantive programmatic changes, as well as responses to crises. Lawmakers are most confident about changes in existing programs, where experience reduces uncertainty—for example, building highways, expanding welfare benefits, raising or cutting taxes, imposing and reforming regulations. They are least confident in new ventures—federal aid to education, pollution controls, health care, housing— and yet often compelled to act because of the seriousness of the issue.

Reorganizations (creating a department or agency) or reforms in processes (war or budget making) suggest at least two phases: (1) the initial reshuffling and adjustments to new requirements; (2) the subsequent effects of these changes on issues. General experience provides lessons about the first. Knowing the full impact of the second is much more problematic.

Finally, crisis can force a decision, with no time to wait for experience or learning by other means. The European Recovery Act was highly speculative but judged necessary, given the economic and political troubles experienced by postwar Europe. More recently, the intelligence failures associated with the 9/11 disasters, bolstered by the report of the National Commission on Terrorist Attacks upon the United States, led to an urgency to reform and reorganize the intelligence services in 2004. A major overhaul was proposed and swiftly enacted by Congress.

That lawmaking is iterative would hardly be a point worth making were it not so often ignored in analyzing presidential-congressional interaction. As expected, there were fewest cases of high iteration in the category of presidential preponderance and most in the category of congressional preponderance. Iteration was moderate to high in a large majority of the cases of balanced institutional participation.

Normally one expects the committees to function in a manner that would reduce the degree of iteration on the floor. That happened in over half the cases in each house. In one instance in the House (the Elementary and Secondary Education Act) and two in the Senate (again, the Education Act, and also the Economic Recovery Tax Act), there was limited iteration at either stage, committee or floor. In a surprisingly high number of instances, iteration continued at a moderate or high rate or actually intensified when the bill was treated on the floor. These include several important pieces of legislation, such as the Taft-Hartley Act, the Omnibus Trade Act, the Energy Policy and Conservation Act, the creation of the Department of Education, COLAs, and the Deficit Reduction Act. And the Civil Rights Act of 1957, which was brought directly from the calendar to avoid the committee stage, thus was highly iterative on the Senate floor.

The rich variety of interparty relations in the congressional lawmaking process is remarkable. There are differences among the four categories of branch participation. The cases of presidential and congressional preponderance show the least variety. In the first, presidents have party support to get their way, are successful in gaining cross-partisan support in advance for overriding issues, or gain that support through the process. In the congressional cases, the greater openness in participation encourages substantially more cross-partisanship in lawmaking. It is not easy for a two-house legislature to form policy solutions through single-party action, particularly given the voters' habitual production of split-party governments. The cases of balanced participation also show substantial cross-partisan activity, either directly or as a result of earlier competitive partisan politics.

These patterns indicate a highly dynamic process of partisan interaction that is not well portrayed by studies of party voting. An intensive look at the process by which the twenty-eight major laws were passed reveals a set of party-based negotiations. The president is often an active participant in this process, but sometimes he is not, even if he was originally responsible for the proposal being negotiated. Therefore in some instances there is a progression from a presidential policy initiative to a congressionally developed proposal that is monitored and responded to by the White House. These developments cannot be captured by roll call votes or by scores based on those votes.

A particularly interesting result of this analysis is the identification of competitive partisan and cross-partisan patterns. There were eighteen such cases in the House and twenty in the Senate (that is, as evidenced in two or more of the committee, floor, and voting stages). Of those cases, twelve in each house occurred in split-party governments. Given that such governments are common, more attention should be paid to how legislation is formed under these circumstances. Just as striking, however, is the fact that six cases of such patterns in the House and eight in the Senate occurred during single-party governments.

In his study of political parties in the postreform House of Representatives, David W. Rohde points out that "partisanship was not muted by divided government, although compromises were eventually reached in some instances. Nor was stalemate the result, and certainly not inaction. Clearly the president did not set this agenda; he opposed it. Yet not only did every one of the ten items on [Speaker] Wright's list of priorities pass the House; every one of them eventually became law in one form or another."[109] Rohde's description of relations between President Reagan and a Democratic Congress in the late 1980s could easily be a summary of legislative interaction between President Truman and the Republican Congress in 1947–49.

The examination of these twenty-eight laws also produces an important distinction between bipartisanship and cross-partisanship. Bipartisanship—where both sides are substantially agreed on and involved in policy development from the first—does not occur often. Cross-partisanship—where a critical portion of one side joins the other to form a majority—occurs frequently. In some cases, the coalition shows up in the early stages of the legislation; in others it is the result of competitive positions taken by each side, followed by compromise and agreement to support a modified version of the proposal.

I have explored the reliability of presidential support scores as indicators of presidential involvement in and success with individual pieces of legislation. Disaggregating these scores for specific pieces of legislation raises serious questions as to what they represent. As I have shown throughout, reliance on them for an important bill often results in a distorted view of the president's role.

There is a stark difference in batting averages between the cases of presidential and congressional preponderance. The presidents suffered no losses for cases in the first category and had wins in just two of the cases in the second category. Clearly these scores do provide gross indicators for distinguishing between the primary involvement of the president and of Congress in major legislation. The presidents' batting averages were impressive in both types of balanced participation, dropping below 78 percent in only three cases. However, throughout this chapter I have raised questions concerning what this scoring means, given the variability, often the incomparability, of the data. For example, the range of votes included for calculating the support score runs from zero, for the Social Security increases in 1972, to nineteen, for the creation of the Department of Education in 1979. The number of votes used for calculating the support score was greater in the Senate than the House, and of course these votes frequently were not directly on the issue, but rather on procedural matters. The weight of a set of votes on a particular issue in relation to the president's overall score for the year varies substantially, from 1 percent to 28 percent (the latter being Kennedy's losses in votes for the Revenue Act of 1962). But the relative weight of any one set of votes depends on how active the president was in making proposals and taking positions along the way. For example, Eisenhower's six wins on the Landrum-Griffin Act of 1959 account for 7 percent of his wins for that year, but Carter's six wins on airline deregulation in 1978 account for just 3 percent of his wins. Support scores should be viewed skeptically as indicators of presidential performance.

This examination of the making of major laws during the postwar era illustrates the true nature of the U.S. national political system. Presidents fit themselves into an ongoing lawmaking process. Often they are key actors, but the process can operate without or alongside them. Those interested in measuring presidential success in lawmaking are advised to refine their measures to account for the important differences in policy, political, and institutional conditions associated with each administration. Even more useful would be the development of a measure of the system's success. For lawmaking in Washington is normally achieved with a substantial amount of cross-institutional and cross-partisan interaction, through elaborate sequences featuring varying degrees of iteration and forms of speculation. A first step in understanding that process is to resist oversimplification.

Applying the Lessons to Clinton and Bush 43

The presidencies of Bill Clinton and George W. Bush supply fascinating cases of lawmaking under conditions of split-party government and narrow-margin politics. Rather than incorporate a sample of these laws into the set of twenty-eight analyzed in the first edition of this book, I have opted to treat them separately, applying the lessons learned in the original exercise.

The presidencies are extraordinary in many ways. Clinton was the first Democrat since Roosevelt to win reelection, the first president since

Woodrow Wilson to be elected twice without receiving a majority of the popular vote, the first Democrat in the twentieth century to lose party control of Congress in his first midterm election, and the only Democrat to be reelected without party control of Congress (a commonality for reelected Republicans in the postwar period). Bush 43 stands out for his failure to win a majority of the popular vote, a historic Supreme Court decision that decided the Electoral College vote in his favor, a net loss for his party of House and Senate seats, a historic tie in the Senate that necessitated a power-sharing agreement with Democrats, loss of party control of the Senate when a Republican senator became an Independent, majority status for Senate Republicans in the 2002 midterm elections, and reelection by the narrowest margins since 1916 accompanied by net increases for his party in the House and Senate. These unusual conditions provided further tests of lawmaking in the separated system, supplying five combinations of party control in just ten years:

—Democratic president, House, and Senate (1993–95)

—Democratic president, Republican House and Senate (1995–2001)

—Republican president and House, tie in the Senate (2001, five months)

—Republican president and House, Democratic Senate (2001–03, nineteen months)

—Republican president, House, and Senate (2003–07)

Could one expect Mayhew's proposition "divided we govern" to hold? Would major laws be enacted? Very definitely. As shown in table 6-2, the quantity of major laws passed does not appear to be adversely affected by split control. During Clinton's presidency, more were passed after the Republicans won the House and the Senate in 1994 (fifteen in the 104th Congress) than when the Democrats were the majority party in both houses (eleven in the 103rd Congress). The decline in production in the 105th and 106th Congresses was likely the result of the Lewinsky scandal and Clinton's impeachment and Senate trial. Republican control of Congress contributed to the partisanship of the time, but the scandal itself was the consequence of the president's personal actions. Before the scandal erupted there had been several signs that legislative production would have been substantial in Clinton's remaining years in office. Notable among these earlier indications were the passage of a historic balanced budget agreement and the robust domestic agenda defined by the president in his 1998 State of the Union message (much of which was worked on in Congress but was then carried over to form the basis of the presidential campaign debate in 2000).

It is early at this writing to analyze the record of Bush 43 beyond his first Congress, the 107th. It can be stated, however, that it was more than ordinarily productive of major legislation. As noted earlier, the results are somewhat confusing to interpret, due to the new domestic security issues in the wake of the 9/11 attacks. The agenda carried over from the 106th Congress—including prescription drugs, education reform, a patients' bill of rights, trade authority, campaign finance reform, energy—was superseded by the war on terrorism. Still, production was high, nearly equaling that of the first Congresses of the Johnson and Nixon presidencies (seventeen compared with twenty-two each for Johnson and Nixon).

These two presidencies illustrate an especially relevant point regarding the separated system. The 104th and 107th Congresses were surely among the most partisan in the postwar era—as a result of the first Republican takeover of Congress in forty years in 1995 and the disputed presidential election and narrow congressional margins in 2001. Yet the imperatives of the agenda resulted in the passage of important legislation (56 percent of the important laws passed in the decade 1993–2003).

To illustrate lawmaking during the Clinton and Bush 43 presidencies, I have chosen six cases taken from the updated list provided by Mayhew. Given their recency, these laws were the result of Mayhew's "sweep one" method only. The three Clinton cases are the Omnibus Deficit Reduction Act (1993), welfare reform (1996), and the Balanced Budget Agreement (1997). The Bush 43 cases are the tax cuts of 2001, education reform (2001), and creation of the Department of Homeland Security (2002). The imbalance—three cases for each presidency, yet eight years for Clinton and just two for Bush—is justified by the range of important legislation enacted in the first two years of Bush's first term.

Not too surprisingly, there are few examples of presidential preponderance in the Mayhew count of major laws for Clinton and Bush 43. Neither one could claim a mandate like that of Johnson. Two proposals might have been cases of presidential preponderance, had they passed: for Clinton, national health care, and for Bush, an elaborate energy initiative. But the health care proposal, the most speculative initiative on Clinton's agenda, was a spectacular failure in Congress. And the Bush energy package passed the House more than once but languished in the Senate. Bush tried for bipartisanship on education reform, but it could not be sustained through the lawmaking process. Accordingly, the six cases selected for discussion here are all examples of joint participation.

Time lines were lengthy in five of the six cases, involving as they did reform (welfare and education) or budgetary issues, including tax cuts. The basic contours of the debate for these initiatives are familiar. The other case, creating a Homeland Security Department, had certain generic elements associated with government reorganization. But the subject at issue—the integration of security programs—was a direct result of 9/11, the first massive terrorist assault on the U.S. mainland.

The political conditions associated with these two presidencies would lead one to expect high levels of iteration, variability in sequence and speculation, and both competitive partisanship and cross-partisanship. Such was the case. Straight partisanship was attempted with just one piece of legislation, the Omnibus Deficit Reduction Act in 1993; only Democrats voted in favor.

Joint Participation—Presidential Initiative

Three cases suit this category: for Clinton, the omnibus deficit reduction package in 1993; and for Bush, tax cuts and education reform, both in 2001.

OMNIBUS DEFICIT REDUCTION. The economy, health care, and welfare reform were designated as the principal issues by the Clinton team in 1993. Selecting which would go first was simple enough, given the recession that had contributed to Clinton's win over an incumbent president. A promised middle-class tax cut proposal was quickly dropped in recognition of the serious deficit problem. A first effort to restore the economy was to offer a stimulus package, but it was thwarted by a filibuster in the Senate. In late spring, Congress began work on a more comprehensive economic package aimed at reducing the deficit. The proposal included tax increases and program cuts. According to Robert E. Rubin, then director of the National Economic Council, the political advisers "expressed serious concerns" because "deficit reduction had no political constituency."[110] The fate of the stimulus package had shown this to be true. Congressional Republicans typically are most united on fiscal issues, especially in opposition to proposed tax increases. Not surprisingly, then, the onus was on the Democrats to bring the package into law.

Nominally, the deficit reduction package followed a standard sequence: president→House→Senate→conference, then on to House→Senate for final approval and signature by the president. Sometimes, however, action within the one chamber influences the other along the way. In this case, a proposed "BTU tax" on energy consumption was controversial, particularly with members of Congress from oil-producing states. Senator David Boren (D-Okla.), a member of the Senate Committee on Finance, advocated eliminating the tax and imposing a cap on entitlement spending while the package was being considered in the House. He and three other senators (one Democrat and two Republicans) cosponsored an alternative. The party split on the Finance Committee was eleven Democrats and nine Republicans. If Boren voted with the Republicans there would be a tie, preventing the package from being reported. Knowing this, House Democrats from oil-producing states were reluctant to "be in a position of walking the plank," as Charles Wilson (D-Tex.) put it, "and then have them [the White House] go over and make a compromise in the Senate."[111]

The size and effect of the legislation required all committees in both houses to act. However, the principal responsibility for drafting the legislation fell to the two taxing committees, Ways and Means in the House and Finance in the Senate. The House Democratic leadership kept the pressure on members not to waver, regardless of what might happen later in the Senate: "Nobody got a pass on this."[112] Oil-state representatives were promised that changes would be made in the Senate but that it was important to move the legislation. The bill passed by just six votes, 219-213. Not one Republican voted in favor; thirty-eight Democrats also voted against.

The political situation in the Senate was even more tentative, starting at the committee level. While the Democrats had a 24-14 advantage in the House Ways and Means Committee, in the Senate Finance Committee the ratio was 11-9. Given unanimous Republican opposition, Boren's defection would kill the bill. Therefore compromises had to be made in the committee. The BTU tax was dropped, as many House members who had voted for it feared—and in spite of the president's promises that it would stay. The president opted out of addressing what would replace this lost revenue. "Adopting a new strategy for dealing with the rebellion among conservative Senate Democrats, Clinton withdrew from the battle over details of the plan. Instead he enunciated a set of broad principles and left the job of working out the specifics to Senate Democratic leaders." As he told reporters before sitting down with Senate Majority Leader George Mitchell (D-Maine) and chair of the Senate Finance Committee Daniel Patrick Moynihan (D-N.Y.), "These guys are going to work it out."[113]

The compromise they reached was to increase the federal gas tax and make further spending cuts. Whereas these changes satisfied the Democratic holdouts on the Finance Committee, Republicans continued their undivided opposition. The floor debate reflected the partisan division. Majority Leader Mitchell stressed the importance of moving the bill to conference as a sign of support for the president in reducing the deficit. His plea was answered by 49 of 56 Democrats but no Republicans; the vote was 49-49. Vice President Gore broke the tie in favor.

"Changes made to pass the bill in the Senate and the narrowness of the vote to pass the bill in the Senate and House guaranteed that reaching a conference agreement on a version passable in both houses would be a delicate and difficult task."[114] The sheer magnitude of the conference—164 House members from sixteen committees, fifty-three senators from thirteen committees—posed problems of organization and coordination. Essentially an ad hoc cross-cameral legislature had been created. The House members formed into subgroups, much like a committee system; senators worked with others from their respective committees.[115] Thus began a third tier iterative process for reaching agreements, still seeking unity among Democrats, given the certainty of Republican opposition.

The hard bargaining was managed by the two tax committee chairs, Daniel Rostenkowski (D-Ill.) in the House and Daniel Patrick Moynihan (D-N.Y.) for the Senate, along with Senate Majority Leader Mitchell. "Hardly a Democrat in Congress . . . was not consulted, cajoled, and in many cases accommodated by the time conferees produced the final bill." Representative John P. Murtha (D-Pa.) noted, "Clinton is dealing with 258 Democrats in the House and 56 in the Senate"—that is, each one on Capitol Hill.[116]

The final roll calls in both chambers were dramatic. House leaders were uncertain on the day of voting whether they could pass the bill. As it happened, the outcome turned on the vote of Marjorie Margolis-Mevinsky (D-Pa.). If she voted against, the result would be a tie and defeat; if in favor, the bill would pass 218-216. She did the latter, at the cost of her reelection in 1994. As with final passage, the result in the Senate was a tie, this time 50-50. And in a repeat performance, the vice president broke the tie in favor.

The presidential support scores suggest a clean sweep for Clinton—eight wins (three in the House, five in the Senate)—and no defeats. The principal defeat, over the BTU tax, was not subject to a roll call vote because it occurred in committee and the president accepted the defeat and endorsed the compromise. In the end, this highly iterative and straight-line partisan legislation was an example of "Democrats . . . working together across the institutional divide."[117] It was a process not replicable for health care the following year. Politically, deficit reduction was a speculative gamble that had short-term costs (losses in the 1994 midterm election) and long-term gains (economic growth).

TAX CUTS. John C. Fortier and Norman J. Ornstein point out that the "compassionate conservatism" proclaimed in George W. Bush's 2000 campaign was a two-pronged strategy, a mix of standard conservative proposals and attention to standard moderate or liberal issues. A "mostly partisan strategy" was relied on for the first set (with tax cuts as the prime example) and a bipartisan or cross-partisan strategy employed for the second (with education reform the central case).[118]

To rely on a mostly partisan strategy for tax cuts was a bold move, given the political conditions under which Bush assumed office. Reagan, too, had proposed a dramatic tax reform package, in 1981. But he had the advantages of a landslide win and the surprise Republican takeover of the Senate. Democrats kept their majority in the House in the 1980 election but had a significant net loss of seats, which led to concern that they might lose their majority in 1982. Bush, on the other hand, won a tie and Republicans had net losses in both House and Senate. There was little margin for error in the House and none in the Senate if the tax bill were to pass by Republican votes only.

As with Clinton's deficit reduction package, the Bush tax cuts followed a standard sequence: President→House→Senate, then to conference→ House→Senate and to the president for signature. The process was much quicker, however. The House completed its initial action by mid-May; the Senate, a week later. The president signed the bill in early June. It was a remarkable achievement for a narrowly divided Congress and a disputed presidency.

The congressional strategy was to push for a straight partisan win in the House, then negotiate a deal in the Senate. House Ways and Means Committee chair Bill Thomas (R-Calif.) split the proposal into three parts: cuts in income tax rates, a tax reduction for married couples, and repeal of the estate tax. "With no pretense of seeking bipartisan support," Thomas got committee approval on a straight party vote of the largest piece, the cut in rates, two days after President Bush delivered his agenda-setting speech to Congress.[119] House approval followed a week later, with no Republican defections and just ten Democrats in support. A similar pattern was followed with the other two pieces, though an effort was made to attract some Democratic votes for the marriage penalty provision. Each provision was approved. Republican votes were lost only on the repeal of the estate tax— one in committee and three on the House floor.

Having passed the various pieces in a demonstration of party unity and strength, the House then passed the tax rate reduction again as a tax reconciliation bill, after the budget resolution passed the House. The purpose of this, according to the Deputy Majority Whip, Roy Blunt (R-Mo.), was "to let the Senate know that a deep cut in the top rate was critically important to the House."[120] (The Senate was at the time considering a higher top rate.) Action then shifted to the Senate, where straight partisanship could not be employed. Deals struck there would have to prevail if a tax cut package were to be enacted. This reality did not sit well with House members, given their constitutional prerogatives regarding taxes. Thomas called it an "outrage that we are told when and how we are to deal with this issue by the other body."[121]

To this point, one might label this a case of presidential preponderance. True, the Senate worked within the basic framework of the Bush tax cut package. But Charles Grassley (R-Iowa) and Max Baucus (D-Mont.), the chair and ranking member, respectively, of the Senate Finance Committee, fashioned a cross-partisan compromise that would attract moderate Democratic support. The first mark of their success came in the committee, when four Democrats joined the Republicans in reporting the bill to the floor.

A fast-track strategy for Senate floor action was made substantially more urgent by rumors that James Jeffords (R-Vt.) would become an Independent and vote with the Democrats for organizing the Senate. Jeffords met with Vice President Cheney and President Bush, who urged him to delay his switch until the tax bill had passed.[122] A dozen Democrats voted with all Republicans to pass the bill. The conference acted swiftly. "Prodded by Bush and cognizant that their unilateral control of the Capitol was about to end, weary Republican leaders in both chambers agreed to a deal with the ever-more-powerful centrist Senate Democrats."[123] The report passed each house the day after it was sent. It received unanimous support from Republicans in the House, and in the Senate all but two Republicans voted for it.

President Bush had a perfect support score on this piece of legislation: seven wins, no losses. Five of the wins were in the House, due to Thomas's decision to split the package into three pieces; two were in the Senate. Party unity among the Republicans was extraordinary: only three were lost on five votes in the House (99.7 percent unity), and just two on two votes in the Senate (97.9 percent unity). Not reflected in these votes were the changes made in the Senate that produced a "package . . . that favored those of modest means far more than Bush and most Republicans advocated."[124] Still, most would agree with Fortier and Ornstein that substantively and politically President Bush had a "huge victory."[125]

EDUCATION REFORM. Fashioning a role for the federal government in education, historically a state and local issue, is now a regular feature of the presidency. The breakthrough came in 1965, with the passage of the Elementary and Secondary Education Act (discussed above). Reagan intended to reverse the trend, but was unsuccessful. Bush 41 sought to be the "education president," as did Clinton. Touting his success as governor of Texas, George W. Bush made education his principal social program—a key element of his compassionate conservatism and an opportunity to poach in traditional Democratic Party territory.

The partisan legislative strategy used for tax cut legislation in the House could not be employed for education reform, however. Democrats had to be invited to participate actively from the start, for at least two reasons: (1) it was an opportunity to cooperate, to reach out at the beginning of a disputed presidency, and (2) Republicans were unlikely to march in lock step as they had for tax cuts, so Democratic votes were essential. Compromises were inevitable. And since the winning coalition was likely to be made up of moderates from each party, the furthest right Republicans were certain to lose their favorite provisions, most notably, school vouchers.

In writing about his experience as a speechwriter for Bush, David Frum observes: "When presidents talk about 'bipartisanship' or 'nonpartisanship,' they usually mean that they wish the other party would roll over and play dead. . . . But [Bush] meant something more by 'bipartisanship' than 'Do as I say.' He meant respect, trust, and a good-faith effort to shrink political differences . . . in a word 'civility.'"[126] In this spirit, President Bush worked from the start with the two Democratic congressional leaders of education reform, Edward Kennedy (D-Mass.) in the Senate and George Miller (D-Calif.) in the House. Initially, the Republican leaders were the two committee chairs: James Jeffords (R-Vt.) of the Senate Committee on Health, Education, Labor, and Pensions and John Boehner (R-Ohio) of the House Committee on Education and the Workforce. Judd Gregg (R-N.H.) became the principal Republican leader on this issue in the Senate when Jeffords switched to Independent status.

The sequence for this legislation was: President→House and Senate→ Conference→House→Senate and then to the president for his signature. This pattern was influenced by signal events along the way, notably Jeffords's leaving the Republican Party and 9/11, which scrambled the existing agenda. The Senate committee acted very early, reporting a bill on March 8 by a 20-0 vote. As agreed to, the bill omitted the most controversial proposals, including school vouchers. Democrats pressed for and Republicans agreed to more money for the neediest schools. Differences over how much discretion to allow states in spending the money were evident, as they had been in previous education policy.

Unanimous support in the House committee was very unlikely. Conservative Republicans were concerned that proposals they favored would be sacrificed in order to get Democratic support. They were right. In fact, Frum reported that President Bush, "not at all an ideological man," was most concerned about "the performance of poor and minority children." He even had doubts about effectiveness of school vouchers.[127] As in the Senate committee, vouchers were dropped. The revised bill was reported out by a cross-partisan vote of 41-7 in early May. Only one of the seven votes against was from a Democrat.

The bills passed by wide margins in the House on May 23 (384-45) and the Senate on June 14 (91-8). More Republicans than Democrats voted against the bill in each chamber. School vouchers were proposed and handily defeated in both houses, as were Democratic efforts to substantially alter the bill. For the most part, the bipartisan compromises shaped in the committees were approved on the floor. Senator Kennedy, who took over management of the bill with the shift in party control in the Senate, declared: "The message is that help is on the way."[128]

The bill might soon have been on its way to the president, but reaching compromises in the conference proved to be a lengthy process, and 9/11 postponed final action until mid-December The conference report was agreed to by very much the same margins as had passed the bills in the House and Senate, though more Democrats than Republicans voted no in the Senate. Judged by presidential support scores, the issue was a huge success for the president: thirteen wins and two losses. Many of the wins came from rejecting Democratic efforts to amend the bill (two of four in the House, seven of nine in the Senate). The two defeats came on vouchers, a proposal about which Bush reportedly had mixed feelings.

The broad support for the compromises should not blind one to the fact that this legislation was the subject of intense negotiations. I have cited education reform in 2001 as a case of competitive bipartisanship. The two parties had well-defined differences that were fully displayed in the bargaining within both houses and during conference deliberations. That leaders of both parties participated throughout and in the end fashioned legislation that garnered 90 percent support is a notable achievement. This bold plan was highly speculative. It was by no means certain how or whether it would be effective.

Joint Participation—Congressional Initiative

The three other cases fit in this category: from the Clinton presidency, welfare reform and a balanced budget agreement; from the Bush presidency, the creation of a new Department of Homeland Security.

WELFARE REFORM. In his 1992 presidential campaign, candidate Clinton had promised to "end welfare as we know it." Along with a middle-class tax cut, welfare reform was part of the strategy to win disaffected Republican and independent voters. Once Clinton was in office, however, priorities had to be set, and it was decided to place national health care ahead of welfare reform (a mistaken choice according to some in the White House, and Clinton himself in an interview in 2004).[129] As a classic case of speculative reform, changes in welfare benefits were bound to be divisive within the Democratic Party, whenever they were proposed. And by starting out with a poorly conceived national health care proposal and scrapping the middle-class tax cut, the administration would seem to Republicans to have abandoned the more moderate policy posture of the campaign. As a result, when Clinton proposed welfare reform, he would likely face a intensely conflicted Congress.

The administration introduced a welfare reform bill in June 1994, but health care, education, and an anticrime bill took precedence and the president's bill was not considered. As it happened, the 1994 midterm elections played an important role. Welfare reform was among the most important substantive policy matters in the Contract with America, the House Republicans' platform. And since Clinton had not designated it a priority and had failed to enact what he had so designated (health care), Republicans took the initiative once they gained control of Capitol Hill. Clinton did not resubmit his proposal in 1995, essentially leaving it to Republicans to take charge of the issue. One White House aide noted: "This gives us more flexibility to work something out." Elizabeth Drew elaborated on this strategy: "Implied, but unstated, was that a bill would do better if it didn't have Clinton's name attached to it." She also observed that the Clinton plan would have cost more for child care, jobs, and job training, and therefore Republicans would have declared it "dead on arrival."[130]

So it was that an issue that might have been a White House initiative came to be treated primarily on Capitol Hill, by the opposition majority party. These circumstances were certain to enhance the partisan conflict characteristic of this issue. Drew reports "a snarling atmosphere" as the House subcommittee began its consideration of the Republican bill.[131] The mood did not improve through the lengthy deliberations. House Republicans, led by Speaker Newt Gingrich (R-Ga.), were anxious to make up for forty years in the minority. Democrats were understandably wary of the effects on constituents of major changes in welfare benefits. Some states had tested "welfare-to-work" plans, but there was considerable uncertainty as to how or whether a national program would work.

The sequence for this legislation was anything but usual. It started in 1994, with a presidential initiative that went nowhere. When the action shifted to Capitol Hill in 1995, the principal initiative came from the House, and was then picked up by the Senate. The first attempt was to incorporate welfare reform into the budget reconciliation package. Speaker Gingrich believed that the 1994 election results would force Clinton to accept a bold Republican budget. But the president vetoed the package late in 1995, even at the cost of closing down parts of the government. A second effort was made with a stand-alone welfare bill, which cleared Congress on December 22, 1995. But President Clinton, judging it too harsh, also vetoed this measure, on January 9, 1996. Thus the first three sequences were: (1) president→no action; (2) House→Senate→conference→House→Senate→veto; and (3) House→Senate→veto.

In his 1996 State of the Union message, Clinton invited Congress to send him a bipartisan welfare reform bill; if Congress did, he would sign it. Republicans therefore had to choose between calling Clinton's bluff or letting his veto stand as a record of failure on one of his major promises. "It was the nation's governors who revitalized Congress' quest to overhaul the welfare program. . . . Meeting in Washington on Feb. 6, the National Governors' Association did what Congress and the president had been unable to do: . . . They reached bipartisan agreement . . . to overhaul welfare and Medicaid."[132] The fourth sequence was thus exceptional: governors→ House→Senate→conference, then returned to the House→Senate, and on to the president for an agonizing decision on whether to issue another veto or sign the bill.

The story of welfare reform in 1996 is one of predictable partisan conflict on an issue that had historically divided the two parties. Yet each of the two parties faced internal strife. For the Democrats, loss of majority status in Congress made them attentive to the popularity of the issue, as well as the prospect of being criticized for not fulfilling one of the president's principal promises of 1992. Further, the president himself was up for reelection and had vowed to sign a bipartisan bill. For the Republicans, resolution of this important issue would deny their presidential candidate an issue in the fall election, and that candidate was to be Senate Majority Leader Bob Dole. Additionally, getting a presidential signature would require removing the Medicaid provisions from the bill, thus substantially reducing its savings. The battle was high-noon politics in a split-party, separated government. It was a prime example of competitive partisanship on a vitally important issue for which serious but speculative change was being proposed.

Jurisdiction for the legislation in the House was distributed over three committees. The Ways and Means Committee was responsible for most of what was being considered, but the Agriculture Committee acted on the food stamp provisions and the Economic and Educational Opportunities Committee addressed work requirements and child care and nutrition. The legislation cleared all three committees, with Ways and Means showing the most serious party splits. The Budget Committee was also active, due to the spending effects of an overhaul of welfare programs. House Republican leaders decided to jettison controversial Medicaid provisions prior to the floor debate. This and other modifications were designed to make the bill more attractive to Democrats, including the president. The bill passed 256-170, with the support of thirty Democrats and all but four Republicans.

In the Senate, the Finance Committee and the Agriculture, Nutrition, and Forestry Committee considered the bill, again, along with the Budget Committee. The bill attracted support from just one Democrat in the two main committees, mostly due to the Medicaid provisions. Once those provisions were removed, Democrats were forced to reassess their positions, but some, like Daniel Patrick Moynihan (D-N.Y.), objected to the stringency of the welfare proposals themselves. Mostly, however, the strategy of offering a straight welfare bill was effective. Following modifications that softened some effects, the bill passed, 74-24, with the Democrats split evenly, 23-23.

The welfare reform proposals having passed both houses by respectable margins, attention shifted to the White House. A conference agreement and passage by both houses was increasingly likely. Therefore President Clinton had to make a choice: press for further changes or signal his support for the legislation. The provisions on food stamps and aid to legal immigrants were especially contentious. Clinton not only was cross-pressured within his own party, but also faced divisions among his White House advisers. Economic adviser Robert E. Rubin, for one, later wrote: "I shared George's [Stephanopoulos] view that the President should not sign the bill."[133] On the other side, domestic policy adviser Bruce Reed and political adviser Rahm Emanuel favored signing. Stephanopoulos described the president's decisionmaking this way: "His heart urged a veto, while his head calculated the risk. They were reconciled by his will—a will to win [in 1996] that was barely distinguishable and basically inseparable from the conviction that what was best for the poor was for him to be president."[134]

The president announced that he would sign the bill "as the best chance we will have for a long, long time to complete the work of ending welfare as we know it."[135] This decision guaranteed acceptance of the conference report in both chambers, by a 328-101 margin in the House and 78-21 in the Senate. The Republicans lost only two votes, both in the House. Many liberal Democrats were furious with the president for signing the bill, even as he promised to propose changes. "Sign it now; fix it later," was how Stephanopoulos summarized the president's view.[136]

The president's support scores for this major piece of legislation reflect the shifts that occurred through the lawmaking process. Clinton had three wins and five losses. Two of the three wins came with the House and Senate agreement to the conference report; the third was on a modification to the food stamp provision. The losses came early, when the Democrats tried to substitute their version of the legislation and on efforts to get waivers for budget rules.

The welfare reform legislation enacted in 1996 provides an example of the flexibility of lawmaking in the separated system. It illustrates the workings of competitive partisanship leading to cross-partisan support, the range of iteration in the service of finding bases for agreements, innovative sequences to take account of political change, and building momentum for taking risks on the bold reform of an entrenched program.

BALANCED BUDGET AGREEMENT. However improbable was the passage of a welfare reform package in 1996, a balanced budget agreement between a reelected Democratic president and returning Republican majorities in the House and Senate was even more unlikely. A president of one party is not expected to find common ground in budget making with congressional majorities of the other party. Yet that is precisely what happened in 1997. It was all the more notable given the fierce budgetary struggles between Clinton and the Republican Congress in 1995–97, which had resulted in the partial shutdown of the government. And that conflict was only the most recent in the "revenge-seeking warfare over the budget that had come to be Congress' chief preoccupation over most of the previous two decades."[137]

What explains this turnabout? Daniel J. Palazzolo explains it as suited to "realist expectations" of the separated system. He views the earlier struggles, and especially the 1995–97 experience, almost as rehearsals that fully displayed partisan positions as well as the limits to what could be achieved by both sides. Associated with this perspective was the reality of the parties' seeking partisan advantage in bipartisan negotiations. What he describes is very much like the competitive bipartisanship observed with the education legislation in the Bush 43 presidency (discussed above). As Palazzolo notes, "leaders constantly wrestle with the difficult tradeoffs between party principles and feasible compromises."[138] In a sense, this balancing act is a commonplace, but there are occasions when the imperative is to cut a deal, as was the case in 1997.

Congressional Quarterly's analysts offer several practical considerations that underlay realist expectations: "sheer exhaustion" from battle-weary opponents, optimistic forecasts in Clinton's 1998 budget proposal, Republicans' reluctance to form their own budget, Clinton's search for a "landmark achievement to help define his second term," and a change of players in the White House, with Leon Panetta leaving the post of chief of staff and a more accommodating team taking his place.[139] Perhaps most important was that the president wanted a deal for a goal long sought by Republicans—a balanced budget. "Clap your hands together" was the reaction of Senator Pete V. Domenici (R-N.M.).[140]

The sequence for this agreement was as unusual as the pact itself. An inclusive progression might properly begin with the development of the Republican budget proposal in 1995, which emphasized a multiyear balancing. At that time Clinton responded with a proposal for balance over a longer period. That aside, the sequence in 1997 started from a cross-partisan working group early in the year, then moved to the House and Senate leadership and respective party members.

Many of the negotiations were behind closed doors, thus producing considerable anxiety among the rank and file, and even some leaders. Democrats, in particular, were concerned about their president's reaching an agreement with the Republicans. But in general, the building of centrist, cross-partisan majorities tends to raise doubts on the edges of both right and left, involving as it does movement away from stalwart positions. Democrats balked at cuts in spending, especially on Medicare, and were keen to ensure that defense would not be immune to reductions and that there would be no downward adjustment of the Consumer Price Index (CPI), on which cost-of-living increases were based. Republicans were just as anxious to promote cuts in domestic spending and preserve tax cuts.

The calendar came to be important because any agreement would be incorporated into the congressional budget resolution and subsequent reconciliation. The resolution was to be enacted by April 15, a deadline often missed on Capitol Hill. On April 7 the chairs of the two Budget Committees and ranking Democrats began serious bargaining with Office of Management and Budget director Franklin Raines, White House congressional relations director John Hilley, and National Economic Council director Gene Sperling. John R. Kasich (R-Ohio), chair of the House Budget Committee, was a key figure among Republicans because of the greater partisanship in the House. He would sponsor the principal budget resolution on the floor. President Clinton was the central player for the Democrats. Among other responsibilities, he had to assure his party that any agreement would not abandon Democratic priorities.

A deal was at hand on May 1, when the Congressional Budget Office (CBO) announced that the fiscal 1997 deficit would be $50 billion less than earlier projected. Further good news was that the increase in income tax revenues that reduced the 1997 deficit would continue to have a positive effect in the five-year period of the agreement. At one stroke, this windfall made the task of creating and holding a cross-partisan majority very much easier. Many of the most contentious issues melted away—for example, reduction in the CPI, per capita caps on Medicaid, and cuts in Medicare. A significant amount would also be earmarked for reducing the deficit.[141]

The windfall eased concerns among liberal Democrats; it did not necessarily win them over. The actuality of a Democratic president having reached an agreement with Republicans on an issue of this magnitude required some getting used to. Clinton announced the deal before a Democratic retreat in Baltimore on May 2. Republicans made their own announcement in the Rotunda of the Capitol. "After five months of negotiating, bargaining, and compromising among the principals and policy leaders, the budget agreement faced its toughest test: winning the approval of majorities in the House and Senate."[142] And it happened. The most tense vote came on a substitute offered by Bud Shuster (R-Pa.) and James Oberstar (D-Minn.) that sought to preserve more money for transportation projects dear to members in their districts. The vote was close, 214-216, but the threat to the agreement was overcome. The Kasich resolution then passed overwhelmingly, 333-99. Only minor amendments were passed in the Senate, which approved the resolution 78-22. The conference report was accepted by similarly large margins in both chambers.

There was no vote on the agreement as such, and thus no presidential support score to reflect a Clinton win or loss. That the four votes on the budget resolution in the two chambers were counted as wins for the president was reasonable enough, given his support for the agreement. What is illustrated yet again, however, is that analysis concentrating on presidential support scores fails to specify who else won. By its very nature, successful competitive bipartisanship counts winners in both parties, a not uncommon result more generally in contemporary separated system politics. It is also difficult to gauge the degree of iteration in closed-door proceedings. No doubt any number of adjustments were made, as evidenced by the time required to get everyone on board, but such dealings are understandably less transparent.

HOMELAND SECURITY DEPARTMENT. Reorganization is a frequent governmental response to crisis. Accordingly it was predictable that the 9/11 attacks would occasion calls for changes in bureaucratic responsibilities. The most recent previous case was the creation of the Department of Energy in response to the OPEC oil embargo and resulting shortages during the Carter presidency. In the Bush 43 presidency, the initiative for combining the federal agencies responsible for domestic security came from the Capitol— the president originally resisted such an elaborate restructuring. The White House had created an Office of Homeland Security in the aftermath of the disaster, headed by Tom Ridge, the Republican governor of Pennsylvania. This arrangement was heavily criticized by members of Congress, because Ridge, not being subject to confirmation by the Senate, declined to testify before congressional committees, on advice from the White House.

In May 2002, Joseph I. Lieberman (D-Conn.), chair of the Senate Committee on Governmental Affairs, introduced a bill to create a Department of Homeland Security and a White House Office for Combating Terrorism. Since the department would have cabinet status, the secretary would be subject to Senate confirmation, and thus accountable to Congress. In June, the White House "abruptly reversed course" and announced a plan for creating a new department—"a sprawling bureaucracy with at least 170,000 employees and a budget of $37.5 billion" that combined units from many departments, offices, and agencies.[143]

And so the issue was joined in the two elected branches of the separated system. There was a majority for taking this action. The debate would focus on preserving jurisdictions, protecting employee rights, and providing executive flexibility in hiring and personnel management. The sequence for the legislation was House/Senate→president→House→Senate stalemate, followed by the 2002 midterm elections and a lame duck session with a sequence of House→Senate→House→president.

A nine-member Select Committee on Homeland Security (five Republicans and four Democrats), chaired by Majority Leader Dick Armey (R-Tex.), was created in the House to write a bill based on recommendations from the standing committees. The White House proposal was sent to eleven committees for their reactions. The responses were then to be assembled within a week. This exercise produced "radically different versions of what a Cabinet-level homeland security department should look like." Predictably, many of the responses were protective of committee jurisdiction over those units being drawn into the new agency. The Select Committee in fact "ignored" many of these recommendations and drafted a bill "that stuck close to the White House plan." The bill was approved by a party-line vote, 5-4, and sent to the floor. Personnel rules and corporate corruption were prominent topics in the floor debate. The White House wanted to preserve as much flexibility as possible on hiring, firing, and management in a department handling security issues. Democrats were successful in getting a provision that would prohibit the department from contracting with businesses headquartered in offshore tax havens. The House bill passed by a substantial margin, 295-132 (with eighty-eight Democrats voting in favor).[144]

Senate action was not nearly so swift. The Committee on Governmental Affairs approved Lieberman's bill, as amended, by a 12-5 vote, but its ranking Republican, Fred Thompson (R-Tenn.), noted: "We have some very fundamental disagreements with regard to the president's authority."[145] This assessment proved to be prescient as the bill was debated on the floor. The White House was anxious to have action completed before the first anniversary of 9/11, but it was not to be. Senator Robert C. Byrd (D-W.V.) deplored the pressure to act quickly and used delaying tactics to prevent a final vote. As in the House, the issue of employee rights was a major roadblock to Democratic support. Final action could not be taken before Congress broke for the midterm elections.

As with Clinton's welfare reform, the outcome of the midterm elections made a difference in getting final approval of the bill. Republicans had net gains in both the House and the Senate, a first for the incumbent president's party in nearly seventy years. When Congress returned, President Bush identified the new department as a priority. Democrats continued their attempts to amend the bill so as to reduce executive flexibility on worker rights, with some limited effect. A redrafted bill passed the House, 299-121, and the Senate, 90-9. There was no conference.

Once the president had signed on to the idea, there was cross-partisan support for a new department. Partisanship was competitive, but in the context of backing for the idea from both sides of the aisle. The degree of iteration was limited, primarily due to party unity among House Republicans, the midterm election results, and the peculiarities of lawmaking in a lame duck session (not the least of which was the anxiety of members to have it over with). Once again, the limitation of presidential support scores is demonstrated. The president batted a thousand by this measure: three wins, no losses. Yet the idea itself originated in Congress, not the White House.

The case of the Department of Homeland Security fits well with other reorganizations noted earlier. The changes made in moving the boxes around were certain enough. What was speculative was whether these organizational adjustments would achieve the substantive policy purposes motivating the changes.

Lessons from the Clinton-Bush Era

What can be learned from the extraordinary politics of the Clinton and Bush 43 presidencies? Do these cases complement or contradict lessons learned from previous postwar presidencies? Perhaps the most telling observation is that lawmaking advances with still more variations in split-party and narrow-margin politics. Gridlock is ever a possibility in a separated system but it is not inevitable, or even consistently probable, when the two parties share powers or are in a position to be credibly competitive. Major pieces of legislation were enacted even as political conditions encouraged analysts to forecast stalemate. Other pieces were stymied for various reasons.

The above examination of six cases, three each in the Clinton and Bush 43 presidencies, produces further observations about how laws are made. Note, for example, that presidential preponderance is not featured in any of these cases, nor is congressional preponderance. All fit within the category of joint participation—three evidencing greater presidential initiative; three, greater congressional initiative. The close margins in Congress and the lack of majorities for the two presidents in the popular vote lessened the chances that Clinton or Bush could dominate lawmaking. Yet both successfully attempted straight partisanship—the Deficit Reduction package for Clinton, the tax cuts for Bush. House Republicans also demonstrated extraordinary party unity and agenda management, thus inspiring a strategy of having the House act first, so as to send the president's proposals on to the Senate in more or less clean form.

This exercise also reveals a variation in partisanship, perhaps a direct consequence of narrow-margin politics. I have argued that bipartisanship is rare in regard to domestic issues, occurring primarily in response to foreign crises and disasters. But the politics of the Clinton and Bush 43 presidencies invited efforts to draw in the other party's leaders at early stages of law-making. Traditional alliances and commitments make it unlikely, however, that bipartisan participants will treat an issue de novo (as they would with a crisis). Thus they work alongside one another competitively. I use the term *competitive bipartisanship* to mark this pattern.

Comments are also merited on the five features emphasized with the other cases: continuity, sequence, speculation, iteration, and partisanship. All six sets of issues had familiar lineages, if not under the political circumstances of these two presidencies. Homeland security had not previously been engaged as a discrete, comprehensive issue to the extent that it was in 2002, but the grouping together of bureaucratic units was very much like that attempted with the creation of the Department of Energy in 1977. Certainly budget and taxing issues were familiar, as were the dimensions of and interests represented by education and welfare reform. Two of the six cases (deficit reduction and the 2001 tax cuts) displayed a standard sequence, from the president to the House, Senate, conference, and presidential signature. Another (education reform) was close, starting with the president working with a bipartisan group of members from both houses. The other three cases (welfare reform, the Balanced Budget Agreement, and the creation of the Homeland Security Department) followed unconventional sequences, with special groups initiating the action for the first two, and Congress doing so for the third.

All of these cases illustrate the speculative nature of lawmaking, though in different ways. The budget and tax set were no more or less speculative than other such cases in the postwar period. Though short-term effects may be understood, few planners or analysts are prepared to identify longer-, or even moderate-, term impacts. That fact does not even prevent partisan guesstimates of bad results; for example, Republican charges that the Clinton tax increases in 1993 would slow the economy or Democratic charges that the Bush 43 tax cuts in 2001 alone produced the deficits of 2002–04. The welfare and education reform packages in 1996 and 2001, respectively, were highly speculative in regard to possible effects. As of this writing, it is still too soon to calculate the full impacts of those changes. Finally, the Homeland Security Department is now in place, but determining its effectiveness is as complex as its mission (which, among other developments, will be affected by reforms in the intelligence services).

Iteration varied in predictable ways: the more controversial, the more iteration. Impressive Republican discipline in the House tended to reduce iteration in committees and on the floor; in the Senate, lesser command and the loss of a majority in 2001 inevitably increased iteration. I noted above two developments in partisan patterns: the use of straight partisanship by presidents with limited political capital and the employment of competitive bipartisanship on issues requiring active bipartisan involvement from the start.

It is a commonplace that politics in the United States has become intensely, even bitterly, divided. Often this interpretation encourages pessimism about lawmaking. That voters have regularly produced split control of the elected branches is a fact of the postwar era. More recently, they have also narrowed the margins of victory, even producing nearly tied results for the House, Senate, and presidency. The scholarly treatment of lawmaking under variable conditions is promoted here as an antidote to prejudgments about the workings of the separated system.

CHAPTER 8

Thinking about Change

The president is authorized to shape the presidency. The presidency is in a continuous search for its role in the government. Ours is a separated system.

The American presidency carries a burden of lofty expectations that simply are not warranted by the political or constitutional basis of the office. Presidents are important actors in national and world politics, but governments here and abroad adjust to their inevitable comings and goings. Effective presidents are those who know and understand their potential and variable place in the permanent and continuing government. One's natural inclination is to make the president responsible for policies and political events that no one can legitimately claim fully to master or manage. Presidents are well advised to resist this invitation to assume a position of power as though it conveyed authority. Rather, they need to identify and define their political capital, and do so repeatedly in a search for the range and limits of their influence.

Why are the status and power of the president exaggerated? Why are the constraints of separated institutions competing for shares of powers often ignored by analysts? And why are presidents commonly expected to overcome these realities? Why are the abundant variations of separation not acknowledged as the system's strengths rather than presidential weaknesses? I have puzzled about these questions throughout this volume. My experience in trying to understand just the president's relationships with Congress may offer partial answers. The complexity of a separated system

339

at work is truly imposing, if not always inspiring. It is like an Escher draw-ing: what rises, from one perspective, sinks, from another. Political ana-lysts, particularly those with deadlines, understandably try to simplify what they observe, and then often complain when the system does not work as simply as has been described.

For scholars, a presidency-centered, party responsibility perspective may be the consequence of historical trends in the frequency of split-party gov-ernment. It was a rarity during the first half of the twentieth century, having occurred often in the latter half of the nineteenth century. Perhaps observers believed that a single-party, presidency-centered government was evolving in the new century, as the solution to problems identified with the separated system. This hypothesis may have been encouraged by the common inter-pretation that the Franklin D. Roosevelt presidencies represented the begin-nings of modern national government and politics. With Roosevelt as the model in an evolutionary system of strong presidential leadership, one can understand the disillusionment accompanying the post–World War II era. Most presidents, and surely those governing with opposite-party majorities in Congress, were bound to fail the FDR test. The frustration of those who believed that presidentialism had arrived, only to discover that the Roo-sevelt years were the exception, not the rule, as has been shown to be the case, can well be imagined.

Sidney M. Milkis offers little comfort to advocates of the evolutionary perspective, and indeed he identifies in the Roosevelt years an emergent separation between presidential government and party government. "Roo-sevelt's party leadership and the New Deal mark the culmination of efforts, which begin in the Progressive era, to loosen the grip of partisan politics on the councils of power, with a view to strengthening national administrative capacities and extending the programmatic commitments of the federal government." For Milkis, "this shift from party to administrative politics" did not secure single-party government, nor did it usher in an "imperial" presidency. Presidents of either party found "themselves navigating a treacherous and lonely path, subject to a volatile political process that makes popular and enduring achievement unlikely."[1] Thus the big govern-ment of the post–New Deal era continues to pose challenges that are not met by reconstituted "responsible" political parties.

Presidents and the Presidency

The analysis in this book supports a number of conclusions regarding the role of presidents in the presidency and the presidency's role in the separated system.

—The separated system is rooted in the separation of elections. Conditions favoring responsible party government are rare, especially in the postwar period. A "government of parties" is more common, associated with several variations of split-party government and narrow-margin politics.

—Several partisan strategies are apparent in the separated system: straight or noncompetitive partisanship, competitive partisanship, bipartisanship, competitive bipartisanship, and cross-partisanship. The greater frequency of split-party government has reduced the likelihood of straight partisanship or bipartisanship and fostered the other forms..

—There are substantial differences in the personal and political background of presidents and how they come to serve in the White House (for example, as elected, reelected, nonelected, and heir apparent presidents or elected vice presidents). These differences can lead to incentives (assertive, compensatory, custodial, guardian, and restorative) that aid in explaining performance in office and how that performance is evaluated.

—Organizing a presidency is an adaptive process associated with the circumstances of how a president enters the White House and the set of problems he then encounters in doing the job. Several observations are relevant. First, many postwar presidencies involve same-party transitions: Roosevelt to Truman, Kennedy to Johnson, Nixon to Ford, and Reagan to Bush 41. These transitions have important organizational implications. In each of these four cases, the new president faced the task of adapting to or replacing an existing structure.

Second, commonly used models of White House organization (the circle or the pyramid) fail to account for the substantial variations experienced by postwar presidencies or the changes that are made through a term in office. The variables that should be taken into account in characterizing the organization of the presidency include the nature of access, the president's organizational concepts (if any), interaction between the president and his staff, relations among the staff, and for takeover presidents, the transition.

Third, cabinet secretaries represent a public manifestation of a president's effort to connect his White House to the permanent government (the bureaucracy and Capitol Hill). But turnover has been high (less so under Clinton and Bush 43), and measuring a president's effectiveness on the basis of a series of one-on-one interactions with the secretaries, while a reasonable approach, is difficult. Most presidents do not meet the challenge of effectively managing the separated system, though not for lack of trying.

—The public standing of presidents, as measured by public approval ratings, is inexactly related to their job performance and effectiveness in working with Congress, as would be expected in a separated system with diffused responsibility and a continuing agenda. Nevertheless, the testing of public approval has increased substantially in recent years, with evaluations typically equating a president's relative standing with his influence in the separated system. Permanent campaigning by presidents has been one response to the quantum increase in the measures taken of their job approval.

—However inapt the concept of a mandate in American national politics, it will continue to be used in interpreting election results. Three renditions—the mandate for change, the status quo mandate, and the mixed or nonmandate—are commonly employed at election time and then become tests for performance. A fourth concept, the unmandate, may accompany midterm losses by the president's party or other negative events later in a presidency.

—Presidents perform important agenda-setting functions by designating priorities, certifying issues, proposing policy solutions, and reacting to the policy initiatives of others. For the most part, the agenda of government itself is continuous from one year to the next. Presidents are judged by their effectiveness as designators, certifiers, and schedulers within the ongoing policy process.

—Lawmaking in the separated system is representative, institutional, and partisan. Statute making is bicameral and cross-institutional. These contexts shape a process that is speculative, continuous, iterative, informative, deliberative, sequential, orderly, and declarative. Most important legislation is worked on over time and is connected with precursory laws familiar to those in the permanent government. To be effective, presidents must take these characteristics of lawmaking into account as they judge how, when, and where to participate.

—An analysis of thirty-four major pieces of legislation (twenty eight from Mayhew's original list, another six from his updated count) in the postwar period reveals the rich variety of presidential-congressional interaction in lawmaking. Presidents are unquestionably important actors. There is, however, substantial variation in whether the White House or Congress is preponderant and also many instances of balanced participation. The engrossing differences in the degree and place of iteration, the extent and form of speculation, the sequence of legislative action, and, above all, the mix of partisan strategies at different stages reveal how little is learned from an analysis restricted to roll call votes (particularly studies based on presidential support scores).

Taken as a whole, these observations advise presidency watchers against isolating one branch from the other or concentrating on only one president or Congress. Understanding the workings of a separated system of diffused responsibility and mixed representation logically requires attention to the institutional context within which any one part of the system does its work. A presidency-centered perspective is insufficiently attentive to the challenge facing the president in finding his place in the permanent government. Often this perspective questions the legitimacy of other participants, who may be identified as obstructionists. This leads to proposed reforms to orient Congress and the bureaucracy more toward presidential policy preferences, or those preferences it is assumed presidents should have.

Much of such presidency-centered analysis concludes that the system is not working well, when in fact only a part of the system has been studied—and one with relatively high turnover, at that. One measure of whether the system is working is the production of important legislation. Mayhew has challenged those who doubt the capacity of the government to produce important laws under conditions that might be expected to result in stalemate. My detailed examination of twenty-eight of Mayhew's list of 267 laws, and six more of those he added in a "sweep one" selection for 1991–2002, shows an astonishing array of sequences, degrees of speculation, patterns of iteration, and partisan strategies. It is said that one does not want to look closely at how either sausage or laws are made. I agree when it comes to sausage. I strongly disagree when it comes to laws. Careful study of how important laws are made reveals the impressive creativity and flexibility of the system of separated institutions competing for shared powers. It is an extraordinarily mature process, with a seemingly infinite number of mutations that are bound to challenge the analyst and the reformer.

Reform and Change

The separated system is constantly undergoing modification as representative and bureaucratic institutions compete for shares of powers in dealing with an agenda. Continual change in the "how" suggests that there is no one method by which the separated and competive institutions cope with the "what." These realities complicate the fashioning and implementation of reforms, defined here as planned alterations to achieve a stated goal. Much is exploratory. Objects of reform are not easy to stipulate, nor are the effects of designed changes all that predictable. The system changes without reforms, and reforms do not necessarily lead to the desired changes. Accordingly, reforms typically are fitted into ongoing change and often become unrecognizable as independent variables explaining outcomes. Regardless, those advocating reforms tend to attribute subsequent change directly to the restructuring they promoted.

It is reasonable to demand that those advocating reform clarify their preferences. Most favor what I have dubbed "unitarianism," an orientation featuring classic responsibility, dominance of the presidency, and single-party wins. The frequency of split-party control in the post–World War II period has been greatly frustrating to unitarians, producing just one pure (Johnson) and one modified (Reagan) case.

I have emphasized "separationism" as an alternative view. This separationist orientation acknowledges diffused responsibility, competition for powers among the branches, and the legitimacy of split-party results. I conclude that separationism fosters a *government of parties*, not party government. This is the perspective of a separated, not a presidential, system, which I judge to be consistent with the constitutional order and historical practices. The original separationist design provided for distinct elections, which in turn allowed various forms of split-party control that contribute partisan checks to supplement the institutional balances already in place. If one accepts that split-party government is as legitimate as single-party government (and some do not), then the analyst as reformer should be interested in making each of these authentic forms work well. If anything, more attention should be paid to the workings of a government of parties than of a party government because it occurs much more frequently.

Normally the system should provide checks on excesses without substantially interfering with the capacity of the government to act on major public problems. This formulation suggests two outcomes that should be avoided: policy escalation, when policy exceeds its real support as a result of a presidency judged to be fully mandated; and policy stalemate, when there is a failure to act on serious policy issues because of—singly or in combination—a weakly supported president, a diminished Congress, and inapt partisan strategies.

Policy Escalation

The electoral conditions leading to broad-scale policy escalation include striking issue differences between the presidential candidates, a landslide for the winner, major gains for the winner's party in Congress, and declarations of support for the new president by his party's leaders on Capitol Hill. The two principal cases in the postwar period occurred in 1964 and 1980, with the elections of Johnson and Reagan. Each president was associated with major policy breakthroughs, substantial enough to affect the agenda for later decades.

These are the elections that come closest to satisfying unitarianism, yet they foster failures of the separated system. Proposals of enormous impact were enacted on a fast track, and thus were not subject to the more common checks and balances associated with the competition and sharing of powers. It is worth noting, however, that it is no simple matter to devise means of curbing an overmandated president, especially given widespread support for that outcome. Not only will a president take advantage of the opportunity provided by such a misreading of his election, but failure to do so may well bring criticism from those in the Washington community who defined the mandate in the first place. There is, in brief, a self-fulfilling quality to the mythical mandate.

The greater responsibility to correct for an overstated mandate lies with Congress, which is constitutionally placed and protected (in that its members are separately elected). As difficult as it may be to accomplish, congressional leaders should devise ways to seriously examine election results for their policy meaning. There is, for example, substantial evidence that in both 1964 and 1980 many voters were casting their ballots against Barry Goldwater and Jimmy Carter, respectively, rather than for the policy programs of the two winners. At the very least, therefore, Congress should resist endorsing the mythical mandate and play its ordinary role in lawmaking.

Of course, no one is eager to stand in front of a speeding truck. The president is commonly expected to have a chance to enact his program (even a president for whom there is no mandate). Yet why should that be assumed without careful analysis of whether voters actually intended that the new president's program be enacted? There is no good constitutional, political, or policy reason for members of Congress to abrogate their responsibilities under any circumstances. When those first readers of election results state that the president has a mandate for large change, members of Congress, as separately certified representatives, have an even greater responsibility to bring their judgment to bear on the formulation and legitimation of these proposals.

A decent case can be made for presidents also to exercise caution when a mandate for change is declared to exist. By enacting the bulk of their program early in the term, overmandated presidents can overdraw their policy "bank accounts," thus leaving little for the remainder of their time in office. Or they may establish expectations that can never again be met. Meanwhile, they may find themselves ill suited to manage the inevitable adjustments that occur as a consequence of policy breakthroughs. In yet another confounding circumstance, there may be a dramatic shift away from the issues at the time of the election toward those for which no mandate could have been foreseen, as was the case with Vietnam for Johnson. In short, mandates can be policy traps for presidents. Presidents may be encouraged to escalate and accelerate lawmaking beyond their real capacity to manage the effects of going too far, thereby threatening their power to persuade and bargain in the future.

Policy Stalemate

Just as serious may be the failure to act when there are pressing public issues. As Mayhew has shown, there are fewer such cases with split-party control than some have imagined. But subsequent studies have shown that split results can affect what agenda items get attention.[2] Stalemate does occur, however, representing a failure of the separated system. If the separation is working well, it can serve as a counterbalancing mechanism. That is, when one institution is not motivated to act, is incapable of acting, or loses political status, the other institution can take the initiative. Legislation can be and is initiated by both the White House and Congress, prompting reaction from the other.

A case of presidential-congressional stalemate occurred during the last two years of the Bush 41 presidency. A look at what happened helps to specify the conditions under which split-party control may thwart lawmaking. President Bush took few initiatives. As during the last years of the Eisenhower and Reagan presidencies, congressional Democrats took control of the agenda. But Bush was still in his first term, and a reelection campaign was forthcoming. The production of major legislation was marginally below that of other presidents in their third and fourth years (though just over half of that during Clinton's first term). The real difference was in the number of bills passed by Congress but then vetoed by Bush, with only one overridden by Congress. Seemingly neither the Republican president nor the Democratic Congress was willing to permit the other side to gain a policy advantage: "gridlock" came to be a common expression during the 1992 presidential and congressional campaigns.

It was the weaknesses of the president and Congress, not their strengths, that explained the gridlock. The president was perceived as having little or no positive program for dealing with an economy that was very slow to recover. Republicans in Congress suffered further losses in the 1990 midterm elections. And the president lost his advantage of expertise in foreign and defense policy issues as a result of the end of the Gulf War and dramatic political changes in Eastern Europe and the former Soviet Union. The problems that might justify rehiring George Bush were dissipating, replaced by economic troubles at home.

Meanwhile, on Capitol Hill congressional Democrats faced a series of scandals, most of which were mismanaged. The most widely publicized one concerned a banking service for the House of Representatives that allowed many members to overdraw their accounts. These revelations encouraged examination of other privileges enjoyed by members of both chambers. And they fueled an already vigorous national movement to limit the terms of legislators. Seldom in recent memory had members of Congress been more concerned about their status and that of their institution. As the election year began, the approval rating of Congress stood at 17 percent, half that of President Bush's low score.

Neither institution was well positioned to take up the slack for the other, as occurred, for example, during the last two years of the Reagan presidency, when congressional Democrats were aggressive in taking policy initiatives. In the case of Bush 41, each institution lacked public confidence even as it perceived weakness in the other. Bargaining can take place when strength is pitted against strength, but it is unlikely to occur between two weak and irritable contenders.

There is no simple remedy to a policy stalemate resulting from low support for leaders and institutions. Of course, elections are always just around the corner in the American version of the separated system. As noted, institutional gridlock came to be a major talking point during the 1992 elections. The problem in the Bush 41 case, however, was that the rational remedy was two-directional: to vote Democratic to correct for a weak president, and Republican to correct for a scandal-ridden Congress.

Can anything be done at the time? Although Congress bears the responsibility for curbing policy escalation, it is not well designed to lead the government out of stalemate. In fact, Sarah Binder has shown that bicameralism itself is often a root cause of stalemate.[3] Only the president can try to break the partisan gridlock of a weakly supported government. It may well be, however, that he cannot succeed, or that he simply is not capable of leading in that manner. After all, there is no constitutional requirement that presidents should know how and when to break a stalemate. Further, some may believe that government is not the solution to a particular problem. But when there is a larger national interest at stake, the president should be willing to forgo short-term political considerations and make a relentless effort to convince congressional party leaders to participate in competitive partisan and cross-partisan politics. This leadership might have to be highly personal, with the president possibly ignoring job approval ratings and the counsel of his political advisers (perhaps less likely in an era of the permanent campaign). In George H. W. Bush's case, his effort in 1990 to get a cross-partisan budget agreement surely was made at the cost of political support within his own party. The risk of such bold actions, however, must be weighed against the effects of not acting or of contributing further to stalemate.

Interestingly, intense partisanship also characterized the third and particularly the fourth years of the Bush 43 presidency. It was not exactly "life father, like son," however. The war on terrorism was not over, insurgency continued to plague Iraq, the economy was in much better shape, Republicans had narrow majorities in Congress, and the president and especially Congress had higher approval ratings. Yet the working relationships between the two institutions were anything but cordial. The political and lawmaking rhetoric and civility deteriorated during the long campaign, thus contributing greater urgency to efforts for a more regular and well-mannered order. It appeared that "sidetrack partisanship" had replaced "mainline partisanship." That is, stylistic and rhetorical matters seemed to have supplanted more substantive policy differences. The result was a loss of the lawmaking imperative to overcome differences through bargaining, so as to solve public problems. In an era of narrow-margin politics, this problem deserves serious attention by leaders of both parties.

A Plurality of Governments

I turn next to the potential for reform and the reality of change in the presidency and its work with Congress. My purpose is less to propose specific reforms than to promote understanding of the plurality of legitimate forms of governing in a two-party separated system—and quite candidly, to discourage illusions that such a system can easily be transformed into a presidential system through institutional or procedural tinkering.

The first point is simply this: universal reforms are discouraged by a constitution that allows for different types of partisan governments. One of the most important lessons from this study is that presidents enter the White House and participate in the policy and lawmaking processes by different constitutionally sanctioned methods. Therefore proposed reforms must account for these permissible variations in legitimate government. I acknowledge that some reformers want to change the constitutional structure itself, so as to prevent this multiplicity of governments.[4] My personal view is that these efforts will, and probably should, fail. Rather than bemoan the legitimate outcomes provided for in the separated system, it is more constructive to judge how the various forms of single- and split-party government might be made to work more effectively. The greater frequency of stalemate in recent years may well be a stimulus for this type of inquiry, which should recognize that the prevention of legislation may also represent effective governance.

The variations in the postwar governments and the strategies that I deduce from the strengths and weaknesses of the presidents upon entering the White House were discussed in chapter 2 (see table 2-4). In a broader perspective, it is useful to identify various patterns of government for the postwar presidents, as I have done in table 8-1. Note, first, that balanced participation is the most common type of government, as would be expected in a separated system with equal branches. Note, further, the tendency for split-party government to move from balanced participation to congressional preponderance. The experiences in single-party government are mixed. Clearly, presidents face different strategic conditions and there is no standard formula for presidential performance. To illustrate, I discuss reform in the three contexts I employed to analyze the cases of major legislation in chapter 7.

PRESIDENTIAL PREPONDERANCE. Presidential preponderance is the situation, relatively rare in recent decades, when an election appears to have conveyed a congruent policy message for both president and Congress: the perceived mandate for change. As has been discussed, such a presidency may result in policy escalation. The cases that fit into this category are the Johnson and Reagan presidencies (principally in their early years).

When presidents have significant political advantages, reforms should strive to preserve the distinctive contributions of the separated institutions and ensure effective communication between the president and his congressional

Table 8-1. *Institutional Interaction and Party Control, 1945–2005*[a]

President and Congress	Institutional interaction	Party control
Truman		
79th	Balanced	Single
80th	Congressional	Split
81st	Balanced	Single
82nd	Balanced/congressional	Single
Eisenhower		
83rd	Balanced	Single
84th	Balanced	Split
85th	Balanced	Split
86th	Congressional	Split
Kennedy-Johnson		
87th	Balanced	Single
88th	Balanced/presidential	Single
89th	Presidential (escalation)	Single
90th	Balanced	Single
Nixon-Ford		
91st	Balanced	Split
92nd	Balanced	Split
93rd	Balanced/congressional	Split
94th	Congressional (stalemate)	Split
Carter		
95th	Balanced	Single
96th	Balanced/congressional	Single
Reagan		
97th	Presidential (escalation)	Split[b]
98th	Balanced	Split[b]
99th	Balanced	Split[b]
100th	Congressional	Split
Bush 41		
101st	Congressional	Split
102nd	Congressional (stalemate)	Split
Clinton		
103rd	Balanced	Single
104th	Congressional/balanced	Split
105th	Balanced	Split
106th	Balanced (stalemate)	Split
Bush 43		
107th	Balanced	Single, then split[c]
108th	Balanced (stalemate)	Single

a. Types of institutional interactions are drawn from the discussion in chapter 7.

b. Split-party control between House and Senate.

c. In the 107th Congress the Senate was initially tied, but then shifted to Democratic control when Senator James Jeffords (Vt.) switched from Republican to Independent.

majority. Because of the difficulty in reading policy messages from diverse and disconnected elections, both institutions must work at deciphering their meaning.

Since policy escalation can be the result of presidential preponderance, stringent tests of representation and responsiveness should be applied, with the members of the president's party in Congress communicating perspectives drawn from their own representational expertise. Congress should never vacate its deliberative and declarative responsibilities. This view undoubtedly will be interpreted as an argument against change. It is not. Rather, it is a brief for change realized through the cross-institutional processes that characterize the separated system. Neither is it counsel against presidential leadership. It is, rather, an acceptance of the special conditions under which leadership works in the separated system, as well as an appreciation of what leeway may offer in getting the best lawmaking result. Put otherwise, presidential power and effectiveness in the separated system are enhanced, not constricted, by active interaction with Congress.

CONGRESSIONAL PREPONDERANCE. In periods of congressional preponderance, the president is substantially weakened by his party's losses in the midterm elections, emboldening the other party in Congress to take policy initiatives. These are most often instances of split-party government, when the president's party has done poorly in a second midterm election, such as the 86th Congress (Eisenhower's last) and the 100th Congress (Reagan's last); or when a takeover president has to manage public dissatisfaction and a mood for change, such as the 80th Congress (Truman's second), the 94th (Ford's post-Watergate Congress), and the 101st and 102nd Congresses (both during Bush 41's term). Clinton's second Congress, the 104th, also fits, a rare case of a president's party losing its House and Senate majorities in the first term, and after forty years of majority status in the House of Representatives.

Under these circumstances, members of Congress are tempted to compensate for a weakened president. However instinctive this reaction may be, reform in such cases should be attentive to the maintenance of the separated system. Therefore an enhanced congressional capacity for setting the agenda, taking policy initiatives, and overseeing executive actions should be constructively developed to prevent the tendency toward policy stalemate noted earlier. However, the opposition majority party in Congress should not assume this role at the expense of further erosion of the president's position or status, particularly given that midterm results cannot, with rare exceptions, reasonably be interpreted as referendums on presidential performance. This is not a recommendation to eliminate politics, but rather a further exhortation to preserve the advantages of the separated system.

The 104th Congress (1995–97) illustrates the usefulness of leeway for congressional leaders, too. Speaker Newt Gingrich (R-Ga.) made an error often attributed to presidents: overestimating the effects of election results on his influence and that of the president. He judged himself more powerful, and the president less so, than could be justified. As a consequence, he failed to realize the benefits of leeway in 1995, which benefits may have avoided confrontations with the president as well as enhanced his own status. Gingrich later acknowledged as much:

> We were committed to the idea of Clinton as a weak President . . . we failed to see the advantageous position he was moving himself into. . . . In the end . . . our seeking an agreement with Clinton in 1995 [by confronting him] was from just about every point of view a fiasco. It cost us damage in public approval that would take most of 1996 and the successful [balanced budget] negotiations of 1997 to overcome.[5]

BALANCED PARTICIPATION. Most often there are balanced advantages between the president and Congress, as befits the separated system. Interestingly, this balance may exist in both single- and split-party government. The source of the equilibrium, however, is not always the same. In single-party cases, balance is associated with the relatively weak electoral performance of a Democratic president and substantial Democratic majorities in the House and Senate (Truman in 1948, Kennedy in 1960, Carter in 1976, and Clinton in 1992) or a marginal, even disputed, win by a Republican president and narrow or no Republican margins in Congress (Bush 43 in 2000). In each of the Democratic cases, the president had advantages associated with a surprise win or the freshness of his message. Yet most congressional Democrats had ample reason to believe that they won independently of the president. Thus the policy connection between the presidential and congressional elections was weak at best. In the case of Bush 43, the president had few sources of power and his party had a net loss of seats in both chambers of Congress. Therefore he could not rely on robust party majorities (indeed, the Senate was tied), and the Democrats were enthused by their net gains.

In split-party cases, balance is associated with congressional Democrats' successfully maintaining their majorities in the face of Republican presidential victories (Eisenhower in 1956, Nixon in 1968 and 1972, and Reagan in 1984). In three of these cases, Democratic House and Senate majorities were returned despite the landslide reelection victories of Republican presidents. The 1996 election provided the reverse: a Democratic president won by a wide margin and Republicans held their House and Senate majorities. One other case was that created when Senator James Jeffords (R-Vt.) declared Independent status in 2001 and voted with Democrats to permit them to organize.

It is vital for comprehending the workings of the separated system in the postwar period to acknowledge that balanced participation is the most frequent of the three situations and that it characterizes both single- and split-party governments. Reforms in this situation should be aimed at strengthening the capacity of both the president and Congress to participate effectively. At times, realizing that goal has meant having to undertake major reforms. In the 1970s, for example, both Congress and the executive made significant changes designed to manage a number of large issues like budget making, civil rights, the environment, energy, the economy, trade, and taxes. It is remarkable how much adjustment does take place when institutions are stimulated to compete for shared powers. This rivalry may arise out of a concern not to lose status, as was the case for Congress in 1946 and in the 1970s.

It is understandable that observers will predict stalemate when seemingly equal rivals contest proposals in the arenas of power. However, the record shows that balanced, competitive participation in the separated system does not produce gridlock very often. Instead, it facilitates the identification and treatment of major public issues, often through intricate processes of competitive partisanship and cross-partisanship (as illustrated in chapter 7). Yet gridlock does occur. As can be seen from table 8-1, three of the four stalemates have come with the most recent three presidents: Bush 41, Clinton, and Bush 43. At the very least, these cases offer conditions under which gridlock can occur: low status for both institutions, scandal and impeachment, and disputed legitimacy and a contentious military commitment.

PERMUTATIONS. For six consecutive years during Reagan's two terms and for nineteen months in 2001–03, Congress itself experienced split-party control: a Republican Senate and a Democratic House of Representatives, in the former; a Democratic Senate and Republican House, in the latter. Although this form of split control had occurred many times in the past, never in the history of the modern two-party system had it been repeated for three successive Congresses. This is another variation in governing, and it has a decent prospect of being repeated, given the recent competitiveness of Senate elections and the persistently narrow margins in the House of Representatives since 1995. One apparent feature of this permutation is the reliance on a legislative sequence that starts with the chamber controlled by the president's party and moves to the chamber controlled by the other party.

Lessons for Presidents

Virtually everything I have written counsels that generic advice to presidents is to be viewed with the utmost suspicion. Presidents differ, and they are free to judge how best to make their personal, political, and policy traits work for them. Still, there are lessons related to the workings of the separated system that may be usefully reiterated. I turn initially to the cases of elected presidents.

The first lesson is the most obvious, yet possibly the one most difficult to absorb in the aftermath of an election. Newly elected presidents come fresh from an experience that is absorbing and extraordinarily self-centered. The perpetual motion of a presidential campaign focuses exclusively on the candidate. Every activity is directed toward decisions that occur by the calendar: primary dates, a convention, debates, election day. The time arrives when the candidate-centered organization can congratulate itself and hand over its victor to the permanent government. It is at that precise point of triumph that a new leader must be the most disciplined in acknowledging the requirements of a transition from candidate to president-elect to president. After heading a temporary, highly convergent, and concentrated organization, he will participate as a central figure in a permanent, divergent, and dispersed structure. The first task, then, for a president in a separated system, is to learn what is required to do the new job.

In the first edition of this book I raised doubts that the campaign experiences of the president and his aides were relevant to governing. Subsequent developments have led me to modify that conclusion. It is generally accepted that permanent campaigning has become a feature of the presidential term. Accordingly, the political consultants from the election campaign have come to play important roles in the policy campaigns of a presidency. In fact, a second generation of political consultants has emerged: those qualified to manage both electoral and policy campaigns, which may be becoming seamless.[6]

A second, related lesson is that presidents should not be misled by the importunings of many in the Washington community about how they want politics to work. For various reasons, these permanent residents may wish the president to exceed his capacity and resources. Presidents are well advised to be stubbornly realistic in understanding who they are, how they came to be in the Oval Office, and what are their own strengths and weaknesses, as well as the strengths and weaknesses of others authorized to participate in decisionmaking. This assessment will help guide prospective achievements.

A third piece of advice is that estimating status and resources is not a one-time activity. Little remains constant in the separated system. The pace of change may have quickened through the postwar era, but there has always been change. That should surprise no one, since a major purpose of representative democracy is to bring the outside in on a continuing basis. Even so, the variety of sources and types of change during a presidency is astonishing, in terms of people, issues, organization, processes, and public support. Presidents typically have more than one presidency; in some cases the change is significant enough to require new leadership. And even with high incumbent return on Capitol Hill, one Congress is seldom exactly like the one before.

Fourth, public support as measured by approval ratings, frequently cited as a source of power, should be viewed skeptically by presidents, for all of the reasons cited in chapter 4. Richard E. Neustadt's concept of public prestige is perhaps more useful, because it rests on more substantial grounds and is tested qualitatively by other actors in the separated system. A high approval rating does not create an advantage in presidential persuasion if it cannot be translated into clear effects for, say, members of Congress. Presidents Bush 41 and Bush 43 can be authoritatively consulted on that point. Likewise, a low approval rating need not result in gridlock or even the judgment that the president has lost prestige as an actor in policymaking. President Clinton, for example, maintained prestige as a knowledgeable policy analyst throughout a year in which his approval rating seldom rose above 50 percent. Later, he received solid job approval ratings even as his personal evaluations were low. Prestige cannot be invented by polls, nor is it likely to be demolished by them.

Fifth, all things considered, presidents are counseled to beware of mandates. They come with high expectations of performance that seldom can be met in a separated system continually in motion. Further, mandates typically last only until those declaring them to exist rediscover how separationist politics works, a process that may take just a few months. In some cases, notably in 1965 and 1981, those declaring a mandate have included members of Congress, who then found it difficult to undo what they had agreed to during the short life of the warrant. Meanwhile, the decisions themselves have lasting effects, even resulting in significant agenda shifts that the mandated presidents may be ill suited to manage (for example, the fiscal politics of huge deficits).

Sixth, an analysis of how laws are made confirms ordinary expectations that the president and members of Congress are legitimate participants in the full range of policy and lawmaking activities. The lesson for presidents is apparent. Whenever powers are shared, attention should be directed to the other authorized decisionmakers. How do they view the problem? What are their present commitments? On what basis will they compromise? The test in a separated system is not simply presidential success. It is, rather, the achievement of the system, with presidents and members of Congress inextricably bound and similarly judged. In the separated system, solo triumphs for presidents are rare. Said differently, failure to explore and incorporate the perspectives of those who share powers sacrifices the leeway offered by the separated system.

Many of these lessons are also applicable to presidents who have been elected previously, but with some additional observations. Reelected presidents have presumably found their place in the permanent government and therefore campaign both as candidates and incumbent leaders. As it has happened, four reelected presidents in the postwar period (Eisenhower, Nixon, Reagan, and Clinton) served in split-party governments. Approval for them occurred within the context of continued public tolerance for that condition. Term limits for reelected presidents alter the policy dynamics, inviting them to indulge and adapt to the policy initiatives of a congressional majority party looking forward to an open presidential election. These circumstances suggest that a president should pay even greater attention to Capitol Hill in formulating and executing a policy program. Bush 43 broke that postwar pattern in 2004 by being reelected with a Republican Congress and also witnessing gains for his party in both houses. This result bolstered his own marginal wins in the popular and electoral votes.

Takeover presidents face enormous challenges in managing an organization created for their predecessor. As vice presidents, they were associated with, and often held responsible for, an administration to which they made marginal contributions. Lacking a concentrated and self-centered campaign experience, they are unlikely to overestimate their status; their campaign activity was oriented toward the presidential candidate. The principal lesson appears to be that such presidents must carefully weigh the complex strategic situation, assessing the expectations of their guardianship and moving cautiously from the designs of their predecessors to make their own connections with the government. Experience suggests that the manner and timing of these developments will vary, depending heavily on the circumstances of the takeover. For Truman, the sheer magnitude and pace of events necessitated decisiveness, virtually to the exclusion of deliberation at times. For Johnson, a substantial agenda awaited his legislative mastery. For Ford, restoration of the president's trusted role in the separated system was required and demanded. The principal lesson appears to be that takeover presidents have to look back to their sponsoring presidency, look in the present to how Congress reacts to changes in executive leadership, and look forward to fashioning a distinctive presidency suited to the new occupant of the Oval Office.

The elected vice presidents (including the one heir apparent) include individuals who could not have been elected on their own before serving as vice president. Harry Truman did not try. There is no evidence that Truman harbored presidential ambitions before he was selected as Roosevelt's running mate in 1944. Lyndon Johnson tried in 1960 and lost badly to his younger Senate colleague. George H. W. Bush tried in 1980 and won just four primaries in competition with Reagan. All three were elected president as a consequence of already being in the White House: Truman and Johnson as president, Bush as vice president and the heir apparent. The six lessons noted for elected presidents are all applicable to these presidents, but there is one more that is especially apt. The rationale for the vice president to serve as president may be more transitory than for an elected president to serve in the first place. Little in the job description or in historical experience suggests that vice presidents are equipped to serve well as presidents. They have their place in the separated system, and that is to serve as the president requests and to be a replacement for elected or reelected presidents should they die or resign. I am not intimating that vice presidents who take over as presidents should stand down at the completion of their predecessor's term. I am, rather, challenging the assumption that they should then be elected to the presidency by reason of their unanticipated incumbency or of being a patient understudy. I similarly question the assumption that a full-service vice president is perforce a logical successor to the president he serves. The increased responsibilities given by their presidents to recent vice presidents—for example, Walter Mondale, Al Gore, and Dick Cheney—do not convince me otherwise. For those moved to seek the presidency anyway, I offer the following advice: establish an independent and personal justification for service as president, displaying qualities of leadership separate from the experience of the vice presidency.

The Presidency in a Separated System

I come away from this study quite in awe of the American national government. That is not to say I believe it is faultless; angels are not available to govern, as James Madison advised long ago. I am, however, impressed with the capacity of a complex of political institutions to adjust to a remarkable variation in political and policy circumstances. E. E. Schattschneider explained that "democracy is a political system for people who are not too sure that they are right."[7] His formulation draws attention to decisionmaking rather than to the decisions themselves. It is no simple matter to create, maintain, or reform a government forged to represent differing versions of uncertainty and to approximate, but not necessarily achieve, policy solutions.

The capacity of the separated system to adjust is reflected in the classifications developed throughout this book. Regardless of the topic—how presidents come to be there, how they organize their presidencies, their public standing and role in agenda setting, and the patterns of partisan and institutional interactions—I have found the differences among and within presidencies to be striking. The manifold determinants of the president's strategic position assist in specifying his advantages for certifying and managing items on a continuous agenda and for participating in a lawmaking process, much of which takes place in another, independent branch of government.

I conclude that it is more important to make the separated system work well than to change the system. The United States has the most intricate lawmaking system in the world. It will not be made better through simplification. Preponderance of one branch over the other should be a cause for concern, not celebration. Presidents are well advised to appreciate the advantages of the separated system and to define their role in it. Most do not have to be counseled on the legitimacy of Congress, but some do. Most know instinctively that their advantages are in certifying the agenda and persuading others to accept their proposals as a basis for compromise, but some have more ambitious conceptions of presidential power. Most understand that they are temporary leaders of a convention of policy choice already in session when they take office, but a few lack the skills to define the limits or realize the advantages of that status. Most realize that patience, persistence, and sharing are required for effective work in the separated system, but some are overly anxious to take immediate credit for change. In essence, most grasp the purposes and benefits of a diffused-responsibility system of mixed representation and shared powers, but some believe that the president is the presidency, the presidency is the government, and ours is a presidential system. Those who believe this may even have convinced themselves that they are right. They will be proven wrong.

Notes

Notes to Chapter 1

1. James W. Ceaser and Andrew Busch, *The Perfect Tie: The True Story of the 2000 Presidential Election* (Lanham, Md.: Rowman and Littlefield, 2001).

2. Quoted in Ruth Marcus, "In Transition Twilight Zone, Clinton's Every Word Scrutinized," *Washington Post,* November 22, 1992, p. A1.

3. Lyndon Baines Johnson, *The Vantage Point: Perspectives of the Presidency, 1963–1969* (New York: Holt, Rinehart, and Winston, 1971), p. 18.

4. "The Johnson Landslide," *New York Times,* November 4, 1964, p. 38.

5. Richard E. Neustadt, personal correspondence to the author.

6. "Republican Renascence," *New York Times,* November 13, 1966, p. E10.

7. David S. Broder, "Somber '68 Message Is a Contrast to Optimism of '64," *Washington Post,* January 18, 1968, p. A13.

8. Johnson, *Vantage Point,* pp. 532–33.

9. " . . . an Empty Landslide," *New York Times,* November 9, 1972, p. 46.

10. Arthur Krock, "The Unmandate," *New York Times,* November 10, 1972, p. 39.

11. "The Nixon Resignation," *New York Times,* August 9, 1974, p. 32.

12. Richard M. Nixon, *In the Arena: A Memoir of Victory, Defeat, and Renewal* (New York: Simon and Schuster, 1990), p. 25.

13. James L. Sundquist, ed., *Beyond Gridlock: Prospects for Governance in the Clinton Years* (Brookings, 1993), p. 25.

14. Johnson, *Vantage Point,* p. 443.

15. Richard Rose, *The Postmodern President: The White House Meets the World* (Chatham, N.J.: Chatham House, 1988), p. 46.

16. Walter Lippmann, *Public Opinion* (New York: Macmillan, 1950), p. 25.

17. Mark J. Rozell, *The Press and the Carter Presidency* (Boulder, Colo.: Westview Press, 1989), p. 4.

18. "Congress and the President," *New York Times,* January 3, 1946, p. 26.

19. "President and Congress," *New York Times,* November 6, 1948, p. 12.

20. David R. Mayhew, *Divided We Govern: Party Control, Lawmaking, and Investigations, 1946–1990* (Yale University Press, 1991), p. 52.

21. "Tuesday's Mandate for the President . . . ," *Washington Post,* November 7, 1974, p. A30.

22. James L. Sundquist, *Constitutional Reform and Effective Government,* rev. ed. (Brookings, 1992), p. 1.

23. Ibid., p. 10.

24. Ibid., p. 11.

25. American Political Science Association, *Toward a More Responsible Two-Party System: A Report of the Committee on Political Parties* (New York: Rinehart, 1950), pp. 1–2.

26. Ibid., p. 89.

27. Robert A. Dahl and Charles E. Lindblom, *Politics, Economics, and Welfare* (New York: Harper and Brothers, 1953), pp. 335–36 (emphasis in original).

28. For party unity scores, see Norman J. Ornstein, Thomas E. Mann, and Michael J. Malbin, *Vital Statistics on Congress, 2001–2002* (Washington: AEI Press, 2002), p. 173.

29. Mark A. Peterson, *Legislating Together: The White House and Capitol Hill from Eisenhower to Reagan* (Harvard University Press, 1990), pp. 8, 9.

30. See Charles O. Jones, *The Speculative Imagination in Democratic Lawmaking* (Oxford University Press, 1999), pp. 13.

31. David R. Mayhew, *Congress: The Electoral Connection* (Yale University Press, 1974).

32. For details on the three types of Senate classes, see Jones, *The Speculative Imagination,* pp. 12–13.

33. Emphasis in original.

34. Interview with Richard E. Neustadt, cited in Charles O. Jones, "Richard E. Neustadt: Public Servant as Scholar," *Annual Review of Political Science* 6 (2003): 1.

35. Richard E. Neustadt, *Presidential Power: The Politics of Leadership* (New York: Wiley, 1960), p. 179.

36. For this application of "position" to Bush 43, see Charles O. Jones, "Capitalizing on Position in a Perfect Tie," in Fred I. Greenstein, ed., *The George W. Bush Presidency: An Early Assessment* (Johns Hopkins University Press, 2003), pp. 173–78.

37. Jones, "Richard E. Neustadt," p. 12.

38. This paragraph borrows from ibid., p. 19.

39. Some might also include nonpartisanship. There are minor issues that are nonpartisan. More important matters, however, fit within bipartisanship, as I define it here.

Notes to Chapter 2

1. Edward S. Corwin, *The President, Office and Powers, 1787–1948: History and Analysis of Practice and Opinion* (New York University Press, 1957), p. 30.

2. *Time,* April 7, 1986, p. 27.

3. An example is Fred I. Greenstein, ed., *Leadership in the Modern Presidency* (Harvard University Press, 1988). Nine very different presidents are analyzed. The concluding essay, by Greenstein, is a "search" for the "modern president," emphasizing the contributions of presidents to the institution.

4. Thomas A. Bailey, *Presidential Greatness: The Image and the Man from George Washington to the Present* (New York: Appleton-Century, 1966), p. 36.

5. Quoted in Michael Nelson, ed., *Guide to the Presidency* (Washington: Congressional Quarterly Press, 1989), p. 148.

6. Fred I. Greenstein, *The Presidential Difference: Leadership Style from FDR to Clinton* (New York: Free Press, 2000), p. 189.

7. See Charles O. Jones, "Nominating 'Carter's Favorite Opponent': The Republicans in 1980," in Austin Ranney, ed., *The American Elections of 1980* (Washington: American Enterprise Institute, 1981), chap. 3, esp. p. 63.

8. For details, see Charles O. Jones, *The Trusteeship Presidency: Jimmy Carter and the United States Congress* (Louisiana State University Press, 1988), chap. 2.

9. For details, see Charles O. Jones, *Clinton and Congress, 1993–1996: Risk, Restoration, and Reelection* (University of Oklahoma Press, 1999), chaps. 4 and 5.

10. *New York Times,* April 15, 1945, p. E3.

11. "President Truman," *New York Times,* April 14, 1945, p. 14.

12. Quoted in David McCullough, *Truman* (New York: Simon and Schuster, 1992), p. 353.

13. "President Johnson," *New York Times,* November 23, 1963, p. 28.

14. "The Next President and Inflation," *Washington Post,* August 9, 1974, p. A30.

15. "The Presidential Pardon," *Washington Post,* September 10, 1974, p. A20.

16. Harry Truman, *Memoirs: Years of Trial and Hope* (New York: Doubleday, 1956), p. 222.

17. Walter Mondale in 1984 might be considered a fourth case. However, he ran four years after his service as vice president and was overwhelmingly defeated by Ronald Reagan.

18. Conditions for an heir apparent may suit what Stephen Skowronek refers to as "the politics of articulation," especially where the predecessor has reconstructed presidential leadership. See Stephen Skowronek, *The Politics Presidents Make: Leadership from John Adams to George Bush* (Harvard University Press, 1993), p. 41.

19. A three-point bonus is awarded to President George W. Bush in the Senate in 2001, because the Republicans had to rely on the vice president's vote for their majority.

20. James David Barber, *The Presidential Character: Predicting Performance in the White House,* 4th ed. (New Jersey: Prentice-Hall, 1992).

21. Garfield had in fact decided to run for the Senate and was so elected in 1880 by the Ohio state legislature at the same time as he was elected president.

22. See Joseph A. Schlesinger, *Political Careers in the United States* (Rand-McNally, 1966), chap. 1; and David T. Canon, *Actors, Athletes, and Astronauts: Political Amateurs in the United States Congress* (University of Chicago Press, 1990), chap. 3.

23. Skowronek, *The Politics Presidents Make*, p. 18.

24. One might identify Bush with a custodial incentive, much like that of Truman following Roosevelt. I decided on the guardian incentive primarily because Bush won on his own in an election that had many features of a reelection, and Bush was more linked to the eight years of Reagan than Truman was to the fourth Roosevelt administration (having served just a few months as vice president before Roosevelt's death).

25. For details, see Jones, *Clinton and Congress*, chap.2.

Notes to Chapter 3

1. For broader treatments, see John P. Burke, *The Institutional Presidency: Organizing and Managing the White House from Roosevelt to Clinton*, 2nd ed. (Johns Hopkins University Press, 2000); James P. Pfiffner, *The Strategic Presidency: Hitting the Ground Running*, 2nd. ed. (University Press of Kansas, 1996); and Charles E. Walcott and Karen M. Hult, *Governing the White House: From Hoover through LBJ* (University Press of Kansas, 1995).

2. President's Committee on Administrative Management, *Administrative Management in the Government of the United States* (Government Printing Office, 1937), p. 5.

3. Bradley H. Patterson Jr., *Ring of Power: The White House Staff and Its Expanding Role in Government* (Basic Books, 1988), p. 11.

4. Peri E. Arnold, *Making the Managerial Presidency: Comprehensive Reorganization Planning, 1905–1980* (Princeton University Press, 1986), pp. 361–63.

5. For corroboration by those with White House experience, see, for example, Clark Clifford, *Counsel to the President: A Memoir* (Random House, 1991), pp. 76–77, and Jack Watson in Samuel Kernell and Samuel L. Popkin, eds., *Chief of Staff: Twenty-Five Years of Managing the Presidency* (University of California Press, 1986), p. 70.

6. Richard E. Neustadt, personal correspondence, July 13, 1993.

7. Paul C. Light, *Thickening of Government: Federal Hierarchy and the Diffusion of Accountability* (Brookings, 1995).

8. Compiling precise data for the White House staff is a daunting task. Figures from the budget do not include detailees from the departments and agencies. Further, there are a number of special funds available to the president that do not get reported as White House expenditures. See John Hart, *The Presidential Branch* (New York: Pergamon, 1987), pp. 97–109.

9. Nelson W. Polsby, "Some Landmarks in Presidential-Congressional Relations," in Anthony King, ed., *Both Ends of the Avenue: The President, the Executive Branch, and the Congress* (Washington: American Enterprise Institute, 1983), p. 3.

10. Hart, *Presidential Branch*, pp. 96–97.

11. Hedrick Smith, *The Power Game: How Washington Works* (Random House, 1988), p. 301.

12. Interview with Eisenhower and Nixon staff person, conducted by Stephen Hess. I have transcribed this and other interviews by Hess cited below with his permission.

13. George E. Reedy, *The Twilight of the Presidency* (New York: World Publishing, 1970), pp. xiv–xv.

14. Interview with Neustadt, as quoted in Charles O. Jones, "Richard E. Neustadt: Public Servant as Scholar," *Annual Review of Political Science* 6 (2003): 11–12. For a critical assessment of this view, see Bert A. Rockman, "Staffing and Organizing the Presidency," in Robert Y. Shapiro, Martha J. Kumar, and Lawrence R. Jacobs, eds., *Presidential Power: Forging the Presidency for the Twenty-First Century* (Columbia University Press, 2000), pp. 159–77.

15. Matthew J. Dickinson, *Bitter Harvest: FDR, Presidential Power and the Growth of the Presidential Branch* (Cambridge University Press, 1997), p. 234.

16. Ibid., chap. 8.

17. Stephen Hess, *Organizing the Presidency,* 2nd ed. (Brookings, 1988), p. xi.

18 The circle and pyramid models are presented in ibid., p. 254.

19. Quoted in Kernell and Popkin, *Chief of Staff,* p. 62.

20 Terry Sullivan, ed., *The Nerve Center: Lessons in Governing from the White House Chief of Staff* (Texas A & M University Press, 2004), p. xiii.

21. Hess, *Organizing the Presidency,* 2nd ed., p. 254.

22. These classifications, primarily those of Richard Tanner Johnson and Roger Porter, are reviewed in John P. Burke, *The Institutional Presidency* (John Hopkins University Press, 1992), pp. 54–58.

23. For purposes of comparison, I limit my discussion to the secretaries of cabinet departments. Every president also appoints other officials to the cabinet, typically reflecting his interest in particular issues or as a signal that the agencies from which they come will be proposed for departmental status. Cabinet secretaries for Presidents Roosevelt through Clinton are listed by department in Michael Nelson, ed., *Guide to the Presidency,* vol. 2, 2nd ed. (Washington: Congressional Quarterly Press, 1996), pp. 1692–97.

24. See Hugh Heclo, "The In-and-Outer System: A Critical Analysis," in G. Calvin MacKenzie, ed., *The In-and-Outers: Presidential Appointees and Transitional Government in Washington* (Johns Hopkins University Press, 1987), p. 195.

25. Dean Rusk, Oral History Interview, Lyndon Baines Johnson Library, July 28, 1969, p. 7.

26. Nelson W. Polsby, "Presidential Cabinet Making: Lessons for the Political System," *Political Science Quarterly* 93 (Spring 1978): 15.

27. Jeffrey E. Cohen, *The Politics of the U.S. Cabinet: Representation in the Executive Branch, 1789–1984* (University of Pittsburgh Press, 1988), p. 169.

28. Richard E. Neustadt, *Presidential Power and the Modern Presidents: The Politics of Leadership from Roosevelt to Reagan* (New York: Free Press, 1990), pp. 222–23.

29. Robert J. Donovan, *Conflict and Crisis: The Presidency of Harry S Truman, 1945–1948* (New York: W. W. Norton, 1977), pp. 22–23.

30. Clifford, *Counsel to the President,* p. 77.

31. Ibid., p. 79. Patrick Anderson contrasted the conflicts in Roosevelt's and Truman's staffs, the former promoted by the president, the latter representing opposing factions battling it out. Patrick Anderson, *The President's Men* (New York: Doubleday, 1968), p. 87.

32. Clifford, *Counsel to the President,* p. 260.

33. Stephen J. Wayne, *The Legislative Presidency* (New York: Harper and Row, 1978), pp. 35–36.

34. G. Calvin Mackenzie, *The Politics of Presidential Appointments* (New York: Free Press, 1981), p. 11.

35. Ibid.

36. Hess, *Organizing the Presidency*, 2nd ed., p. 41.

37. Quoted in Kernell and Popkin, *Chief of Staff*, p. 67.

38. Dwight D. Eisenhower, *Mandate for Change: The White House Years, 1953–1956* (New York: Doubleday, 1963), p. 87.

39. Fred I. Greenstein, *The Hidden-Hand Presidency: Eisenhower as Leader* (New York: Basic Books, 1982), pp. 140, 141.

40. Louis W. Koenig, *The Chief Executive* (New York: Harcourt, Brace and World, 1964), p. 403.

41. Having Adams in charge did not mean that others were denied access. In an interview with Stephen Hess, one White House staff aide found Eisenhower "highly approachable."

42. Eisenhower, *Mandate for Change*, p. 134.

43. Patterson, *Ring of Power*, p. 29.

44. Eisenhower, *Mandate for Change*, p. 99 (emphasis added).

45. Wayne, *The Legislative Presidency*, p. 39.

46. Interview conducted by Stephen Hess (see note 12).

47. Neustadt is cited in Hess, *Organizing the Presidency*, 2nd ed., p. 75 (emphasis in original); Clifford, *Counsel to the President*, p. 329. Neustadt's memos are published in Charles O. Jones, ed., *Preparing to be President: The Memos of Richard E. Neustadt* (Washington: American Enterprise Institute Press, 2000); see in particular the essay on "Roosevelt's Approach to Staffing the White House," pp. 54–60.

48. Quoted in Kernell and Popkin, *Chief of Staff*, p. 76.

49. Arthur Schlesinger, *A Thousand Days: John F. Kennedy in the White House* (Houghton Mifflin, 1965), p. 687.

50. Theodore Sorensen, *Kennedy* (New York: Harper and Row, 1965), p. 258 (emphasis in original).

51. Lyndon B. Johnson, *The Vantage Point: Perspectives of the Presidency, 1963–1969* (New York: Holt, Rinehart and Winston, 1971), p. 19.

52. Wayne, *The Legislative Presidency*, p. 42.

53. Harry McPherson, Oral History Interview, Lyndon B. Johnson Library, December 19, 1968, p. 17.

54. Doris Kearns Goodwin, *Lyndon B. Johnson and the American Dream* (New York: Harper and Row, 1976), pp. 174–75.

55. See ibid., p. 173.

56. Hess, *Organizing the Presidency*, 2nd ed., p. 103.

57. Quoted in Schlesinger, *A Thousand Days*, p. 127.

58. Eric F. Goldman, *The Tragedy of Lyndon Johnson* (New York: Alfred A. Knopf, 1969), p. 264.

59. Kearns Goodwin, *Lyndon Johnson and the American Dream*, p. 253.

60. Hess, *Organizing the Presidency*, 2nd ed., pp. 104–05.

61. Kernell and Popkin, *Chief of Staff*, p. 46.

62. Hess, *Organizing the Presidency*, 2nd ed., pp. 106, 113.

63. H. R. Haldeman (with Joseph DiMona), *The Ends of Power* (New York: Times Books, 1978), p. 58.

64. Interview with former Nixon White House staff aide, conducted by Stephen Hess.

65. Haldeman, *Ends of Power*, p. 52.

66. John Ehrlichman, *Witness to Power: The Nixon Years* (New York: Simon and Schuster, 1982), p. 78.

67. Author's notes from a presentation by Ehrlichman at the White Burkett Miller Center, University of Virginia, November 20, 1984.

68. Haldeman, *Ends of Power*, pp. 59, 61.

69. Gerald R. Ford, *A Time to Heal: The Autobiography of Gerald R. Ford* (New York: Harper and Row, 1979), p. 148.

70. Mark J. Rozell, *The Press and the Ford Presidency* (University of Michigan Press, 1992), p. 12.

71. Ford, *A Time to Heal*, p. 24.

72. Rumsfeld, quoted in Kernell and Popkin, *Chief of Staff*, p. 74.

73. Henry Kissinger, *Years of Upheaval* (Boston: Little, Brown, 1982), p. 435.

74. Ehrlichman, *Witness to Power*, p. 110.

75. Richard M. Nixon, *RN: The Memoirs of Richard Nixon*, vol. 1 (New York: Warner Books, 1978), p. 418.

76. Ibid.

77. Ehrlichman, *Witness to Power*, p. 88 (emphasis in original).

78. Ibid., p. 111. See also ibid., pp. 92–101, 104–10, for accounts of the earlier removal of Walter Hickel, secretary of the interior, and George Romney, secretary of housing and urban development.

79. Stephen E. Ambrose, *Nixon: Ruin and Recovery, 1973–1990* (New York: Simon and Schuster, 1991), p. 14.

80. Henry Kissinger, *The White House Years* (Boston: Little, Brown, 1979), pp. 1406–07.

81. Ford, *A Time to Heal*, p. 126.

82. Philip W. Buchen, "Reflections on a Politician's President," in Kenneth W. Thompson, ed., *Portraits of American Presidents: The Ford Presidency* (University Press of America, 1988), p. 29.

83. Ibid., p. 32.

84. Richard B. Cheney, "Forming and Managing an Administration," in Thompson, *Portraits of American Presidents: The Ford Presidency*, p. 68.

85. The volume of lawmaking is shown by David R. Mayhew, *Divided We Govern: Party Control, Lawmaking, and Investigations, 1946–1990* (Yale University Press, 1991), pp. 61–67.

86. James P. Pfiffner, *The Strategic Presidency: Hitting the Ground Running*, 2nd ed. (University Press of Kansas, 1996), p. 24.

87. Kernell and Popkin, *Chief of Staff,* pp. 70, 71.

88. Hess, *Organizing the Presidency,* 2nd ed., 254.

89. Jimmy Carter, *Keeping Faith: Memoirs of a President* (New York: Bantam Books, 1982), pp. 40, 41, 42.

90. Finley Lewis, *Mondale: Portrait of an American Politician* (New York: Harper and Row, 1980), p. 239.

91. Erwin C. Hargrove, *Jimmy Carter as President: Leadership and the Politics of the Public Good* (Louisiana State University Press, 1988), pp. 23–24.

92. Ibid., p. 26.

93. Haynes Johnson, *In the Absence of Power: Governing America* (New York: Viking Press, 1980), pp. 154–55.

94. John H. Kessel, "The Structure of the Carter White House," *American Journal of Political Science* 27 (August 1983): 460.

95. Charles O. Jones, *The Trusteeship Presidency: Jimmy Carter and the United States Congress* (Louisiana State University Press, 1988), pp. 7–8 (emphasis in the original).

96. Hargrove, *Jimmy Carter as President,* p. 31.

97. Carter, *Keeping Faith,* p. 115.

98. Ibid., p. 117.

99. Joseph A. Califano Jr., *Governing America: An Insider's Report from the White House and Cabinet* (New York: Simon and Schuster, 1981), pp. 430–31.

100. Kessel, "Structure of the Carter White House," p. 461.

101. Hargrove, *Jimmy Carter as President,* p. 32.

102. Carter, *Keeping Faith,* p. 58.

103. Hess, *Organizing the Presidency,* 2nd ed., p. 156.

104. Califano, *Governing America,* pp. 429–30.

105. Neustadt, *Presidential Power,* 287.

106. Ronald Reagan, *An American Life: The Autobiography* (New York: Simon and Schuster, 1990), pp. 222, 225.

107. Lou Cannon, *President Reagan: The Role of a Lifetime* (New York: Simon and Schuster, 1991), p. 70.

108. Ibid., pp. 70, 71.

109. David Gergen, *Eyewitness to Power: The Essence of Leadership* (New York: Simon and Schuster, 2000), p. 181.

110. Colin Campbell, *Managing the Presidency: Carter, Reagan, and the Search for Executive Harmony* (University of Pittsburgh Press, 1986), pp, 94, 101–03.

111. Donald T. Regan, *For the Record: From Wall Street to Washington* (New York: Harcourt Brace Jovanovich, 1988), pp. 223–29, quote on p. 227; also see Cannon, *President Reagan,* pp. 558–59.

112. Cannon, *President Reagan,* p. 564.

113. *Report of the President's Special Review Board,* February 27, 1987, p. IV-11.

114. Reagan, *An American Life,* pp. 536–37 (emphasis in orginal).

115. The changeover was abrupt, as discussed by Howard Baker in Sullivan, *The Nerve Center,* p. 49. Baker had intended to get his affairs in order over the weekend but was called to the White House immediately because "Nobody's in charge."

116. Hess, *Organizing the Presidency,* 2nd ed., p. 151.

117. Cannon, *President Reagan,* p. 733.

118. Gergen, *Eyewitness to Power,* p. 181.

119. Neustadt, *Presidential Power,* p. 312.

120. Walter Dean Burnham, "The Legacy of George Bush: Travails of an Understudy," in Gerald M. Pomper, ed., *The Election of 1992: Reports and Interpretations* (Chatham, N.J.: Chatham House, 1993), p. 2.

121. Michael Duffy and Dan Goodgame, *Marching in Place: The Status Quo Presidency of George Bush* (New York: Simon and Schuster, 1992), pp. 112, 116–17.

122. Stephen Hess, *Organizing the Presidency,* 3rd ed. (Brookings, 2002), p. 153.

123. For details, see ibid., p. 154.

124. For other details of the Baker shift and an analysis of reelection campaigns more generally, see Kathryn Dunn Tenpas, *Presidents as Candidates: Inside the White House for the Presidential Campaign* (New York: Garland Press, 1997), especially pp. 114–15.

125. Cannon, *President Reagan,* p. 183.

126. William Earl Walker and Michael R. Reopel, "Strategies for Governance: Transition and Domestic Policymaking in the Reagan Administration," *Presidential Studies Quarterly* 16 (Fall 1986): 734.

127. Martin Anderson, *Revolution* (New York: Harcourt Brace Jovanovich, 1988), pp. 197–99.

128. Pfiffner, *The Strategic Presidency,* p. 61.

129. Peter M. Benda and Charles Levine, "Reagan and the Bureaucracy: The Bequest, the Promise, and the Legacy," in Charles O. Jones, ed., *The Reagan Legacy: Promise and Performance* (Chatham, N.J.: Chatham House, 1988), p. 108.

130. John H. Kessel, "The Structure of the Reagan White House," *American Journal of Political Science* 28 (1984): 246.

131. Anderson, *Revolution,* p. 226.

132. James P. Pfiffner, "Establishing the Bush Presidency," *Public Administration Review* 50 (January–February 1990): 68.

133. Reprinted in Jones, *Preparing to be President,* p. 125. The advice was given to Kennedy in 1960 in a more elaborate memo, also reprinted in ibid., pp. 24–26.

134. James Bennet, "Clinton's New Year's Eve: Looking Back," *New York Times,* January 3, 1997, p. A20.

135. Hess, *Organizing the Presidency,* 3rd. ed., p. 153.

136. Bill Clinton, *My Life* (New York: Alfred A. Knopf, 2004), p. 454.

137. Thomas Preston *The President and His Inner Circle: Leadership Style and the Advisory Process in Foreign Affairs* (Columbia University Press, 2001), p. 224.

138. Shirley Anne Warshaw, *Powersharing: White House–Cabinet Relations in the Modern Presidency* (State University of New York Press, 1996), p. 210.

139. For details, see Bob Woodward, *The Agenda: Inside the Clinton White House* (New York: Simon and Schuster, 1994).

140. Gergen, *Eyewitness to Power,* p. 264.

141. Clinton, *My Life,* p. 521.

142. Hess, *Organizing the Presidency,* 3rd ed., p. 158; Preston, *The President and His Inner Circle,* p. 225.

143. Quoted in Charles O. Jones, *Passages to the Presidency: From Campaigning to Governing* (Brookings, 1998), p. 91.

144. Clinton, *My Life,* p. 454.

145. David Frum, *The Right Man: The Surprise Presidency of George W. Bush* (New York: Random House, 2003), pp. 16, 18, 20.

146. Quoted in Mike Allen, "Optimistic Bush Meets with Potential Cabinet," *Washington Post,* November 11, 2000, p. A15.

147. Donald F. Kettl, *Team Bush: Leadership Lessons from the Bush White House* (New York: McGraw-Hill, 2003), p. 36.

148. Ibid., p. 41.

149. Karen M. Hult, "The Bush White House in Comparative Perspective," in Fred I. Greenstein, ed., *The George W. Bush Presidency: An Early Assessment* (Johns Hopkins University Press, 2003), pp. 76-77.

150. The Neustadt memos are published in Jones, *Preparing to be President.*

151. For details of the Bush 43 transition, see the following: Sullivan, *The Nerve Center,* pp. 125–66; Martha Joynt Kumar and Terry Sullivan, eds., *The White House World: Transitions, Organizations, and Office Operations* (Texas A & M University Press, 2003); and Charles O. Jones, "The Presidential Transition into a Fifty-Fifty Government," in Byron E. Shafer, ed., *The State of American Politics* (Lanham, Md.: Rowman and Littlefield, 2002), pp. 93–124.

152. Quoted in Bob Woodward, *Bush at War* (New York: Simon and Schuster, 2002), pp. 256, 259.

153. Quoted in Hugh Heclo, "The Political Ethos of George W. Bush," in Greenstein, *The George W. Bush Presidency,* p. 17.

154. As cited in Dana Milbank, "Bush Seeks to Rule the Bureaucracy," *Washington Post,* November 22, 2004, p. A4.

155. Tenpas, *Presidents and Candidates,* p. 116.

156. Bradley Patterson has codified and described many of these positions and units in *The Ring of Power.*

Notes to Chapter 4

1. George C. Edwards III, *Presidential Approval: A Sourcebook* (Johns Hopkins University Press, 1990), p. 1.

2. For an excellent review and analysis, see Robert M. Eisinger, *The Evolution of Presidential Polling* (Cambridge University Press, 2003).

3. George C. Edwards III, *On Deaf Ears: The Limits of the Bully Pulpit* (Yale University Press, 2003), p. 241.

4. Unless otherwise noted, the approval ratings referenced in this chapter are from polls conducted by the Gallup Organization.

5. "That Was the Easy Part," *The Economist,* November 12, 1988, p. 9.

6. David Frum, *The Right Man: The Surprising Presidency of George W. Bush* (Random House, 2003), pp. 9-10.

7. Haynes Johnson, "A Nation's Sense of Failure Swept Away by Victory," *Washington Post,* March 1, 1991, p. A2.

8. Jeffrey H. Birnbaum, "Politics and Policy: Bush's Surging Across-the-Board Popularity May Translate into Greater 'Clout' in Congress," *Wall Street Journal,* March 4, 1991, p. A10.

9. Mark J. Rozell, *The Press and the Ford Presidency* (University of Michigan Press, 1992), p. 209.

10. Quoted in Birnbaum, "Politics and Policy," p. A10.

11. Quoted in Richard L. Berke, "Democrats to President: Focus on Issues at Home," *New York Times,* March 5, 1991, p. A18.

12. John C. Fortier and Norman J. Ornstein, "President Bush: Legislative Strategist," in Fred I. Greenstein, ed., *The George W. Bush Presidency: An Early Assessment* (Johns Hopkins University Press, 2003), pp. 156–60.

13. Charles O. Jones, "Capitalizing on Position in the Perfect Tie," in Greenstein, *The George W. Bush Presidency,* p. 184.

14. Fortier and Ornstein, "President Bush," p. 160.

15. Janet Hook, "Bush Inspired Frail Support for First Year President," *Congressional Quarterly Weekly Report,* December 30, 1989, p. 3543.

16. "Bush Calls on Postwar Congress for Reform and Renewal," *Congressional Quarterly Weekly Report,* March 9, 1991, p. 624.

17. Quoted in Chuck Alston, "Bush's High Public Standing Held Little Sway on Hill," *Congressional Quarterly Weekly Report,* December 28, 1991, p. 3751.

18. Charles O. Jones, "Richard E. Neustadt: Public Servant as Scholar," *Annual Review of Political Science* 6 (2003): 17.

19. James W. Ceaser, "The Reagan Presidency and American Public Opinion," in Charles O. Jones, ed., *The Reagan Legacy: Promise and Performance* (Chatham, N.J.: Chatham House, 1988), p. 207.

20. Richard A. Brody, *Assessing the President: The Media, Elite Opinion, and Public Support* (Stanford University Press, 1991), p. 19.

21. Norman J. Ornstein and Thomas E. Mann, "The Permanent Campaign and the Future of American Democracy," in Norman J. Ornstein and Thomas E. Mann, eds., *The Permanent Campaign and Its Future* (Washington: American Enterprise Institute and Brookings, 2000), p. 219.

22. Quoted in Rozell, *The Press and the Presidency,* p. 220.

23. Richard A. Brody and Benjamin I Page, "The Impact of Events on Presidential Popularity: The Johnson and Nixon Administrations," in Aaron Wildavsky, ed., *Perspectives on the Presidency* (Boston: Little, Brown, 1975), p. 146.

24. Calculated from poll data provided by the Polling Report, at www. pollingreport.com.

25. Charles O. Jones, *Clinton and Congress, 1993–1996: Risk, Restoration, and Reelection* (University of Oklahoma Press, 1999), pp. 87–93.

26. Corey Cook, "The Permanence of the 'Permanent Campaign': George W. Bush's Public Presidency," *Presidential Studies Quarterly* 32 (December 2002): 762.

27. As reported in Bob Woodward, *The Agenda: Inside the Clinton White House* (New York: Simon and Schuster, 1994), pp. 248, 141.

28. Charles W. Ostrom Jr. and Dennis M. Simon, "Promise and Performance: A Dynamic Model of Presidential Popularity," *American Political Science Review* 79 (June 1985): 356.

29. Douglas Rivers and Nancy L. Rose, "Passing the President's Program: Public Opinion and Presidential Influence in Congress," *American Journal of Political Science* 29 (May 1985): 187.

30. George C. Edwards, III, *At the Margins: Presidential Leadership of Congress* (Yale University Press, 1989), p. 125.

31. Personal interview, March 27, 1991.

32. Harvey G. Zeidenstein, "Varying Relationships between Presidents' Popularity and Their Legislative Success: A Futile Search for Patterns," *Presidential Studies Quarterly* 13 (Fall 1983): 547.

33. Harvey G. Zeidenstein, "Presidents' Popularity and Their Wins and Losses on Major Issues in Congress: Does One Have Greater Influence over the Other?" *Presidential Studies Quarterly* 15 (Spring 1985): 287.

34. Edwards, *At the Margins*, p. 114.

35. Jon R. Bond and Richard Fleisher, *The President in the Legislative Arena* (University of Chicago Press, 1990), p. 194.

36. Samuel Kernell, *Going Public: New Strategies of Presidential Leadership* (Washington: Congressional Quarterly Press, 1986), pp. 1, 98.

37. Ibid., pp. 3–4, 37.

38. Lyndon B. Johnson, *The Vantage Point: Perspectives of the Presidency, 1963–1969* (New York: Holt, Rinehart and Winston, 1971), p. 450.

39. Edwards, *On Deaf Ears*.

40. Ibid., chap. 10.

41. John E. Mueller, "Presidential Popularity from Truman to Johnson," *American Political Science Review* 64 (March 1970): 21.

42. Samuel Kernell, "Explaining Presidential Popularity," *American Political Science Review* 72 (June 1978): 520, 521.

43. Barbara Hinckley, *The Symbolic Presidency: How Presidents Portray Themselves* (New York: Routledge, 1990), chap. 1; and Lyn Ragsdale, "The Politics of Presidential Speechmaking, 1949-1980," *American Political Science Review* 78 (December 1984): 971–84.

44. See Edwards, *Presidential Approval*, table 1.2, p. 119.

45. Dean Keith Simonton, *Why Presidents Succeed: A Political Psychology of Leadership* (Yale University Press, 1987), pp. 91–92.

46. Harry S. Truman, *Memoirs: Years of Trial and Hope* (New York: Doubleday, 1956), p. 196.

47. Dick Morris, *Behind the Oval Office: Winning the Presidency in the Nineties* (New York: Random House, 1997), pp. 143, 338.

48. Brody, *Assessing the President*, p. 44.

49. Unless otherwise noted, I rely on David R. Mayhew's count of major legislation in the postwar period in *Divided We Govern: Party Control, Lawmaking, and Investigations, 1946–1990* (Yale University Press, 1991), pp. 52–73, with updates available at pantheon.yale.edu/~dmayhew/.

50. Richard E. Neustadt, *Presidential Power: The Politics of Leadership* (New York: Wiley, 1960), chap. 5.

51. James L. Sundquist, *Politics and Policy: The Eisenhower, Kennedy, and Johnson Years* (Brookings, 1968), p. 470.

52. Paul C. Light, *The President's Agenda: Domestic Policy Choices from Kennedy to Carter* (Johns Hopkins University Press, 1982), pp. 42, 45.

53. Mayhew, *Divided We Govern*, pp. 89–90.

54. Ceaser, "The Reagan Presidency," p. 198.

55. Thomas P. O'Neill Jr. (with William Novak), *Man of the House: The Life and Political Memoirs of Speaker Tip O'Neill* (New York: Random House, 1987), p. 344.

56. Quoted in Gail Gregg, "Reagan Proposes Dramatic Role in Federal Role," *Congressional Quarterly Weekly Report,* March 14, 1981, p. 445.

57. As reported in "Congress's Ratings at an All-Time Low," *American Enterprise* 3 (November–December 1992): 86–87.

58. David W. Brady, John F. Cogan, and Douglas Rivers, "How the Republicans Captured the House: An Assessment of the 1994 Midterm Elections" (Hoover Institution, Stanford University, 1995), p. 19.

59. Quoted in Michael Kelly, "You Ain't Seen Nothing Yet," *New Yorker,* April 24, 1995, p. 41.

60. Gary C. Jacobson, "The Bush Presidency and the American Electorate," in Greenstein, *The George W. Bush Presidency.*

Notes to Chapter 5

1. Raymond E. Wolfinger, "Dealignment, Realignment, and Mandates in the 1984 Election," in Austin Ranney, ed., *The American Elections of 1984* (Washington: American Enterprise Institute, 1985), p. 293.

2. Henry Jones Ford, *Representative Government* (New York: Henry Holt, 1924), p. 271.

3. Robert A. Dahl, *A Preface to Democratic Theory* (University of Chicago Press, 1956), pp. 124, 125, 126, 130.

4. Robert A. Dahl, "Myth of the Presidential Mandate," *Political Science Quarterly* 105 (Fall 1990): 358–59.

5. Ibid., p. 360.

6. Woodrow Wilson, *Constitutional Government in the United States* (Columbia University Press, 1908), pp. 70, 67–68.

7. Ibid., pp. 70, 68.

8. Quoted in Donald Smith, "Transcript of Carter's Interview," *Congressional Quarterly Weekly Report,* September 4, 1976, pp. 2380–83.

9. Jimmy Carter, *Keeping Faith: Memoirs of a President* (New York: Bantam Books, 1982), p. 88.

10. Dahl, "Myth of the Presidential Mandate," p. 363.

11. Ibid., p. 365.

12. Personal interview, July 17, 1989.

13. Dahl, "Myth of the Presidential Mandate," pp. 365–66.

14. Frank R. Baumgartner and Bryan D. Jones, *Agendas and Instability in American Politics* (University of Chicago Press, 1993), p. 4.

15. Chalmers M. Roberts, "Goldwater Takes Five of Southern States, Witholds Concession," *Washington Post,* November 4, 1964, pp. A1, A12; "The Vote: Mandate, Hard and Clear," *Time,* November 4, 1964, p. 3.

16. Arthur Krock, "In the Nation: Two Questions in the Wake of the Landslide," *New York Times,* November 5, 1964, p. 44; "The Johnson Landslide," *New York Times,* November 4, 1964, p. 38; and "The Voters' Answer," *Washington Post,* November 4, 1965, p. A20.

17. "Reagan Coast-to-Coast," *Time,* November 17, 1980, p. 24.

18. James Reston, "Reagan's Startling Victory," *New York Times,* November 5, 1980, p. 31.

19. David Broder, "A Sharp Right Turn," *Washington Post,* November 6, 1980, p. A1; and "Tidal Wave," *Washington Post,* November 6, 1980, p. A18.

20. Arthur Krock, "Personal Victory," *New York Times,* November 6, 1952, p. 1; *Time,* November 10, 1952, p. 11; "Landslide Sweeps Eisenhower into the White House," and "Significance: It Was Time for a Change," *Newsweek,* November 10, 1952, pp. 3, 7. The phrase "a mandate for change" is from "The Will of the People," *Time,* November 17, 1952, p. 25.

21. Walter Lippmann, "A Mighty Majority," *Washinton Post,* November 6, 1952, p. 11.

22. Paul C. Light, *The President's Agenda: Domestic Policy Choice from Kennedy to Carter* (Johns Hopkins University Press, 1982), p. 218.

23. "The Landslide," *Newsweek,* November 12, 1956, p. 62; Dole is quoted in Haynes Johnson, "Democrats Battered but Strong," *Washington Post,* November 9, 1972, p. A1; and Haynes Johnson, "Voters Send Up Caution Flags," *Washington Post,* November 8, 1984, p. A48.

24. As cited in Marjorie Randon Hershey, "The Congressional Election," in Gerald M. Pomper, ed., *The Elections of 1996* (Chatham, N.J.: Chatham House, 1997), p. 233.

25. "The Winner's Burden," *Washington Post,* November 7, 1956, p. A22.

26. Arthur Krock, "The Unmandate," *New York Times,* November 10, 1972, p. 39; and ". . . an Empty Landslide," *New York Times,* November 9, 1972, p. 46.

27. *Time,* November 19, 1984, p. 39.

28. David Broder, "Victory Shows Broad Appeal of President," *Washington Post,* November 7, 1984, p. A1; and "The Mandate, the Mandate," *New York Times,* November 8, 1984, p. A30.

29. Gerald M. Pomper, "The Presidential Election," in *The Elections of 1996,* p. 200.

30. David Broder, "Voters Again Opt for a Divided Government," *Washington Post,* November 9, 1988, p. 1; David Broder and Paul Taylor, "Once Again Democrats Debate about Why They Lost," *Washington Post,* November 10, 1988, p. 1; Larry Martz, "The Tough Task Ahead," *Newsweek,* November 21, 1988, p. 9; and "A Mandate to Make Sense," *New York Times,* November 11, 1988, p. A30.

31. Arthur Krock, "President Can Claim Big National Triumph," *New York Times,* November 7, 1948, p. E3.

32. Raymond Moley, "The Road Ahead," *Newsweek,* November 8, 1948, p. 8.

33. Sources are, respectively, James M. Naughton, "A Victory but Not a Mandate," *New York Times,* November 4, 1976, p. 21; "The President's Election," *New York Times,* November 10, 1960, p. 46; and "President-Elect Richard M. Nixon," *Washington Post,* November 7, 1968, p. A20.

34. Walter Lippmann, "On the Day After," *Washington Post,* November 10, 1960, p. A25.

35. David Broder, "Democratic Edge in the House, Senate Trimmed Slightly," *Washington Post,* November 7, 1968, pp. A1, A6.

36. "The Presidency. . . ." *Washington Post,* November 5, 1992, p. A22.

37. Michael Kramer, "What He Will Do," *Time,* November 16, 1992 (emphasis in original).

38. Helen Dewar, "On Hill, Clinton Will Find Neither Gridlock Nor Compliance," *Washington Post,* November 5, 1992, p. A25.

39. Robert J. Samuelson, "The Great Political Tune-Out," *Washington Post,* November 30, 2000, p. A37.

40. James W. Ceaser and Andrew E. Busch, *The Perfect Tie: The True Story of the 2000 Presidential Election* (Lanham, Md.: Rowman and Littlefield, 2001), p. 20.

41. Nancy Gibb, "In Victory's Glow," *Time,* November 15, 2004, p. 34.

42. Charles Krauthammer, "Using All of a Mandate," and E.J. Dionne Jr., ". . . He Did Not Get," both in *Washington Post,* November 5, 2004, p. A25.

43. "Bush Gets Mandate to Be Strong Abroad," *Financial Times,* November 4, 2004, p. 12.

44. "Mr. Bush's Victory," *Washington Post,* November 4, 2004, p. A24.

45. Quoted in Mike Allen, "Confident Bush Vows to Move Aggressively," *Washington Post,* November 5, 2004, p. A1.

46. "The Republican Tide," *New York Times,* November 9, 1966, p. 38.

47. Bruce I. Oppenheimer, James A. Stimson, and Richard W. Waterman, "Interpreting U. S. Congressional Elections: The Exposure Thesis," *Legislative Studies Quarterly* 11 (May 1986): 227, 243.

48. *New York Times,* November 9, 1950, p. E32; William S. White, "Rayburn to Be Speaker: No Clear Mandate Seen in Results," *New York Times,* November 4, 1954, p. A1.

49. "Tuesday's 'Mandates': For the President . . . " *Washington Post,* November 7, 1974, p. A30.

50. James L. Sundquist, *Politics and Policy: The Eisenhower, Kennedy, and Johnson Years* (Brookings, 1968), p. 6.

51. Neustadt, *Presidential Power*, p. 5.

52. Bert A. Rockman, *The Leadership Question: The Presidency and the American System* (Westport, Conn.: Praeger, 1984), p. 185.

53. Erwin C. Hargrove and Michael Nelson, *President, Politics, and Policy* (Johns Hopkins University Press, 1984), pp. 196, 197, 198.

54. Baumgartner and Jones, *Agendas and Instability, p. 237.*

55. Light, *The President's Agenda*, p. 10.

56. Neustadt, *Presidential Power*, p. 8.

57. John W. Kingdon, *Agendas, Alternatives, and Public Policies* (Boston: Little, Brown, 1984), p. 25.

58. Baumgartner and Jones, *Agendas and Instability*, p. 241.

59. Ibid., p. 250.

60. Kingdon, *Agendas, Alternatives, and Public Policies*, pp. 3–4.

61. Baumgartner and Jones, *Agendas and Instability*, p. 239.

62. For details, see Charles O. Jones, *Clinton and Congress 1993–1996: Risk, Restoration, and Reelection* (University of Oklahoma Press, 1999), chap. 4.

63. Dwight D. Eisenhower, "State of the Union Message," *Public Papers of the Presidents of the United States; Dwight D. Eisenhower, 1960–61* (Government Printing Office, 1961), p. 930.

64. Sundquist, *Politics and Policy*, p. 507.

65. Theodore Sorensen, *Kennedy* (New York: Harper and Row, 1965), p. 340.

66. A. James Reichley, *Conservatives in an Age of Change: The Nixon and Ford Administrations* (Brookings, 1981), p. 325.

67. Congressional Quarterly, *Congress and the Nation, 1973–1976*, vol. 4 (Washington, 1977), p. 6.

68. Congressional Quarterly, *Congress and the Nation, 1977–1980*, vol. 5 (Washington, 1981), p. 3.

69. Ryan J. Barilleaux and Mark J. Rozell, *Power and Prudence: The Presidency of George H. W. Bush* (Texas A & M University Press, 2004), chap. 2.

70. For details, see ibid., pp. 33–35.

71. Beth Donovan and Congressional Quarterly staff, "Partisanship, Purse Strings Hobbled the 102nd," *Congressional Quarterly Weekly Report*, October 31, 1992, p. 3451.

72. James L. Sundquist, ed., *Beyond Gridlock? Prospects for Governance in the Clinton Years—and After* (Brookings, 1993), p. 25.

73. Ibid., p. 19.

74. Gerald M. Pomper, "The Presidential Election," in Pomper, ed., *The Election of 1992* (Chatham, N.J.: Chatham House, 1993), p. 146.

75. See Nicol C. Rae and Colton C. Campbell, *Impeaching Clinton: Partisan Strife on Capitol Hill* (University Press of Kansas, 2004). A broader treatment of the effects of character on leadership that examines several presidents is James P. Pfiffner, *The Character Factor: How We Judge America's Presidents* (Texas A & M University Press, 2004).

Notes to Chapter 6

1. John B. Bader, "The 86th and 100th Congresses: Changing Goals and a New Definition of Success in Presidential Relations," paper prepared for the annual meeting of the American Political Science Association, 1992. See also John B. Bader, *Taking the Initiative: Leadership Agendas in Congress and the "Contract with America"* (Georgetown University Press, 1996).

2. Charles O. Jones, "A Way of Life and Law," *American Political Science Review* 89 (March 1995): 1.

3. J. Willard Hurst, *The Growth of American Law: The Lawmakers* (Boston: Little, Brown, 1950), pp. 11, 13.

4. T. V. Smith, *The Legislative Way of Life* (University of Chicago Press, 1940), pp. 29, 72, 73, 93.

5. Jeremy Waldron, *Law and Disagreement* (Oxford University Press, 1999), p. 16.

6. A portion of what follows is a revision of the argument in Jones, "A Way of Life and Law," pp. 4–8.

7. Elijah Jordan, *Theory of Legislation: An Essay on the Dynamics of Public Mind* (University of Chicago Press, 1930), p. 313.

8. Quoted in Dana Priest, "Where Health Care Reform Effort Failed," *Washington Post*, August 27, 1994.

9. Smith, *The Legislative Way of Life,* p. 13.

10. Hurst, *The Growth of American Law,* pp. 23–24, 25, 26.

11. Keith Krehbiel, *Information and Legislative Organization* (University of Chicago Press, 1991), pp. 71, 76.

12. Jordan, *Theory of Legislation,* p. 153.

13. Ibid., pp. 346, 349.

14. Woodrow Wilson, *Congressional Government: A Study in American Politics* (Boston: Houghton Mifflin, 1885), pp. 216, 219.

15. See Sarah A. Binder, *Stalemate: Causes and Consequences of Legislative Gridlock* (Brookings, 2003), pp. 70–71. See also her *Minority Rights, Majority Rule: Partisanship and the Development of Congress* (Cambridge University Press, 1997), pp. 195–201.

16. Jordan, *Theory of Legislation,* p. 314.

17. Steven A. Shull, *Domestic Policy Formation: Presidential-Congressional Partnership?* (Westport, Conn.: Greenwood Press, 1983), chap. 1.

18. Jon R. Bond and Richard Fleisher, *The President in the Legislative Arena* (University of Chicago Press, 1990), p. x.

19. Recent studies include Kenneth R. Mayer, *With the Stroke of a Pen: Executive Orders and Presidential Power* (Princeton University Press, 2001); and William G. Howell, *Power without Persuasion: The Politics of Direct Presidential Action* (Princeton University Press, 2003).

20. Lawrence H. Chamberlain, *The President, Congress and Legislation* (Columbia University Press, 1946).

21. Ibid., p. 454.

22. Ibid., p. 453.

23. Ibid., p. 463.

24. Quotes are, respectively, from Arthur M. Schlesinger Jr., *The Imperial Presidency* (Boston: Houghton Mifflin, 1973); and James MacGregor Burns, *Presidential Government: The Crucible of Leadership* (Boston: Houghton Mifflin, 1965).

25. Samuel P. Huntington, "Congressional Responses in the Twentieth Century," in David B. Truman, ed., *The Congress and America's Future* (New Jersey: Prentice-Hall, 1965), pp. 7, 8.

26. Ronald C. Moe and Steven C. Teel, "Congress as Policy Maker: A Necessary Reappraisal," *Political Science Quarterly* 85 (September 1970): 467–68, 469.

27. R. Douglas Arnold, *The Logic of Congressional Action* (Yale University Press, 1990), p. 269.

28. *Congressional Quarterly Almanac* (Washington: Congressional Quarterly Press, 1989), p. 28b.

29. George C. Edwards III, *At the Margins: Presidential Leadership of Congress* (Yale University Press, 1989), chap. 2; Mark A. Peterson, *Legislating Together: The White House and Capitol Hill from Eisenhower to Reagan* (Harvard University Press, 1990), app. B; and Bond and Fleisher, *President in the Legislative Arena*, pp. 60–66.

30. Bond and Fleisher, *President in the Legislative Arena*, p. 64.

31. W. H. Lawrence, "President Backs U.S. Court Order," *New York Times*, September 10, 1957, p. 29.

32. Edwards, *At the Margins*, p. 20.

33. Ibid., p. 25.

34. Bond and Fleisher, *President in the Legislative Arena*, pp. 71–80.

35. Peterson, *Legislating Together*, 151.

36. Edwards, *At the Margins*, pp. 223, 217; Bond and Fleisher, *President in the Legislative Arena*, pp. 225–29.

37. Woodrow Wilson, *Constitutional Government in the United States* (Columbia University Press, 1911), p. 60.

38. James L. Sundquist, "Needed: A Political Theory for the New Era of Coalition Government," *Political Science Quarterly* 103 (Winter 1988–89), pp. 629–30.

39. James MacGregor Burns, *Congress on Trial: The Legislative Process and the Administrative State* (Staten Island, N.Y.: Gordian Press, 1966), p. 45, and Burns, "U.S., Model for Eastern Europe?" *New York Times*, February 8, 1990, p. A29.

40. James MacGregor Burns, *The Deadlock of Democracy: Four Party Politics in America* (New Jersey: Prentice-Hall, 1963).

41. David R. Mayhew, *Divided We Govern: Party Control, Lawmaking, and Investigations, 1946–90* (Yale University Press, 1991), p. 4.

42. Ibid., p. 35.

43. Examples include Binder, *Stalemate*; George C. Edwards III, Andrew Barrett, and Jeffrey Peake, "The Legislative Impact of Divided Government: What Failed to Pass in Congress?" *American Journal of Political Science* 41 (May 1997): pp. 545–63; William Howell, Scott Adler, Charles Cameron, and Charles Riemann, "Divided Gov-

ernment and the Legislative Production of Congress," *Legislative Studies Quarterly* 25 (May 2000): pp. 285–312.

44. Mayhew, *Divided We Govern,* p. 122.

45. Chamberlain, *President, Congress, and Legislation,* p. 453; John W. Kingdon, *Agendas, Alternatives, and Public Policies* (Boston: Little, Brown, 1984), p. 210; Richard E. Neustadt, *Presidential Power: The Politics of Leadership* (New York: Wiley, 1960), p. 3; Baker quoted in Hedrick Smith, *The Power Game: How Washington Works* (New York: Random House, 1988), p. 652; and Richard Rose, *The Postmodern Presidency: The White House Meets the World* (Chatham, N.J.: Chatham House, 1991), pp. 175–76.

46. Quoted in Neil MacNeil, *Dirksen: Portrait of a Public Man* (New York: World Publishing, 1970), p. 238.

47. Personal interview, March 26, 1991.

48. Richard F. Fenno Jr., *Home Style: House Members in Their Districts* (Boston: Little, Brown, 1978), pp. 249–57.

49. Mayhew, *Divided We Govern,* p. 198.

50. Neustadt, *Presidential Power,* p. 33.

Notes to Chapter 7

1. David R. Mayhew, *Divided We Govern: Party Control, Lawmaking, and Investigations, 1945–1990* (Yale University Press, 1991).

2. These types are close to those relied on by Lawrence H. Chamberlain, *The President, Congress, and Legislation* (Columbia University Press, 1946), pp. 450–52. Chamberlain also has a category "pressure group preponderant" that I do not employ here.

3. William G. Howell, *Power without Persuasion: The Politics of Direct Presidential Action* (Princeton University Press, 2003); and Kenneth R. Mayer, *With the Stroke of a Pen: Executive Orders and Presidential Power* (Princeton University Press, 2001).

4. David McCullough, *Truman* (New York: Simon and Schuster, 1992), pp. 561, 562.

5. Ibid., p. 565.

6. Harold F. Gosnell, *Truman's Crises: A Political Biography of Harry S. Truman* (Westport, Conn.: Greenwood Press, 1980), pp. 354, 356.

7. Harry S. Truman, *Memoirs: Years of Trial and Hope* (New York: Doubleday, 1956), p. 119.

8. Dwight D. Eisenhower, *Mandate for Change, 1953–1956* (New York: Doubleday, 1963), p. 548.

9. Martha Derthick and Paul J. Quirk, *The Politics of Deregulation* (Brookings, 1985), pp. 118, 121, 123.

10. As reported in Ivor P. Morgan, "Toward Deregulation," in John R. Meyer and Clinton V. Oster, eds., *Airline Deregulation: The Early Experience* (Boston: Auburn House, 1981), p. 51.

11. Gilbert Y. Steiner, *The State of Welfare* (Brookings, 1971), p. 203.

12. Randall L. Ripley, "Legislative Bargaining and the Food Stamp Act, 1964," in Frederic N. Cleaveland, ed., *Congress and Urban Problems* (Brookings, 1969), p. 295.

13. Steiner, *The State of Welfare*, p. 209.

14. Frank J. Munger and Richard F. Fenno Jr., *National Politics and Federal Aid to Education* (Syracuse University Press, 1962), p. 19.

15. Hugh Douglas Price, "Race, Religion, and the Rules Committee: The Kennedy Aid-to-Education Bills," in Alan Westin, ed., *The Uses of Power* (Harcourt, Brace and World, 1962), pp. 2–71.

16. Quoted in Eugene Eidenberg and Roy D. Morey, *An Act of Congress* (New York: W. W. Norton, 1969), p. 93.

17. Randall Strahan, *New Ways and Means: Reform and Change in a Congressional Committee* (University of North Carolina Press, 1990), p. 127.

18. Truman, *Memoirs: Years of Trial and Hope*, p. 29.

19. *Congressional Quarterly Almanac* (Washington: Congressional Quarterly Press, 1947), p. 280.

20. James T. Patterson, *Mr. Republican: A Biography of Robert A. Taft* (Boston: Houghton Mifflin, 1972), p. 360. This is an especially good account of Taft's struggle on the bill.

21. Robert J. Donovan, *Conflict and Crisis: The Presidency of Harry S. Truman, 1945–1948* (New York: W. W. Norton, 1977), p. 302.

22. "The Labor Bill," *New York Times*, June 5, 1947, p. 24; "Slave Labor," *Washington Post*, June 6, 1947, p. 18.

23. Patterson, *Mr. Republican*, p. 365.

24. Donovan, *Crisis and Conflict*, p. 302.

25. Samuel C. Patterson, *Labor Lobbying and Labor Reform: The Passage of the Landrum-Griffin Act* (Indianapolis: Bobbs-Merrill, 1966), p. 1.

26. Ibid., p. 13.

27. *Congressional Quarterly Almanac*, 1959, p. 162.

28. Alan K. McAdams, *Power and Politics in Labor Legislation* (Columbia University Press, 1964), pp. 72–73.

29. Quotes from "Meany Sees Deal in Labor Bill," *New York Times*, September 8, 1959, p. 41; and "President Is Pleased," *New York Times*, September 6, 1959, p. 29.

30. Martha Derthick, *Policymaking for Social Security* (Brookings, 1979), p. 364.

31. Ibid., p. 365.

32. *Congressional Record*, June 30, 1972, p. 23733.

33. R. Kent Weaver, *Automatic Government: The Politics of Indexation* (Brookings, 1988), p. 77.

34. Marjorie Hunter, "President Signs Bill for 20 Percent Increase in Old-Age Benefits," *New York Times*, July 2, 1972, pp. 1, 15.

35. Paul R. Portney, "Toxic Substance Policy and the Protection of Human Health," in Portney, ed., *Current Issues in U.S. Environmental Policy* (Johns Hopkins University Press, 1978), p. 106.

36. "Senate Action: Toxic Substances," *Congressional Quarterly Weekly Report*, April 3, 1976, p. 764; and Margaret Horblower, "Senate Votes Toxic Controls," *Washington Post*, March 27, 1976, p. A1.

37. Mary Russell, "Ford Signs Bill on Toxic Substances," *Washington Post,* October 13, 1976, p. A3.

38. Congressional Quarterly, *Congress and the Nation, 1985–1988* (Washington, 1989), p. 142.

39. Richard J. Whalen and R. Christopher Whalen, eds., *Trade Warriors: A Guide to the Politics of Trade and Foreign Investment* (Washington: Whalen, 1990), pp. 27, 28.

40. Ibid., p. 26.

41. Robert A. Katzmann, "War Powers: Toward a New Accommodation," in Thomas E. Mann, ed., *A Question of Balance: The President, the Congress, and Foreign Policy* (Brookings, 1990), p. 35.

42. Congressional Quarterly, *Congress and the Nation, 1969–1972* (Washington, 1973), p. 856.

43. "Veto Override: A Hint of Watergate, but No Trend Yet," *Congressional Quarterly Weekly Report,* November 10, 1973, p. 2943.

44. James M. Naughton, "Curb on Spending Gains in Congress," *New York Times,* April 17, 1973, p. 24.

45. Congressional Quarterly, *Congress and the Nation, 1973–1976* (Washington, 1977), p. 75.

46. Quoted in "Congress Gains Wide Budget Role," *New York Times,* July 13, 1974, p. 6.

47. Richard M. Nixon, *In the Arena: A Memoir of Victory, Defeat and Renewal* (New York: Simon and Schuster, 1990), p. 206.

48. James L. Sundquist, *Politics and Policy: The Eisenhower, Kennedy, and Johnson Years* (Brookings, 1968), pp. 302–08.

49. Ibid., p. 317.

50. Wilbur J. Cohen, Oral History, Lyndon B. Johnson Oral History Project, December 8, 1968, tape 2, p. 2.

51. Eric Davis, "Building Presidential Coalitions in Congress: Legislative Liaison in the Johnson White House," Ph.D. diss., Stanford University, 1977, p. 159.

52. John F. Manley, *The Politics of Finance: The House Committee on Ways and Means* (Boston: Little, Brown, 1970), p. 150.

53. Davis, "Building Presidential Coalitions," pp. 162–63.

54. Jimmy Carter, *Keeping Faith: Memoirs of a President* (New York: Bantam Books, 1982), p. 76.

55. Joseph A. Califano Jr., *Governing America: An Insider's Report from the White House and the Cabinet* (New York: Simon and Schuster, 1981), p. 284.

56. Congressional Quarterly, *Congress and the Nation, 1977–1980* (Washington, 1981), p. 670.

57. Sources relied on for the Department of Education legislation include: Beryl A. Rabin and Willis D. Hawley, *The Politics of Federal Reorganization: Creating the U.S. Department of Education* (New York: Pergamon Press, 1988); and David Stephens, "President Carter, the Congress, and NEA: Creating the Department of Education," *Political Science Quarterly* 98 (Winter 1983–84): 654.

58. Carter, *Keeping Faith,* p. 111.

59. *Congressional Quarterly Almanac,* 1979, p. 47E.

60. Richard H. K. Vietor, *Energy Policy in America since 1945: A Study of Business-Government Relations* (Cambridge University Press, 1984), p. 44.

61. Walter A. Rosenbaum, *Energy, Politics, and Public Policy,* 2nd ed. (Washington: Congressional Quarterly Press, 1987), p. 94.

62. Quoted in Adam Clymer, "Republicans Call Energy Speech Political and Vague," *New York Times,* July 16, 1979, p. A11; and Ann Pelham, "Congress 'Ahead of Game' on Energy," *Congressional Quarterly Weekly Report,* July 21, 1979, p. 1436.

63. Thomas P. O'Neill Jr., with William Novak, *Man of the House: The Life and Political Memoirs of Speaker Tip O'Neill* (New York: Random House, 1987), p. 260.

64. John E. Chubb, *Interest Groups and the Bureaucracy: The Politics of Energy* (Stanford University Press, 1983), p. 129.

65. Quoted in *Congressional Quarterly Almanac,* 1975, p. 235.

66. Quoted in ibid., pp. 244–45.

67. Gerald R. Ford, *A Time to Heal: The Autobiography of Gerald R. Ford* (New York: Harper and Row, 1979), p. 339.

68. Pietro S. Nivola, *The Politics of Energy Conservation* (Brookings, 1986), p. 49.

69. William E. Simon, *A Time for Truth* (New York: McGraw-Hill, 1978), p. 79.

70. *Public Papers of the President of the United States: Ronald Reagan, 1983,* vol. 1 (Government Printing Office, 1984), p. 107.

71. "The Rush to Misjudgment on Crime," *New York Times,* February 6, 1984, p. A18.

72. Harry S. Truman, *Memoirs: Years of Decisions* (Doubleday, 1955), p. 512.

73. Martin Meyerson, Barbara Terrett, and William L. C. Wheaton, *Housing, People, and Cities* (McGraw-Hill, 1962), p. 287.

74. Patterson, *Mr. Republican,* p. 433.

75. Robert J. Donovan, *Tumultuous Years: The Presidency of Harry S. Truman, 1949–1953* (New York: W. W. Norton, 1982), p. 127.

76. John F. Witte, *The Politics and Development of the Federal Income Tax* (University of Wisconsin Press, 1985), p. 138.

77. Quotes are, respectively, from "Excess Profits Tax: Background," *Congressional Quarterly Almanac,* 1950, p. 671; and *New York Times,* December 6, 1950, p. 21.

78. Witte, *Politics and Development of Federal Income Tax,* p. 139.

79. J. W. Anderson, *Eisenhower, Brownell, and the Congress: The Tangled Origins of the Civil Rights Bill of 1956–1957* (University of Alabama Press, 1964), p. 1.

80. Eisenhower, *Mandate for Change,* pp. 235, 234.

81. Sundquist, *Politics and Policy,* p. 233.

82. Ibid., pp. 234–35.

83. William S. White, "President Bars Ballot on Rights, Would Hear Foes," *New York Times,* July 4, 1957, pp. 1, 20.

84. Stephen E. Ambrose, *Eisenhower: The President,* vol. 2 (New York: Simon and Schuster, 1984), p. 407.

85. Ambrose, *Eisenhower,* vol. 2, p. 410.

86. Witte, *Politics and Development of the Federal Income Tax*, p. 157.

87. Quotes are, respectively, from John D. Morris, "Senate Approves Tax Bill in Diluted Form, 59 to 24," *New York Times*, September 7, 1962, p. 1; and *Congressional Quarterly Almanac*, 1962, p. 504.

88. Nelson W. Polsby, *Political Innovation in America: The Politics of Policy Initiation* (Yale University Press, 1984), p. 18.

89. Mark Hertsgaard, *Nuclear Inc.: The Men and Money behind Nuclear Energy* (New York: Pantheon Books, 1983), p. 30.

90. Harold P. Green and Alan Rosenthal, *Government of the Atom: The Integration of Powers* (New York: Atherton Press, 1963), p. 159.

91. James T. Patterson, *America's Struggle against Poverty, 1900–1985* (Harvard University Press, 1986), p. 126.

92. Ibid., p. 127.

93. Sundquist, *Politics and Policy*, p. 87.

94. Quoted in Randall B. Ripley, "Congress and Clean Air: The Issue of Enforcement in 1963," in Frederic N. Cleaveland, ed., *Congress and Urban Problems* (Brookings, 1969), p. 235. The present account of clean air legislation relies heavily on Ripley; Sundquist, *Politics and Policy*, pp. 351–55; and Charles O. Jones, *Clean Air: The Policies and Politics of Pollution Control* (University of Pittsburgh Press, 1975), pp. 71–76.

95. Ripley, "Congress and Clean Air," pp. 248–49.

96. Ibid., p. 251.

97. Ibid., pp. 277–78.

98. Graham K. Wilson, *The Politics of Safety and Health: Occupational Safety and Health in the United States and Britain* (Oxford: Clarendon Press, 1985), p. 36.

99. Martha Derthick, *Agency under Stress: The Social Security Administration in American Government* (Brookings, 1990), pp. 91–92.

100. Paul C. Light, *Artful Work: The Politics of Social Security Reform* (New York: Random House, 1985), p. 101.

101. Ibid., pp. 122–23.

102. Richard E. Neustadt and Ernest R. May, *Thinking in Time: The Uses of History for Decision Makers* (New York: Free Press, 1986), p. 21.

103. Light, *Artful Work*, p. 24; and David A. Stockman, *The Triumph of Politics: How the Reagan Revolution Failed* (New York: Harper and Row, 1986), p. 191.

104. Light, *Artful Work*, p. 232.

105. Barbara Sinclair, "Governing Unheroically (and Sometimes Unappetizingly): Bush and the 101st Congress," in Colin Campbell and Bert A. Rockman, eds., *The Bush Presidency: First Appraisals* (Chatham, N.J.: Chatham House, 1991), p. 176.

106. Text in *Congressional Quarterly Almanac*, 1990, p. 131.

107. Quoted in ibid., p. 134.

108. Sinclair, "Governing Unheroically," p. 181.

109. David W. Rohde, *Parties and Leaders in the Postreform House* (University of Chicago Press, 1991), p. 175.

110. Robert E. Rubin, *In an Uncertain World: Tough Choices from Wall Street to Washington* (Washington: Random House, 2003), p. 123.

111. Quoted in *Congressional Quarterly Almanac,* 1993, p. 111.

112. Barney Frank (D-Mass.), quoted in ibid., p. 111.

113. Ibid., p. 114.

114. Barbara Sinclair, *Unorthodox Lawmaking: New Legislative Processes in the U.S. Congress* (Congressional Quarterly Press, 1997), p. 167.

115. For details, see ibid., pp. 167–69; and *Congressional Quarterly Almanac,* 1993, pp. 118–22.

116. *Congressional Quarterly Almanac,* 1993, p. 118.

117. Sinclair, *Unorthodox Lawmaking,* p. 173.

118. John C. Fortier and Norman J. Ornstein, "President Bush: Legislative Strategist," in Fred I. Greenstein, ed., *The George W. Bush Presidency: An Early Assessment* (Johns Hopkins University Press, 2003), p. 145.

119. *Congressional Quarterly Almanac,* 2001, p. 18-4.

120. Ibid., p. 18-7.

121. Quoted in ibid., p. 18-7.

122. Fortier and Ornstein, "President Bush," p. 150.

123. *Congressional Quarterly Almanac,* 2001, p. 18-9.

124. Ibid., p. 18-9.

125. Fortier and Ornstein, "President Bush," p. 151.

126. David Frum, *The Right Man: The Surprise Presidency of George W. Bush* (New York: Random House, 2003), p. 55.

127. Ibid., pp. 57–58.

128. Quoted in *Congressional Quarterly Almanac,* 2001, p. 8-7.

129. Interview, "Larry King Live," CNN, June 24, 2004.

130. Elizabeth Drew, *Showdown: The Struggle between the Gingrich Congress and the Clinton White House* (New York: Simon and Schuster, 1996), p. 92.

131. Ibid., p. 141.

132. *Congressional Quarterly Almanac,* 1996, p. 6-4.

133. Rubin, *In an Uncertain World,* p. 200.

134. George Stephanopoulos, *All Too Human: A Political Education* (Boston: Little, Brown, 1999), p. 421.

135. Quoted in *Congressional Quarterly Almanac,* 1996, p. 6-24.

136. Stephanopoulos, *All Too Human,* p. 421.

137. *Congressional Quarterly Almanac,* 1997, p. 2-18. For a full account of these struggles, see Daniel J. Palazzolo, *Done Deal: The Politics of the 1997 Budget Agreement* (Chatham, N.J.: Chatham House, 1999), chap. 2.

138. Palazzolo, *Done Deal,* p. 9.

139. *Congressional Quarterly Almanac,* 1997, pp. 219–20.

140. Quoted in ibid., p. 2-18.

141. For details, see ibid., p. 2-22; and Palazzolo, *Done Deal,* chap. 5.

142. Palazzolo, *Done Deal,* p. 94.

143. *Congressional Quarterly Almanac,* 2002, p. 7-3.

144. Ibid., pp. 7-5, 7-6.

145. Ibid., p. 7-6.

Notes to Chapter 8

1. Sidney M. Milkis, *The President and the Parties: The Transformation of the American Party System since the New Deal* (Oxford University Press, 1993), pp. viii, ix.

2. See, for example, George C. Edwards III, Andrew Barrett, and Jeffrey Peake, "The Legislative Impact of Divided Government: What Failed to Pass in Congress?" *American Journal of Political Science* 41 (May 1997): 545–63; and William Howell and others, "Divided Government and Legislative Productivity of Congress," *Legislative Studies Quarterly* 25 (May 2000): 285–312.

3. Sarah A. Binder, *Stalemate: Causes and Consequences of Legislative Gridlock* (Brookings, 2003), pp. 104–05.

4. The Committee on the Constitutional System, for example, has proposed many such changes, as reported in James L. Sundquist, *Constitutional Reform and Effective Government,* rev. ed. (Brookings, 1992).

5. Newt Gingrich, *Lessons Learned the Hard Way: A Personal Account* (New York: HarperCollins, 1998), pp. 59–60, 63.

6. For a discussion of these developments, see Norman J. Ornstein and Thomas E. Mann, eds., *The Permanent Campaign and Its Future* (Washington: American Enterprise Institute, 2000). George C. Edwards III also discusses the limits of public campaigning in *On Deaf Ears: The Limits of the Bully Pulpit* (Yale University Press, 2003).

7. E. E. Schattschneider, *Two Hundred Million Americans in Search of a Government* (New York: Holt, Rinehart and Winston, 1969), p. 53.

Index

ABM Treaty. *See* Anti-Ballistic Missile Treaty

Abortion, 215

Accountability and responsibility: in the American political system, 21–22; of cabinet members, 76; congressional accountability and responsibility, 19, 21; constitutional issues of, 20–21, 177; elections and, 21; governmental responsibility, 19, 20, 21; lawmaking and, 224; in parliamentary systems, 74; of political parties, 19, 21–22, 26; presidential accountability and responsibility, 19, 20, 21, 66, 140, 143, 182–83, 232, 287

Acheson, Dean, 259, 260

Adams, Sherman, 85–86, 107, 108

AEC. *See* Atomic Energy Commission

Afghanistan, 132

AFL-CIO. *See* American Federation of Labor-Congress of Industrial Organizations

AFT. *See* American Federation of Teachers

Age Discrimination Act (*1967*), 154

Agencies. *See* Government—departments and agencies; individual departments and agencies

Agendas. *See* Congress; Presidents; individual presidents

Agnew, Spiro T., 31, 46, 244, 282, 290

Agricultural issues, 173

Aid for Health Maintenance Organizations (*1973*), 157

Airline industry, 160, 173, 252, 259, 261–63, 318

Air Quality Act (*1967*), 154

Alaska, 151, 157, 160

Albert, Carl (D-Okla.), 290

Alfred P. Murrah Federal Office Building (Oklahoma City), 169

Allen, Richard, 113

Alliance for Progress, 153

AMA. *See* American Medical Association

Ambrose, Stephen E., 299, 300

American Federation of Teachers (AFT), 287–88

American Medical Association (AMA), 284, 285

American Federation of Labor-Congress of Industrial Organizations (AFL-CIO), 272, 284

American Political Science Association (APSA), 11

Americans with Disabilities Act (*1990*), 166

American Vocational Association (AVA), 304

AmeriCorps program, 170

Amtrak. *See* Rail Passenger Service Act

Anderson, Clinton (D-N.M.), 285

Anderson, John, 40

Anderson, Martin, 113, 114

Anti-Ballistic Missile (ABM) Treaty (*1972*), 157

Anticrime package (*1984*), 290, 293–94

Anti-Drug Abuse Act (*1988*), 164

Appalachian Regional Development Act (*1965*), 154

APSA. *See* American Political Science Association

Area Redevelopment Act (*1961*), 153, 304

Armey, Dick (R-Tex.), 334

Arms Control and Development Agency, 153

Armstrong, William (R-Colo.), 310

Arnold, Peri E., 67–68, 70